LIKE WATER

LIKE WATER

A CULTURAL HISTORY OF BRUCE LEE

DARYL JOJI MAEDA

NEW YORK UNIVERSITY PRESS

NEW YORK

NEW YORK UNIVERSITY PRESS
New York
www.nyupress.org

References to Internet websites (URLs) were accurate at the time of writing. Neither the author nor New York University Press is responsible for URLs that may have expired or changed since the manuscript was prepared.

Library of Congress Cataloging-in-Publication Data
Names: Maeda, Daryl J., author.
Title: Like water : a cultural history of Bruce Lee / Daryl Joji Maeda.
Description: New York : New York University Press, [2022] |
Includes bibliographical references and index.
Identifiers: LCCN 2021057771 | ISBN 9781479812868 (hardback) | ISBN 9781479812899 (ebook) |
ISBN 9781479812875 (ebook other)
Subjects: LCSH: Lee, Bruce, 1940–1973. | Lee, Bruce, 1940–1973—Influence. | Chinese American actors—Biography. | Martial artists—United States—Biography. | Martial artists—China—Hong Kong—Biography. | Martial arts films—History and criticism.
Classification: LCC PN2287.L2897 M34 2022 | DDC 791.4302/8092 [B]—dc23/eng/20220218
LC record available at https://lccn.loc.gov/2021057771

New York University Press books are printed on acid-free paper, and their binding materials are chosen for strength and durability. We strive to use environmentally responsible suppliers and materials to the greatest extent possible in publishing our books.

Manufactured in the United States of America

10 9 8 7 6 5 4 3 2 1

Also available as an ebook

BE FORMLESS, SHAPELESS, LIKE WATER

—BRUCE LEE

CONTENTS

Bruce Lee with fresh scratch marks on his face and chest in the mirror room in *Enter the Dragon* (1973). (Photo by Warner Bros. via Getty Images)

INTRODUCTION

In the climactic scene of Bruce Lee's final film, the 1973 martial arts movie *Enter the Dragon*, Lee pursues the archvillain Han with the hope of finishing their fight in a hall of mirrors. The two stalk each other through the maze of reflections and refractions, the screen filled with one Lee, two, a dozen, or none at all, as he slinks in and out of the frame. Some of the images are complete, others only fragmentary slivers. The multiple Lees always move in unison, sometimes in the same direction, sometimes toward or away from each other. A distorted image of Han lies in wait for Lee and strikes him in the face with a backhand blow. Lee swings back at the reflection but finds only air as Han retreats invisibly farther into the funhouse.

As Lee moves forward, his back to the camera, Han emerges from the reflections and slashes Lee on the shoulder with a bladed claw before disappearing again. The camera alternately captures images of Lee and Han reflected in long mirrored panels that break them up into a dozen overlapping images. Tension builds as the viewer is never sure of whether the image onscreen is the real Lee or a mere reflection. The fragmented Lee delivers a side kick that sends a dozen Hans flying, after which the real Han rolls across the screen.

Lee, frustrated by his inability to locate his foe, backs up against a set of mirrors as a voice-over of his *sifu* (teacher) intones, "Remember, the enemy has only images and illusions behind which he hides his true motives. Destroy the image, and you will break the enemy."

Inspired by this brief philosophical refresher, Lee delivers a backhanded fist to an image of Han, in the process splintering the mirror containing Han's reflection. Using fists and feet, he shatters mirror after mirror until he can move forward confidently, for the shards of broken glass reveal the falseness of the Hans they reflect and leave the true Han visible and vulnerable. Lee rushes triumphantly toward the exposed villain and side-kicks him across the room, impaling him on a spear protruding from the wall.

According to Robert Clouse, the film's director, the hall of mirrors scene was not included in the original script but was dreamed up by him and his wife. The set consisted of a large room paneled completely in mirrors. Three shallow bays, each about five feet wide, were covered with narrow vertical slats of mirrors that created dozens more reflections. The camera sat inside a mirror-covered box about six feet square in the center of the room behind a mirrored sheet of plywood with a cutout for the lens that enabled it to shoot anywhere without capturing its own reflection.

Some $8,000 worth of mirrors—two truckloads' worth—were used to construct the set, an undertaking that took three days. The scene, which lasts for just five minutes in the movie, took two days to shoot. Clouse claims that after filming on *Enter the Dragon* ended, Lee spent two more weeks in Hong Kong, where the film was made, shooting additional scenes on the mirrored set.[1]

In many respects, this intricate scene represents the complexity of both Bruce Lee's life and his career. Never before had the entire world had a chance to see Bruce so clearly, but *Enter the Dragon* elevated his profile to unimaginable heights. Though he was already Hong Kong's biggest movie star, his final film hit occupied the top spot on the United States box-office chart for three weeks and took in more than $90 million worldwide. But just as the images of the fictional Lee seesaw between reality and illusion, unity and multiplicity, perception and deception, the figure of Bruce Lee remains as elusive and contradictory in real life as he was in that hall of mirrors on the big screen. Hometown hero or global icon, Chinese nationalist or universal humanist, disciple of kung fu or heretic, ascetic or hedonist, devoted father and husband or playboy: the iconic martial arts practitioner and pop-culture hero vacillated between being all of these and none.

Take, for example, the question of what country can rightly claim him as its own. Hong Kong loves its native son, who grew up in the colony and in the 1970s became the first global Chinese superstar. A bronze statue of the martial artist and actor holds pride of place on the Avenue of Stars on the Kowloon waterfront, where tourists flock to strike martial arts poses for photographs framed by the blue waters of Victoria Bay and the soaring downtown skyline. The *Bruce Lee: Kung Fu, Art, Life* exhibit mounted at the Hong Kong Heritage Museum in 2013 told the story of a local boy and child movie star who learned Wing Chun style of kung fu and fought atop rooftops, decamped to the United States for a few years, then returned to Hong Kong to become Asia's biggest movie star and win worldwide acclaim.[2]

Chinese America also loves its native son, who was born in San Francisco in 1940, worked as a busboy in a Chinese restaurant while attending a technical school in Seattle, developed a reputation as a martial artist in Oakland, and struggled to make a name for himself in Hollywood. On the Bruce Lee walking tour of Seattle, sightseers visit the playground where the young martial artist worked out and dined on his favorite dish of beef with oyster sauce at Tai Tung, his favorite Chinese restaurant. The *Do You Know Bruce?* exhibit at the Wing Luke Museum in 2015 traced Lee's Seattle roots and stressed his development as a martial artist, teacher, and actor on the US West Coast. Yet neither of these two competing local stories—of a Hong Kong boy who ventured out into the world or a Chinese immigrant struggling to make it in the United States—captures what is most compelling about this iconic figure.

As the often riveting details of Bruce Lee's life reveal, his story is endlessly fascinating, and for many different reasons. He became a global phenomenon due to his incessant traversals across the Pacific, a vast region across which peoples of various nationalities, races, and cultures have confronted each other as adversaries, trading partners, and neighbors over four centuries. Transpacific migrations shaped Lee and his world.

Movements and migrations across the Pacific Ocean structured the histories and cultures he inherited, the milieu he occupied, the martial arts practices he developed, the films he made, and the world that he left behind after his death in Hong Kong on July 20, 1973, a year that will also be remembered as the one that witnessed the Yom Kippur War, the Arab oil embargo, and the start of the Watergate hearings in Washington, DC. Lee's death, blamed on an overdose of a prescription pain killer, was officially ruled "death by misadventure," which in turn became the title of a 1973 documentary about Lee's turbulent life and times. He was thirty-two years old.

The conditions that enabled Lee to become an icon celebrated around the globe were created by a variety of forces—European and US trade with China in the sixteenth through nineteenth centuries, the British colonization of Hong Kong in 1841, the discovery of gold in California in 1848, Cold War deployments of US troops throughout Asia in the last half of the twentieth century, the counterculture of the 1960s, and Lee's own incessant shuttling between Hong Kong and the West Coast of the United States until the abrupt end of his richly multifaceted career in 1973.

Within the turbulence of people, cultures, and identities roiled by transnational capitalism and militarism, Lee combined Taoism and Western philosophies; synthesized fighting styles from China, Japan, Okinawa, the Philippines, Korea, and the West; and blended Hong Kong and Hollywood cinema to create a fusion all his own. He pioneered new ways to use the body as a weapon, advocated martial arts as a path toward harmony among strangers, and articulated interlinked critiques of colonialism and racism.

≈

Bruce Lee's colorful and dramatic story is worth examining for a number of important reasons. Because Lee embodied the transpacific flows of people, culture, and ideas that began in the sixteenth century and have accelerated ever since, his story provides a lens through which to understand how peoples confront each other, intermingle, and produce wondrous new cultural forms and alliances in an era of globalization that itself confronts continuing inequality, racism, and xenophobia.

Bruce Lee's story is a quintessential illustration of how larger forces have shaped an increasingly globalized world. Lee was an extraordinary person, to be sure, but his story could not have unfolded at any other moment in history. The forces of mercantile capitalism, colonialism, Cold War militarism, and globalization fundamentally reordered the world in the nineteenth and twentieth centuries, giving rise to the intricately intertwined and thoroughly transnational planet we inhabit today. Humans have crossed geographical and political boundaries since time immemorial but never at the pace and frequency seen in the twentieth and twenty-first centuries.

Migrations and contacts, whether friendly or belligerent, produce new forms of culture. Whenever peoples meet others whom they consider to be different from themselves, regardless of whether the distinctions are drawn along tribal, ethnic, religious, or national lines, they exchange, adopt, adapt, co-opt, and incorporate ideas, beliefs, technologies, and cultural practices and create new identities. As the Roman Empire grew through conquest, it not only spread its religion throughout Europe and Africa but also incorporated new local deities that coexisted alongside the old gods. The Manchus who conquered China strategically embraced the native ideology of Confucianism as an instrument of rule. What could be more English than tea served in a fine China pot? Yet both the beverage and the vessel that typify Britannia originated in China.

It is impossible to imagine US music or world music for that matter—jazz, rock-and-roll, hip-hop—without hearing the voices of enslaved African peoples. The borderlands of the Southwest of the United States boast a unique hybrid culture that combines Mexican, Spanish, Indigenous, and European influences and, where these borderlands abut the Pacific, Asian influences as well. Where could the Korean taco have emerged except in Los Angeles?

THE FRAMEWORK

The emerging fields of Pacific history and transpacific studies provide frameworks that illuminate how studying Bruce Lee can show how China and the United States exist in entangled ways. Pacific history bridges the different yet overlapping histories of Asia, Oceania, Europe, and the Americas to help us understand the Pacific as a far-flung and diverse entity that is nevertheless worth considering as a whole.

In the afterword to *Pacific Histories: Ocean, Land, People*, an important 2014 overview edited by the historians David Armitage and Alison Bashford, Matt K. Matsuda characterizes the Pacific as a zone defined by "currents, flows and markers of adjacent, intersecting colliding cultures."[3] The contributors embrace the messiness of tracing connections between Asian, Western, and Oceanic historians and historical writing and avoiding attempts to create a unified vision of the Pacific.

In contrast, monographs by the American historians Matt K. Matsuda and David Igler embrace the Herculean task of envisioning narratives of the Pacific centered on environments, explorations, passages, and exchanges. The Hong Kong scholar Elizabeth Sinn has similarly shown how the growth of both Hong Kong and California, which she sees as interlinked "translocalities," was propelled by the increasing flow of people, goods, and capital impelled by the Gold Rush.[4]

Transpacific studies shares with Pacific history an interest in mobility and flows, examining what Janet Hoskins and Viet Thanh Nguyen call "the movements of people, culture, capital, or ideas within regions and between nations."[5] The discipline draws from area studies, American studies, and Asian American studies but critiques these fields for being overly bounded by the concept of nation-states. As Hoskins, a professor of anthropology at the University of Southern California, and Nguyen, a professor of English, American studies and ethnicity, and comparative literature at USC, explain in the introduction to their pioneering 2014 collection, *Transpacific Studies: Framing an Emerging Field*, the discipline is founded on an explicitly critical stance toward transnational capitalism, continuing neoimperialism and militarism, and the logics of racism, sexism, and nationalism that have created and continue to create systems of inequality in the Pacific.

Continuously riding transpacific currents driven by labor migration, capitalism, and militarism made Bruce Lee a nomad in the literal sense, but he also embodied the notion of the nomad as described by Gilles Deleuze, the French philosopher, and Félix Guattari, a French psychoanalyst and political activist. Deleuze and Guattari describe nomads as entities that destabilize both borders and boundaries despite the state's efforts to create clearly delineated territories.[6] Considering Pacific history and transpacific studies in the context of the theories of Deleuze and Guattari suggests that capitalism, imperialism, and nationalism are instruments that impose racial, gender, and sexual hierarchies to define and regulate groups of people. Nomads travel through the spaces demarcated by these ideologies but defy and blur the boundary lines they impose.

Lee's most famous dictum, "Be formless, shapeless, like water," argues that water pliantly takes on the form of its container—a teapot, a cup—but can also resist, like a river carving a canyon or ocean waves pounding cliffs into sand. Like water, Lee refused to be captured by either East or West but instead flowed between and shaped both. His peripatetic life and career contributed to the continuing entanglement of China and the United States across great distances, interweaving and unraveling structures involving nationalism, colonialism, race, and gender.

My goal in this book is to examine the figure of Bruce Lee as a way to connect the relatively discrete bodies of scholarship in American studies, Asian studies, and Asian American studies. To speak of Bruce Lee is to speak of the various images of "Bruce Lee" that oscillate between scholarly fields just as Bruce Lee himself shuttled like a vagabond back and forth across the Pacific.[7] "Bruce Lee" entangles the individual—whose life has been illuminated by memoirs of those who encountered him and biographies ranging from hagiographies describing an ever-devoted husband and father to hit pieces portraying a drug-addled egomaniac—with the onscreen figure that has been interpreted variously as an "Oriental," a Chinese nationalist, and a body devoid of race.[8] Studying Bruce Lee involves the challenging task of bringing together scholarship from a range of fields and analyzing the distortions produced by differing perspectives.[9]

When studying the impact and significance of Bruce Lee's life, Asian American and American studies scholars focus primarily on issues involving race and gender within the context of US culture and history. The Chinese American scholar Jachinson Chan, author of *Chinese American Masculinities: From Fu Manchu to Bruce Lee*, places Lee alongside the fictional characters Fu Manchu and Charlie Chan, arguing that Lee strove to overcome "the ways in which mainstream American society marginalized him because of his race" by constructing a "Chinese American masculinity" that emphasized physical domination over other men. Chan alleges, however, that Lee's masculinity adheres to Western stereotypes of Chinese men by remaining "asexual."[10]

Celine Parreñas Shimizu, a professor of cinema at San Francisco State University whose specialty is the study of race and sexuality as represented in global popular culture, counters this emasculated representation of Lee, interpreting the sexuality he projects on film as an "ethical masculinity" not built on the domination of women and emblematized by his care for others and vulnerability amid violence.[11] Sylvia Chong, a professor of English and American studies at the University of Virginia, examines Bruce Lee the person and his screen persona as emblems of the racial violence of the Vietnam War, arguing that his body plays contradictory roles as an exemplar of "the transcendence of racial categories and the epitome of racialized masculinity."[12]

While Asian studies scholarship shares Asian American and American studies' concern with Lee's masculinity, it tends to locate Bruce Lee within the confines of Asia and emphasize colonialism rather than race. David Desser, a professor emeritus of cinema studies at the University of Illinois at Urbana-Champaign and an expert in Asian cinema, traces the impact of samurai films and the Japanese film industry on Hong Kong cinema and sees Lee's masculinity as an instance of the emergent "muscular Mandarin" genre of filmmaking in Hong Kong in the 1970s.[13] Stephen Teo, a professor of communication and information at Nanyang Technological University in Singapore, emphasizes Lee's status as a symbol of Chinese resistance to colonial degradation.[14]

Studying Bruce Lee also illuminates the scholarly literature on Afro-Asian encounters. Most notably, Vijay Prashad, a professor of international studies at Trinity College in Connecticut and the author of *Everybody Was Kung Fu Fighting: Afro-Asian Connections and the Myth of Cultural Purity*, depicts Lee as a "polycultural figure who demolished the high walls of parochialism and ethnonationalism through a potent dialectic of cultural presence and antiracism." In other words, he fought against ethnocentrism and racism by drawing from multiple cultural influences and traditions. This antiracism, born of his own struggles against white supremacy, enabled Lee to become an icon to people of color around the world.[15] Prashad describes Lee as polycultural because he rejected stale notions of purity and authenticity in favor of intermingling and syncretism. Although the notion of polyculturalism accurately represents Lee's mixing of various influences, it does not explain the precise ways that Lee encountered different ideas about movement, humanity, and existence or the larger social forces that brought these ideas into conversation around him. Prashad points out that Lee's polycultural kung fu brought together African and Asian peoples in the realm of antiracist and anti-imperialist struggle.

The historians Robin D. G. Kelley and Betsy Esch, authors of "Black like Mao: Red China and Black Revolution," highlight the racial, national, and political intertwinings of Black radicals like Robert F. Williams with the People's Republic of China. Williams spent three years in exile in China, a country he praised for its opposition to Western imperialism, and he urged Mao Zedong to issue his famous "Statement Supporting the Afro-Americans in Their Just

Struggle Against Racial Discrimination by U.S. Imperialism." Williams's admiration of Mao inspired an entire generation of Black radicals, including the Black Panther Party.

As Robeson Taj Frazier, director of the Institute for Diversity and Empowerment at the University of Southern California, shows, China figured prominently as a beacon of antiracism not only for Williams but also for Black radical intellectuals including W. E. B. and Shirley Du Bois, William Worthy, and Vicki Garvin.[16] The Panthers inspired by the Mao-admiring Williams in turn influenced the formation of Asian American radical groups like as the Red Guard Party of San Francisco. The Red Guards, who claimed Mao as their ideological leader and pledged allegiance to the People's Republic of China, did so initially not simply out of ethnic nationalism but also as an expression of solidarity with the Panthers.[17]

Diane C. Fujino, a professor of Asian American studies at the University of California, Santa Barbara, further demonstrates how participation in the Black Power movement galvanized Asian American radicals by examining the lives of Richard Aoki, a pivotal and controversial figure who bridged the Black Panther Party and a germinal organization, the Asian American Political Alliance, and Yuri Kochiyama, whose association with Malcolm X launched her on a lifelong journey of advocacy for rights and self-determination for people of color in the US and abroad.[18]

Black and Asian American radicals built imperfect solidarities with leftist Asia during the Vietnam War era, at times overly romanticizing China and Vietnam, as the historian Judy Tzu-Chun Wu argues.[19] Bill V. Mullen, a professor of English and American studies at Purdue University, locates writer-activists W. E. B. Du Bois, Richard Wright, and Williams as Afro-Asian figures, a roster to which he adds the Detroit radicals Grace Lee and James Boggs and the jazz musician Fred Ho.[20] Rychetta Watkins, author of *Black Power, Yellow Power, and the Making of Revolutionary Identities*, analyzes how African American and Asian American activists and writers coalesced around the rubric of "Power" in the late 1960s to demand "self-determination," or the ability to control their own destinies. While China looms largest in the scholarly works on the post-1949 era, prior to that, Japan and its campaign against Western imperialism held a fascination for Black radicals before World War II, as demonstrated by Yuichiro Onishi, a professor of African American and African studies at the University of Minnesota, and Gerald Horne, a professor of history at the University of Houston.[21]

Examining Bruce Lee entails incessant crossing of scholarly boundaries, just as Lee himself shuttled across the Pacific, entangling bodies of literature rather than proclaiming the supremacy of any single one. Like a quantum particle whose state remains ambiguous until it becomes determined by an observer's act of measurement, Lee exists in multiple states—as person and film image, racial minority and colonial subject, artifact of Hollywood and product of Hong Kong—until critics fix him in place with their interpretations. I aim to show how a transpacific lens that refracts images embracing multiple locations and literatures can reveal how migration and border crossings enabled Lee to synthesize various martial arts and combine critiques of racism and colonialism.

Although this book is a cultural history, it necessarily converses with the innumerable biographies of Bruce Lee, which fall into three main waves. The first wave includes brief works rushed into print in the 1970s to capitalize on the kung fu frenzy. Alex Ben Block's *The Legend of Bruce Lee* and Felix Dennis and Don Atyeo's *Bruce Lee: King of Kung-Fu* appeared in 1974, just a year after Lee's death. Despite their brevity, both represent creditable work by journalists who interviewed figures around Bruce Lee.

The second wave includes accounts published from 1978 to 1989 by people associated with Lee. Linda Lee tells her husband's story from the vantage point of his wife and family in *Bruce Lee: The Man Only I Knew* and *The Bruce Lee Story*. The longtime martial arts publisher Mitoshi Uyehara recalls him in *Bruce Lee: The Incomparable Fighter*. Robert Clouse's *Bruce Lee: The Biography* offers unique perspectives on the filming of *Enter the Dragon* by the film's director.

The third wave of biographies includes in-depth works published from 1994 to 2018. In *Bruce Lee: Fighting Spirit*, the dedicated and thoughtful fan Bruce

Thomas draws on abundant sources published in the two decades after Lee's death to produce the first serious full-length biography. Matthew Polly's *Bruce Lee: A Life*, which stands as the unarguably definitive biography of Lee, mines previous accounts, published sources, and innumerable in-depth interviews conducted by the author. In contrast to the earlier works, which appealed to martial arts fans and tended to be published by specialty houses, *Bruce Lee: A Life* tells a story aimed at general-interest readers, carries the imprint of a major New York publishing house, Simon & Schuster, and features deft writing and storytelling that mark it as exceptional in the field.

THE ENDURING RELEVANCE

Bruce Lee died in 1973, yet he is arguably more famous today than at any point in his lifetime. At the close of the twentieth century, *Time* magazine named him as one of twenty "Heroes and Inspirations" on "Time 100: The Most Important People of the Century," a roster that also included such luminaries as Winston Churchill, Mohandas Gandhi, Albert Einstein, Helen Keller, the Wright Brothers, and Mother Teresa.[22] *Forbes* ranked him as the ninth-highest earner among deceased celebrities in 2014, with his estate garnering $9 million.[23]

In 2017, the Museum of Modern Art in New York City screened a series of films titled "Eternal Bruce Lee," a retrospective of *The Big Boss*, *Fist of Fury*, *The Way of the Dragon*, and *Enter the Dragon*, the four movies Lee starred in as an adult, as well as the ludicrously exploitative *Game of Death*, which was released after his death. The event marked the premier of splendid digital restorations of these films and drew multigenerational audiences composed of both fans who remembered his heroics in the 1970s and those born decades after his death. Recent documentaries on his life include *I Am Bruce Lee* (2012) and *Be Water* (2020). Perhaps nothing demonstrates Bruce Lee's enduring relevance better than his ability to generate passionate debate nearly half a century after his death.

In 2019, the director Quentin Tarantino stoked controversy with his portrayal of Bruce Lee (Mike Moh) in the film *Once Upon a Time in Hollywood*, a fictional reimagining of 1960s Hollywood that follows the actress Sharon Tate (Margot Robbie) as she approaches what the audience dreads will be a tragic confrontation with the Manson Family. On the night of the planned massacre, the fictional aging, semiemployed stuntman Cliff Booth (Brad Pitt) intervenes, killing Manson's followers and saving Tate and her friends.

Tarantino correctly places Lee within the Hollywood orbit of figures like Tate, whom he had trained while serving as a fight consultant for the 1968 film *The Wrecking Crew*; Tate's husband, the director Roman Polanski, who attempted to study martial arts with Lee; and Lee's students, who included the actor Steve McQueen (Damian Lewis) and the hairdresser and Tate confidant Jay Sebring (Emile Hirsch). The dispute over Lee's representation lies in the space between accuracy and imagination, just as the film hovers between a realistic depiction of the social relations around Lee and a fairy-tale version of reality in which the princess-like Tate lives on, presumably happily ever after.

The most contentious scene depicts a fight between Lee and Booth on a movie set. Lee is boasting to a crowd that he could beat the legendary heavyweight Muhammad Ali. Booth scoffs at the assertion, Lee takes his response as a challenge, and the two men square off to settle their disagreement. Lee wins round one by knocking Booth to the ground with a kick. Booth takes round two by hurling Lee against a car door so violently that his body leaves a large dent in the metal. The bout ends in a draw when the stunt coordinator arrives and fires Booth for fighting.

Lee loyalists objected to Tarantino's portrayal of Lee as excessively arrogant. As Dan Inosanto, a longtime Lee disciple, put it, "He was never, in my opinion, cocky. Maybe he was cocky in as far as martial arts because he was very sure of himself. He was worlds ahead of everyone else. But on a set, he's not gonna show off." Inosanto also argued that Lee would never have disrespected the heavyweight champion "because he worshiped the ground Muhammad Ali walked on." Lee's daughter, Shannon, acknowledged the fact that her father possessed a deep level of confidence, but she too rejected the characterization of him as arrogant. Inosanto also scoffed at the idea that an aging stuntman could fight Lee to a draw. In response to these criticisms of the film's take on Lee, Tarantino doubled down, saying, "Bruce Lee was kind of an arrogant guy," adding, "The way he was talking, I didn't just make a lot of that up. I heard him say things like that, to that effect." Perhaps more important, he claimed that Linda Lee in her biography of her late husband quoted Bruce as saying that he could beat Ali.[24]

On this point, Tarantino is wrong. Linda Lee never represents her husband as boasting about being able to beat Ali but attributes that notion to unnamed observers. Tarantino probably misremembers a passage in which she quotes a television critic who commented on Lee's performance on *The Green Hornet*: "Those who watched him would bet on Lee to render Cassius Clay senseless if they were put in a room and told that anything goes."[25] In addition, Linda Lee backs Inosanto's memory of Bruce's deep admiration for The Greatest, noting that he pored over footage of Ali's fights to glean insight into the boxer's techniques.

Furthermore, Yang Sze, who played the heavily muscled Bolo in *Enter the Dragon*, recalls seeing Bruce studying film of Muhammad Ali bouts. He had set up a full-length mirror to watch the image in reverse so that his own south-paw stance would match Ali's and carefully mimicked every movement. "I'm studying every move he makes. I'm getting to know how he thinks and moves," Bruce commented, because he thought he might fight Ali someday. But he harbored no illusions about who would prevail. "Look at my hand," he concluded. "That's a little Chinese hand. He'd kill me."[26]

Tarantino's portrayal dismisses a man who continues to be one of the most highly visible Asian or Asian American icons even nearly half a century after his death. The objections of Shannon Lee and Dan Inosanto can be seen as the protestations of people who have a vested interest in his legacy—Shannon as his daughter and beneficiary of his estate, as well as chair of the board of the Bruce Lee Foundation, and Inosanto as Lee's most famous student and inheritor of the Jeet Kune Do martial arts discipline he created. Tarantino also makes a valid point about Bruce's famous self-assurance, which could be interpreted by various observers in different situations as confidence, swagger, chutzpah, braggadocio, or even hubris.

However, the major problem with Tarantino's fiction is that it depicts un-bridled ego as Lee's main characteristic (the fight scene constitutes his pri-mary appearance in the film) while doing nothing to humanize the fighter or establish his backstory. How much self-assurance must it have required for a five foot seven migrant from Hong Kong who wore elevator shoes to augment his height to persevere in a Hollywood hell-bent on keeping him in his place as a bit player whose primary claim to fame was his membership in a specific racial group? Bruce's urge to seize the spotlight whenever possible ruffled more than a few feathers and incited power players to wonder at the audacity of this strange "Chinaman" with his dreams of stardom.

Indeed, Bruce Lee's life story is one of repeated setbacks followed by a dogged refusal to capitulate that could only have arisen from deep wells of re-solve and belief in himself. The tragedy is that by showing Lee being forced to fight to maintain his image of masculinity and invincibility, Tarantino comes tantalizingly close to, but shies away from, showing Bruce as a vulnerable yet resilient human being. Instead, *Once Upon a Time in Hollywood* diminishes Bruce Lee to a comical aside.[27]

Rather than reducing Bruce Lee to a caricature, as has happened so often, my goal is to humanize him and, more important, to show how he was both a product of his times and a harbinger of the future. As uncommonly deter-mined, physically gifted, talented, and brilliant as he may have been, Lee rose to fame by riding transpacific currents that circulated before his birth and have accelerated ever since. An equally extraordinary person born decades earlier could not have developed into the man or the icon that Bruce Lee became. And though one born decades later might still encounter some of the barriers Lee faced, that person would be following in the footsteps of a trailblazer: the first Asian / Asian American global superstar.

THE STORY

The Bruce Lee story, which began a century before his birth, is remarkable, even in a nutshell. To understand that story, one should start by examining how Hong Kong and California came to be nodes in a transpacific network of migration and commercial and artistic exchange. Hong Kong was a hybrid society structured by British colonialism and European mercantile capitalism, both of which influenced the creation of the cast of multiracial people known as Eurasians, and Bruce descended from the wealthiest and most prominent Eurasian clan, the Ho family. It was the journey of Chinese opera across the Pacific to California that led to Bruce's birth in San Francisco in 1940. And as a result of the transpacific origins of Chinese cinema, which was tightly connected to the opera, Bruce made his film debut in San Francisco at the age of three months, playing an infant in the Chinese film *Golden Gate Girl*.

Bruce grew up in Hong Kong as the son of privilege and a child movie star who also dabbled in the disreputable world of street fighting. Because he earned fame as a martial artist, it is useful to examine his martial arts pedigree as an adherent of Wing Chun kung fu. Far from being an accomplished master of an ancient art, he was a relatively nonadvanced student of Yip Man, the grandmaster of Wing Chun, who revised the style he taught to Bruce and others.

At the age of eighteen, Bruce Lee migrated to the West Coast of the United States, where he confronted new challenges and absorbed new influences. There he faced US racism for the first time and remade his philosophy, fighting style, and body in response to both the barriers he faced and the influences he encountered. He learned to move in new ways as he confronted martial arts styles from around the world.

As a working-class immigrant in Seattle, he attended school and worked in a Chinese restaurant. He began teaching Wing Chun and encountered many more martial arts styles than he ever would have in Hong Kong. As it turns out, his evolving approach to fighting would be mirrored in his philosophy as expressed in his notebooks from his time as a student at the University of Washington and even his romantic life, as he began dating Linda Emery, whom he would wed in defiance of widespread prejudice against interracial marriages.

Bruce changed his martial art dramatically during his time on the West Coast. His time in Oakland was marked by continual change as he met and befriended martial artists whose styles were drawn from all across Asia and intermixed in the crucible of the United States. Unsurprisingly, given that all martial arts are hybrid forms, Bruce Lee's was shaped by his own migration as well as the transnational forces of militarism and colonialism.

Throughout his time in Seattle and Oakland, Bruce Lee dreamed of finding fame and fortune as a martial arts teacher, but in 1965, at the age of twenty-five, he returned to his childhood vocation of acting and pursued a career in television and film that took him from Hollywood to Hong Kong, while struggling against Hollywood stereotypes of Chinese people and Asian Americans generally that limited his choices.

Upon returning to Hong Kong, however, he made three groundbreaking martial arts films that transformed him into Asia's biggest movie star. This trilogy examined nationalism and transnationalism, showcased the martial arts philosophy that Bruce had developed while on the West Coast, and galvanized audiences not only in Asia but throughout the world. The success of these movies also enabled Bruce to fulfill his long-standing goal of starring in a Hollywood blockbuster, albeit one filmed in Hong Kong.

This movie, *Enter the Dragon*, blended stories of resistance to US-style racism with narratives that resonated with the colony's audience for martial arts films, which were known as *wuxia*. But before the film was released, Bruce Lee collapsed and died, leaving friends, family, and fans around the world to grieve and wonder about the perplexing circumstances of his premature death at the age of thirty-two.

Bruce Lee willed himself to worldwide superstardom through supreme self-possession, dogged determination, and astonishing physical skills. By any measure, he was an extraordinary individual. Yet it was his preternatural ability to absorb the ideas, atmosphere, and styles of movement surrounding him and to synthesize them so that they were uniquely his own that enabled him to become the first global icon to emerge from outside the West. He was exposed to these influences by his incessant travels across the Pacific, impelled by the transnational processes of militarism and capitalism, and melded them into a potent blend of justice-seeking and personal empowerment that has proved inspirational for half a century.

Since his death, Asian martial arts have suffused filmmaking and cultural practices throughout an ever-more-globalizing world. Yet despite an army of imitators and wannabes, there will never be another Bruce Lee.

1

NEITHER EAST NOR WEST

BRUCE LEE AND TRANSPACIFIC CURRENTS

> Oh, East is East, and West is West, and never the twain shall meet,
> Till Earth and Sky stand presently at God's great Judgment Seat;
> But there is neither East nor West, Border, nor Breed, nor Birth,
> When two strong men stand face to face, tho' they come from the
> ends of the earth!
> —Rudyard Kipling, "The Ballad of East and West" (1889)

Bruce Lee was born in San Francisco on the morning of November 27, 1940. Much is made of the fact that the man who would become known worldwide as The Dragon was born in the Chinese year of the dragon during the hour of the dragon. Lee certainly fulfilled his astrological forecast, for in Chinese tradition, dragons are purported to be ambitious, driven, and passionate as well as headstrong and impulsive—all qualities that Lee embodied in abundance. But less is made of the historical circumstances that led to his birth and what they imply for understanding the world from which Lee emerged and in which we live today. Bruce Lee's birth, life, and career resulted from and furthered centuries-long processes of globalization that created the Pacific as a unique transnational zone of contact between Asia and the West.

In the 1889 poem "The Ballad of East and West," the English writer Rudyard Kipling famously wrote, "Oh, East is East, and West is West, and never the twain shall meet," an oft-quoted statement about the incompatibility of the so-called Orient and the Occident and one that is sometimes taken as evidence of Kipling's racism. The statement seems to argue for what the celebrated scholar Edward Said decried as "Orientalism"—a way of understanding the world as structured by a stark divide, with the East seen as weak, passive, ancient, ossified, mysterious, and superstitious and the West as powerful, active, dynamic, modern, scientific, and logical.

Orientalism claims that the Orient is the negation of the Occident—the shadow to its sunshine, the subjugated to its conquerors, the witch doctors to its scientists, the feminine to its masculine—and as such, the two are incompatible and in permanent opposition to each other. Critically, as Said argues, Orientalism is a pattern of thought and action that legitimizes and perpetuates unequal relations of power, namely, Western colonial, military, and intellectual domination of Asia. But studying Bruce Lee as a transpacific figure, one whose life straddles both the East and the West, reveals Orientalist notions to be simplistic and in fact mistaken, for constant oceanic crossings of people, goods, ideas, and cultures rendered the barrier between East and West highly permeable.

Although Kipling was indeed deeply imbued with all the self-righteousness and belief in white supremacy expected of the Victorian-era British imperialist that he was, "The Ballad of East and West" paints a more complex picture than first meets the eye. Set in a remote region of colonial India in the late nineteenth century, the poem tells the story of how a brown-skinned man steals the cherished horse of a British officer. The officer's son pursues the thief through hostile territory, but when the antagonists confront each other, they reach a détente and exchange tokens of mutual respect.

The poem concludes that "there is neither East nor West, Border, nor Breed, nor Birth" when "two strong men" engage in honorable combat. Kipling raises the notion of an impenetrable barrier between Asia and Europe in the oft-quoted first line of his poem only to subvert it at the end, arguing that the nobility of battle erases distinctions of race and nationality. Yet the unspoken threat of the power of empire lurks behind the seeming egalitarianism described in the ballad, for in the end, the officer's son recaptures the mare by threatening British military retaliation. Kipling's poem thus sets up a framework for understanding East-West relations as bifurcated, on the one hand, yet eminently broachable, on the other, and always plagued by questions of race, nation, and power.

≈

Bruce Lee is often understood within the East-West dichotomy that Kipling sets up, as a Chinese martial artist who shattered barriers to enter the Western imagination. This book argues instead that Lee emerged within a thoroughly transpacific world that had long been swept up in processes of globalization that rendered geographic, national, cultural, and racial boundaries between East and West thoroughly permeable. While Kipling imagines the meeting of East and West as the meeting of "two strong men" in conflict, Lee was a single individual in whom the "ends of the earth" came together through the synthesis of the fighting arts.

Bruce Lee's birth, life, career, and death and the enduring resonance of his life and his achievements existed within processes of globalization that began half a millennium ago and have accelerated dramatically in the past century. These processes created the Pacific as a zone of contact, exchange, and mixture, interconnecting Asia and the West into a progressively tighter network over time, with people, cultures, ideas, goods, technologies, and capital traveling in every conceivable direction. If we were to trace these oceanic crossings on a map over time, our diagram would become an increasingly dense network of lines, arcs, and loops that would eventually leave virtually no place untouched.

Transpacific currents washed Lee both eastward and westward from his birth in San Francisco in 1940 to his death three decades later in Hong Kong and his burial in Seattle and so incessantly that any attempt to pin down his one true point of origin is futile. Rather than existing as a product of either Hong Kong or the United States, Bruce Lee came into being through processes that interconnected the two. His cultural identity defies neat categorization because he developed a sense of self, a philosophy of life, and a style of fighting all structured by his constant traversals.

What was Bruce Lee's family background? How did he happen to be born in the United States? How does his background reflect the emerging concept of Asia-America? How did he become part of the thriving world of Chinese opera that had rooted itself in San Francisco after the start of the Gold Rush? And how did he come to make his debut as an infant in a 1941 Chinese film shot in San Francisco?

The story of the early years of the man who would become Bruce Lee is complex, often laced with myths and falsehoods, and in some cases dauntingly hard to unravel. Nonetheless, answering these and similar questions provides an excellent starting point for understanding both the importance of transpacific flows to creating the world Lee entered and the forces that drove those currents.

≈

The 2010 biographical film *Bruce Lee, My Brother*, based on the book of the same title written by Bruce's younger brother, Robert Lee, opens with the boys' father, Lee Hoi Chuen, standing on a stage in San Francisco. He is wearing an elaborate golden brocade silk robe, a beautifully beaded hat, and dramatic makeup—white pancake covering his face, accented by shoe-polish-black eyebrows, eyeliner, and mustache, deep red lips, and pink cheeks. Under a bright spotlight, with a spare instrumental accompaniment, he sings of life as a poor farmer who cannot read poetry. As he delivers his final line, he basks in the applause of a large and enthusiastic audience. The scene establishes Hoi Chuen as a Cantonese opera performer, which is one important strand of the story of how Bruce Lee came to be the iconic transpacific figure that he did.

Backstage after the performance, Lee Hoi Chuen receives word that his wife, Grace Lee, is in labor, and he dashes off to the Tung Wah Dispensary, a San Francisco institution established in 1899 to serve the city's immigrant Chinese population. Anxiously smoking cigarettes as he paces outside the delivery room, the father-to-be hears a white nurse repeatedly urging Grace to "push" in English. When the nurse asks for the baby's name for the birth certificate, a semiconscious Grace murmurs, "Push," which the nurse records as "Bruce."

This nativity scene, touching as it might be, skirts historical accuracy in at least three respects. First, when Bruce was born, Lee Hoi Chuen was performing with his opera company in New York and so could not have rushed to his wife's side. Second, Bruce was not born at a dispensary or clinic but at Chinese Hospital, a major medical facility and source of pride for San Francisco's Chinese American community. Finally, it was not a nurse but Dr. Mary Glover, the attending physician, who bestowed the English name "Bruce" on the infant so it could be recorded on his birth certificate.[1]

Setting aside quibbles with cinematic representation, the scene focuses on Lee Hoi Chuen while relegating his wife to a background role, despite the fact that her fascinating family history provides a second key line of inquiry into her son's true origins. But more important than the details of Lee Hoi Chuen's vocation and his wife's ancestry is the idea that Asia and the West, rather than existing discretely and in opposition to each other, have for centuries been deeply intertwined by forces of mercantile capitalism, colonialism, and racism. And it is this complexity that provides the best lens through which to tell the story of one of the most celebrated people to emerge from that world.

ASIA-AMERICA

The United States, and indeed the Americas writ large, can scarcely be imagined without also conjuring the idea of Asia. Asian commodities, people, and cultures have played important roles in the development of the Americas since the sixteenth century. In addition, ideas about Asia, known then as "the Orient," shaped the European quest for the Americas and the ways that its new inhabitants conceived of themselves. In the nineteenth and twentieth centuries, large-scale immigration created a significant Asian presence in the United States on the West Coast. Travel in both directions of merchants, workers, and artists, as well as information, capital, and culture, transcended national and racial boundaries, creating the transpacific world as a site of mixture, fusion, and hybridization.

The foundational stories of the New World were already intertwined with Asia, particularly through trade and exchange. Christopher Columbus famously set off from Spain in 1492 on a quest for a new sea route to the East Indies in Asia that would enable the Spaniards to gain an upper hand in the spice trade. Columbus mistook the Caribbean islands he landed on for the East Indies, even dubbing the indigenous people he encountered "Indios," and he died convinced that he had reached the coast of Asia. Asian commodities, people, and cultures played critical roles in the conquest and incorporation of the Americas into the world system of capitalism from the sixteenth century onward. Beginning in 1565, Spanish galleons plied the Pacific between Manila and Acapulco, exchanging Chinese spices, porcelain, and silk for Mexican silver.

Just as early encounters with the Americas were linked to the so-called Orient, the establishment of the United States as an independent nation was interwoven with Asia. Perhaps no incident is more emblematic of the burgeoning American revolutionary spirit than the famed Boston Tea Party, which was motivated by a dispute with Britain over trade with Asia. When white colonists swarmed aboard three British ships and dumped their cargo of tea into Boston Harbor on December 16, 1773, they did so to protest the imposition of a British tax on imports of Chinese tea, a highly popular drink in the Colonies.

Colonists opposed the Tea Act, as the legislation was known, because it kept American merchants out of the tea trade and continued a tea tariff that Americans considered to be taxation without representation. This emblematic moment in the movement toward the nation's independence revolved around a Chinese import good and a desire to trade directly with China without British interference.

And just as the Americas could not be imagined without Asia, China has been infiltrated by the West for over half a millennium, primarily through the mechanisms of trade and imperialism. Until the rise of seafaring mercantilism, China to Europeans remained a distant, mythical realm for more than two hundred years after Marco Polo's fabled overland travels along the Silk Road in the thirteenth century.

≈

The first Europeans to begin regular trade with China were the Portuguese, who visited the port city of Canton in 1516 and in 1557 established a permanent trading outpost at the Chinese city of Macao. The Dutch and British followed more than a century later, but Chinese rulers rebuffed overtures from the foreigners, whom they regarded as barbarians, and restricted their activities to Macao and Canton.

Direct trade between the United States and China began in 1784, just one year after the end of the Revolutionary War, with the voyage of the *Empress of China* from New York to Canton. American merchants traded gold bullion, ginseng, and furs for Chinese tea, silk, and porcelain. To the British, by contrast, China seemed like a bottomless pit into which they dumped silver in exchange for Chinese goods. To offset this trade deficit, the British East India Company began exporting to China opium grown in India, and British merchants continued to smuggle the narcotic into the country even after the Chinese government banned its importation.

In response, in an act of rebellion reminiscent of the Boston Tea Party, the Chinese blockaded opium-bearing ships near the Canton River, seized the drugs on the ships and in the port's warehouses, and destroyed more than one thousand tons valued at over £2 million. The British government declared that this action violated the rights of its subjects and began the First Opium War, in which it decisively defeated the Chinese and in 1842 forced them to sign the Treaty of Nanking. The first of many national humiliations for China, the treaty opened up four additional ports and ceded Hong Kong to Great Britain.[2]

The Second Opium War concluded similarly in 1858, with China ceding trading rights in eleven cities to Britain, France, Russia, and the United States. Many more nations rushed in to take advantage of Chinese vulnerability, and by the early 1900s, Austria-Hungary, Belgium, France, Germany, Great Britain,

Italy, Japan, Portugal, and Russia held concessions or outright colonies in China.

Throughout the nineteenth century, the Pearl River Delta functioned as China's primary gateway to the rest of the world. The Guangdong province and its central city of Canton (known today as Guangzhou) had long formed the heart of a vibrant mercantile economic system that incorporated nearby Macao and Hong Kong, and Pearl River Delta merchants had traded extensively throughout Southeast Asia for centuries before European colonialism in the area.

From 1757 until the end of the First Opium War, Canton was designated as the sole port for international trade.[3] Even after Western powers forced the opening of other ports, the Pearl River Delta continued to be a thriving center of transpacific commerce, a place where traders from England, France, Holland, Denmark, Sweden, Spain, Austria, and the United States rubbed elbows with both one another and the Chinese as they bought and sold their wares.

≈

Across the Pacific, the western terminus of the transpacific trade was another bustling city: San Francisco. Just as Europe opened China to trade by force, the United States appropriated California by conquest. The indigenous Ohlone people lived on and around the peninsula on which the city eventually grew, undisturbed for centuries until the arrival of Spanish invaders. In 1776, an expedition led by Captain Juan Bautista de Anza pushed its way northward from what was then Sonora (now Arizona) to the tip of the San Francisco peninsula. The invaders planted the Spanish flag atop the bluff that towers over the entrance to the magnificent bay and farther inland established the Mission San Francisco de Asis.

Spanish colonization decimated the indigenous population. Under the mission system established by the Franciscan Father Junípero Serra, the Ohlone and other Native Americans in Alta California were victims of kidnapping, forced conversion to Christianity, coerced labor, and devastating disease. Yerba Buena, as the settlement on the peninsula was then called, remained a Spanish possession until Mexico attained independence in 1821. By the 1830s, US ships regularly arrived to buy cattle hides and tallow from California ranchos, which they transported to tanneries and factories in New England. But although a few Yankees trekked overland to California, drawn to the region's temperate climate and fertile soil, California remained Mexican territory until two closely spaced events occurred in early 1848.

On January 24 of that year, in what would prove a transformative moment for the region, the nation, and regions far distant and in many respects would set the scene for the creation of the world in which Bruce Lee would be born, a carpenter named James Wilson Marshall, who was building a sawmill on the American River in the Sierra Nevada foothills, spied flakes of gold in the riverbed. Nine days later, Mexico and the United States concluded the US-Mexico War by signing the Treaty of Guadalupe Hidalgo.

As the victor, the United States claimed Mexico's northern territories, including what would become the states of California, Nevada, Utah, and parts of New Mexico, Arizona, Colorado, and Wyoming, in exchange for a paltry payment of $15 million. California became a US territory just as Hong Kong had become a British colony—as spoils of war.

The ensuing Gold Rush transformed San Francisco from a sleepy port to a boom town and, eventually, a cosmopolitan city filled with migrants from the eastern United States, Europe, and, most important for the purposes of our story, China. Word about the spectacular troves to be found in the California dirt spread so widely throughout southern China that California came to be known as "Gum San," or Gold Mountain.

Chinese migration to the United States began with a trickle but soon swelled into a rushing stream. In 1849, 325 Chinese gold seekers arrived in California, followed by 450 in 1850 and 2,716 in 1852. Then the floodgates opened. More than 20,000 would-be miners landed in Gum San, and by 1870, roughly 48,500 Chinese lived in California, with another 14,500 in other parts of the United States.[4] In 1890, when the country's total population exceeded 62 million, 103,620 Chinese resided in the United States, with 21,745 of them living in San Francisco, which they called "dai fou," or "big city."[5]

These immigrants came overwhelmingly from the Pearl River Delta and spoke the Cantonese dialect. According to the 1880 census, more than nine in ten residents of San Francisco's Chinatown came from the Guangdong province.[6] They joined countless Americans, many of whom were immigrants from Europe, who had journeyed westward to gather nuggets and flakes of gold from the rich California soil.

CANTONESE OPERA

Cantonese opera was one of the first major cultural imports to follow Chinese immigrants to California. A dramatic art form developed during the late Ming and early Qing Dynasties (around 1600 CE), Cantonese opera incorporates "loud drums and gongs, high-pitched falsetto, colorful painted faces and embroidered costume, ferocious fighting and delicate dancing."[7] Although Cantonese opera revolves chiefly around singing, speaking, and some dancing, the genre called "martial drama" highlights acrobatics, fighting, and weaponry.[8] Cantonese opera, known as *yueju*, emerged in the coastal districts of Guangdong and Guangxi and was viewed as more provincial than the more sophisticated, nationalized Beijing form, which was known as *jingju*.

But because early Chinese migrants were mostly poor Cantonese speakers from southern China, Cantonese opera became the dominant form to cross the Pacific to North America. By the 1920s, the opera had spread even more widely, creating a transnational network with centers in both Southeast Asia, including Indonesia, Thailand, Myanmar (formerly known as Burma), India, Vietnam, and the Philippines, with an especially strong presence in Singapore, and the Americas, notably New York City, Vancouver, Peru, Mexico, and Cuba.[9]

The first well-documented Cantonese opera performance in the United States occurred in 1852, when the Tong Hook Tong Dramatic Company traveled from Guangzhou to San Francisco.[10] Bankrolled by Chinese merchants to the tune of £2,000, the troupe of 123 actors and musicians transported their instruments, sumptuous costumes, and even an elaborate, prefabricated theater building across the ocean. Once arrived, they began performing immediately, even before they could assemble their theater. On the opening night, October 18, a mixed audience, mostly Chinese but including some whites, crowded into the American Theater on Sansome Street, paying two dollars apiece to sit in the gallery or six dollars for a seat in a private box.

The lineup featured dramatic staples of Cantonese opera such as "The Eight Genii Offering Their Congratulation to the High Ruler Yuk Hwang, on His Birthday" and "Too Tsin Made High Minister by the Six States." The Chinese in the audience—thousands of *li* away from kith and kin—thrilled to these familiar mythical epics performed to the music and in the language and costumes of home by actors with Chinese faces.

While Chinese audiences found these performances comfortingly familiar, white observers experienced Chinese theater as an alien albeit exotic spectacle. They found the costumes—made of satin, silk, and painted cotton and adorned with tinsel and ornaments—to be "magnificent," "splendid," and "gorgeous." After the Tong Hook Tong troupe's initial run, it assembled the building that it had brought from China, which seated more than a thousand patrons and was, according to newspaper accounts, an object of wonder, a "curious pagoda-looking edifice" that was "painted, outside and in, in an extraordinary manner." Despite the pleasing visual spectacle of Cantonese opera, white audiences found its sounds intolerably grating. According to nineteenth-century accounts, the orchestra produced "an interminable humming, banging, scraping, and screeching of Chinese fiddles, pipes, cymbals and gongs" that was so "incessant," "discordant and deafening" that it "severely tortured the white man to listen to." Chinese singing was no more pleasing to American ears than were the instruments: one newspaper critic described the vocal performances as "howl[s]" and "shriek[s]," the "wailings of a thousand love-lorn cats, the screams, gobblings, brayings and barkings of as many peacocks, turkeys, donkeys and dogs." And if the music of Cantonese opera sat poorly with white audiences, the acting and plotting fared no better. "Chinese acting has no dignity, no repose, no beauty," *Harper's Weekly* opined, adding that "the plots are of almost childish simplicity."[11]

The conventions of Chinese opera also perplexed white audiences. Viewers were surprised to see the musicians sitting on the stage wearing ordinary street clothing rather than being hidden away in an orchestra pit. During breaks in the music, the musicians casually smoked or drank tea in full view of the audience, then picked up their instruments to resume their performance. Stagehands sauntered across the stage in everyday garb to hand swords or teacups to the actors as the play demanded.

In addition, the Chinese style of staging was exceedingly spare, with no scenery or curtains and very few props. If an actor wished to convey the fact that he had entered a house and slammed the door, he simply carried a chair to the middle of the stage and thumped it down onto the floor. A character would be shown to cross a bridge simply by walking across a plank set between two tables.

And the behavior of the Chinese audience seemed out of place to white theatergoers. During performances, the Chinese chatted casually, smoked cigars, snacked on melon seeds, and even kicked off their shoes to lounge comfortably on the bench seating. Only an especially dramatic climax to a scene could draw the crowd's full attention. This minimalist staging and the blurring of the boundary between the stage and the audience would not become familiar to Westerners until the emergence of avant-garde theater in the late nineteenth century.

By the Tong Hook Tong Company's third performance, it began adjusting its offerings, emphasizing in English-language advertisements in the *Alta California* newspaper that they would present "feats of skill, vaulting, tumbling and dramatic performance."[12] The emphasis on acrobatics and bodily dexterity rather than drama suggests something important about the way white audiences viewed Cantonese opera. Rather than embracing its universal human elements—narratives of conflict and triumph, for example—white Californians were drawn instead toward the physical spectacle of flying bodies and flashing weapons.

One observer deemed the "most exciting part" of the Tong Hook Tong performance to be an exhibition in which a man spread-eagled himself against a door while half a dozen others pelted the door with knives from a distance of fifteen to twenty feet, "putting a knife into every square inch of the door, but never touching the man." The spectator added with wry understatement, "It was very pleasant to see."[13]

≈

The world of Cantonese opera, an art form that became a staple of life in San Francisco from 1852 onward, would profoundly shape Bruce Lee's early years, thanks to his father's deep involvement in the art form as a celebrated opera star. Numerous touring companies followed the Tong Hook Tong troupe in the 1850s, and several permanent companies opened in the city, ensuring that Cantonese opera was performed continuously in San Francisco's Chinatown for the next several decades.

The most renowned permanent company, the Hing Chuen Yuen, or Royal Chinese Theatre, opened in 1868, and by the early 1880s, four theaters featuring Cantonese opera operated in Chinatown simultaneously. Rivalries between troupes sometimes became so heated that they spilled into riots in the streets, with allegations flying back and forth of kidnapping, arson, and even murder.

For Chinese immigrants, opera provided one of the chief forms of entertainment and social interaction. To begin with, it was eminently affordable, with tickets in 1880 priced at twenty cents apiece for Chinese and fifty cents for non-Chinese. A single ticket to the day's show could provide hours of entertainment, for performances began at seven in the morning and, breaking only for meals, continued nearly nonstop until two or three the next morning. Not surprisingly, crowds at the Royal Chinese Theatre often topped twelve hundred at a time.

Ah Quin, a San Francisco resident who was one of the city's myriad opera habitués, recorded in his diary that he would sometimes go to performances twice a day and stay up to several hours each time.[14] In addition to being a bargain, the theater also provided a place where lonely migrants could socialize in a relaxed, familiar, and convivial atmosphere. Audience members like Ah Quin would gather there with friends to chat, tell jokes, compliment the performers, smoke, drink, snack, and even occasionally give full attention to the drama onstage.

Some white producers printed programs entirely in English, a clear indication of an intention to draw white Americans into the audience. For example, the program for a three-day run at the American Theater in 1878 promised "Dramatic, Acrobatic and Gymnastic Company, from the Imperial Theatre, Canton (China), comprising the largest and most Wonderful Company of first-class male and female Artists that ever left THE FLOWERY KINGDOM."[15] In addition to being printed in English, the wording and point of view of the program (explaining that Canton is in China and referencing the "flowery kingdom") indicate that the theater was seen as a zone of interracial contact where whites would encounter unexpected cultural oddities.

Indeed, visitors regularly noted the many peculiarities of Chinese opera. Besides being dazzled by the spectacular sights, jarring sounds, and formalistic differences from European theater that could be observed onstage, they also expressed puzzlement or even distaste for what occurred backstage. Visitors were appalled by the immodesty of the actors, who milled about in a state of half-dress or even near nudity as they changed costumes. One white actress was dismayed by the startling indifference of the brown-skinned men who disrobed in her presence. "I had some difficulty in finding a nook I could fix my eyes on without being shocked," she told a reporter.[16]

The living arrangements of actors came in for criticism as well, as the entire company performed, slept, cooked, and ate within the four walls of the theater. The same white actress was disgusted by more than just the dressing room. "I then visited the kitchen," she said, "for, *mon ami*, the Chinese actors live in the theatre and, and their sleeping dens—pah, I sicken as I think of them." At the Royal China Theatre, where the combination dining and dressing room was located in the basement, another white visitor complained about the "dense, greasy vapors and smells" of cooking that were "even more uncanny than those which salute [patrons'] noses above."[17]

≈

The strangeness of Cantonese opera in the eyes of whites was due not simply to its foreignness, for Gold Rush–era California was heavily populated by migrants of all kinds: the Chinese, to be sure, but also Mexicans, Europeans from many nations, and American Forty-Niners. San Francisco became a sophisticated, cosmopolitan city with stunning rapidity after gold was discovered nearby, and European opera was first performed there in 1851, just one year before the Tong Hook Tong debuted.

Throughout the 1850s, Italian, French, and German operas were performed regularly in the city.[18] These European operas were seen as magnificent or enthralling, rather than racial spectacle. Although whites regularly attended Cantonese opera, Chinese were decidedly unwelcome at white venues. The attendance of two Chinese men and a Chinese woman at a European opera in 1877 was so noteworthy that the *San Francisco Post* reported that the "unprecedented spectacle . . . gave rise to good deal of comment among the fashionable audience in attendance, much of which was of a decidedly hostile character."[19] White fascination with and revulsion to Cantonese opera reflected a racial hierarchy that positioned the Chinese as inexorably alien to the United States, perpetual foreigners who could never be assimilated into the US body politic.

Opposition to the presence of Chinese newcomers in the United States began almost immediately after their arrival. In 1850, California enacted a Foreign Miners' Tax, which primarily targeted Chinese.[20] White workers depicted the Chinese as "coolies," or unfree laborers, who served as tools of capitalists by providing cheap labor and thus threatened the ability of white men to earn a decent living.

In fact, Chinese immigrants to the United States were not indentured or unfree. Nevertheless, the Workingmen's Party of California, led by the Irish immigrant Denis Kearney, adopted the slogan "The Chinese must go!" The Workingmen's Party stoked the flames of anti-Chinese sentiment at rallies across the state, where speakers spewed invective such as, "Are you ready to march down to the wharf and stop the leprous Chinamen from landing?" and "Judge Lynch is the judge wanted by the workingmen of California. I advise all to own a musket and a hundred rounds of ammunition."[21]

The reference to lynching was much more than mere hyperbole. During these years, Chinese throughout the western United States were the victims of widespread violence, including roundups, expulsions, arson, beatings, and even murder. In 1871, seventeen Chinese were lynched by a mob in Los Angeles. In 1880, rioting whites burned the Chinese section of Denver and murdered one Chinese man. The violence of 1885 alone included vigilantes rounding up and expelling the three-hundred-member Chinese community in Eureka, California; a mob ransacking the Chinese enclave in Tacoma, Washington, and marching its eight hundred to nine hundred residents marched out of town; and white miners in Rock Springs, Wyoming, killing twenty-eight Chinese miners, injuring fifteen more, and chasing hundreds of Chinese into the desert.[22] And these episodes represent only a few of the 153 documented instances of anti-Chinese violence that occurred in the United States between 1852 and 1908.[23]

In addition to claiming that the Chinese represented an economic threat, the anti-Chinese movement depicted Chinese women as prostitutes and Chinese men as depraved, opium-addicted sexual predators who especially threatened white women. Grotesque images of Chinese as filthy, diseased, and debauched circulated widely in popular magazines, further contributing to their vilification as threats to the nation.[24]

The anti-Chinese movement had great success in legalizing discrimination against Chinese immigrants. As Governor John Bigler of California exhorted, "Measures must be adopted to check this tide of Asiatic immigration." Chinese were forbidden from testifying against whites under an 1854 ruling of the California Supreme Court, in which the majority opinion interpreted an existing California statute stating that "no Black or Mulatto person, or Indian, shall be allowed to give evidence for or against a white man" to also forbid Chinese testimony. (The court's chief justice tortuously reasoned that "Indians" referred to the people Columbus encountered when he mistakenly believed that he had reached the Indies, that China was a part of the Indies, and therefore "Indians" included Chinese.)[25]

The Page Act of 1875, which prohibited the entry of Asian women suspected to be prostitutes, was enforced against nearly all would-be female Chinese immigrants. But the crowning achievement of the anti-Chinese movement came in 1882 with the passage of the infamous Chinese Exclusion Act, which barred the entry of Chinese laborers, a group that comprised the vast majority of men in the immigrant stream. Despite such measures, however, touring opera performers, regarded as visiting artists, were able to travel to San Francisco and other Chinese enclaves on the West Coast and New York City until the beginning of World War II, when travel across the Pacific was interrupted by hostilities between Japan and the United States.

BRUCE LEE'S PARENTS AND TRANSPACIFIC OPERA

On November 18, 1939, Lee Hoi Chuen and his wife boarded the SS *President Coolidge* in Hong Kong bound for San Francisco. The other passengers were mostly students and merchants—both classes exempted from the Chinese Exclusion Act—and a few Chinese Americans who held citizenship by virtue of their birth in the United States. The ship steamed eastward for twenty days, making port calls in Shanghai, Kobe, and Honolulu before docking at the San Pedro pier in Los Angeles on December 7. The couple proceeded to San Francisco by train, arriving the next day.

As aliens subject to the Chinese Exclusion Act, the Lees and other Chinese citizens endured an arduous process to gain permission to enter the United States on a temporary basis. The case files for Chinese immigrants who came to the United States under the Exclusion Act, which were maintained by the US Immigration and Naturalization Service, detail the various steps in this process.

In the application of Bruce's father, Lee Hoi Chuen, for a temporary one-year, nonimmigrant visa, he listed his age as thirty-five years old, his birthday as February 18, and his place of birth as Kongmee, Shuntak, Kwantung, China. Elsewhere, he stated that he had been an actor for eighteen to nineteen years.

MANDARIN THEATRE, CHINATOWN

© STANLEY A. PILTZ

Postcard circa the 1930s illustrating the Mandarin Theatre in San Francisco, an important venue for Cantonese opera performances and Chinese film screenings. (Artist: Stanley A. Piltz)

Bruce's mother listed her name as Ho Oi Yee, her age as twenty-eight years old, her birthday as November 8, and her place of birth as Canton, China, despite, as we shall see, research suggesting that she was born in Shanghai. The fact that Lee's mother, who was named Grace when she was born and is called Grace in the film about Lee that was made by his brother, officially identified herself to immigration officials as Ho Oi Yee will become a critical element when it comes to unraveling the complex story of her famous son's origins.

To obtain visas, the couple presented affidavits signed by a representative of the elegant Mandarin Theatre, which had been established in 1924 at 1021 Grant Avenue and whose modern amenities and Chinese architectural flourishes signaled that it was arguably Chinatown's preeminent entertainment venue. While Lee signed his application in Chinese, his wife's signature appears in English, her ability to write English being further evidence of her own origins, specifically that she had received an education because she had grown up as a member of the Eurasian caste in Hong Kong.

Bruce Lee's parents were able to land in San Francisco due to a provision in the law that allowed employed actors and other artists to enter the United States temporarily on the condition that they post a bond of $1,000 per individual, to be forfeited if they failed to leave when their visas expired. The affidavits for them affirmed that they would be employed by the Mandarin and pledged a $1,000 bond for each of them.[26]

～

Immigration officials subjected passengers on ships departing from China to considerable scrutiny, carefully screening them and logging their arrival on a form titled "List or Manifest of Alien Passengers for the United States Immigrant Inspector at Port of Arrival." Even Chinese Americans with US citizenship were included on the list of aliens subjected to heightened inspection. On the ship's manifest, Lee Hoi Chuen was described as a five-foot-three thirty-five-year-old Chinese actor and his wife as a five-foot-one twenty-eight-year-old Chinese actress and wardrobe caretaker.

Lee and his wife both affirmed that they were married, neither polygamists nor anarchists, literate in Chinese, and in possession of at least fifty dollars apiece. Most important, they disavowed any intention of becoming US citizens (which would have been illegal for Chinese nationals) and stated that they planned to remain in the United States for just one year. The ship's surgeon found both to be in good mental and physical health, with yellow complexions, black hair, and black eyes.

While all biographers agree that Bruce's mother accompanied his father on the opera tour, the ship's manifest and the Immigration and Naturalization Service case files provide three bits of new information about the couple. The first tidbit is that although Lee's mother was named Grace, she apparently traveled under the name Ho Oi Yee. How can we be sure that Ho Oi Yee and Grace are the same person? Immigration documents provide convincing, if slightly inconsistent, evidence.

In the case files, Lee and Ho referred to each other as husband and wife. In the ship's manifest, both listed Lok Shee of Hong Kong as their nearest relative, with Lee listing her as his mother and Ho listing her as her mother-in-law. Another indication comes from a naturalization petition filed decades later, in 1976, under the name Ho Oi Yue (not identical to Ho Oi Yee but similar), which stipulates that the woman who would become Bruce's mother was born on December 29, 1911, in Shanghai (not on November 8 of that year in Canton) and requests that her name as a US citizen be entered as Grace Lee. Also of interest is the typewritten ship manifest, which lists her occupation as actress, with a handwritten note adding the words "wardrobe caretaker." Her visa application echoes this ambiguity, listing her as an actor and wardrobe tender. These documents provide the only known indication that Bruce's mother may have been an opera performer but are not fully convincing because her entry to the United States would have been considerably smoothed by claiming an official role with the theater troupe.

≈

On December 8, 1939, Lee Hoi Chuen and his wife departed from the immigration facilities in San Francisco and, along with another actor, two actresses, and a wardrobe woman, headed for the Mandarin Theatre, which had paid for their passages from Hong Kong and posted their bonds.[27] The little group then settled in a house at 18 Trenton Street, an alley located directly behind the Chinese Hospital, just a few blocks west of the Mandarin. The white actress of the nineteenth century who was sickened by the living conditions of Chinese opera performers probably would have cried "pah" again in 1940 had she seen what went on at 18 Trenton Street, for a total of nearly thirty actors and actresses lived in the cramped Trenton Street abode.

Many Bruce Lee biographers have described Lee Hoi Chuen as a Cantonese opera star. While he became a well-known performer later in his career, at the time of his arrival in the United States, he was no luminary. Nor was he particularly rich. The annual salaries of the performers living in the house on Trenton Street ranged from $200 to $800, at a time when the average American earned $1,368 per year. Lee's earnings of $360 ($6,629 in 2020 inflation-adjusted dollars) placed him below both the average income of $446 and the median income of $400 of those who lived in the house.

Interestingly, on average, actresses outearned their male counterparts by $15 per year and enjoyed a $20 higher median salary. Furthermore, opera performers must have taken their rewards in applause more than in money, as their wages lagged behind those of the Chinese manual laborers who lived in the same census tract. For example, a Chinese houseboy, a hotel janitor, and a hotel cook living in a house across the street from the house where the actors lived reported annual salaries of $650, $750, and $1,000, respectively. However, all of the actors and actresses reported receiving $50 or more in nonwage sources, probably in the form of food and lodging provided by the opera company.[28] The relative poverty in which Grace Lee found herself as an opera performer's wife may have explained why her wealthy father had discouraged her from marrying Lee Hoi Chuen.

EURASIAN ENCOUNTERS

One of the effects of nineteenth-century colonial and commercial contact between China and Europe was interracial mixing, as European businessmen sometimes married Asian women or took them as concubines. The children of these unions, known as Eurasians, constituted an important caste in Hong Kong, as argued by the historian Emma Jinhua Teng, a professor at the Massachusetts Institute of Technology specializing in Asian studies. "Eurasians were despised and feared," she writes, "for in blurring the color line they radically destabilized . . . racial hierarchies," by bridging the social distance between Europeans and Chinese. Eurasians did serve what Teng describes as "vital intermediary functions" by serving as compradors (middlemen between European and Chinese traders), interpreters, and trade officials. But although Eurasians derived prestige and wealth from their intermediate status, they nonetheless existed in a sort of liminal space, for they were never seen as equals by Europeans, nor were they accepted into Chinese society.[29]

Many biographers, including Bruce's wife, Linda, assert that Bruce's mother, Grace Ho, was half German.[30] That claim remains unverified except as family lore. Grace's lineage may or may not have included European genes, but she was undeniably the product of a hybrid Eurasian society that brought East and West together in complex and intimate ways. This hybrid society would become an essential strand of what became the Bruce Lee story.

≈

Since the early 1900s and continuing to the present day, the most prominent group of Eurasian families in Hong Kong has been the sprawling and wealthy Ho clan. Its patriarch, Charles Henri Maurice Bosman, was a Dutch Jew born in Rotterdam in 1839 who arrived in Hong Kong around 1859 and initially worked for a Dutch trader named Cornelius Koopmanschap. Bosman established an import-export business that traded rice and other commodities and eventually rose to such prominence that he served as the Dutch consul to Hong Kong in the late 1860s.

In addition to trading in goods, Bosman brokered Chinese laborers; his joint venture with his old mentor, Koopmanschap & Bosman, exported Chinese laborers to California to work on the railroad.[31] Because the United States by then prohibited slavery, these workers were free, even if they endured dreadful working conditions and were paid less than their white counterparts. Koopmanschap & Bosman did, however, export indentured laborers to Cuba and other places in the Caribbean.[32]

The matriarch of the Ho family was Shi Tai (who was also known by the surname Sze), a Chinese woman who was born on Chongming Island near Shanghai around 1841.[33] Her bound feet indicate that she came from wealth, but her family fell on hard times. According to Eric Peter Ho, a Hong Kong government official and descendant of the Ho clan, after Shi Tai's father died and a blight killed the mulberry trees that the family relied on for their silk-growing business, her uncles sold her in Shanghai to alleviate the family's poverty.

Shi Tai ended up in Hong Kong around 1855, probably after having been bought and sold several times. It must have been a frightening and disorienting experience for a young girl who had probably never left her village to be bought and sold as chattel, to be shipped to a distant island, and to end up in a place where people spoke the strange language of Cantonese, so different from her native dialect. Probably around 1860 she became the concubine of Charles Bosman with the legal status of a "protected woman."[34] As such, she received a salary, a house, and money to support their children, although Bosman lived elsewhere and her children were not recognized as his legal heirs.[35]

Shi Tai bore Bosman either five or six children (the first critical discrepancy when it comes to tracing Bruce Lee's possible European ancestry). The family adopted the last name of Ho in accordance with the usual practice of Eurasian families of the time, who commonly took Chinese surnames linked to their European lineage. For example, the daughter of a MacLean might have the surname Mak, and the son of a man with the first name of Stephen might adopt the surname of Sin. In addition to honoring a father who came from Holland, Ho is a common Chinese surname.[36]

≈

Eurasian families like the Hos occupied an intermediate position in Hong Kong society, encountering discrimination both from Europeans, who were loath to accept people of mixed blood as equals, and from Chinese, who had their own prejudices. Hemmed in from both directions, Eurasians formed their own social caste, intermarrying among other Eurasian families and generally keeping silent about their European ancestry.

Though Eurasian families may have not been fully Chinese by blood, they were completely immersed in Chinese culture. They spoke Cantonese in the home, observed Chinese customs, and practiced traditional ancestor worship, probably due to the fact that Chinese mothers raised the children. Even the white fathers underwent Sinification for ceremonial purposes: Charles

Bosman was dubbed Ho Si-Man and bore a title from the imperial Qing Dynasty, probably purchased from an official in Guangzhou.[37]

Eurasian children were socially marginal. But as the scions of wealthy foreigners, even if not officially recognized as such, they received high-quality bilingual educations that enabled them to rise into Hong Kong's upper class, and many of them held positions of influence in business and government.[38] Sir Robert Ho Tung, the eldest son of Bosman and Shi, became the most prominent Eurasian of the late nineteenth and early twentieth centuries. Born as Ho Tung in 1862, he matriculated at Government Central School, which admitted select Chinese pupils and instructed them in English in most subjects, although in Chinese in Chinese language, literature, and history classes.[39]

Ho Tung completed the eight-year curriculum in just five years and in 1878, on the strength of his English skills, entered government service as a customs officer in Canton. He resigned in 1880 to join the British firm of Jardine Matheson & Co., an importer and exporter of opium, tea, and many other goods that was one of Asia's largest trading companies. At Jardine, he rose to the position of chief comprador, serving as a middleman who brokered transactions between foreigners and local Chinese.

Although Ho Tung earned healthy brokerage commissions, his extensive trading on his own account proved even more lucrative.[40] He was perhaps the wealthiest individual in Hong Kong in the decades before World War II, and he became one of the first Chinese people to be knighted (first by King George V in 1915 and again by Queen Elizabeth II in 1955). Due to his wealth and prominence, the man who would come to be known as Sir Robert became the first non-European allowed to live in Victoria Peak, a racially segregated district that normally excluded Chinese.[41] His generous patronage of schools, hospitals, and war-relief efforts earned him esteem as a philanthropist and public figure.[42]

Ho Tung was also a racially ambiguous figure whose appearance varied depending on the setting in which he found himself. When he traveled to the United States in 1901 under the name H. T. Bosman to evade US discrimination against Chinese people, the *New York Times* commented, "No one would suspect Mr. Bosman's identity from reading his autograph which appears in bold English hand upon the register" at the Waldorf-Astoria hotel. "Indeed," the *Times* continued, "it is hard to realize even after meeting him that he is Asiatic in blood as well as by birth, although he has all the physical characteristics of the Oriental."[43] As H. T. Bosman in the United States and Europe, he wore Western garb, but his grandnephew recalls him dressing exclusively in Chinese robes as Ho Tung in Hong Kong, where he cultivated an image of himself as a Chinese gentleman.

A Hong Kong description of Sir Robert as "completely European" in appearance, with "pale pink skin, piercing blue eyes and reddish hair," contrasts with the *Times'* assertion that he had "all the physical characteristics of the Oriental."[44] Even portraits fail to resolve his racial identity; perhaps not surprisingly, a portrait of Sir Robert in the Hong Kong Museum of History shows that his appearance represents a blend of Asian and European features.

The case of Sir Robert's younger brother further demonstrates the racial ambiguity of Eurasians. Ho Kai-kai, the youngest son of Bosman and Shi, won early distinction as the top scholar in his senior class at Victoria College under the name of Walter Bosman. He studied engineering in London, worked for the Natal Government Railways in South Africa, married an Englishwoman, and finally returned to visit Hong Kong in 1938, more than half a century after he had left.

The Hong Kong press devoted extensive coverage to the illustrious visitor but never mentioned that Walter Bosman was the brother of Sir Robert Ho Tung, an omission that suggests a taboo on openly discussing people of multiracial backgrounds.[45] Yet despite the silence about their identities, their racial and cultural amalgam ideally situated Eurasians like the Ho family to interact with both Europeans and Asians and elude hard-and-fast categorizations.

≈

Between the births of Ho Tung and Walter Bosman, Shi Tai bore a son named Ho Kom Tong. Establishing Kom Tong's identity is important because he was

Bruce Lee's maternal grandfather, and his identity would provide one key to determining whether Bruce Lee was multiracial.

Ho Kom Tong's paternity is the subject of speculation for two reasons. First, Kom Tong was born on September 16, 1866, but Charles Bosman had been away from Hong Kong for all of 1865 and returned only in January 1866, calling into question whether he could have been Kom Tong's father. Second, Kom Tong's contemporaries thought that he looked entirely Chinese with no trace of European features, and indeed, portraits of him seem to bear out that judgment.

Kom Tong's father was probably a Chinese merchant named either Kwok Chung or Kwok Hing-yin. During Bosman's extended absence, Shi ran short of money, a situation perhaps compounded by the fact that she was reputedly an avid gambler, and she may have turned to Kwok for support. In any case, after Bosman returned from abroad, Shi brought Kom Tong into the Ho household with the presumption that he was Bosman's son, and he was treated as if he were a brother to Bosman and Shi's other children.

Shortly thereafter, Bosman ran into financial difficulties and fled Hong Kong permanently, thus depriving Shi and her children of support.[46] He ended up in Britain, where he fathered five more children with an American wife, gained naturalized British citizenship, and died in 1892.[47] After Bosman's departure, Shi turned again to Kwok, who took her as his fourth concubine and fathered three more children by her. Shi died in 1896 at the age of fifty-five.

Ho Kom Tong followed in the footsteps of his illustrious brothers. A few years after he graduated from the Central School, his brother Ho Tung brought him aboard as an assistant comprador, an agent for foreign organizations involved in financial or other activities, at Jardine Matheson & Co. Ho Tung, Ho Kom Tong, and a third brother, Ho Fook, built their fortunes as compradors and merchants in their own right who controlled much of the sugar and cotton trade between China and Southeast Asia.

Ho Kom Tong spent the enormous wealth he earned as a middleman and a trader on lavish residences and an expansive family life. In 1914, he built the palatial Kom Tong Hall in the exclusive Mid-Levels, an area from which

Chinese families were normally excluded. Construction of the three-story architectural marvel cost what was then the astounding sum of HK$300,000. Its grand façade incorporated red brick, granite columns, arched portals, and curving balconies with filigreed iron railings. The interior featured Art Nouveau stained-glass windows, a cantilevered floating staircase, and a magnificent crystal chandelier hanging above large Persian rugs. Chinese furniture filled the main ceremonial room, which was used for weddings, funerals, and Chinese New Year's receptions. The French parlor, which was used for Christmas celebrations and receptions for foreign dignitaries, boasted a gilded ceiling, French provincial furniture, and decorative objects imported from Europe.[48]

In keeping with the privileges of an enormously wealthy man, Ho Kom Tong took a number of concubines. Family lore says that each time he acquired a new concubine, he appeased his first wife with expensive jewelry; given that he had thirteen occasions to make such gifts, her collection must have been extraordinary.[49]

In the early 1900s, the concubines and their children occupied several separate residences, but in 1924, Kom Tong built a massive new home to accommodate his sprawling family. It was named "Sai Uk," or Small House, in deference to Kom Tong Hall, which was called "Dai Uk," or Big House, to honor the fact that it was the home of Ho Kom Tong's first wife and her children. Small House was a decided misnomer, however, for a compound with three buildings containing twenty-five bedrooms, twelve sitting rooms, sixteen bathrooms, six kitchens, an ancestral shrine, eleven rooms for servants, and an immense terraced garden overlooking Hong Kong's harbor.[50]

Ho Kom Tong lived a thoroughly hybrid life in both the private and the public spheres. His Shanghai-born wife, Edith McClymont (Sze Lin Yut), was also Eurasian, the daughter of a Scottish tea merchant and a mother who may have been a Parsi Eurasian. In Kom Tong's public life, he generously supported many causes, both Chinese and British. In Hong Kong, he helped to establish hospitals that served Chinese people, founded the St. John Ambulance Brigade, served as a director for the Po Leung Kuk shelter for young Chinese women who were kidnapped or sold into slavery or prostitution, and contributed to the creation of the Tsuen Wan Chinese Permanent Cemetery, a burial ground for the Chinese community. He also funded relief efforts for Chinese victims of floods and war, and the Chinese government conferred decorations on him for his support of the Chinese revolution and humanitarian efforts.

Ho Kom Tong also pursued an impressive array of avocations. He assembled a vast collection of Chinese art and antiques, practiced feng shui and Chinese herbal medicine with great acumen, earned prizes for his photography, won competitions for the cultivation of sweet peas and chrysanthemums, and as a horse-racing aficionado became the first Chinese owner to win the Hong Kong Derby.[51]

But most important for the Bruce Lee story, Ho Kom Tong took great interest in Cantonese opera, the world that would have such a profound effect on his celebrated grandson's early years. He regularly attended performances, befriended stars, and even took to the stage himself at charity events.[52] His thirteenth concubine was an opera star from Guangzhou named So Yin-Ching.[53] According to her daughter, So was the star of a revolutionary opera troupe that was closely linked to Dr. Sun Yat-sen's nationalist organization, the Tong Meng Hui (Revolutionary Alliance), and performed under the patriotic stage name of So Xing-Qun, which means "awaken the public."

The troupe was revolutionary for its politics but perhaps even more because its productions featured all-female casts in defiance of the old norm that prohibited women performers. The women toured Southeast Asia for several years, raising money for the revolution and daringly smuggling guns and grenades in their costume trunks and dynamite fuses in their clothing. After the 1911 Chinese revolution, So Yin-Ching and her comrades were viewed as heroines; they rode triumphantly into one victory celebration with grenades hanging from their belts. Despite her derring-do, however, after So Yin-Ching became Ho Kom Tong's concubine, she agreed to give up performing.[54]

≈

Unsurprisingly, given the family's illustrious past, the mighty branches of the Ho family tree have been thoroughly documented. Consequently, much is known about the wealthiest and most prominent brothers, Ho Tung, Ho Fook, and Ho Kom Tong, because their descendants have dutifully recorded their history. But it is an obscure and relatively unexplored twig of the family tree that provides the link to Bruce Lee.

According to family lore, during Ho Kom Tong's extensive business travels, he took a mistress in Shanghai, a Russian Eurasian woman with the surname of Cheung. Although Ho paid her a stipend, he never formally married her nor made her a concubine. Cheung bore two daughters, Grace and Josephine, who became nearly the last of Ho Kom Tong's twenty-seven children. Cheung, along with Grace, who was nineteen years old in 1930, and Josephine moved to Hong Kong, where they lived at one of Sir Robert Ho Tung's homes. Perhaps they did not live at Sai Uk with Ho Kom Tong's other concubines and their children because Cheung ranked as a mere mistress.

In any case, Grace regularly attended Cantonese opera in Hong Kong with her father. At these performances, she made sure to sit where a certain comic performer who had caught her eye would notice her. Her efforts paid off. She met Lee Hoi Chuen, and the two soon eloped. Grace occupied a very junior position in the family due to her mother's status and because she was one of the last of Ho Kom Tong's daughters—hence her near-complete absence from family histories.[55] In addition, because her father disapproved of Lee Hoi Chuen, Grace and Lee and appear to have lost contact with the family subsequently.

Ho Kom Tong died of prostate cancer in 1950 and was buried in one of the most elaborate funerals that Hong Kong had ever seen.[56] The Church of Jesus Christ of Latter-day Saints acquired Kom Tong Hall and maintained it for many years before turning it over to the Hong Kong government. Today, Kom Tong Hall houses the Dr. Sun Yat-sen Museum, and visitors to the Mid-Levels may tour the exquisitely restored mansion.

Competing versions of Bruce's genealogy suggest that he may have had as much as one-quarter European ancestry or as little as an eighth; the story is dauntingly complicated. According to Ho family documentation, Bruce's half-Dutch maternal grandfather, Ho Kom Tong, contributed an eighth and a half-Russian maternal grandmother contributed another eighth, although that fraction would be reduced to an eighth total if the Chinese Kwok, rather than Bosman, was the father of Ho Kom Tong.

Alternately, Linda Lee's biography of her husband asserts that Grace was the daughter of a German father (that is to say, not Ho Kom Tong) and a Chinese mother, making Bruce one-quarter European on his mother's side. Depending on which figures one relies on, Bruce may have been one-eighth Dutch and one-eighth Russian, or one-eighth Russian, or one-quarter German.

Understandably, finding the truth among all these competing lineages is difficult. As unreliable as photographs may be as diagnostic tools for determining the socially fraught question of race, in photographs Grace does not look like a half-European woman, adding doubt to the assertion that her father was German.

At any rate, there is no question that Bruce Lee's roots included some European ancestry, and his mother definitely came from the Eurasian caste. This multiracial background speaks to the presence of intimate marital and familial relations engendered by the mercantile and colonial forces that rendered Hong Kong a vital zone of contact between Asia and the West. And if interracial sexuality constituted one form of contact, the transpacific cinema industry that would play such a large role in transforming Bruce Lee into a worldwide phenomenon would constitute another equally powerful one.

TRANSPACIFIC CHINESE CINEMA

Just as Lee Hoi Chuen followed the well-established route of Cantonese opera performance when he toured the United States, his appearance in the 1941 film *Golden Gate Girl* illustrated the transpacific nature of Chinese cinema and the porous boundary between cinema and opera. The history of films in China and Chinese-language filmmaking involves myriad transoceanic crossings and a complex transnational network of actors, technicians, promoters, and financiers.

Scholars debate the precise date when movies debuted in China. Although ambiguous evidence points to August 11, 1896, when Shanghai newspaper articles suggest that an entertainment show in Xu Garden included what were described as "Western shadow plays" showing scenes of Europe, it is unclear whether these shadow plays were actually films. Contrary to this hypothesis, the film historians Law Kar and Frank Bren, the authors of the 2004 book *Hong Kong Cinema: A Cross-Cultural View*, argue that the first reliably documented screenings occurred on April 28, 1897, in Hong Kong, when a French entrepreneur named Maurice Charvet enthralled large audiences with five showings a day of moving images at City Hall. Local accounts proclaimed the moving images to be "extraordinary" and "life-like" but complained about the "irritating quiver" of the projections. About a month later, an American hotel-keeper named Lewis M. Johnson introduced films to the mainland, showing eager audiences in Shanghai scenes of busy thoroughfares, a train arriving at a station, and a turbulent sea. Another Western entrepreneur, Harry Welby Cook, introduced movies to Beijing, Tianjin, Shanghai, and Hong Kong in 1897.[57]

From the late nineteenth century onward, a number of Western promoters and filmmakers toured Chinese cities with their fantastical new moving-image machines. But if the technology of moving pictures was a Western importation, the Chinese rapidly adapted this technology as their own and began creating Chinese content. The first natively made film was shot in 1905 in Beijing (known then as Peking) and consisted of three scenes of a Chinese opera. Many early Chinese films—initially silents and subsequently talkies—incorporated the older form of opera by adapting its narratives and scenes into movies, and operatic stars frequently became cinematic stars as well. Opera pictures constituted perhaps a fourth of all Hong Kong films as late as the 1930s and enjoyed popularity into the 1960s.[58]

≈

One of the most colorful figures in this hybrid milieu of Chinese and Western entrepreneurs and artists was a man named Benjamin Brodsky, who may be called the "Western Uncle of Chinese Cinema."[59] A poor Russian Jew born in Odessa in the late 1800s, he claimed to have stowed away on an England-bound freighter as a fourteen-year-old. After surviving the sinking of the ship, he made his way to New York and ended up traveling with a circus. After settling in the United States and amassing considerable wealth, he returned to visit his homeland but fled when Russian authorities tried to press him into military service.

After the end of the Spanish-American War of 1898, Brodsky set up shop in Manila as a ship supplier. He later bought a circus in Canada and took it on tour in China. During the Russo-Japanese War of 1904–5, fought in part over rival claims to Manchuria, Brodsky worked as a translator for the Russians. He popped up next in San Francisco, where he built a theater and narrowly survived the 1906 earthquake. After hearing of the popularity of the moving pictures, Brodsky opened one nickelodeon in San Francisco, then another and another.

Brodsky was a transnational figure whose ventures oscillated across the Pacific, which he clearly saw as a zone rife with untapped commercial opportunities. Passenger manifests show that Brodsky shuttled among the United States, Japan, China, Hong Kong, and Russia throughout the early 1900s. Most important for our story, the entrepreneurial Brodsky bought films, projectors, and a tent for a barnstorming tour through China.

A fire in Tianjin destroyed his equipment, but the undaunted Brodsky returned to the United States, bought moviemaking equipment, and returned to China, this time as a producer. He based his new company, the Variety Film Exchange Company, in Shanghai and Hong Kong. The film historian Ramona Curry, who teaches at the University of Illinois at Urbana-Champaign, argues that Brodsky relied on connections he had made with Chinese university students studying in the United States and US-educated Chinese intellectuals and businesspeople to get his company off the ground.[60]

≈

Brodsky may or may not have produced Hong Kong's first commercial movies in 1909, *Stealing a Roast Duck* and *The Haunted Pot*, both with plots adapted from well-known Chinese operas and both the product of elaborate cross-cultural collaboration.[61] Brodsky provided the financial backing, equipment, and film stock, but the creative talent was Chinese: Leung Siu-bo (Liang Xiabo) directed and starred as the thief, while Lai Buk-hoi (Li Beihai) played the part of the policeman.[62]

The fledgling Chinese artistic form of filmmaking was closely associated with the 1911 Chinese revolution, republicanism, and modernization. Lai Buk-hoi (the policeman of *Stealing a Roast Duck*) and his brother, Lai Man-wai (Li Minwei), along with their associate Lo Wing-cheong, had been active members of a new, Western-influenced artistic movement promoting *wenmingxi* (civilized drama), a form in which lines were spoken rather than set to music. Defining itself as modern, in contrast to traditional forms like opera, *wenmingxi* argued for modernization along Western lines and opposition to the outdated governmental system of imperial rule.

Lo and the Lai brothers were part of the earliest "civilized drama" troupe in Hong Kong, the Ching Ping Lok Theatre Company. The company's name, translated as "When the Qing Dynasty falls, happiness comes," bespoke its pro-republican stance. Fittingly, Lai Man-wai became one of the first members in the Hong Kong branch of Sun Yat-sen's nationalist movement. Brodsky in turn produced the 1912 film *The Chinese Revolution*, a dramatization of the 1911 rebellion.

Shortly thereafter, Lo and the Lai brothers collaborated with Brodsky in the creation of *Chuang Tsi Tests His Wife* (1913), the first two-reel feature made in Hong Kong. *Chuang Tsi* was a truly transpacific creation—produced by the Variety Film Exchange Company, financed by Brodsky, shot by R. F. Van Velzer (an American cinematographer and associate of Brodsky) with assistance from Lo, written by Lai Man-wai, directed by Lai Buk-hoi, and starring both Lai brothers along with Man-wai's wife Yim Shan-shan.

Brodsky screened both *Stealing a Roast Duck* and *Chuang Tsi* in Los Angeles in 1917, but he achieved much-greater acclaim in the United States with *A Trip through China*, an epic two-hour travelogue that he shot from 1912 through 1915 in Hong Kong and seven Chinese cities. The film played to eager crowds across the United States from 1916 to 1919 and generated considerable press coverage.

≈

Lai Man-wai, known as the "Father of Hong Kong Film," was a figure nearly as cosmopolitan as Brodsky. Born in Japan and educated at two of Hong Kong's best English-language colleges, he came from a wealthy merchant family that imported and sold rice. In 1921, the Lai brothers built World Theatre in Hong Kong, the first venue to show both Chinese and Western films. Two years later, they established Hong Kong's first studio, China Sun (Minxin) Film Company. Occupying a three-story building, the studio was fully outfitted with cameras, equipment for developing and processing film, and editing rooms.

In 1925, China Sun produced *Rouge* (also known as *Love Is Dangerous*), Hong Kong's first full-length feature film. Its familiar crew dated back to the days of *Stealing a Roast Duck*: it costarred Lai Man-wai and his other wife, Lam Cho-cho (who went on to become a major film star), along with Leung Siu-bo; Lai Buk-hoi directed, and Lo Wing-cheong was the cinematographer.

Just as had been the case with "civilized drama," the Lai brothers believed in film as an activist art form with the power to educate audiences and convince them to support Chinese nationalism. Although they used Western equipment and Japanese techniques in making *Rouge*, China Sun adapted local source materials in the form of fantasy tales written by a Qing-era author to make a uniquely Chinese film. Yet the China Sun coterie that was so dedicated to creating a Chinese cinema for the edification of Chinese audiences was composed of thoroughly transnational individuals: as mentioned before, Lai Man-wai had been born in Japan and received a Western education, Lam Cho-cho was born and educated in Canada, Lai Buk-hoi had attended Queen's College (the Eton of Hong Kong, with notable alumni including Sun Yat-sen), and Lo Wing-cheong had been educated at an English-language college in Hong Kong.

One of the new faces on the *Rouge* set belonged to Moon Kwan (Kwan Man-ching), an émigré from Guangzhou who attended the University of California, Berkeley, before moving in 1915 to Los Angeles, where he learned film-industry techniques while working on various productions as a writer, cook, and extra.[63] He became known around Hollywood as an expert on China and served as a consultant to D. W. Griffith on *Broken Blossoms*, the famed director's yellowface drama starring Lillian Gish. Kwan returned to China in 1921 and two years later brought his Hollywood expertise to China Sun, where he taught scriptwriting and acting and contributed to the script of *Rouge*. In addition, as a makeup artist, he introduced Max Factor products and techniques to Hong Kong. But although *Rouge* broke all box-office records, China Sun subsequently faltered and eventually closed.

Kwan nonetheless continued to contribute to the creation of transpacific Chinese cinema. He directed a film in Guangzhou in 1926, then worked in California on a travelogue called *Pieces of China* that was shot in China by an American producer with postproduction in Los Angeles.

In the early 1930s, Kwan made two films for Lianhua, a financially struggling Hong Kong studio, which charged him with distributing its films in the United States and raising capital to enable the studio to buy sound equipment. He packed four films into his baggage and set off for San Francisco, which promised abundant Chinese American audiences and potential investors. There he met an aspiring filmmaker named Joe Chiu (Chiu Shu-sun), yet another transnational figure, who was born to a wealthy family in Guangdong in 1904 and educated in California.

Together, Kwan and Chiu founded Grandview Film Company, which would become one of the most important producers of transpacific cinema. The company, established in 1933 at 12 Ross Alley in San Francisco's Chinatown, had a board of directors made up of eleven Chinese American investors, with Chiu's father as chairman and Joe Chiu as general manager.[64]

≈

Grandview's first film, *Romance of the Songsters*, may have been the world's first Cantonese talkie. A love story of two opera singers set in San Francisco, it featured singing, dancing, and comic interludes, all captured with high-quality cinematography and sound recording. The film reflected the transpacific nature of Chinese cinema, with a cast drawn from the plentiful pools of Cantonese opera performers based in San Francisco or passing through the city with touring companies. Two touring opera singers starred in the main male and female roles, and the film propelled the female lead, Wu Dip-ying, to Hong Kong cinematic stardom.[65]

Released in 1933, *Romance of the Songsters* captivated audiences in Chinatowns across the US. Hong Kong audiences received it eagerly as well, which opened new opportunities for Kwan and Chiu to extend their production and distribution across the Pacific. And *Romance of the Songsters* tied both ends of the transpacific Chinese migration stream together in another way; as Law Kar notes, "It was also one of the first films to depict the lives of overseas American-Chinese" to audiences on both sides of the Pacific.[66] Funded by San Francisco investors, Kwan and Chiu created a new company, called Grandview Film Company (Hong Kong) to further their reach into the Hong Kong market, and from 1935 until the start of World War II, it produced sixty-five films.

During the 1930s, Grandview addressed one of the most important social issues of the day: Japanese imperial aggression in China. Japan had begun encroaching in Manchuria in 1905 and dramatically escalated its belligerence in 1937 with the Marco Polo Bridge Incident, an event that sparked the second Sino-Japanese War and resulted in Japanese occupation of much of China.[67]

Grandview (Hong Kong)'s *Lifeline*, produced by Chiu and written and directed by Kwan, debuted at the Lai brothers' New World Theater in 1935 as the first Hong Kong film to foment resistance to Japanese aggression, and it broke box-office records in both Hong Kong and Guangdong. Another of the company's productions, *48 Hours*, produced and directed by Chiu in 1937, decried the Marco Polo Bridge Incident almost immediately after its occurrence.

In 1939, Chiu returned to San Francisco to raise capital for new equipment and was stranded there when the Japanese bombed Pearl Harbor on December 7, 1941. After Hong Kong fell under Japanese occupation, Grandview shifted its productions entirely to California for the duration of the war and from 1939 to 1945 produced about twenty films in California.

≈

One of Grandview's directors was an intrepid woman named Esther Eng (Ng Kam-ha), whose life story is so dramatic that it in fact reads like a movie plot.[68] Born in San Francisco in 1914 to immigrant parents from Guangdong province, Eng grew up thoroughly enmeshed in Chinese American society and culture. As a teenager, she worked at the box office of the Mandarin Theatre, the same landmark Chinatown venue where Lee Hoi Chuen, the man who would become Bruce Lee's father, performed in 1940, the same year that the son who would one day achieve extraordinary worldwide fame was born.

The Mandarin staged Cantonese opera and screened Cantonese films, and Eng grew to love both artistic forms. She consistently defied gender and sexual norms; she was a woman in a man's industry, presented herself in such a masculine way that friends sometimes addressed her as "Brother Ha," and was involved in romantic relationships with women. Her films addressed the role of women in society and promoted Chinese patriotism, often through tragic romance stories.

Grandview's patriotic film *Lifeline* made its way from Hong Kong to San Francisco, where it inspired Eng to fuse her passion for film with her love of China, which, though the country of neither her birth nor her citizenship, was central to her identity as an ethnic Chinese woman. With the backing of her merchant father, Eng established a film company at the age of twenty-one, a remarkable achievement for a woman of her background in that time and place. She moved with friends to Hollywood, rented a studio, and there produced *Heartaches* (*Sum Hun*, 1935).

The first pro-China patriotic film made in the United States, *Heartaches* argues that true love must sacrifice itself for the nation. Its protagonist, a female Cantonese opera singer in the United States (played by Eng's childhood friend and midlevel opera star Wai Kim-fong) falls in love with a military pilot but urges him to go to China to fight against the Japanese. He returns from China safely but is now married, and the opera singer falls ill from love sickness. The singer and the pilot eventually reunite just in time for her to die in his arms.

Despite the film's melodrama, *Heartaches* marked the debut of a remarkable talent. Eng became the first Chinese filmmaker to produce a movie in Hollywood, and her initial effort was even shot partially in color. The film drew such large audiences in Chinatowns across California that Eng was inspired to take it to Hong Kong.

Along with Wai, who was both Eng's star and her lover, she traveled to Hong Kong in 1936 and decided to remain and make movies there. Eng's first Hong Kong film starred Wai as a woman who joins the Chinese army to fight against Japanese invaders, a timely subject because women were beginning to make important contributions to the war effort. Eng made several more films in Hong Kong, one of which, *Woman's World*, featured an entirely female cast. Her success as a filmmaker, however, contrasted with her personal travails, as she suffered from malaria and separated from Wai over a fling with another woman. In 1939, with the Japanese army surging southward toward Hong Kong, Eng returned home to San Francisco.

≈

Esther Eng's return to California brings us back full circle to Bruce Lee's debut as an infant in *Golden Gate Girl*, a 1941 film on which Eng collaborated with Grandview's Joe Chiu and Moon Kwan. In this romantic tragedy, a young woman falls in love with and marries a Cantonese opera performer over her father's objections, then dies giving birth to a baby girl. Years later, the now-grown daughter reconciles with her grandfather. Eng codirected with Kwan, who wrote the script and played a supporting role, while Chiu served as the cinematographer.[69]

The setting in the opera world and the doomed romance revisit themes common to both Cantonese-language films of the era and Eng's earlier work. The final reunion is further sweetened when it is revealed that unbeknownst to each other, the granddaughter had performed in a benefit concert for Chinese war victims and the grandfather had donated $3,000 to the cause.[70] Bruce landed the brief role because his father appeared in the film carrying the baby.

Unsurprisingly, Eng found few opportunities for a Chinese American lesbian woman to make films in Hollywood, a world that from its inception would be dominated almost entirely by white males. She concentrated instead on distributing Cantonese films throughout North America and Latin America, and after the war, she continued directing for Grandview.

In 1951, at the age of thirty-seven, Eng retreated to New York, where over the next two decades she opened a series of Chinese restaurants and mostly stayed away from the camera. When she died in 1970, obituaries reminded readers of her pioneering role in creating and promoting Chinese films and Cantonese opera. And though Esther Eng died just one year before Bruce Lee made waves in Hong Kong filmdom, it is appropriate that this pioneering traverser of oceans and transgressor of gender and sexual norms gave the world its first glimpse of the incipient phenomenon.

≈

In retrospect, it is clear that three transpacific strands—commercial and racial crossings, Cantonese opera, and Chinese cinema—intertwined to create the conditions that led to Bruce Lee's birth in San Francisco.

When the time came for Grace Lee to deliver her baby, she went to the Chinese Hospital, one of the Chinese American community's most important institutions. Built on Jackson Street in Chinatown with money raised by fifteen community organizations, the hospital had opened in 1925 and boasted the period's most modern medical equipment. At the opening of the hospital, whose five Chinese American doctors were all trained in Western medicine, Chinese children sang "The Star-Spangled Banner," the crowds listened to speeches by the mayor of San Francisco and other dignities, and the community celebrated with a ten-day festival of parades, well-baby contests, and banquets.[71]

The Chinese Hospital and its elaborate opening festivities demonstrate the changing position of the ethnic Chinese community in San Francisco. By both birth and culture, they were in the process of combining Chinese culture and US national identity. Some of these Chinese Americans performing the lion dance through the Chinatown streets and pledging allegiance to the United States may have been descendants of the laborers exported by Grace's grandfather Charles Bosman. In any case, Bruce's birth at the Chinese Hospital thus reflected the transpacific migrations that brought China and the West into intimate contact, illuminated the intermixture of Chinese and American identities, and foreshadowed Bruce's many further crossings of the Pacific.

When Lee Hoi Chuen and Grace Lee left San Francisco in 1941, they did so as aliens who were barred from becoming naturalized US citizens by virtue of an 1878 federal court ruling. A district court in California had denied the application for naturalization from a Chinese immigrant named Ah Yup, decreeing that all members of the "Mongolian" race were ineligible for naturalization.

The question of whether people of Chinese ancestry who were born in the United States held US citizenship came before the Supreme Court two decades later. In the *United States v. Wong Kim Ark* case, involving a Chinese man who had been born in San Francisco, left to visit family in China in 1894, and was denied reentry to the United States the following year under the Chinese Exclusion Act, the court in 1898, citing the Fourteenth Amendment's Equal Protection Clause, ruled that birth in the United States automatically conferred birthright citizenship, even to the Chinese.[72]

Thus, although Bruce's parents left the United States as unnaturalizable aliens, he departed with them as a citizen of the United States by the principle of what is called *jus soli* (right of the soil). This status would come to matter enormously when he reached young adulthood. And fittingly, although Dr. Glover dubbed the infant Bruce, Grace named the child Jun Fan, meaning "return again," for she believed that he would one day return to the land of his birth.

2

A HONG KONG CHILDHOOD

On April 7, 1941, the infant Bruce Lee accompanied his parents aboard the SS *President Pierce* to begin their journey across the Pacific to the uniquely hybrid society and culture of Hong Kong, which combined Chinese and British influences to create what the novelist Ian Fleming, creator of James Bond, once called "the most vivid and exciting city" he had ever seen: "a gay and splendid colony humming with vitality and progress, and pure joy to the senses and spirits."[1] Fleming's description of Hong Kong as a "colony" suggests that its frissons resulted in part from the unequal yoking of Chinese people and culture with British control.

The territory of Hong Kong lies at the mouth of the Pearl River, directly across the border from the Chinese city of Shenzen in Guangdong Province in southern China. It consists of the Kowloon district and New Territories on the Asian mainland and the densely populated Hong Kong Island, along with over two hundred sparsely peopled islands. Great Britain had taken possession of Hong Kong during the first Opium War (1839–42) as British forces scored victories across southern China. Captain Charles Eliot, the plenipotentiary to China, and Qishan, the imperial viceroy, entered into an agreement called the Convention of Chuenpi, which, among other things, transferred ownership of Hong Kong to the British.

On the morning of January 26, 1841, an expeditionary force had landed at a spot on the northwest coast of the island, just inside the mouth of the magnificent bay, and marched inland. Meeting no resistance, they advanced to a bluff that came to be known as Possession Point, where they claimed the island for the Crown by hoisting the Union Jack, savoring a celebratory salvo from the ships below, and toasting the queen.[2] However, both the British and Chinese governments rejected the Chuenpi agreement and relieved Eliot and Qishan of their posts for having negotiated it. As a result, the status of the territory remained unresolved for several months until China formally ceded Hong Kong with the signing of the Treaty of Nanking in 1842.

A similar process unfolded at the conclusion of the Second Opium War, with China relinquishing the southern portion of the Kowloon Peninsula on the mainland, giving the British landholdings on both sides of the valuable deep-water harbor. The final colonial expansion occurred in 1898, when Great Britain acquired a ninety-nine-year lease on the remainder of Kowloon and the rural New Territories on the mainland.

Under British rule, Kowloon rapidly grew from a series of small villages with just a few thousand residents to one of the most densely populated urban regions in the world. Today, more than two million people cram into a scant eighteen square miles that encompass everything from wealthy enclaves and middle-class neighborhoods to tenements and red-light districts. The Kowloon waterfront offers peaceful repose away from the scrum of the streets; visitors frequently stand there transfixed by the stunning view of Hong Kong skyscrapers across the tranquil blue waters of Victoria Harbour.

Although commuter trains connect the island and the peninsula through tunnels bored beneath the water, the Star Ferry offers perhaps the world's greatest value in tourist transportation. A scant HK$2.70 (about 35 cents in US dollars) buys a ticket for a ten-minute ride in a historic vessel across the waters of the harbor, with a view of the soaring Victoria Peak and the island's skyline. After disembarking at the Star Ferry Pier in Kowloon, visitors can follow a walkway wending across the harbor front to the Avenue of the Stars.

Like Hollywood Boulevard, the Avenue of the Stars honors cinematic luminaries with plaques in the sidewalk. One features Lai Man-Wai, the Brodsky collaborator and "Father of Hong Kong Cinema." Another pays tribute to Sir Run Run Shaw, longtime chief of Shaw Brothers Studio, Hong Kong's most important moviemaker. A third honors Raymond Chow, who signed Bruce to a two-film contract for Golden Harvest studios in 1971. More recent additions celebrate modern stars, including Chow Yun Fat, Jackie Chan, Jet Li, and Michelle Yeoh.

But the most popular attraction by far is the eight-foot-tall bronze statue of Bruce Lee posing shirtless in a kung fu stance, which was installed in 2005. In 1941, Lee Hoi Chuen and Grace Lee would have had no idea that their son would become famous enough to be honored with such a monument, but a visitor retracing Bruce's steps today can stroll northward from his statue, across lanes of rushing traffic on Salisbury Road, to the site of the Lee family home on Nathan Road.

≈

Although Grace Lee came from the powerful Ho clan, Bruce did not grow up surrounded by vast wealth. Family histories by Eric Peter Ho and Frances Tse Liu both state that Grace's father, Ho Kom Tong, disapproved of her marriage to Lee Hoi Chuen and imply that she did not participate in family events after their elopement. Furthermore, both Ho and Liu mention Bruce only in passing, a clear indication that he did not spend time with the extended family or share in its fortune. But while the Lees did not enjoy the Ho affluence, neither did they live in poverty. Lee Hoi Chuen earned a good living from acting in operas and films and supplemented with income from several rental properties. The family employed live-in servants and paid parochial school tuition, although Bruce complained that he never received any spending money from his tight-fisted father.[3]

The Lee family settled in a two-bedroom flat at 218 Nathan Road, one of the first major streets to be developed by the British in Kowloon. Located above shops on the second story of an older building, the apartment overlooked a bustling four-lane boulevard. Nathan Road runs northward from Salisbury Road near the harbor, past the Chunking Mansions, infamous as a den of drugs and petty criminals, Kowloon Mosque, and tranquil green spaces of Kowloon Park in Tsim Sha Tsui and continues past the Temple Street Night Market in Yau Ma Tei and the Ladies Market in Mong Kok. It terminates at Boundary Street, which from 1860 to 1898 marked the border between the British colony and China. Today, the street's dazzling neon signs, electronics shops, fashion boutiques, and restaurants open past midnight make Nathan Road one of Hong Kong's most popular shopping destinations, though tourists are warned to be wary of pickpockets and unscrupulous merchants.

The Lee apartment accommodated Bruce; his mother and father; his older sisters, Agnes and Phoebe; his older brother, Peter; and his younger brother, Robert. Lee Hoi Chuen's sister-in-law and her five children also shared the flat, as he had dutifully taken them in after his brother died. As if that were not enough, several live-in servants completed the household. The Lees also unofficially adopted the son of two servants, Wu Ngan, who went on to appear in a small role in *The Way of the Dragon* and to serve as Bruce's valet in the 1970s. This throng of up to twenty people coexisted with a menagerie of dogs (including Bruce's favorite, a white Alsatian named Bobby who slept under his bed), cats, birds, fish, and even a chicken.

A narrow outer stairway connected the flat to the street below, and homeless people often set up camp in the ground-level entryway, though metal bars and an inner door secured the second-floor landing. Inside the apartment, a large room with a refrigerator and table served as a combined kitchen, dining room, and living room by day and a sleeping area at night. Two bedrooms were crammed full of bunks and beds. A veranda off one bedroom held potted plants, a chicken coop, and a bathtub concealed behind a curtain. Amazingly, a single bathroom accommodated the needs of the entire twenty-member household.[4]

Family members called Bruce "Sai Fon," or "Phoenix," a name traditionally given to girls. Because Hoi Chuen and Grace had lost their first son, the female moniker was intended to fool malevolent spirits into leaving Bruce undisturbed.

He earned another nickname, "Mo Si Tung," or "never sits still," for his bound-less energy. He epitomized perpetual motion, always talking, running, jumping, or fidgeting. He even walked in his sleep; on many nights, Agnes saw him climb down from his top bunk and wander away without waking.

≈

Bruce channeled his restlessness into practical jokes that he played on every-one around him, children and adults alike. His younger brother, Robert, recounts Bruce enticing him into a game called Submarine, in which Bruce held the sleeve of a jacket through which Robert was supposed to peer upward like a periscope and call out "Fire One!" when he spied an enemy ship pass by. Each time Robert cried out, Bruce told him that he was too late, and Robert concentrated harder, until the final turn, when he was doused by a pitcher of ice water poured down the sleeve. Bruce helpfully explained that he had been too slow, and the ship had dropped a depth charge on the submarine.

Bruce's older sisters also recall his impish sense of humor. Bruce gave Phoebe a special book that he said she needed to read, which gave her an electric shock when she opened it, sending him running away with peals of laughter. Agnes remembers that he delighted in sending the maids to the store to buy ridiculous items that he knew it did not carry. Grace remembers an occasion when a maid left the apartment and Bruce surreptitiously rearranged all the furniture in one room. When the maid returned after dark, she stumbled into every chair and table as she groped for the light. Reading was the one thing that slowed Bruce down; he would curl up for hours with a book, often deep into the night.[5] This combination of the seemingly opposite qualities of hyperkinetic activity and thoughtful contemplation would characterize Bruce over the course of his life.

Besides being energetic, the young Bruce Lee also exhibited an empathetic side. His mother once observed him staring intently down at Nathan Road from the family's living room. Suddenly, he dashed out the door, down the stairs, and into the street. When she went to the window to see where he had gone, she saw him leading a blind man across the street. He later told his mother that he could not simply stand by as crowds of people ignored the

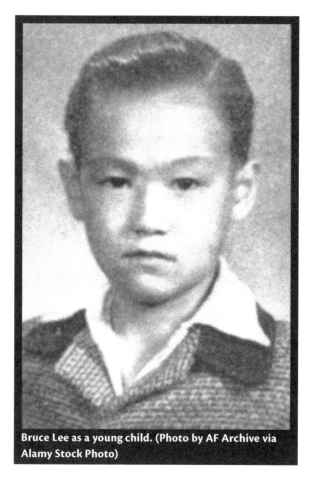

Bruce Lee as a young child. (Photo by AF Archive via Alamy Stock Photo)

frustrated and helpless old man. And his empathy also made him protective. If a boy ever teased Agnes, whom Bruce called the "Little Queen," he would rush to her defense, despite being the younger sibling. Agnes was the one who bestowed on her pugnacious younger brother the nickname that would follow him throughout his life: Siu Lung, or "Little Dragon."[6]

According to Linda Lee, Bruce once shook his fist defiantly at a Japanese plane flying over Nathan Road during the Japanese occupation of Hong Kong during World War II.[7] This anecdote is often repeated to emphasize Bruce's fierce pride in being Chinese. It is not particularly revealing, however, for Bruce was just one year old when the British governor surrendered Hong

Kong to the Japanese on December 25, 1941, and was not yet five when the occupation ended on August 15, 1945. Nevertheless, the image of Bruce as an insolent toddler challenging the hated Japanese would in years to come reflect his cinematic expressions of Chinese pride.

Lee Hoi Chuen was an aloof father whose children approached him "like an emperor," as Robert Lee remembered.[8] Grace herself recalled her husband as a distant father who spent most of his time at home alone in his room, working or studying.[9] According to Bruce's wife, Linda, the father's relationship with Bruce was "neither nurturing nor supportive," due in part to the fact that the elder Lee's hectic schedule of performing in operas and movies frequently took him away from the family. Perhaps more to the point, Linda also notes that he was an opium smoker and, even when physically present, "was often not mentally there for Bruce." Despite it all, she said, Bruce loved, respected, idolized, and feared his father in various measures.[10] And despite being detached as a father, Lee Hoi Chuen deeply influenced his son in one crucial respect: he introduced Bruce to acting.

CHILDHOOD IN THE MOVIES

Like many opera performers, the elder Lee also acted extensively in movies. The Hong Kong Movie Database credits Lee Hoi Chuen with appearances in ninety-six movies between 1939, when he was thirty-three years old, and 1963.[11] He often brought Bruce backstage at plays and to the sets of films, and a four-year-old Bruce, along with his older sisters, Phoebe and Agnes, performed briefly in one of his plays. The acting bug bit Bruce hard, and even as a child, he visited his father at work whenever possible. On one visit, a keen-eyed movie director caught sight of young Bruce busily charming everyone on the set. The director offered him a part in the film, which he and his father accepted on the spot. Bruce thus began his Hong Kong film career in 1946 at the age of six in the otherwise unremarkable *The Birth of Mankind*.[12]

Bruce appeared in a total of twenty Hong Kong films as a child actor, most often playing a scrappy kid, street urchin, orphan, or juvenile delinquent. Stills from these mostly forgotten movies show Bruce to already be matinee-idol handsome, displaying both the dazzling smile and scowling sneer that he would later flash on screens worldwide. His heartfelt, charismatic performances encouraged audiences to root for him whether he was the good guy or the bad guy.

His role in the 1950 film *The Kid*, which in 2011 was honored by the Hong Kong Film Archive as one of its "100 Must-See Hong Kong Movies," represented the most important of Lee's early childhood career. It was not only the first movie in which he starred but also the first in which he was credited as Lee Siu Lung, or Lee Little Dragon. A ten-year-old Bruce plays the Kid Cheung of the title, an orphan living with his out-of-work uncle and running in the streets with a gang of adult criminals who take him under their wing. When the uncle discovers that the kid has stolen a golden necklace from a rich girl, he marches him to her house to return the pilfered loot.

In gratitude, the girl pressures her father (played by Lee Hoi Chuen) into hiring the uncle and enrolling the child in school. Beset by bullies at school, the child defends himself and gets expelled for fighting. Going to work in a factory (as a ten-year-old, no less), he faces down a menacing foreman and defends a young woman from sexual harassment. His protective relationships with girls and women, which teeter from friendship toward romantic interest, his dedication to justice for the underdog, straddling the line between heroism and criminality, and even his gesture of defiantly thumbing his nose at an opponent all foreshadow themes and movements in the movies Bruce would make as an adult.

In Bruce's final and most prominent role before leaving Hong Kong, the eighteen-year-old would star in the 1960 film *The Orphan* as a budding hoodlum taken in by a compassionate school director who tries to coax him away from the gangster life. In his most emotionally mature performance, Bruce glowers his way through tough-guy scenes but flashes signs of vulnerability as an alternate path to a new life opens before him.

Acting provided an important outlet for Bruce's prodigious energies, and his mother recalled that he never complained about working, even at odd hours. "At two o'clock in the morning," she recalled, "I'd call out, 'Bruce, the car is here,' and he'd leap up and put on his shoes and go out very cheerfully."[13]

But while Bruce relished acting, school was another matter entirely. Despite his evident intelligence, teachers could not contain his energetic outbursts, and he constantly got into trouble. Today it is commonly understood that people who suffer from what is now called attention deficit disorder have trouble focusing on subjects that fail to capture their interest yet can maintain extraordinary focus on those that do. Although Bruce never received such a diagnosis, he certainly exhibited the traits that resemble its symptoms. Art and history interested Bruce to a certain degree, but he hated math and science, for the most part earning poor grades; and although he chafed at the regimen of school, he read voraciously on his own for hours at home.[14]

INTRODUCTION TO WING CHUN KUNG FU

In 1951, Bruce enrolled as a fifth-grader at La Salle College, a Catholic boys' school where a primarily Chinese student body took classes taught in English. His mischievousness and inability to sit still in class quickly earned him a reputation for being a troublemaker. One perceptive teacher recognized Bruce's intelligence, however, and tried to divert his energies into running errands, cleaning blackboards, and opening windows, all tasks he performed eagerly, but these efforts could not transform him into a conventionally successful student. Bruce preferred fisticuffs to academics.

The Chinese boys of La Salle developed a fierce hatred of the British boys who attended the nearby King George V School and relished an activity they labeled "Limey Bashing." After school let out, Bruce and his gang would gather on a hill to taunt the British boys, heaping abuse on them until a fight broke out. Then they would brawl until one side or the other was defeated or until bystanders called the police and the combatants scattered. Untrained in martial arts, Bruce and his comrades won some battles and lost others. Unsurprisingly, these shenanigans eventually caught up to Bruce and resulted in his expulsion from La Salle in 1956.[15]

In the decade after World War II, the population of Hong Kong skyrocketed from six hundred thousand to two and a half million.[16] Although the new residents included some entrepreneurs and capitalists fleeing from the 1949 Communist revolution on the mainland, most of those who came were unskilled laborers. Even as the colony's economy rebounded in the 1950s, countless thousands of refugees struggled for survival.

Many of these refugees lived in wooden squatter huts built on open hillsides without electricity or running water and under constant threat from fires and mudslides. In December 1953, the disastrous Shek Kip Mei fire burned a shanty town, leaving fifty-eight thousand people in Kowloon homeless and spurring government efforts to resettle refugees into public accommodations. By the 1960s, nearly a third of Hong Kong's population lived in government housing, which offered scant improvement over the shanties. In these unsanitary spaces, families of five crammed into an average space of 120 square feet and smaller families into an average of 86 square feet.[17] Predictably, these substandard conditions produced an abundance of alienated juvenile delinquents who dabbled in petty crime and fighting.

≈

The impetuous Bruce dove eagerly into the maelstrom of youth gang fights. On the street, he looked for trouble and started fights without provocation. He would walk up to a kid and stare him down until insults flew, followed quickly by fists. As he told *Black Belt* magazine years later, "I was a punk and went looking for fights. We used chains and pens with knives hidden inside." He secreted these weapons away in a closet at home and carried them on his body in the streets. Bruce also begged his mother to enroll him in martial arts lessons, claiming that he had to defend himself from bullies. But like many myths about a man who would become a legend, this was an unlikely story considering how willingly and frequently Bruce fought. Years later, he volunteered a more convincing explanation: "One day, I wondered what would happen if I didn't have my gang behind me if I got into a fight. I decided to learn how to protect myself, and I began to study gung-fu."[18]

At around the age of fourteen, Bruce Lee began his formal martial arts training. He had practiced Tai Chi Chuan with his father a few times, but the slow pace and deliberate movements of the style did not satisfy the spirited youngster. His mother succumbed to Bruce's badgering and agreed to pay for lessons with Yip Man, the grandmaster of the Wing Chun style of kung fu in Hong Kong.

≈

Today, Wing Chun is among the world's most famous and widely practiced martial arts, largely because it is known as the one Bruce Lee studied first. But in the mid-1950s, it was but one style of kung fu among many, no more popular than any of its southern Chinese rivals like Choy Li Fut and Hung Gar. No matter the style, all kung fu remained obscure outside of China, a situation that would not change until Bruce Lee erupted onto movie screens across the globe.

As is the case with most martial arts, the historical roots of Wing Chun are shrouded in legend. The origin myth of Wing Chun begins with the destruction of the Shaolin Temple, a Buddhist monastery in the central province of Henan. In the early 1700s, a jealous emperor, fearful of the tremendous fighting power being developed there, slaughtered the monks and burned the temple. One nun, Ng Mui, escaped and was taken in by a family with a daughter named Yim Wing Chun. Although Wing Chun was in love with a local boy, she had caught the eye of a gangster who threatened to force her into marriage. Ng Mui intervened, telling the thug that he could marry Wing Chun if he could defeat her in battle.

The nun trained the girl assiduously for months, simplifying her fighting system down to its core and modifying it to suit a woman. When the bully returned, Wing Chun beat him badly and then married her sweetheart, whom she trained in Ng Mui's fighting system. Although scholars put little stock in the accuracy of that myth, it conveys elemental principles, such as the notion that Wing Chun teaches flexibility and sensitivity rather than brute power because it was created by a woman for a woman to fight a bigger and sturdier man.[19]

Wing Chun emphasizes principles such as economy of motion, simultaneous attacking and defending, and protecting the "center line" of the body running vertically through the nose and groin. Most suited to close-quarters combat rather than attacking from afar, it prioritizes operating from a stable base called a "horse stance" as opposed to incorporating long acrobatic leaps and roundabout movements. Because it relies on quick, direct punches and kicks within confined areas, it tends to be visually brutal, in contrast to styles that flow and circulate through space.

Wing Chun instruction builds on three forms, or slow, choreographed routines intended to teach the style's basic positions and movements. The first, *siu lim tao*, or "little idea," because it comprises the kernel of Wing Chun philosophy, teaches the stance and hand movements. The second, *chom kiu*, adds footwork and kicking. The final form, *biu gee*, conveys advanced techniques only shared with trusted students. Practicing forms enables students to adopt correct positions and practice essential movements to mastery. Running through the forms also imbues the mind-set of the style, as the motions encapsulate its philosophy of fighting. The "wooden dummy" serves as a training tool. Practitioners who have achieved intermediate or higher competency use the dummy's wood limbs and torso to rehearse their blocks and strikes and toughen their hands, forearms, legs, and feet. In addition to empty-handed combat, Wing Chun includes training with an elongated pole and short swords.

As a martial art steeped in a creation myth that lauds the strength of femininity, Wing Chun embraces the dichotomies of masculinity/femininity and firmness/flexibility. It is appropriate that the man who came to be seen as its grand master also embodied seemingly opposed forces of traditionalism and modernity. Yip Man was born into a wealthy family in 1893 in Foshan in southern China, and despite being a member of the upper class and sickly to boot, he insisted on studying what was considered the socially disreputable activity of kung fu. When he was fifteen, his family sent him to study in Hong Kong at an elite English boarding school, where he received a Western education. By happenstance, he met a Wing Chun instructor, with whom he studied more advanced forms than he had mastered in Foshan. But when he returned to his hometown in 1917, he found the Wing Chun community in disarray.[20]

While Yip Man was in Hong Kong, the Chinese revolution of 1911 had resulted in the overthrowing of the emperor and the establishment of a republic. Throughout the 1920s and 1930s, the ruling Nationalist Party imposed an ideology of rationality to reform the martial arts, attempting to unify the panoply of local and regional variations into a standardized Guoshu (national arts) form. This movement originated in the sophisticated urban centers of Shanghai and Nanjing in northern China but extended to the southern hinterlands of Foshan in the Guangdong province, where an unruly myriad of schools and styles proliferated.

Rather than being static and unchanging styles, all martial arts are malleable and evolving practices due to how they propagate. Teachers train students who advance to high-enough levels of mastery that they in turn become qualified to teach on their own. (In some forms, such as karate and tae kwon do, students earn belts signifying their acquired skills through passing examinations, but belts are not part of the kung fu tradition.) Successive generations of teachers incorporate their owns experiences and philosophies, and the social context around them, as they teach their students slight modifications to movements or place different emphases on core principles of their disciplines. Over time, students taught within various lineages will inevitably practice the style differently.

Yip Man, with his traditional training and Western education, stood astride the divide between traditionalism and modernism.[21] When he began teaching Wing Chun, he started with the martial art he had learned as a boy in Foshan and a student in Hong Kong, yet he revised it according to principles of rationality and practicality. He discarded mystical terminology referring to the "five elements" and eliminated all superfluous movements, paring down the style to its essential principles and movements. He embraced an empirical outlook that demanded that all ideas must be proven in practice (i.e., hand-to-hand combat). Although Yip Man adopted a scientific approach to revising and reforming Wing Chun, he remained a traditionalist in other respects. Far from being enthusiastically pro-Western, he always dressed in Chinese garb and embraced Buddhist, Taoist, and Confucian philosophies.[22]

≈

Yip Man brought a modified Wing Chun to Hong Kong when he fled China after the Communist revolution of 1949. The streamlined form he taught was not one transmitted without alteration from Ng Mui to Yim Wing Chun to the present. Instead, the Wing Chun he taught in Hong Kong in the 1950s had been influenced by the Chinese revolution that overthrew the emperor as an outdated relic of the past and sought to replace it with a modern, rationally constituted republic. In turn, the Chinese revolution gained authority in part because of the Qing Dynasty's inability to resist Western imperialism. Benjamin Judkins and Jon Nielson, the authors of the best scholarly history of the style, *The Creation of Wing Chun*, demonstrate how Wing Chun evolved in response to the social and political conditions surrounding it.

With Yip Man having lost his family fortune, he began teaching Wing Chun as his main source of income for the first time in his life. Kung fu was closely associated in the public mind with the underground criminal organizations known as the "triads," which used the fighting arts to wage turf wars and intimidate civilians, and perhaps not surprisingly, Yip Man's first students tended to be delinquents and street toughs. Wong Shun Leung, one of his most senior pupils, came from this first generation of students and made a name for both himself and Yip Man in the brutal challenge fights that pitted adherents of various schools against one another in unregulated fights on the rooftops of Hong Kong.

Using the Wing Chun that Yip Man had streamlined according to scientific pragmatism, Wong proved himself and his martial art to be effective against all challengers. And as Yip Man became more famous, he attracted new students, included some middle- to upper-class youth quite different from the hooligans of Wong's cohort. Bruce Lee's aspiration to learn Wing Chun partially signaled that he was dabbling in the world of street violence, but it was also an index of the growing popularity of the martial arts among the middle class.

Bruce persuading his mother to pay for Wing Chun lessons was one thing, but persuading the school to admit him was another. Yip's senior student Wong Shun Leung recalls meeting Bruce and rejecting the arrogant "Elvis like youngster," as he described him, who wandered into the studio and leaned casually against the wall, legs crossed, with one hand in his back pocket. Bruce showed proper respect when he returned to the school a few months later, however, and Yip Man accepted him as a "disciple." But as Wong remembers dryly, "From then on, he brought me a lot of trouble."[23]

≈

Kung fu focused Bruce in a way that nothing else could. He attended classes every day after school, never missing a session. He practiced incessantly, throwing punches and kicks while walking down the street to the bewilderment of passersby, and pounded a stool while eating dinner in order to strengthen his arms and toughen his hands. Phoebe recalls that he was always trying to teach her to break bricks, though she never succeeded.[24]

And Bruce studied the philosophical aspects of kung fu just as assiduously as he practiced its physical side. Yip Man introduced him to reading Buddha, Confucius, and Lao-Tzu, the founder of Taoism. From Lao-Tzu, Bruce learned the principle of yin and yang—opposition and complementarity—that would characterize his later teachings. Indeed, in the 1960s, he incorporated the yin-yang symbol into the emblem he designed for Jeet Kune Do, the martial art form that he created in the United States. Although Bruce had enrolled in Wing Chun lessons to become a better fighter in a rough-and-tumble world, studying it also engaged his philosophical mind and provided him with a basis for his further evolutions.

After his expulsion from La Salle College, Bruce transferred to another Catholic school, Francis Xavier Intermediate School. True to form, he developed a reputation as a troublemaker and earned the moniker "Gorilla" for his muscularity and willingness to mix it up. While Bruce intimidated most of the students at Francis Xavier, only his closest friend, Hawkins Cheung, dared to mock his skinny lower body by calling him "Chicken Legs."

Bruce and Hawkins were inseparable. Living only a couple of blocks apart, they slept over at each other's houses on weekends, studied for exams together, and egged each other on in mischief. They spent innumerable hours together practicing Wing Chun under Yip Man and his senior students. Like many close friends, their relationship vacillated between competition and cooperation. When one learned a new Wing Chun technique, rather than sharing the knowledge, he would spring it on the other during sparring to see if it would work. If it did not work, though, they would return to cooperation, asking their teacher or more advanced students to show the technique again. Bruce would engage with the teacher while Hawkins watched. Then they would trade positions. Afterward, they compared notes and tried sparring again until they worked out the kinks.

Yip Man encouraged this practical-minded way of learning and empirically testing Wing Chun concepts, telling his students, "Don't believe me, as I may be tricking you. Go out and have a fight. Test it out." Bruce and Hawkins took this admonition to heart, not only by sparring with each other but also by taking on unsuspecting outsiders. To instigate a fight, they would approach a target, bump or push him, and curse his mother if necessary to provoke him into throwing a punch. Undoubtedly this was the behavior of teenage ruffians, but it was also a way to test and polish their art. While one stepped into the fight, the other would stand aside to observe what techniques worked best under different circumstances.[25]

 Contentions over whose fighting skills were best arose frequently among the vast array of kung fu teachers and styles that proliferated in 1960s Hong Kong. The only way to settle such disputes was through test battles, in which champions would fight for the honor of their respective schools, teachers, and styles. These informal bouts would be arranged through challenges issued and answered through a neutral party. One fighter might send a message: "Hey, I hear you think you're pretty tough." The answer could be, "I'll be at Kowloon Park at 4 p.m. on Thursday. Let's find out who's tough."

The challenge fights took place in parks or on rooftops with a neutral party acting as referee and arbitrator. Before the fight, contestants agreed on rules, such as what would constitute victory—drawing first blood, a knockdown, or submission. The fights would draw a crowd of onlookers who had heard about the challenge or were members of the schools represented. As one of Yip Man's senior students, Wong Shun Leung represented the school on many occasions, earning a reputation as a fearsome challenge fighter.

≈

In Wing Chun, as with most martial arts, lineage and seniority matters a great deal. Practitioners trace their pedigree through their masters and their masters' masters. It is common practice for a *sifu* (master) to deputize a *sihing* (elder brother, or advanced student) to teach more junior students. Although Wong Shun Leung was only six years older than Bruce Lee, he was considerably more advanced in Wing Chun. Both were students of Yip Man, but Lee took most of his direct instruction from *sihing* Wong.

In contrast to the image of Bruce as a fearless gangster, according to Wong's student *Sifu* Clifford Ah-Yeung, Wong stated that Bruce initially shied away from challenge matches and had to be prodded to overcome his fears. Wong himself recounts a fight on the rooftop of a Kowloon apartment building in which Bruce took on an assistant teacher at a rival school. After the first round, in which Bruce suffered a bruised eye and bloody nose, Bruce, who after all was an actor, voiced concern about risking further damage to his face and proposed quitting. Wong admonished him. "If you withdraw, how will you answer your fellow-learners?" he demanded. "You will regret it. As a matter of fact, whether you win or not is not important, but you must try your best. If you fight on, you will win." In response, Bruce took part in the second round and knocked his opponent bloody.[26]

Sifu Ah-Yeung also tells an amusing story about Bruce's deviousness in pursuit of Wing Chun knowledge. Apparently, Bruce desperately wanted to take private lessons from Wong, who told him to just come with other students, but Bruce concocted a clever ploy. Wong gave lessons in his apartment on an upper floor of his building. Bruce showed up early and waited at the ground-floor entrance. As other students arrived, he told them that Wong was not around and sent them on their way. After all the other students left, he went upstairs, told Wong that no one else had come, and received his one-on-one lessons. Wong caught on after a few days, and the jig was up.[27] Wong Shun Leung himself confirmed in an interview that he rejected Bruce's "selfish" request for private lessons and discovered his ruse.[28]

Hawkins Cheung, Bruce's best friend, recalls that Francis Xavier did not have a boxing team, but when an interscholastic boxing championship tournament was announced, one of the Irish teachers who had sparred with Bruce suggested that he represent his school. Although Bruce had not boxed before, he may have been persuaded to agree by the fact that the tournament would be hosted by the hated King George V School and the reigning champion was a King George V student.

Bruce turned for advice to his *sihing*, Wong Shun Leung, with whom he had been studying for six months. Wong encouraged Bruce to enter and trained him for several months. Despite having no experience with Western boxing, Wong helped Bruce adapt Wing Chun to its rules, identify his weaknesses, and build his strengths. On the night of the tournament, Bruce entered the ring to face the three-time reigning champion. British boys and girls jeered from the crowd as he settled into a Wing Chun stance but fell silent as the fight turned from an expected rout into a victory for the Chinese underdog.

Bruce used the principles of Wing Chun to get inside his opponent's reach and deliver a series of rapid alternating left-right-left-right punches to his face. This technique is known as chain punching in Wing Chun and is practiced endlessly in training. He knocked down the champ in the first round, won his first boxing match, and in the process seized the championship for himself and his school.[29]

Despite Bruce's successes on rooftops and in the ring, Wong did not see him as doggedly devoted to Wing Chun. "He was not an exceptional student," he recalled, "only being a bit more diligent than most. Instead he was teaching people dancing, like Cha Cha."[30] Indeed, dancing occupied an important place in Bruce's adolescent life. He was a gifted performer, which should come as no surprise to anyone who has marveled at his precise yet fluid movements in his martial arts films. Once he discovered his passion for the cha-cha, he pursued it doggedly, keeping a list of 108 moves in his wallet and practicing every day after school with Pearl Tso, a close family friend.[31]

Bruce's rivalry with his best friend, Hawkins Cheung, extended from Wing Chun to dancing, and Cheung turned the tables on Bruce's attempt to monopolize a teacher. Knowing how proud Bruce was of his cha-cha moves,

Cheung showed off some new steps he had learned from Filipino school friends. But when Bruce turned up with new steps of his own, Cheung tracked down his Filipino instructor and tried to convince him not to teach Bruce anything more.[32]

Bruce's dedication paid off, as he won the Crown Colony Cha-Cha Championship in 1958. Although many biographies mention this triumph, few name his dancing partner, leaving readers to assume that it was one of his girlfriends.[33] The truth is more interesting: Bruce's dancing partner was his little brother, Robert. Robert's biopic, *Bruce Lee, My Brother*, depicts them stepping lively and pirouetting their way to victory, with Bruce effortlessly tossing and catching his nine-year-old sibling. The film explains that Bruce selected Robert in order to avoid having to choose between two girls who were infatuated with him.

Photographic evidence backs up Robert's role. A picture published in *Black Belt* magazine the year after Bruce's death shows the brothers accepting the championship banner, both clad in dapper suits, Robert wearing a newsboy hat and Bruce his thick-framed black glasses.[34] *The Orphan*, the final film Bruce made in Hong Kong before decamping to the United States, highlights his cha-cha skill. In contrast to most of his films, which were shot in black and white, *The Orphan* treats viewers to a glorious rendition of his graceful, rhythmic dancing captured in full color.

EXIT HONG KONG

By 1959, at the age of eighteen, Bruce had become a recognizable actor, accomplished dancer, and rising fighter, but by May, he would be living overseas in the United States. What precipitated this drastic change? As with many questions regarding Lee's life, this one is difficult to answer definitively. According to his wife, Linda, whom he would marry in Seattle in 1964, Bruce had engaged in a rooftop challenge match with a student of the Choy Li Fut kung fu school that ended with Bruce brutalizing his opponent. Under pressure from the losing fighter's parents, the local police forced Grace to sign a statement guaranteeing

Bruce's good conduct in exchange for not arresting him. Knowing how bleak his future looked, she decided that Bruce must leave Hong Kong.[35]

Other versions purport that Bruce was becoming too embroiled in gang fighting and fled to escape retribution from the underground criminal organizations known as the triads.[36] It is also possible that his parents simply thought he needed a fresh start. Whatever the reason, in the spring of 1959, Bruce readied himself to depart from Hong Kong, the only home he could remember. As he prepared to leave, Bruce realized how limited his martial arts training had been thus far. Wong Shun Leung has said in a videotaped interview that Bruce studied Wing Chun with him for about a year and a half and in a written account has estimated that he had about two years of training, while sources suggesting that he began studying Wing Chun at around the age of fourteen would credit him with nearly four years of training.[37] His best friend, Hawkins Cheung, indicates that when Bruce left Hong Kong, the two of them had learned only two of the three Wing Chun forms, *siu lim tao* and *chom kiu*, along with about forty moves on the wooden dummy.[38]

In any case, Bruce spent his final days in Hong Kong learning other flashier styles of kung fu in the hope that they could prove useful in the United States. Wong declares that Bruce studied northern-style kung fu for about ten days before his departure so that he could perform it onstage.[39] Similarly, Cheung recounts that he and Bruce began training with Shiu Hon Sang, a *sifu* of the northern styles, because Bruce thought it might be good to be able to teach kung fu in the US. Although Cheung dropped out after a few days, Bruce continued for two additional months and learned several northern-style forms.[40] Together, these accounts make clear not only that Bruce Lee was an unfinished product when he left Hong Kong but, more important, that he strove to extend his training by learning stylistically diverse forms of kung fu before he arrived in the United States. He would commit even more fully to this course in the years to come.

≈

Bruce Lee and his parents, Lee Hoi Chuen and Grace Lee, in Kowloon, Hong Kong, circa the late 1950s. (Photo by Michael Ochs Archives via Getty Images)

On April 29, 1959, an eighteen-year-old Bruce Jun Fan Lee, the little dragon who could not remain still, the phoenix and one destined to return again to the place of his birth, headed down to the wharf in the Hong Kong harbor on route to his future. Relatives and friends bid him bon voyage as he boarded the SS *President Wilson* bound for San Francisco. Among the 193 passengers, he was one of only 32 US citizens. He set off on his grand adventure with only $100 and change in his pocket, traveling under the US passport he held by virtue of his birth in the US and booked into a lower-level Class E/Tourist berth. Like the ship that had borne Lee Hoi Chuen and Grace Lee to the United States two decades earlier, the *President Wilson* made port calls in Japan and Honolulu before steaming on to California.

The letters that Bruce wrote on board to friends reveal him as a naïve and inexperienced traveler. He worried that he would become seasick from the swaying motion of his bed and was surprised that the ship's bar charged for Coca-Cola. When he showered, he alternated between scalding-hot and freezing-cold water, only later learning that they could be combined.

The *President Wilson* arrived in San Francisco on May 17, 1959. After clearing immigration, Bruce was met by a close friend of his father's from the Cantonese opera, who took him to live at his apartment at 654 Jackson Street in Chinatown.[41] At this address, Bruce would be living, at least temporarily, just two blocks east of the Chinese Hospital, the place where he had been born. As Bruce returned to the land of his birth, his future remained opaque even to him, although he had envisioned a career in health care before he sailed from Hong Kong.

In 1958, around Bruce's eighteenth birthday and on the advice of his mother, he had written to a friend of his father's asking for advice on how to become a doctor or pharmacist, saying, "I planned [*sic*] to come to the States next year and finish High School, I intend to take medicine."[42] Shortly before he left, he had informed his school pal Hawkins Cheung that he was going to become a dentist in the US. "You, a dentist?" Cheung scoffed. "Your patients would lose all their teeth."[43] Jun Fan Lee had returned to the US as his mother had foreseen, but he would not go on to seek his fortune through a career in medicine.

3

AN IMMIGRANT IN SEATTLE

Bruce Lee arrived in Seattle in mid-1959 as a brash, skinny, eighteen-year-old kid with no job skills or concrete plans, a meager understanding of the harsh realities of race and class in the United States, and most important, only limited martial arts training, and that drawn overwhelmingly from the Wing Chun style of kung fu. Although he had come to Seattle expecting to be a guest in the home of one of his father's opera friends, he was stripped of the comfortable, middle-class lifestyle and minor celebrity he had enjoyed in Hong Kong. In this new environment, he encountered influences from around the world that forced him to confront the limitations in his Wing Chun training and exposed him to new ways of fighting and thinking—and loving. These influences transformed his martial arts practices and enabled him to challenge barriers of racism and nationalism.

In Seattle, Bruce attracted a coterie of friends and pupils who admired both his martial arts virtuosity and his outsized personality. A charismatic show-off who craved the spotlight, in part because performing was one of the chief ways he related to people, he radiated self-confidence to the brink of arrogance. Yet he was also open, vulnerable, funny, and generous with his friends. And in his five years in the city, Bruce would eagerly drink in new experiences, begin combining his Chinese kung fu practices with Japanese and Western forms, develop ambitious plans to open martial arts schools around the country, and, in defiance of what were powerful social norms of the era, fall in love with and marry a white woman.

Bruce's experiences in Seattle reveal a great deal about his personal journey. Although San Francisco may be thought of as the quintessential "Asian" city on the West Coast, the one with the largest Asian population, in fact, Seattle was early on a major magnet for Asian immigrants and became home to a flourishing Asian community that in turn attracted more émigrés from Asia, Bruce Lee famously among them. His experiences in Seattle are also a reminder of the virulence of anti-Asian feelings that permeated the United States in the nineteenth and twentieth centuries, feelings that are critical to understanding the Bruce Lee story.

The story of Bruce's teenage years is also a reminder that the man who became a legendary, world-famous figure during his short life of just thirty-two years took his first steps toward making his way in his adopted country and taking what would prove to be his early steps toward stardom by working as a busboy and waiter in a Chinese restaurant in Seattle. This might not seem an auspicious way to begin what would ultimately be such a glamorous career. Nonetheless, Bruce's experiences in Seattle would further reveal the twisted and complex transpacific ties that would shape and define both his personal life and his professional life.

≈

Bruce's journey to the Pacific Northwest retraced a route that had been traversed by migrants from the south of China for more than a century. Seattle's first recorded Chinese resident, Chin Chun Hock, had been born in 1844 in the city of Toisan (Taishan) in the Canton (Guangdong) province. At the age of sixteen, Chin sailed to San Francisco, then traveled north to Seattle, where he found work either as a houseboy or in the cookhouse of a lumber mill—accounts vary.

In 1868, Chin established the Wa Chong Company in a wooden structure set on stilts in a tidal flat on Puget Sound. The company sold sugar, silk, rice, tea, herbs, fireworks, and opium (which was then legal) and manufactured cigars and clothing. Chin also served as a labor recruiter and contractor, providing Chinese workers for logging operations, canneries, railroads, and road-repair projects. The Wa Chong Company facilities functioned as an important community center, replete with a post office, labor hall, and worker housing. Workers could also gamble and smoke opium in adjacent buildings. Before returning to Toisan in 1900, Chin had amassed what was reportedly a million-dollar fortune.[1]

But such success stories were the exception during an era in which Chinese immigrants faced discrimination, harassment, and often violence. During the nineteenth century, Seattle and what would become the state of Washington, along with the entire western United States, vilified Chinese immigrants as unfair competition for white workers and a moral threat to the nation. This anti-Chinese movement sought to bar Chinese from entering the United States, restrict them from public spaces, prevent them from working in occupations deemed to be the province of whites, and deny them the rights of citizenship.

According to the historian Beth Lew-Williams, an associate professor at Princeton whose specialty is Asian American history, by the 1880s violent expulsion was the "method of choice" for driving Chinese out of communities.[2] White mobs invaded Chinatowns and Chinese settlements across the West, setting fire to buildings, beating residents, and marching them out of town. Vigilantes also engaged in bombings and murders of Chinese. These round-ups or "pogroms," as Jean Pfaelzer, a now-retired professor at the University of Delaware, calls them, reached a fevered pitch in 1885 and 1886, when mobs forcefully expelled thousands of Chinese residents from at least 168 communities in eight western states. Criminal acts of violence reflected a broad hostility toward Chinese immigrants; in 1879, an astonishing 99 percent of California voters described themselves as "against Chinese immigration."[3]

≈

The two most notable expulsions in the Puget Sound region occurred in Tacoma and Seattle, though neither matched the homicidal fury unleashed in Rock Springs, Wyoming, where on September 2, 1885, some 150 white coal miners stormed the Chinese quarter of town, driving out its occupants, burning buildings, and shooting Chinese miners as they fled. Twenty-eight Chinese people died, fifteen were injured, and some six hundred were driven from the area in what proved to be the worst incidence of anti-Chinese violence the western territories had ever seen.[4]

The Rock Springs massacre inspired anti-Chinese agitation in Washington Territory. Chinese people who were expelled from mining settlements, towns, and cities by white vigilante gangs gravitated to port cities like Tacoma and Seattle, where other Chinese immigrants had settled to help build the extension of the Northern Pacific Railroad. In Tacoma, on November 3, 1885, Mayor R. Jacob Weisbach and Pierce County Sheriff Lewis Byrd watched as an armed mob marched into the Chinese section of town, knocked on doors, demanded that the Chinese leave, and dragged resisters into the street.

In this attack, reminiscent of the attacks on Jews in the pogroms of the Russian Empire under the tsar, the Chinese were marched through a driving rainstorm and abandoned eight miles outside of town. Although white residents of Tacoma crowed about having executed what they described as a "peaceful expulsion," some Chinese were beaten, two died from exposure, and Chinatown was burned to the ground three days later.[5]

And in Seattle, on February 7, 1886, a mob forcibly marched several hundred Chinese to the docks, intending to make them board a steamer bound for San Francisco. Over the next two weeks, roughly three hundred Chinese departed from Seattle by ship and train, intimidated into leaving by the threat of violence from both the mob and the city police.[6]

≈

Even as anti-Asian racism in Seattle eased significantly, Asian Americans remained racially marked as outsiders, and the city's Asian American population grew and diversified throughout the late nineteenth and early to mid-twentieth century in response to the shifting whims of US immigration policy. The pattern of migration that typified Asian immigration to the United States as a whole was reproduced in microcosm in Seattle. Following the ban on the immigration of Chinese workers imposed by the 1882 Chinese Exclusion Act, legislation that would go down in history as the nation's most discriminatory law barring immigrants from the United States, Japanese immigrants filled the need for cheap labor.

Throughout the twentieth century, Japanese Americans established businesses and residences in Nihonmachi (Japan Town) adjacent to Chinatown. After Japanese immigrants were excluded through the Gentlemen's Agreement of 1907–8, the ending of so-called picture bride migration in 1920, and the Immigration Act of 1924, which banned all immigration from Asia, Filipinos formed the third wave of Asian immigrants. As subjects of the US colony of the Philippines, they were neither citizens nor aliens and thus were able to immigrate until the Tydings-McDuffie Act of 1934 barred their entry. Filipino migrants also occupied the section of town that was known as Chinatown but boasted a thriving multiethnic Asian community that included neighborhood businesses, restaurants, and hotels.[7] Hemmed in because of housing discrimination, Chinese, Japanese, and Filipino Americans clustered in the Jackson Street corridor that encompassed Chinatown and Nihonmachi, along with Beacon Hill to the south.[8]

RUBY CHOW'S RESTAURANT

Upon Bruce Lee's arrival in the United States, Bruce's father called on his durable transpacific Cantonese opera connections to look after his wayward son while Bruce was so far from home. He turned to Ping Chow, a fellow opera performer who with his wife, Ruby, had in 1948 founded Ruby Chow's, Seattle's most prominent Chinese restaurant. In turn, Chow reached out to Fook Young, who was then working for the restaurant as a cook.

Young, another of Lee's old opera connections, had lived with Bruce's father in San Francisco while they performed at the Mandarin Theatre. The man whom

Bruce had called "Uncle Fook" when he visited the Lee home in Kowloon had retired from opera, and although he continued to take amateur roles in local performances, his primary occupation was working at Ruby Chow's, a restaurant whose own history reveals a great deal about how Chinese immigrants typically fared in a major US city not long after the end of the Korean War.

Young drove to San Francisco to bring his old friend's son to Seattle, where Bruce expected to live as an honored guest in the home of a family friend.[9] Instead, the Chows put him to work as a busboy and housed him in the attic of the building in which their restaurant was located. For a pampered young man whose family had employed live-in servants in Kowloon, being thrust into the life of a working-class Chinese immigrant in the United States must have come as a rude awakening.

Ruby Chow's, which had opened in 1948 and was the first Chinese restaurant located outside the boundaries of Seattle's Chinatown, was a trailblazing establishment that introduced many of the city's white residents to Chinese cuisine. The menu, which offered complete Cantonese-style meals for $2.50 per person, described exotic-sounding dishes and unfamiliar ingredients for uneasy diners. Won ton was described as "Chinese ravioli," and Ruby Chow's egg rolls were proclaimed to be "one of the leading specialties of the house." The section of the menu labeled "Exotic Recipes of the Far East" included "Chicken Curry" and "Fresh Whole Cracked Crab Curry." Less adventurous diners could opt for "Chef Chow's Special Steaks" ($2.25) or "Disjointed Half Fried Chicken" ($1.75).[10]

Though just five feet tall, Ruby Chow cut a larger-than-life figure, bustling about in her extravagant bouffant and leaving in her wake a trail of charmed customers and chastened waiters and busboys. When Bruce began working at the restaurant, the woman known throughout Chinatown as "Auntie Ruby" had already risen from dire poverty but had not yet broken all the barriers she was destined to break. Born in 1920 on a fishing dock on the Seattle waterfront, she gained prominence as a restaurateur, went on to become a power broker in Chinatown, and became the first Chinese American women to serve on the King County Council, the jurisdiction of which includes Seattle.

Ruby's appearance as a kindly Chinese aunt masked a steel spine and sharp elbows. Charming and cajoling, imperious, fiercely loyal, and furious when she felt betrayed, Ruby Chow was a polarizing figure who dominated settings from banquet halls to council chambers.[11] As one newspaper profile said of her, "She's a living legend in Seattle's Chinese community, but got there the all-American way. She elbows for power one moment, then becomes 'Auntie Ruby,' the social worker, the next."[12]

≈

Ruby Chow's father, Jim Mar, had immigrated to the United States from Guangdong in 1883 at the age of nineteen to work on the railroad. In Seattle, he rose to the position of foreman at the San Juan fish cannery. In a hostile climate in which Chinese immigrants faced legal discrimination and overt discrimination in labor and housing, family associations and mutual aid societies organized to provide support and services. Tongs, or secret societies, offered legitimate job opportunities and business loans to members, but they also presided over illegal activities such as gambling, smuggling, prostitution, and drug trafficking. Mar founded the Seattle branch of the Hop Sing Tong, which on one occasion survived an attack from a competing tong member who fired twelve shots at him in front of a store in Chinatown.

Mar married a woman thirty-three years his junior, and together they had ten children, the fourth of whom, Seung Gum, became known as Ruby. Mar returned to China when the youngest child was a baby, leaving his wife and children to fend for themselves.[13] To make ends meet, Ruby's mother sold lottery tickets in Chinatown, and despite the family's dire situation, she rejected monetary offers from wealthy families who wanted to adopt Ruby, retorting angrily that she would feed her children out of garbage buckets before she parted with any of them.

When Ruby's mother died during her junior year of high school, she dropped out to support the family by waiting tables in restaurants and working as a salesgirl. She then moved to New York and found employment in a Chinese restaurant, where her future husband, Ping, was working as a cook.

Ping had come to New York as a performer in a Cantonese opera touring company but became ill and was stranded when the company returned to Hong Kong shortly before the beginning of World War II. After their marriage, Ruby and Ping moved to Seattle, where they worked at the Hong Kong Cafe, Ruby as a manager and waitress, Ping as a cook.

Ping continued to perform in Cantonese opera, and the restaurant became a gathering spot for local opera people and touring companies. When the couple saved enough money to start their own restaurant, they bought a site on Broadway and Jefferson Street, where Ruby Chow's opened in 1948 and quickly became a hot spot that attracted politicians ranging from the governor to city council members, along with visiting celebrities, foreign dignitaries, and business leaders. Over the years, the Chows expanded the restaurant from its initial seating capacity of sixty-five to over three hundred. One politician described it as the unofficial clubhouse of the Seattle Democrats.

Ruby's influence in the Chinese American community grew along with her business success. For decades, the Chong Wa Benevolent Association, one of Seattle's most important community institutions, had helped manual laborers find work on the docks and railroads, obtain exit permits to visit or return to China, and bury those who died destitute. And for decades, the organization had been run by elderly men. But in 1958, Ruby, along with six other women, won election to Chong Wa's board of directors, and nearly two decades later, she became the first woman in the world to be elected president of a Chong Wa chapter.

Ruby's leadership in the Chinese American community convinced her that the community needed better political representation, so she turned her considerable influence toward supporting a young assistant district attorney named Wing Luke in his campaign for a seat on the Seattle City Council. To raise his name recognition, Ruby coordinated a fortune-cookie publicity campaign, convincing all two hundred Seattle Chinese restaurants to serve customers fortune cookies containing slips of paper reading, "Wing Luke says . . ." followed by supposedly Confucian adages. Whether or not because of this unusual campaign tactic, Luke became the first Chinese American elected to the council of a major US city.

When Ruby herself ran for a seat on the King County Council in 1973, she won and went on to serve three terms. She also groomed a generation of Asian American politicians, including her son Mark, who became a King County district court judge; her daughter Cheryl, who served on the Seattle School Board and Seattle City Council; and Gary Locke, who cut his teeth on Ruby's campaign, won election as Washington's first Asian American governor, and served as secretary of commerce and US ambassador to China in the Obama administration.

≈

When Bruce Lee arrived at Ruby Chow's, he was promptly put to work as a waiter and busboy. The Chows lived above the restaurant and designated for Bruce a tiny, third-floor space under the stairs, a Spartan forty-square-foot enclosure that was more like a walk-in closet than a room. He slept on a mattress on the floor under a sloping ceiling that made it impossible to stand up. A wooden fruit crate held books and a few family photographs. At night, he pulled a string that dangled from a bare bulb to turn off the light.[14]

One can only imagine the confrontations between the imperious boss who brooked no loafing or backtalk and the headstrong teenager who had previously worked only as an actor. Recalling how Bruce responded to manual labor, Ruby's son Shelton admitted tactfully, "He didn't cotton to that very well." Her daughter Cheryl added, "He was like any teenage boy working at our restaurant—he worked hard when he saw my mom coming around the corner."[15]

But as much as Bruce hated working at the restaurant, he loved having a new audience for his martial arts. During breaks, he showed off his moves and taught kung fu to waiters, cooks, and busboys in an alley behind the restaurant (a scene he later re-created in *The Way of the Dragon*, in which his character trains the staff of a Chinese restaurant in Rome in a back courtyard).

BRUCE LEE, AMERICAN HIGH SCHOOL STUDENT

In the fall of 1959, at the age of eighteen, Bruce enrolled at Edison Technical School, a vocational high school that also offered an adult education program that helped both foreign students needing to hone their English-language skills and adjust to the US educational system and veterans returning to complete their high school studies and prepare for college. Edison was a good academic fit for Bruce, who had completed the equivalent of high school in Hong Kong but was not yet ready to matriculate at a US university. It was also a good fit given his nonacademic interests because a vibrant martial arts scene flourished at Edison due to the presence of many foreign students and veterans who had learned martial arts in Asia.

Jesse Glover, a fellow student at Edison, became Bruce's closest friend for the next three years and, most important, his first student. Glover, who was born in 1935, had grown up in nearby Yesler Terrace, a public housing project notable not only as Seattle's first but also as the nation's first racially integrated project when it opened in 1941. Despite the idealism underpinning Yesler's racial mix, Glover was familiar with police harassment and brutality. As a twelve-year-old boy, he and two friends had encountered a racist cop who called them "little niggers" and beat him with a nightstick, leaving him hospitalized with a broken jaw that had to be wired shut. Sickly as a child, Glover had tried to overcome his sense of vulnerability by teaching himself the Japanese art of jiu jitsu by studying books. But he discovered that books were no substitute for personal instruction, and he tried desperately to enroll in judo classes taught by Japanese Americans, first in Seattle, then in California, where he moved to live with his father. In both cases, he was rebuffed as an outsider.[16]

Joining the US Air Force unlocked the door to formal judo instruction as Glover enrolled in classes while stationed at Ramstein Air Base in Germany. After his enlistment, he returned home to Seattle and to the dojo, or training studio, that had rejected him earlier. This time, the skills he had learned in the Air Force gained him acceptance as a member of the dojo, where he eventually earned a brown belt in judo. As his proficiency grew, however, he began to question the usefulness of judo as a weapon for self-defense, and by 1960, he was eager to explore other options.[17]

≈

One of Glover's judo friends, Leroy Porter, loaned him a book on the Chinese art of kung fu by James Yimm Lee (no relation to Bruce but an important friend in years to come), a teacher with training in both karate and kung fu. Glover tirelessly practiced the techniques shown, but as before, he found it impossible to learn a physical art from a book.

Some weeks later, Glover heard that a kung fu demonstration was going to be held by Seattle's Chinese Youth Club at the Seafair festival. He and his roommate, Ed Hart, made their way to the front of a crowd eagerly awaiting a martial arts performance. Instead, the demonstration opened with a graceful couple dancing the cha-cha. When the kung fu finally started, the most impressive performer was the male cha-cha dancer, whom the announcer named as Bruce Lee. "I was totally fascinated with Bruce's moves, and vowed that I was going to learn to move the same way," Glover would say later. "Little did I know that only a year later I would be performing on the same stage as Bruce's No. 1 student."[18]

Glover was pleased to discover that Bruce attended Edison Tech and lived nearby. He began planning ways to introduce himself and found an opening when he noticed that Bruce walked to school each morning. Glover began taking the same route, walking ahead of Bruce and punching and kicking telephone poles to show off his chops. When that failed to attract Bruce's attention, he approached Bruce directly, told him that he had seen the kung fu demonstration at Seafair, and requested lessons. Bruce agreed, but on the condition that the lessons occur in private away from prying eyes. Jesse Glover thus became Bruce Lee's first martial arts student. They trained at Glover's house when his roommates were absent, under a staircase at Edison Tech, and behind Ruby Chow's restaurant.[19]

After a month of secret workouts, Glover persuaded Bruce to work with his close friend and roommate, Ed Hart, who was also a student at Edison and became Bruce's second student.[20] A former professional middleweight boxer, Hart was a powerful puncher who could knock down a two-hundred-pound man with either a left- or right-handed punch. Glover once tested his roommate by asking Hart to punch him in the stomach with only half his strength and ruefully recalls both the "deep pain and gasping that followed Ed's blow" and the agonizing three minutes he spent on the floor trying to recover.[21] But even Hart's extensive fighting experience and power did not prepare him to deal with Bruce, who handled him with ease in their first workout, repeatedly thwarting Hart's attacks, tying up his hands, and preventing him from getting away safely.[22]

Glover also introduced Bruce to the person who would become his third student, Skip Ellsworth, another friend and Edison student. Upon meeting Ellsworth, Bruce gave a little demonstration: he smacked Ellsworth in the chest with two palms so hard that the much larger man flew across the room and slammed against a wall, instantly converting him into a true believer in the power of Bruce's martial art.[23]

The group grew as Glover and Hart introduced Bruce to more of their friends and fellow fighters. Howard Hall, who had accompanied Glover on his kung fu pilgrimage to the Bay Area, asked whether they might put in a good word with Bruce. In addition, Glover introduced Bruce to Leroy Porter, who had lent Glover the James Lee book, and to Pat Hooks, a military veteran whom he knew from judo circles. Charlie Woo, who had told Glover about the first demonstration, also joined the crew.[24]

James Demile became yet another early member of Bruce's group. A 220-pound former undefeated heavyweight champion of the US Air Force, Demile had enrolled at Edison Tech to complete a few high school credits before starting college.[25] After watching Bruce give a demonstration, Demile told him that Wing Chun did not seem useful for real fighting. Bruce invited him to throw a punch, but as Demile recounts, "Unfortunately for me, when I tried to punch him, I was totally unsuccessful. He was able to trap me and counter me and hit me. There was nothing I can do. So this was my first introduction to Bruce Lee."[26]

The initial group of Jessie Glover, Ed Hart, Skip Ellsworth, Howard Hall, Leroy Porter, Pat Hooks, Charlie Woo, James Demile, and Leroy Garcia were young, accomplished fighters who had earned credibility both on the streets and in the boxing ring. They tended to be, as Demile put it, "kind of, in a way, street punks," and several of them were military veterans.[27] The group around Bruce now looked "kinda like the United Nations," as Glover put it, a motley assemblage of "Japanese guys, Chinese guys, Black guys, white guys, [and] Hispanic guys."[28] They constituted Bruce's first inner circle.

≈

These young men were far more than students to Bruce. Although everyone acknowledged his superior skill, Bruce acted as the leader of the pack rather than as a revered master. They were his primary social outlet and closest friends, who not only trained with him but also helped him adapt to life in the United States. As Glover summed up their relationship, "Bruce was never an idol to me." Glover never called Bruce *sifu*, the respectful title used for a kung fu teacher, nor did any other members of this circle, sensing that Bruce did not expect such veneration.[29] Ellsworth agrees but cited one notable exception: Bruce asked his friends to bow to him and call him *sifu* at martial arts exhibitions. Adding these formal elements added to the showmanship of the performance, so they were happy to acquiesce.[30]

Bruce's dedication to teaching did not match his passion for practicing the martial arts. Rather than devote himself to his students' improvement, he used them as props to hone his own skills. Glover notes that Bruce "didn't consider himself to be a good teacher because he was far too caught up in his own development and had little time and patience for answering or teaching those who were not quick to learn." Indeed, Bruce "made no secret of his distaste for teaching."[31] Hart agrees. "I don't think he liked teaching a lot," he said, "but he did like to do *chi sao*, and he did like to show closing moves."[32] *Chi sao*, or "sticking hands," is a foundational Wing Chun drill in which two partners facing each other touch the other's forearms and "roll" through a sequence of prescribed movements while seeking opportunities to attack and defend. It teaches the essential Wing Chun principles of sensitivity (one must feel windows to strike as they open and withdraw as they close) and mutuality and reciprocity (partners moves in concert with each other and respond to the other's advancement or retreat). Bruce's love of closing moves—quickly moving from a safe distance into striking range—spoke to his eagerness to exchange blows.

Demile puts it best when he concludes, "I was a training partner, a dummy."[33] Nevertheless, Bruce's students could not help but benefit from serving as his active punching bags because he had such deep knowledge of kung fu, a style none of his students were familiar with, and was advancing his own understanding of fighting so rapidly.

Initially, Bruce and the gang trained wherever they could find free space. He visited Jesse Glover's apartment for one-on-one sessions, sending the much bigger man "flying about the living room" and in the process breaking every piece of furniture.[34] They practiced in the parking garage of the Blue Cross Insurance building and in the parking lot of Ruby Chow's. Cheryl Chow recalls once hearing a commotion in the yard behind the restaurant and going outside to see what it was all about. Bruce, who was there training with a group, had boasted that he could beat any of them with his eyes closed. One ambitious fighter sneaked up on Bruce from behind and punched the back of his head. Bruce lost his temper, opened his eyes, and smashed the miscreant into the garage wall.[35]

Bruce and his pals acted like a typical crew of young men, hanging out, eating together at restaurants, going to movies. After living under Ruby Chow's roof for six months, Bruce felt the need for more freedom and moved into the house where several of his students lived. This house, located on Sixth Avenue and Cherry Street, just a few blocks from both the restaurant and Edison Tech, became a central gathering place for the gang, where they talked, argued, hung out, and of course, practiced martial arts.[36]

The group formed tight bonds of friendship, and several members helped Bruce with his homework and various jobs. Hart provided assistance on many of Bruce's school papers.[37] Ellsworth lent a hand washing dishes and sweeping and mopping the floor at Ruby Chow's.[38] Glover and Demile pitched in with Bruce's other job, stuffing advertising inserts into the Sunday edition of the *Seattle Times*.[39]

≈

Bruce loved Chinese food almost as much as he loved practicing martial arts. After workouts, he and his friends would often troop out for a meal in Chinatown (now called the International District). They frequented several restaurants, each selected for a particular specialty: Yin Lin for beef with oyster sauce (his favorite dish),[40] Baby Three Grands for tomato beef, and Gim Ling for Chinese pastries. But they congregated most regularly at Tai Tung on South King Street, which offered a good variety of dishes and served generous portions for reasonable prices.[41]

Although Tai Tung has been renovated since Bruce's day, fans can still visit the restaurant and see the memorabilia and posters displayed in what is called the "Bruce Lee corner." Tourists taking part in the Bruce Lee's Chinatown Tour can sample cabbage soup, beef with oyster sauce, garlic-sauce shrimp, sweet and sour pork, broccoli, green beans, and root beer.

In addition to sparring and eating, Bruce and his cohorts frequently went to the movies. Theaters in Chinatown screened kung fu films and Japanese samurai films, both of which they watched by the dozens. Bruce scrutinized these films, incessantly commenting on them and critiquing then as to the realism of their fight scenes. The good ones impressed him, but the inferior ones elicited mild cursing that could be heard throughout the theater. Glover believes that these samurai films influenced Bruce's kung fu movies a decade later.[42] As for American films, no one cracked up Bruce like Jerry Lewis, who tickled his slapstick sense of humor.[43]

Bruce enjoyed clowning around himself, sometimes doing crude and often unkind impressions that appealed to negative stereotypes of disabled people and gay men. Wearing a pair of glasses with cloudy trick lenses that made him appear to be blind, he would buy a movie ticket just to see the look of surprise on the cashier's face.[44] At non-Chinese restaurants, he would pose as a son of the Chinese ambassador and pretend that he did not speak English.[45]

These attention-grabbing performances not only echoed Bruce's previous life as a minor celebrity in Hong Kong but also foreshadowed his later quest for worldwide acclaim. But during these early Seattle years, Bruce was simply a young man surrounded by rowdy friends, tentatively groping his way toward the future.

Bruce tended to fashion as seriously as he did to martial arts, food, and films; he owned at least twenty suits and ten pairs of shoes. When he left Hong Kong, his father had given him a raccoon coat, which he reluctantly put into mothballs upon learning that such coats were not in style in the United States. Photographs from his Seattle years show Bruce as a dapper young man, often wearing a sharp suit with thin lapels and a skinny tie. His vanity extended to his height. To disguise being just five foot seven, he wore boots and shoes with Cuban heels that boosted him by an inch.[46] When he later enrolled at the University of Washington and joined the ROTC, a friend recalled that Bruce enjoyed knowing how good he looked in his military uniform.[47]

The ultimate accessory for a stylish young man was a car. Bruce did not know how to drive when he arrived in Seattle, but his friend Leroy Garcia taught him in Garcia's Fiat. Bruce drove with the same abandon he used when practicing martial arts, zooming up on other cars, tailgating impatiently, and whipping around to pass another vehicle. "Bruce was as poor at driving as he was good at Gung Fu," Glover remembered. "Every time that I rode with him I felt like the trip might be my last." When Bruce had finally saved up enough money, he bought a 1957 black Ford, which he washed so often that, in Glover's words, he "almost wore off the paint."[48]

In addition to learning how to drive in Seattle, Bruce also learned how to shoot firearms. Garcia and Ellsworth introduced him to pistols, revolvers, rifles, and shotguns. Mainly they shot cardboard targets in the mountains outside Seattle, but Ellsworth suggests that they "may have" shot at less appropriate targets in the city as well; Bruce reportedly used a .25-caliber semiautomatic handgun he had received as a birthday present to shoot at pigeons outside his window at Ruby Chow's.[49]

≈

Bruce Lee's most important and loyal Seattle acolyte was a Japanese American man named Takauki "Taky" Kimura. When he met Bruce, Taky was thirty-eight years old, was married with a son, ran a small market near Edison Tech and Ruby Chow's, and bore psychological scars from having been imprisoned during World War II.

Kimura had been born in 1924 and grew up in Clallam Bay, a tiny town near the tip of the Olympic Peninsula separating the Pacific Ocean from Puget Sound. His parents were Japanese immigrants who had come to Washington in the early twentieth century and raised seven children there. His father had worked on a railroad track maintenance crew and eventually rose to the rank of foreman.

In early 1942, the federal government began incarcerating Japanese Americans living on the Pacific Coast into what were euphemistically called "relocation centers" that resembled nothing so much as prison camps. The Kimura family was initially shipped to a camp in Tule Lake in California, then transferred to one in Minidoka, Idaho. Taky recalls substandard food and housing too flimsy to provide protection from harsh and frequent sandstorms. He volunteered for the US Army, hoping to join the all–Japanese American 442nd Regimental Combat Team, but was rejected because of poor eyesight.

When the family was finally released, and with nothing to return to in Clallam Bay, they moved to Seattle, home to the largest Japanese American community in the Pacific Northwest. The family of nine lived in a one-bedroom house, the only accommodation they could find in a city still suspicious of people who looked like the enemy. They bought a small grocery store, which they made thrive by grueling labor. For decades, Taky worked six days a week.[50]

Glover knew Kimura from training at the Seattle judo dojo and introduced him to Bruce. Kimura was hardly Bruce's most athletically gifted student, but he was the one most affected by working with Bruce. The two developed a deep friendship that lasted until Bruce's death, and Bruce rewarded Kimura's fealty and devotion by naming him as his assistant teacher. Having been stripped of his dignity and sense of self-worth by his World War II incarceration, Kimura developed new confidence as he practiced martial arts with Bruce. "Bruce made me realize that I am a human being and I have equal rights," he recalled years later. "He changed my way of thinking and looking at myself. He told me I'm just as good as anyone else and I began to believe in myself."[51]

MARTIAL ARTS INNOVATION IN SEATTLE

The subtitle of Jesse Glover's memoir, *Bruce Lee: Between Wing Chun and Jeet Kune Do*, provides an excellent framework for understanding Bruce's development during his Seattle years. He began with a strong base in the southern Chinese Wing Chun style of kung fu but rapidly began developing new methods of fighting that incorporated a myriad of influences as he moved away from martial arts orthodoxy and toward forging his own fusion style.

As Bruce Lee fans would come to learn, Wing Chun is designed to enable a smaller, weaker person to defeat a stronger opponent. And while its charming origin story is best understood as a fable, it is true that Wing Chun teaches its practitioners to deflect and redirect, rather than directly oppose, their opponent's blows. For this reason, Wing Chun is sometimes referred to as a "soft" style, in contrast to "hard" styles such as karate that teach practitioners to attack by crashing through their opponents' blocking movements and defend by directly blocking their blows.

Wing Chun emphasizes short, direct movements intended to attack and protect from the so-called center line, the vertical line that proceeds from the space between the feet to the crown of the skull. Because Wing Chun stresses directness and compact movements, its movements can appear less graceful than the longer, more flowing motions of some other styles.

When Bruce began working at Ruby Chow's, his primary training consisted of a maximum four years (and possibly fewer) of studying Wing Chun in Hong Kong. Before departing for the United States, he had picked up a few forms from various northern styles of kung fu, and in Seattle, he learned some

Tai Chi and Southern Mantis style from "Uncle Fook" Young, his father's opera friend who became the chief instructor at the Chinese Youth Club.[52] In other words, Bruce possessed superficial knowledge of other varieties of kung fu, but he was far from proficient in them, let alone accomplished. It is understandable that when Jesse Glover approached Bruce about becoming his first student, Bruce began by teaching Glover Wing Chun.

≈

When Bruce showed up at Glover's door for their first session, he suggested that they test the efficacy of his method by saying to Jesse, "Hit me any way you can." Jesse threw jabs, hooks, and roundhouses. Bruce blocked every attempted strike and followed each one with a fist that stopped just short of Jesse's face. When they turned to short-range combat, Jesse found himself hopelessly blocked, unable to strike, move, or even retreat. "Every time that his hands made contact with mine," he recalls, "I was unable to do anything."[53]

In this short-range exercise, Bruce was showing Glover a Wing Chun drill called *chi sao*, or sticking hands, one of the style's primary training tools. When Wing Chun practitioners want to engage in *chi sao*, they will invite a partner to "touch hands." They begin by facing each other and making contact with their forearms in mirrored positions, then they begin a cadence of scripted movements. However, *chi sao* is not simply a drill but rather an improvisational exercise from which either participant may deviate at any time. If one participant attempts a strike, their partner can parry, initiate their own attack, or return to the rhythmic movements. Unlike American football, in which teams alternates possessing the ball and one team is chiefly responsible for trying to score at any given time, Wing Chun teaches that offense and defense flow into and from each other.

One point of sticking hands is to develop solid positions. A person who allows their elbows to drift too far outward will soon receive a thump on the chest from a partner who has sensed an opening along the center line; one who drops the hands too low will find a fist grazing their nose. The other point is to develop sensitivity, as partners continually feel each other's energy and probe for openings. Pushing forward too emphatically will result in an opponent who lets you tumble off balance, while blocking too gently will allow a punch to come crashing toward your face.

Bruce's *chi sao* skill was what enabled him to tie up Glover. "His hands controlled mine with a kind of friction that stopped any kind of forward movement," Glover recalls. "Whenever I tried to nullify this friction by changing my angle of attack, Bruce would also change his angle of defense and my hands were still unable to move forward. . . . Next I attempted to disengage and go around his hands, but this strategy was met with direct strikes to my chest."[54] After *chi sao*, Bruce taught Glover *siu lim tao*, the first form of Wing Chun. As the basis for Wing Chun teaching, its name translates to "little idea," because it rehearses in slow motion all the positions and movements necessary to learn the basic style.

By beginning Glover's instruction with *siu lim tao* and *chi sao*, Bruce was following Wing Chun orthodoxy. In his first two years in Seattle, Bruce continued to see forms as invaluable building blocks for teaching the martial arts. He taught forms to all his students and insisted that they be performed flawlessly. Even as he contemplated creating a new martial art, he discussed creating forms to reflect his burgeoning ideas. However, by the following year, he had lost faith in forms and viewed them as impediments to true learning.[55] The reason for this sudden change of heart lies in the diversity of the martial arts scene in Seattle.

≈

Many different martial arts styles, Chinese and other, rubbed elbows in Seattle's martial arts scene. Bruce had learned some northern kung fu forms before leaving Hong Kong and had studied a number of others with Fook Young in Seattle. Although he still considered Wing Chun to be superior overall, he admired various elements of kung fu styles like Hung Gar, Eagle Claw, Southern Mantis, Northern Mantis, and Choy Li Fut.[56] He customized his instruction by teaching one form from a non–Wing Chun style to each

individual student. This ensured that his school could put on visually striking and variegated performances at the martial arts demonstrations that they
always seemed to be performing. Perhaps more important, having students
well versed with the forms drawn from a variety of different styles enabled
Bruce to scrutinize their movements to probe for strengths and vulnerabilities.

Although Bruce did not relish teaching, his student Ed Hart said, he enjoyed pitting himself against students using different styles. "He liked to
practice against any kind of attack," Hart said. "He was always practicing
against any kind of attack at all to try and find a weak spot."[57] Bruce would
have been able to study all these Chinese styles of kung fu in Hong Kong, but
in Seattle, he encountered the Japanese martial arts that were dominant in
the United States at the time: judo and karate. Although Japanese Americans
had practiced their martial arts in the United States since their arrival in the
late nineteenth and early twentieth centuries, Japanese martial arts became
popularized after World War II by US military veterans returning from the
deployments in Japan and Okinawa.

In contrast to the Japanese styles, Chinese martial arts were virtually unknown in the United States in the early 1960s. "At first Gung Fu sounds like
a variety of Chow Mein," began an article in the *Seattle Times*. "And after you
think about it, you're pretty sure it is—but it really isn't." This article about
Bruce and his efforts to publicize kung fu is perhaps best understood as an artifact of its time, as its (erroneous) headline reads, "Mike Lee Hope for Rotsa
Ruck," and its conclusion explains that Bruce would be "velly happy" if he
could help gung fu become well known. Today, the casual racism of the article's broken-English parody—which is based on the idea that Asian people
cannot enunciate the *r* sound properly—seems as surprising as the notion
that kung fu was totally unfamiliar to the newspaper's audience. But in the
early 1960s, many Americans had yet to be introduced to the Chinese martial
arts and certainly had not come to grips with deeply entrenched racist stereotypes of Asians and Asian Americans.[58]

To build greater awareness of kung fu, Bruce and his students spent considerable time and effort putting on martial arts demonstrations at gyms, street

festivals, and high schools and colleges around the city and sometimes even appearing on television.[59] Because of kung fu's obscurity, these exhibitions were billed as judo or karate demonstrations. Spectators who came to see the more familiar Japanese arts were indeed treated to displays of judo and karate but were also introduced to various kung fu styles. Bruce and his students learned Japanese sets and ran through them as smoothly at these events as the Chinese sets that Bruce taught his students.

≈

Even while studying kung fu with Bruce, Jesse Glover continued to train in judo at the YMCA, where Bruce occasionally worked on his judo forms as well. Two Japanese students at Edison Tech—Tak Miaybi and Masafusa Kimura, both black belts in karate—also practiced at the YMCA. Watching Bruce performing an unfamiliar style piqued their interest, and when he explained that he was doing "Chinese boxing," they asked to learn more. He agreed to teach them, and they joined his circle.[60] But relationships between practitioners of Japanese and Chinese styles were not always so cordial.

One karateka (practitioner of karate) who also attended Edison Tech and had seen Bruce performing kung fu took a particularly dim view of it and made no effort to conceal his disdain. At a demonstration at the Yesler Terrace gymnasium, he sent a friend over to deliver a message that he wanted to fight Bruce. For the next couple of weeks, the challenger sneered at Bruce in the school's lounge, gestured at him to come over and fight, and tried to block his way in the hallways. Bruce studiously ignored all these insults— quite a feat for the normally quick-tempered youngster—until the karate man went too far. He had a friend deliver a message that said that if Bruce wanted to go to the hospital, all he had to do was walk over to where the karate man was standing.

This spark ignited the fury that Bruce had been assiduously tamping down until then and sent him searching for Jesse Glover to serve as a referee. Bruce wanted to fight right there at school, but Glover cautioned that they might be expelled and suggested meeting instead at the YMCA. Bruce, Glover, Ed

Hart, and Howard Hall gathered outside the school, Bruce's anger burning hotter by the minute. When the karateka showed up with two of his friends, Bruce avoided eye contact, trying to keep from exploding, while the karateka goaded him by repeatedly moving into his line of sight.

With the tension skyrocketing, it seemed as if the fight might erupt right there; but a bus arrived, and both groups clambered aboard for the ride to the YMCA. En route, the karateka tried to establish rules for the fight, but the infuriated Bruce, who looked like "he was going to burst a blood vessel," waved them off and spat out his intention to go full force. The two groups converged in a handball court at the YMCA and agreed on a three-round fight, each round lasting two minutes, with Glover serving as the referee and Hart as the timekeeper. When Glover waved for the fight to begin, Bruce assumed a Wing Chun stance, the challenger a classic karate stance. The karateka went on offense first, launching a foot toward Bruce's midsection. Bruce parried the kick with his right forearm and simultaneously landed a punch to the face with his left, then followed up with a volley of punches to the head, each one so hard that it looked as though the man's face "was being distorted by the force of gravitational pull," according to Glover.[61]

As the punches drove the challenger backward, he desperately tried to strike back, but all his punches glanced harmlessly off Bruce's arms. Bruce had seized control of the center line, which allowed him to punch from the inside and concurrently deflect blows aimed at his head and torso. Seeing the futility of his tactics, the karateka reversed course and tried to grab the arms that were pummeling him, but as he did so, Bruce unleashed a devastating double punch—one to the man's face, the other to his chest. The force of these blows catapulted the challenger six feet through the air. Bruce moved forward as the man flew backward and, at precisely the moment his opponent landed, kicked him viciously in the nose, knocking him senseless. The challenger laid motionless on the court, his face battered as if by a baseball bat, looking as if he were dead. When he finally stirred, the first thing he did was ask how long the fight had lasted. The timekeeper replied that it was twenty-two seconds, not having the heart to tell him that it had only taken only eleven seconds.

Astoundingly, the karateka requested a rematch, which Bruce declined, saying that he had not wanted to fight in the first place. But the swiftly spreading news about the showdown at the YMCA firmly established Bruce's reputation as a fearsome fighter.[62]

≈

Gaining respect for kung fu proved to be a critical goal for Bruce and a key way to express his pride in Chinese culture. In addition to the showdown at the YMCA, he had many chances to demonstrate the efficacy of this unknown martial art. Doug "Jake" Palmer, a seventeen-year-old about to start his senior year of high school, became "mesmerized" watching a demonstration by Bruce and his students in Chinatown in the summer of 1961. Palmer had boxed since the fifth grade but had never seen Asian martial arts and asked one of the students about studying with the young master.

A week later, at the Bon Odori festival (a Japanese celebration of the dead), Palmer felt a tap on the shoulder and turned around to see Bruce. "I heard you were looking for me," Bruce said. The two discussed martial arts, and Bruce invited Palmer to observe a workout. Palmer was delighted to do so and soon joined the school. The year after Palmer graduated from Garfield High School, Bruce visited the school to give a guest lecture on Chinese philosophy. His talk was greeted by yawns and amusement by several beefy football and basketball players, who scoffed at the insistence by a slight, 130-pound young man that this philosophy undergirded a powerful martial art. In response, Bruce picked out the biggest, most dismissive guy in the room and asked him to "volunteer" for a demonstration. As the skeptic sauntered to the front of the room, Bruce told him that he would demonstrate a one-inch punch. He stood with his arm extended, an inch from the volunteer's chest, then as if spontaneously thinking of it, dashed around to set a chair five feet behind the increasingly nervous athlete, "just in case," he said. By now all eyes were focused on the action, as Bruce set up again. When his fist shimmered an inch forward, the kid went flying backward into the chair, flipped over, and skittered against the wall. Bruce continued his lecture to a rapt audience.[63]

As Bruce continued to build a name for himself, he took his first tentative step toward becoming a martial arts teacher. His informal circle of friends and students had been training in backyards, parking lots, garages, alleys, and apartments. Seeking a more permanent location, they pooled their money to rent a space in Seattle's Chinatown, at the intersection of Weller Avenue and Maynard Street. The two-story storefront sat amid other shabby storefronts and decrepit hotels but had the advantage of being just around the corner from the Tai Tung restaurant.

Bruce and his friends practiced in a long, narrow, first-floor room while curious onlookers and passersby on the sidewalk gawked through the large display windows. After practice, the fighters could retreat to the second floor to hang out, shoot the breeze, or nap.[64] Although much of Bruce's social life centered around teaching kung fu to his friends, the idea of making a career as a martial arts instructor had yet to crystallize for him. Instead, like many young people, he and his student Skip Ellsworth often commiserated about not knowing what they wanted to do with their lives and careers.[65] Though Bruce no longer hoped to become a doctor or pharmacist, a wide range of possible futures spread before him.

Living in Seattle presented Bruce with just as many options in martial arts styles as potential career paths. Palmer remembers deeply eclectic training sessions: "Every time I came back he had everything he taught before, and another layer on top of it. It was not Wing Chun. He was watching boxing movies and fights, from Dempsey or Sugar Ray Robinson, over and over, and would take elements from them. It wasn't as if he was just taking a move from them; he was doing something more fundamental. He was looking at principles, or approaches he could use."[66] When it came to martial arts, Bruce realized that rather than having to choose one, he could sample many.

"INTERRELATED AND INSEPARABLE": COLLEGE, PHILOSOPHY, AND ROMANCE

At the age of twenty, Bruce Lee enrolled at the University of Washington for the Spring 1961 quarter. Although he never completed his undergraduate major in philosophy, the three years he spent as a college student represented a pivotal period in which he experienced romance and heartbreak, further developed his approach to martial arts, and launched plans to become a world-famous martial arts teacher.

Bruce's social life as a college student continued to center around kung fu and his circle of students. His student Skip Ellsworth often invited him to parties hosted by his fraternity, Delta Kappa Epsilon. A nonstop showboat, Bruce was the center of attention at these parties, demonstrating one-finger push-ups and his one-inch punch, demonstrating various kung fu forms, and teaching the cha-cha.[67]

Bruce was far from a stellar college student. As had been the case in Hong Kong, he focused his keen intellect on the things that interested him while neglecting other subjects, and during his college years, he was most preoccupied by practicing and teaching martial arts. His report card for the winter of 1962 included a C in composition (perhaps understandable for a nonnative English speaker) and astoundingly, given his athletic prowess, a C in gymnastics. The 1.33 GPA he earned that quarter lowered his cumulative GPA to 1.84 out of a possible 4.0.[68]

Bruce's lackluster academic performance did not stem from a lack of intelligence or inquisitiveness. On the contrary, Bruce was a voracious reader who consumed books on a variety of topics, including philosophy and self-improvement. But he read intently to find ideas and lessons to apply to his favorite topic: martial arts.

≈

Bruce admired the Chinese philosophy of Taoism and drew on it extensively, copying passages from its foundational text, the *Tao Te Ching*, into his personal notebooks and quoting its author, Lao Tzu, in his college essays. In "The Tao of Gung Fu: A Study of the Way of the Chinese Martial Art," an essay he wrote in May 1962, most likely as an assignment for one of his classes, Bruce argued that tao should be understood as the core principle of kung fu.[69] But what is tao? Bruce rejected a common translation of *tao* as "the way," opting for a more expansive notion that he drew from a quotation from Lao Tzu: "The Way that can be expressed in words is not the eternal Way; the Name that can be uttered is not the eternal Name. Conceived of as nameless it is the cause of Heaven and earth. Conceived of as having a name it is the mother of all things." This ineffable principle incorporates the two complementary and mutually dependent forces of yin and yang, where yin is epitomized by darkness, weakness, coldness, femininity, softness, and emptiness, and yang is typified by lightness, strength, warmth, masculinity, hardness, and existence. Though conceived of as opposites, at certain points yin becomes yang and vice versa, as surely as night gives way to day at dawn, only to have day cede to night at dusk. Rather than being irreconcilable opposites, yin and yang form harmonious complements to each other, both dependent on each other for their existence, each flourishing alternately but not resisting the rise of the other.

Despite embracing the principle of tao, Bruce recognized the absurdity of trying to use language to describe its inexpressible qualities. As he put it, "Even Lao-tzu, the author of the *Tao Te Ching*, and the man who wrote, 'He who knows does not speak. He who speaks does not know,' wrote 5,000 words to explain his doctrine."[70] For Bruce, teaching and practicing kung fu was a critical way to explore the elusive yet all important nature of *tao*. Doug Palmer remembers that Bruce recited Taoist aphorisms that could be applied to the martial arts and encouraged his students to strive to attain the mind-set that the aphorisms conveyed.[71]

This metaphysical approach convinced another of his students, Pat Strong, that Bruce was, in his words, "an astute philosopher" in addition to being a talented martial artist and that the two were deeply interrelated. Strong observes that Bruce's "study of martial art had taught him powerful principles, strategies and philosophy," adding, "I was struck at the way he was able to interpret the physical realities of his gung fu into illustrations of universal principles. It seemed to me that his gung fu and philosophy were interrelated and inseparable."[72]

Applying the principle of tao to fighting, Bruce asserted that a kung fu artist who understands tao does not seek to impose unilateral will in a fight but instead strives to attain a form of harmony with the opponent. A fighter who confronts resistance must react with softness rather than charge in relentlessly. One whose opponent creates emptiness by retreating must respond by filling the void and attacking. Neither aggression nor restraint should be valued over the other; instead, both must be used judiciously, in concert with and in response to the opponent. Although associated with strength, yang can extend a beguiling invitation to death, and yin, thought of as weakness, can lead to survival.

To make this point, Bruce quotes Lao Tzu: "The stiffest tree is readiest for the ax. The strong and mighty topple from their place; the soft and yielding rise above them all." Lao Tzu's metaphor of the pliant, enduring tree was one that Bruce returned to repeatedly over the years when explaining the nature of kung fu.

As might be expected of a philosophy major, Lee filled his college notebooks with essays and notes addressing canonical Western philosophers, including Plato, Socrates, St. Thomas Aquinas, and René Descartes. Lee critiqued Aquinas and Descartes on similar grounds, despite their divergent commitments to the divine and reason, respectively. Bruce objected to Aquinas's rigid dichotomization of cause and effect, which he saw as an example of the particularly Western proclivity to wrongly cleave incompatible halves out of what should be considered complementary wholes.[73] He also turned a jaundiced eye toward Descartes, the father of modern rationalism, whose iconic axiom "Cogito, ergo sum," or "I think, therefore I am," established a firm dichotomy between mind and body. Lee objected to a rigid rationalism that prioritizes the mind and its ability to reason over the body and its ability to feel and move.[74] To a martial artist who believed in the complementary unity of mind and body and strove to attain the state of *wu wei*, or acting without intention, it seemed that attributing human existence to our capacity for thought overlooked the possibility that we can verify our existence through our abilities to feel, sense, and move. Bruce privileged neither faith nor reason, finding both to be incomplete in isolation.

≈

The theme of water saturated Bruce's college notebooks. Drizzly Seattle was an appropriate setting for these ruminations, surrounded by Puget Sound and a waterfront at Lake Washington that he loved because it reminded him of the harbor in Hong Kong.[75] In his essay "The Tao of Gung Fu," Bruce quoted a passage from the *Tao Te Ching*:

> Nothing is weaker than water,
> But when it attacks something hard
> Or resistant, then nothing withstands it,
> And nothing will alter its way.

His commentary on the passage notes that water cannot be grasped, struck, or harmed and exists in mighty forms as liquid, ice, and steam. Rather, he wrote, "It has no shape of its own but molds itself to the receptacle that contains it." In another essay, "A Moment of Understanding," Bruce recounted experiencing an epiphany about water's powerful adaptability while sailing on a junk in Hong Kong. Frustrated by Yip Man's oblique advice to "learn the art of detachment," he punched the water. As the ripples widened, he realized, "This water, the softest substance in the world . . . only seemed weak. In reality it could penetrate the hardest substance in the world. That was it! I wanted to be like the nature of water." Bruce wrote about water in his poetry as well as his essays on martial arts. In "All Streams Flowing East or West," he traced the dual nature of water: "Streams born from mountain snows" go on to "flow into the sea," form waves that become "Hammer to sculpture rocks," and eventually settle into gentle tide pools that nestle sea life like jellyfish.

The verse invokes the manifold nature of water as relentless in its creative destruction and essential to life. He would spend the next decade rehearsing various forms of that sentiment onscreen and in interviews.[76]

≈

Bruce was obsessed with martial arts, but he was also interested in women. Such a charismatic, handsome, and muscular young man would remain single only for as long as he wished. And when Bruce had delivered his guest lecture on Chinese philosophy at Garfield High School and bowled over the skeptical audience, unbeknownst to him, he had also caught the eye of a shy, blond, seventeen-year-old cheerleader.

Linda Emery spied Bruce laughing and sparring good-naturedly with several students down the hallway and wondered who the attractive man might be.[77] He seemed sophisticated and mysterious, older than the high school students but younger than the teachers, modish in a narrow-brimmed hat and long beige trench coat. Susan Kay, a Chinese American friend of Linda's, informed her that the intriguing young man was her kung fu teacher, Bruce Lee.

Like most Americans at the time, Linda had never heard of kung fu, but one day, on a dare, she accompanied her friend to Chinatown to see it in action. Sue Ann led her down a dark stairwell to a bare, concrete basement where Bruce was preparing to teach about a dozen students and introduced her to the young *sifu*. From then on, Linda regularly attended Bruce's class on Sunday mornings, then accompanied Bruce and other students for lunch at a local Chinese restaurant.

Linda was nearly as unfamiliar with Chinese cuisine as she had been ignorant of Chinese martial arts but grew to relish the dim sum delicacies that Bruce and his students enjoyed. Bruce commanded as much attention while dining as he did when teaching, holding forth, arguing, demonstrating, and cracking jokes. After lunch, the group often proceeded to a theater in Chinatown, where they watched Japanese samurai films, accompanied by Bruce's endless stream of comments. Once they saw *The Orphan*, the final film Bruce had made in Hong Kong.

≈

Bruce returned to his childhood home for the first time in the summer of 1963.[78] No longer a juvenile delinquent, he was now a twenty-two-year-old college student and kung fu teacher in his own right. He had spent four years in the United States being exposed to new influences, widening his social circles, and becoming a man. One of his students, Doug Palmer, was majoring in Chinese at Yale University, an interest sparked in part by his kung fu studies. Knowing of Palmer's interest in Chinese culture, Bruce invited him to visit Hong Kong.

Palmer borrowed $600 from his father and arrived in July, during a sweltering heat wave. He was eager to practice the Mandarin dialect he had been studying in college but was disappointed to discover that everyone in Hong Kong spoke Cantonese. Despite the language barrier, the stifling heat and humidity, the teeming crowds, and the dank tropical aromas, Palmer relished the opportunity to experience Bruce's childhood environment.

The Lee family welcomed Palmer as a guest in their already-bursting Nathan Road apartment. Mornings began with Bruce meticulously ironing his shirt and pants for the day because the maid's ironing did not meet his impeccable standards. Due to water restrictions imposed during the drought, bathing was restricted to sponge baths taken behind a curtain on the veranda facing the street, although the steamy tropical heat left everyone soaked by perspiration in minutes.

This vacation may have been the most carefree period of Bruce's life. He was far from the demands of college and had yet to incur the obligations of a family and a career. He and Palmer hung out with his show-business friends and ate at many Chinese restaurants with various regional specialties. They even went on double dates together, and Palmer remembers that Bruce showed him how to make the moves on Hong Kong girls.

One of Bruce's goals while visiting Hong Kong was to test the progress he had made as a martial artist during his four years of practicing in the United States against his Wing Chun elders. He took Palmer to a high-rise apartment building to meet his old teacher, Yip Man, who welcomed Palmer graciously and allowed him to observe as he and Bruce worked out. When Bruce and Yip stripped down to their undershirts and began to practice *chi sao* together, Palmer observed that elderly *sifu*'s remarkable fitness.

More significantly, Palmer saw that the slight teacher and his bigger, stronger former student were evenly matched. But Palmer concluded that Bruce was clearly more skilled than the other Wing Chun students. Because Bruce was not ready to let on that he was teaching kung fu to non-Chinese students, Palmer feigned ignorance and did not get the chance to test his kung fu while in Hong Kong. En route home to Seattle, during a layover in Honolulu, Bruce used Palmer in an exhibition at an all-Chinese kung fu school. Yet even outside of Hong Kong, the students were unsettled to learn that Bruce was teaching their martial art to a white man, who they believed should not be made privy to these Chinese secrets.

In September 1963, the Palmer family returned Bruce's generosity by letting Bruce live in their Seattle-area home for six weeks after he was evicted from his apartment. Palmer's parents, Ida and Doug Senior, found Bruce a courteous houseguest who ironed his clothes, cleaned his room, did his chores, and encouraged the younger Palmer boys to do theirs as well, although he sometimes tired of Mrs. Palmer's potato-heavy dinners and told her that he had to go to Chinatown to eat rice.

The Palmer boys, Mike, Kevin, and Cam, were impressed by other sides of Bruce, seeing him as an incandescent star, show-off, and jokester. They were amazed by his brick-breaking chop, one-handed push-ups with the 195-pound Mike lying on his back, and the strength of his grip that could put a paralyzing, vise-like hold on the clavicle of an unfortunate victim. He kept Mike up at night telling corny jokes and laughing at his own punch lines, impressed Kevin with his fastidious grooming regimen that included generous applications of Brylcreem, and terrorized Cam by trying to perfect the clavicle hold on the ten-year-old.

The boys recalled, "Bruce could be overbearing, but not in a haughty way. He was very sure of himself, and that came across strongly when you spent time with him."[79] That supreme sense of self-possession assured that Bruce was always the center of attention, no matter where he went.

≈

In the autumn of 1963, Linda Emery enrolled as a freshman at the University of Washington, where she discovered that Bruce was holding court at lunchtime every day at the school's student center, known as the HUB. His kung fu students who were attending college, along with others attracted to the spectacle, listened to his discourses on philosophy, laughed at his boisterous jokes, and admired his martial arts demonstrations.

By now, Linda had a major crush on Bruce, and she became the most regular attendee at these lunchtime events. Her classwork as a premed student began to falter as she moved closer into Bruce's orbit and began devoting more time to being around him than to her science classes.

Bruce and Linda's relationship took a dramatic turn one autumn afternoon. The kung fu crew worked out regularly at the Sylvan Theater, a grassy field framed by four stately Greek columns. As the pair were running across the field, away from the rest of the group, Bruce tackled Linda as if to show her a new move. But instead of letting her go, he held her down and invited her to dinner at the spectacular revolving restaurant atop the Space Needle, the futuristic tower built for the 1962 World's Fair.

"You mean all of us?" she asked, assuming that he meant the entire group. "No," he replied, "only you and me."

The budding romance between the eighteen-year-old Linda and twenty-three-year-old Bruce began in an era of widespread condemnation of interracial dating and marriage. Although Linda attended the racially integrated Garfield High School and had several Asian American girlfriends, her mother had drawn the line when Linda went out briefly with a Japanese American boy, making clear that interracial dating was forbidden in their family.

This objection reflected the prevalent sentiment of the time, a time when nearly every white American objected to interracial marriages. In a Gallup poll taken in 1958, only 4 percent of white Americans approved of "marriages between white and colored people." Linda's willingness to enter a relationship with Bruce made her an unusual young white woman; a 1942 nationwide poll of high school students showed that 73 percent would refuse to marry a Chinese person. Only members of the group defined as "Negroes" were less acceptable as potential spouses, with 92 percent of the respondents stating that they would refuse such a union.[80]

Linda, to evade her mother's certain disapproval, got dressed at a friend's house and instructed Bruce to pick her up there. He arrived for what would be their first date, on October 25, 1963, in his gleaming black Ford, looking debonair in a black Italian silk suit, purple shirt, and black tie. His hair was slicked back on the sides, and a curl dangled on his forehead. In the restaurant atop the Space Needle, as they were rotating slowly five hundred feet above the city, the ever-voluble Bruce overcame Linda's reticence by talking enough for the both of them, telling her about his childhood and plans for the future. Their evening ended with a chaste kiss.

≈

As students returned to the university in the fall of 1963, Bruce was increasingly preoccupied by being a teacher, not a pupil. He had decided that his path forward lay in becoming a full-time martial arts instructor, and he rented space for what he was calling the Jun Fan Gung Fu Institute. The name of the school revealed much about the evolution of Bruce's martial arts prowess. It still referenced "gung fu," the art that he had studied in Hong Kong, but by branding it with Bruce's Chinese name, Jun Fan, he made clear that the style being taught bore his individual imprint.

Bruce rented space at 4750 University Way NE, on the main commercial corridor adjacent to the university, which is known affectionately to locals as "The Ave." The three-thousand-square-foot ground floor of an apartment building located just two blocks northeast of campus contained a large open room facing the street where Bruce taught classes; a dark, windowless space at the rear that served as his bedroom; and a gymnasium-style restroom that contained a communal shower area, which he liked to turn into a makeshift steam room by opening all the shower heads at full heat. Regular members paid $22 per month and junior members enrolled at a discount rate of $17 a month to study techniques that Bruce promised would be "smooth, short, and extremely fast" and "stripped down to their essential purpose without any wasted motions."[81]

Bruce and Linda continued to date secretly throughout the fall of 1963 and into the spring of 1964, becoming nearly inseparable. In the morning, she would come to his room in the back of the Jun Fan Gung Fu Institute to wake him for classes. After school, the two would rush back to his room to watch the soap opera *General Hospital*. Most evenings, they went out to dinner at the Chinese restaurant across the street, always ordering Bruce's favorites: beef with oyster sauce and shrimp with black bean sauce.

≈

In the summer of 1964, Linda's relationship with Bruce moved to a new level.

At the end of his junior year, Bruce decided to put college on hold to pursue his dream of becoming a nationally known martial arts teacher. The dream had been percolating in his head for at least two years; in September 1962, he had written to a friend in Hong Kong about his plan to "establish a first gung fu institute that will later spread out all over the U.S. . . . within 10–15 years." He likened this growth to a pebble thrown into a pond that sends ripples dispersing across the water.[82] Having tossed the first stone in Seattle, he now intended to see its first ripple appear in the Bay Area of California.

Bruce had been discussing plans for several months with James Yimm Lee, a highly respected kung fu teacher and martial arts publisher who agreed to collaborate with Bruce in opening the second branch of his Jun Fan Gung Fu Institute in Oakland. Bruce closed the school on The Ave, named his student Taky Kimura as the head instructor of the Chinatown branch of the Jun Fan Gung Fu Institute, sold his beloved '57 Ford, and shipped his furniture to Oakland.

In July 1964, Linda drove Bruce to the airport. Although the two had discussed marriage, no commitments had been made. As Bruce boarded the plane, he looked Linda in the eyes and said, simply, "I'll be back." Throughout the summer, they corresponded regularly. Linda harbored doubts that she would ever see Bruce again, but over the summer, he made the momentous decision that they should get married.

"Finally, Bruce wrote that he wanted me with him and would return to Seattle to get me," she recalled. "If it sounds like a one-sided decision, I guess it was. I *knew* I wanted to be with this man forever. It was a matter of Bruce deciding if he could handle the idea of marriage."[83] What goes unspoken in Linda's account is that she must have discovered that she was pregnant, a state of affairs that would certainly help to explain Bruce's sudden willingness to commit his life to hers. In any case, he returned to Seattle on August 12, 1964.

≈

Although the two lovers were ready to be married, Linda's family continued to present a challenge because of their opposition to interracial unions. Linda suggested that she and Bruce elope, move to Oakland, then inform her mother about the marriage over the telephone, but Bruce convinced her that they should have a proper wedding. Obtaining a marriage license in Seattle required applying at the King County Courthouse and waiting three days while the applications were published in the newspaper.

Linda's sharp-eyed Aunt Sally spotted an announcement in the Vital Statistics section that Linda C. Emery and Bruce J. F. Lee intended to wed, and she informed Linda's mother. At the family gathering convened to discuss the matter, Bruce introduced himself by saying, "I want to marry your daughter. By the way, I'm Chinese."

The family saw it differently. Linda's deeply religious aunt and uncle claimed that race-mixing was an abomination prohibited by the Bible.[84] Linda's mother worried that as an interracial family, Bruce, Linda, and their future children would be subjected to prejudice and discrimination. Linda's mother was also hurt and angry; not only because her precious daughter had fallen in love with a Chinese man but also because he had such poor prospects. After all, who had ever heard of kung fu, let along teaching kung fu as a career?

Over the course of the conversation, Linda's mother came around to accept the fact that the marriage would occur, regardless of her feelings. A flurry of hasty arrangements culminated on August 17, 1964, with a Christian ceremony in a church, with Bruce in a rented suit, Linda wearing an ordinary dress, no photographer, and no floral arrangements. The only guests were Linda's family and Bruce's student Taky Kimura, who proudly served as the best man.[85]

Shortly after the wedding, Bruce returned with Linda to Oakland, where they would live with James Yimm Lee—Bruce's partner in the Oakland branch of the Jun Fan Gung Fu Institute—and his family. The headstrong teenager who had arrived in Seattle five years earlier was now a young man, a husband, and a father-to-be, with martial arts schools already established in Seattle and Oakland and ambitions to open more. His years in the Emerald City had launched him on a journey toward success and stardom. A pivotal turning point on this pathway had occurred during the summer of 1964, between the time Bruce departed from a tearful Linda at the Seattle-Tacoma Airport and the time he returned to marry her. It was the moment Bruce Lee burst onto the national stage of martial arts in the United States.

4

OAKLAND TRANSITIONS

Bruce Lee's reputation as an up-and-coming martial artist preceded him to Oakland, California, the city just east of San Francisco Bay. For at least a year before dropping out of college in 1964, he had been visiting and making connections in the San Francisco Bay Area, which had become the epicenter of martial arts in the United States. The Bay Area enjoyed its preeminence in part because of the number of kung fu teachers who lived in San Francisco, the city that had been the unofficial capital of Chinese America since the Gold Rush days, but also because several influential teachers from the poly-ethnic melting pot of Hawaii had migrated to California after World War II.

This volatile mixture sparked a reaction that fused elements of traditional Chinese, Okinawan, Japanese, and Western fighting styles with a modern ethos of pragmatic innovation. Bruce, who had already begun breaking from Wing Chun orthodoxy in Seattle, found the ferment of the Bay Area intoxicating.

San Francisco's Chinatown, a densely populated neighborhood of roughly thirty blocks, lies south of Telegraph Hill and a few blocks west of the waterfront. Home to historic Portsmouth Square and the iconic Grant Avenue, in the 1960s the neighborhood was the largest Chinese community outside of

Asia and the oldest Chinatown in North America. More important for the Bruce Lee story, it was also the domain of traditional kung fu teachers, two of whom formed its most prominent pillars.

The first, Lau Bun, lived a life that reflected the quintessential story of Chinese America.[1] His father was part of the wave of Chinese migrants who flocked to the United States before the passage of the 1882 Chinese Exclusion Act. These men, for the population was overwhelmingly male, found work on the West Coast and dutifully sent remittances to the families they had left behind.

Lau Bun was born in 1891 and raised in the city of Taishan (formerly Toisan), in Guangdong province, where the money his father sent from Gum San (Gold Mountain, as the Chinese called California) allowed him to study the Choy Li Fut style of kung fu. This style, which combines the short, direct strikes typical of southern styles with the longer, rounder, and more flowing movements that characterize northern styles, was one of the most popular forms of kung fu in southern China and was renowned for its ability to enable a single man to defend himself against multiple attackers.

When Lau Bun decided to follow his father to the United States, he traveled via Mexico to evade the immigration restrictions in place during the era of Chinese exclusion, which extended from 1882 to 1943. He made it to Los Angeles, where immigration agents tried to apprehend him. The legend of Lau's dramatic escape—he reportedly fought off four or perhaps five agents, possibly killing two, and leaped to safety from a second-story window—burnished his reputation as a fearsome fighter. He fled to San Francisco, where the Hop Sing Tong recruited him as an enforcer and trainer for its soldiers.

Lau's role as a Choy Li Fut teacher both established his importance to the tong and cemented his place in the wider community. His Hung Sing kung fu studio was a community institution for decades, and the lion dancing team he trained at the school became a staple of Chinatown parades, an elaborately stylized lion head leading the way, followed by dancers undulating like a human centipede beneath the brightly colored fabric symbolizing the body. By the time Bruce Lee returned to the Bay Area, Lau Bun was in his late sixties or early seventies, an elder esteemed for his knowledge of herbal medicine and his ability to mediate disputes. But despite his mastery of the healing arts, he remained convinced that kung fu should be proven in battle. Like Yip Man in Hong Kong, Lau Bun regularly dispatched his students to test their training and their mettle in the streets. And like Yip's pupils, Lau's usually returned victorious.

≈

If Lau Bun was the elder statesman of orthodox Chinatown kung fu, Wong Tim Yuen (also known as T. Y. Wong) represented its future. Fifteen years younger than Lau Bun, Wong also learned his fighting craft in China, where he studied for a decade under a legendary itinerant teacher named Leong Tin Chee, "traveling China and often fighting in his share of the brutal *le tai* competitions, the full-contact platform matches that ended for many participants in serious injury or maiming."[2] While Lau left China to seek better fortunes and Wong fled to escape the Japanese invasion, their fates converged in San Francisco.

Like Lau, Wong earned a reputation as an enforcer for the Hop Sing Tong by handling the drunken, unruly soldiers and sailors who made trouble in the bars and streets of Chinatown while on leave during World War II. His standing enabled him to open a kung fu school, where he taught the Sil Lum style. Wong called his school, which was located at 142 Waverly Place, the Kin Mon Physical Culture Studio.

The use of the term *kin mon*, or "sturdy citizen," underscored Wong's philosophy that martial arts should be used to maintain a stable and moral society. As he taught, "The proper use of the good long fist is to punish lawbreakers and to eliminate violence." But he also preached that kung fu should be used to "vanquish humiliation and get revenge."[3] Wong understood that kung fu would have to adapt to its new setting in the twentieth-century United States and that part of that adaptation meant avoiding secrecy in favor of embracing new media.

Perhaps not surprisingly, it was the younger Wong, not the older Lau, who introduced Chinese martial arts to a national television audience for the first time. A photograph on the wall of Kin Mon commemorated the kung fu demonstration that he and his students gave in 1955 on NBC's popular daytime program *Home*, a demonstration that marked an important milestone in US martial arts.

≈

One of Wong's students, James Yimm "Jimmy" Lee (no relation to Bruce), helped pioneer the fusion of martial arts practice with strength training. Lee had been born in Oakland in 1920, the son of a Chinese American father who established several successful businesses and a mother who immigrated from China.[4] In high school, he developed a passion for physical fitness, spending more time lifting weights than studying, and he set a Northern California weightlifting record for his weight class, an achievement that later earned him nicknames like "Shoulders Lee" and "Lee the Vee man" for his broad shoulders tapering to a narrow waist.

After high school, Lee took a welding apprenticeship at a local shipyard, then requested a transfer to Hawaii, arriving just a week before the Japanese attack on Pearl Harbor on December 7, 1941. During the early years of World War II, he repaired ships in the harbor by day and in his off-hours trained rigorously in judo and jujitsu with Seishiro Okazaki, a prominent Japanese American teacher in Honolulu. Lee joined the army in 1944, fought in the Philippines, and after the war returned to Oakland, where he worked as a welder and resumed strength and martial arts training with renewed vigor. He studied Sil Lum kung fu with Wong throughout the 1950s while continuing his rigorous program of weightlifting.

CHANGES FROM AFAR

Even as traditional kung fu continued to flourish in San Francisco's Chinatown, winds of change were blowing eastward from Hawaii, "the first great melting pot of Asian martial arts," as Dan Inosanto, the Filipino martial arts instructor who would become one of Bruce's most important students and closest friend, described it.[5] And it was the rich and complex history of martial arts in the Hawaiian Islands that led indirectly to Bruce Lee's emergence and phenomenal success.

Like San Francisco and Hong Kong, the island nation of Hawaii was acquired by its colonial master through conquest and grew due to transoceanic trade. Indeed, its introduction to the West incorporated both trade and violence. On July 12, 1776, just eight days after the American colonies adopted the Declaration of Independence, the British explorer Captain James Cook set off from Plymouth, England, on his third Pacific expedition with a secret mission from the British Admiralty: to discover the fabled Northwest Passageway, a sea route thought to join the Atlantic and the Pacific Oceans.

Three centuries after Christopher Columbus stumbled upon the Americas while trying to reach Asia, Europeans were still seeking a direct route that would confer a competitive advantage over trading rivals by allowing them to avoid the long southern detour around Africa. To locate the Pacific gateway to the Northwest Passage, Cook and his two ships, the HMS *Resolution* and HMS *Discovery*, sailed southward from England, around the Cape of Good Hope at the southern tip of Africa, eastward to New Zealand and Tahiti, then northward toward the western coast of North America.

In the middle of the Pacific Ocean, sailors spotted sea turtles and birds, both signs of land. And on January 18, 1778, three islands loomed into view: Oahu, Niihau, and Kauai, the northernmost major islands of the Hawaiian archipelago. The local inhabitants paddled long canoes to the ships and amicably traded pigs and potatoes for nails, and although a British sailor broke the peace by fatally shooting a man in a scuffle over goods, the Hawaiians continued to visit the ships and allowed Cook to land at Waimea Bay on the island of Kauai. Cook and his ships set sail after a fortnight, heading eastward again until they reached landfall in what today is Oregon. They then traveled up the western coast of North America until they reached the ice-filled, impassable Bering Straits.

The Northwest Passage was not to be found. But almost two centuries later, the islands that Cook had unexpectedly stumbled upon, over fifty-seven hundred miles east of Hong Kong and nearly twenty-five hundred miles west of

California, would provide a critical piece of the complicated jigsaw puzzle that helped shape both the man and the myth that was Bruce Lee.

≈

On the journey home, the *Resolution* and *Discovery* returned to the island chain that Cook had named the Sandwich Islands in honor of his sponsor, the First Lord of the Admiralty, John Montagu, the Fourth Earl of Sandwich. At anchor in Kealakekua Bay on the Big Island of Hawaii, so called because it is the biggest island in the archipelago, the British initially enjoyed being fed and feted by island residents, but tensions grew as their stay was prolonged and finally exploded over a purported theft by a Hawaiian and a British attempt to kidnap the island's king in retaliation. In the battle that erupted on February 14, 1779, Captain James Cook died in the fighting.[6]

One of the participants in the skirmish was the nephew of the Hawaiian king, an ambitious young nobleman who had already built a reputation as a fierce warrior. This man, whose name was Kamehameha and who would unify the Hawaiian islands into a kingdom, rose to power in response to the archipelago's increasing integration into the global economy, and he used the tools of colonialists to do so. With the islands now indelibly recorded on Western maps, warships and trading vessels from Britain, France, Russia, and the United States made regular stops at their mid-Pacific harbors. Kamehameha in turn employed Western military advisers and deployed Western weaponry, including ships, cannons, and muskets stockpiled through trade. His power base grew as he conquered Hawaii island by island, and in 1810, he became the supreme sovereign of the entire island chain.[7] His triumph was due in no small part to his ability to adapt to the changing strategies and weapons brought by Western incursion.

Today, an eight-and-a-half-foot statue of King Kamehameha stands on a pedestal in downtown Honolulu, opposite Iolani Palace, the former royal residence, and every year on June 11, well-wishers festoon the statue with enormous leis to celebrate Kamehameha Day, the state holiday that commemorates his birthday. The giant figure, which has become a beloved symbol of Hawaii, bears unwitting witness to Kamehameha's ability to combine disparate influences.

Designed in 1880 by the American sculptor Thomas Ridgeway Gould and cast in brass in Paris, the sculpture combines indigenous elements with a Roman-inspired pose to create what the artist and the commissioning committee conceived as a "Pacific Hero" who led the transition of the islands from "barbarism" (as the artist terms it) to becoming a republic. Kamehameha wears the sash, cloak, and brilliant yellow helmet befitting a Hawaiian king, but he stands in a "classic stance of a Roman emperor," his right arm extended in a welcoming gesture and his left hand cradling an upright spear. A second version of the sculpture stands in the town of Kapaau near Kamehameha's birthplace on the Kohala Coast of the Big Island, and a third appears in the United States Capitol Building in Washington, DC, that one commissioned in honor of Hawaii's statehood in 1959.[8]

≈

The incorporation of the Kingdom of Hawaii into the United States proceeded through settler colonialism and conquest fueled by capitalism. Word of the islands' friendly climate and fertile soil attracted wealthy Americans who wished to establish plantations, while reports of a land of nonbelievers drew Christian missionaries eager for converts. The haole (white) planters and missionaries wrought changes that transformed Hawaii's economy, stripped its indigenous occupants of their lands, attracted waves of migrants from across Asia, and ultimately overthrew its monarchy. Rising to positions of influence as advisers to the crown, they advocated far-reaching changes to the systems of government and land tenure. In 1840, in response to their efforts, Hawaii adopted a Western-style constitutional monarchy featuring an executive branch, a judicial branch, and a bicameral legislature. But reconfiguring the monarchy ultimately proved far less consequential than rewriting the laws of land ownership.

Although burgeoning West Coast markets craved the agricultural products, sugar in particular, that were grown on the bountiful islands, would-be investors balked because the indigenous Hawaiian system of land stewardship did not recognize the notion of private ownership under which land could be conveyed from one owner to another but instead regarded land as something that belonged to the monarch.

However, the Great Mahele (Division) of 1848, which would prove to be a profoundly important event in Hawaii's history, divided land into parcels owned variously by the king, the noble class, and commoners. As a result, land could be bought and sold in a way that had never before been possible, and ownership of vast portions of the islands passed from native to haole hands, with foreigners possessing two-thirds of all privately held land by 1886. In turn, securing land titles emboldened planters to establish the sugar plantation system that would undergird the island economy for the next century.[9] This plantation system would eventually lead to the islands' multiethnic composition, which helped create the world in which Bruce Lee achieved prominence.

≈

If land fulfilled the first prerequisite for the establishment of plantations, cheap labor was a close second. Growing sugarcane on an industrial scale requires a myriad of workers to perform the arduous labor of planting, tending, and harvesting. Native Hawaiians proved to be an inadequate labor force because rampant disease had reduced their population to one-sixth of what it had been before contact with the outside world, and the remainder preferred traditional agriculture and fishing over highly regimented, low-wage work.[10] As a result, planters turned to Asia to fill their vast needs. Between 1850 and 1920, more than three hundred thousand Asians migrated to Hawaii, lured by labor recruiters proffering dreams of riches that would deliver them from poverty and stultified futures in their native lands.[11]

The first wave of workers came from China. By 1890, Chinese formed nearly one-fifth of Hawaii's population.[12] Japanese workers also flocked to the islands, with some 200,000 arriving between 1885 and 1924.[13] Okinawan immigrants counted among the Japanese arrivals because Japan had formally colonized the former Ryukyu Kingdom in 1879. Korea, which became an unwilling protectorate of Japan in 1905, sent fewer workers to the islands, as the Japanese government gave preferences to its own citizens, but more than 118,000 Filipinos migrated to Hawaii from 1909 to 1934, a period during which the Philippines was a US colony.[14] As a result of this influx, Hawaii was by 1940 home to nearly a quarter of a million ethnic Asians.[15]

Not surprisingly, interethnic rivalries ran rampant among the workers, whom planters sought to keep divided as a strategy to prevent unified strikes and uprisings. Yet ironically, the fighting arts provided an arena that brought together people of all ethnicities. In the melting pot of Hawaii, as Dan Inosanto points out, "Chinese trained Japanese, Japanese trained Chinese, Chinese trained Filipinos, and then Hawaiians themselves got involved in all those arts too."[16] The picture is complicated further by the fact that Okinawans and Koreans made unique contributions too. The migrants to the shores of these islands in the middle of the Pacific wove together myriad threads of martial arts.

~

The art of *kenpo* illustrates how multiple migrations and crossings of national and cultural boundaries drove the evolution of a style, and Dr. James Mitose is an example of how this evolution worked. Mitose was born in Hawaii in 1916 to Japanese immigrant parents who sent him to Japan to be educated. There he studied his family's martial art, which according to lore had been brought from China around 1600, modified by successive generations of Mitoses, and formalized under the name *kosho-ryu kempo*. Mitose returned to Honolulu and taught *kosho-ryu kempo* for more than a decade, beginning in 1942.[17] The Japanese American Mitose conferred black belts on five students, including the Chinese American William S. K. Chow.

Prior to working with Mitose, Chow had explored a variety of fighting forms, including kung fu learned from his father, jujitsu, sumo, and karate as well as boxing and wrestling. When Chow began teaching in 1949, the five-foot-two man known as "Thunderbolt" combined Mitose's Japanese *kosho-ryu kempo* with Okinawan-influenced karate into a form he called *kenpo*.

Studying under Chow could be a brutal experience; at least one student re-members suffering broken ribs.[18]

Although Chow trained many influential students, only one went on to become one of the most pivotal leaders in popularizing karate in the United States, in part by migrating from Hawaii to the mainland. Edmund Kealoha "Ed" Parker studied *kenpo* with Chow but left Honolulu to attend Brigham Young University in Utah, where he gave a halftime demonstration during a basketball game between Brigham Young and the University of California, Los Angeles (UCLA). As word of the exhibition spread, Parker fielded invita-tions from prospective students and began teaching in Provo.

After graduating from Brigham Young, Parker moved to Pasadena, California, and opened what eventually become a series of *kenpo* schools. In the shadow of Hollywood, he taught movie stars and celebrities including Elvis Presley, Blake Edwards, Robert Wagner, and Warren Beatty. Parker be-came a minicelebrity in his own right, appearing in *Time* magazine as "High Priest of Hollywood's Karate Sect" in 1961, on television in an episode of *The Lucy Show* in 1963, and in movies such as Blake Edwards's 1963 film *The Pink Panther*.[19]

≈

Like Parker, Ralph Castro trained with William Chow in Hawaii, and though Parker and Castro never met there, they became close friends and colleagues when they later crossed paths on the mainland. Castro taught *kenpo* out of his school on Valencia Street in San Francisco's Mission District and played host to Parker when he visited the Bay Area. Through Castro, Parker grew to know the close-knit brotherhood of like-minded martial arts tinkerers and experimenters in the region, a group that included James Lee and Wally Jay, two students of the influential teacher Seishiro "Henry" Okazaki.[20]

Okazaki's journey began in his native Japan and continued in Hawaii, where he immigrated in his teens. He started practicing martial arts to recover from tuberculosis and bouts of depression, mastering three different styles of the Japanese art of jujitsu. His catholic appetite drove him further to study

Chinese kung fu, Okinawan karate, "Filipino knife fighting, Western wrestling, and the native Hawaiian martial art of lua."[21] Chosen to represent the local Japanese community in a match against an arrogant English boxer who proclaimed himself a better fighter than any Japanese, Okazaki scrutinized Western boxing to identify its vulnerabilities. He won the match by adopting an extremely low stance, reasoning that boxers are not accustomed to kicking.

In Okazaki's quest for perfection, he developed his own style of jujitsu, drawing on all of the arts he had studied. The name he selected for his creation, *danzan ryu*, paid homage to his Chinese kung fu teacher while simultaneously invoking hybridity and combination: *danzan ryu* means "Cedar Mountain Style" in Japanese, a reference to "Sandalwood Mountain," the Chinese name for Hawaii. The name combines the histories of Japanese and Chinese migrations to Hawaii, and its meaning can be decoded only by understanding both the Japanese language and the Chinese terminology.

At the Honolulu YMCA, Okazaki taught thousands of American GIs. During the war, he was confined to a prison camp for three months for being an influential member of the Japanese American community, even though on the morning of Pearl Harbor, he had charged into the streets wielding a samurai sword to fight any Japanese invaders.[22]

Okazaki also taught civilian students, one of whom was Jay, a Chinese American born in Hawaii to immigrant parents. Jay had trained as a boxer during high school and college before studying jujitsu under Okazaki and earning his black belt in 1944. He combined his boxing and jujitsu training with instruction in judo from Ken Kawachi, the islands' reigning judo champion. After Jay and his family moved to the Bay Area in 1950, he formed the Island Judo Jujitsu Club, which trained in a gym he built behind his house in Alameda.

The poor performance of Jay's club members in competitions on the large stage of the mainland forced him to return to the drawing board. He incorporated Kawachi's insights on how to gain and use leverage to break holds and throw opponents more effectively into his own creation, Small Circle Theory, which eventually yielded national championships for members of the club. Twice a year between 1957 and 1972, he threw huge fundraiser luaus, which

attracted former residents of Hawaii from throughout the Bay Area and became fixtures on the martial arts calendar, with advertisements appearing
regularly in *Black Belt* magazine.[23]

The foods served at Wally Jay's luaus reflected migration and intermixture
as surely as the island's martial arts. Guests enjoyed the traditional delicacies of kalua pig roasted in the earthen pit, mounds of the signature taro
starch known as poi, and platters of lomi-lomi salmon, a ceviche-like dish
that combines salted salmon and tomatoes, neither items native to Hawaii.[24]
The incorporation of these incongruous elements into a must-serve dish of
Hawaiian celebrations shows how people create remarkable new traditions in
the face of cultural disruptions wrought by migration and colonialism. Just as
surely as a dish made of nonnative salmon and tomatoes became a beloved
delicacy of Hawaii, Wally Jay and his cohorts in the Bay Area during the post-
war period intermixed fighting styles from different nations and cultures and
transformed traditional martial arts into thoroughly modern forms. By 1962,
the only missing ingredient was Bruce Lee.

≈

Wally Jay used the luau proceeds to take the Island Judo Jujitsu Club to various regional tournaments. In May 1962, the club toured the Pacific Northwest,
competing in Vancouver, Portland, and Seattle. By chance, the mother of one
club member had taken cha-cha lessons from Bruce in San Francisco when he
first arrived in the US in 1959, and she asked Jay to look him up in Seattle. Jay
put out feelers about Bruce in Chinatown, discovered that he was developing
quite a reputation, and located his *kwoon* (training studio) in the basement of
a Chinese church.

Jay and his students visited the *kwoon* during one of Bruce's classes, filing
in quietly and respectfully to allay any sense that they were spoiling for a fight.
Bruce greeted them cautiously but warmed up after realizing their peaceful in-
tentions. He described his increasingly flexible, nondogmatic approach to martial arts, which he demonstrated by easily controlling Jay's largest student. Jay
surprised his students by engaging skillfully in *chi sao* with Bruce, and by the

time Jay left, the two men sensed that they shared a common approach to martial arts and should keep in touch. When Jay returned to Alameda and called James Lee to tell him about the new Wing Chun teacher in Seattle, he was surprised to learn that James had already heard about the impressive young buck from his brother, who had also taken cha-cha lessons from Bruce in 1959.[25]

When James Lee learned that Allen Joe, his best friend since childhood, was planning to visit Seattle, he asked Joe to further observe the upstart. Allen Joe had grown up across the street from James in Oakland's Chinatown, and the two had bonded over a shared love of martial arts and bodybuilding.[26] The fabled fitness guru Jack LaLanne had opened his first gym in Oakland in 1936, and it was there that the legendary trainer Ed Yarick had produced champions like the 1947 Mr. America, Steve Reeves.

Joe had begun lifting weights as a sixteen-year-old in 1939 after spotting a Charles Atlas advertisement in a magazine and started trained with Yarick after being introduced to him by James Lee.[27] Joe served in the army during World War II and saw action across the Pacific from the Philippines to Okinawa, all the while doing makeshift weight training by lifting scrap metal and parts from wrecked vehicles.[28] After returning to Oakland, he won the 1946 Mr. Northern California title in his weight class at a competition judged by LaLanne, becoming the first Asian American to win a bodybuilding championship in the United States.[29]

≈

In June 1962, Allen Joe took his family to the World's Fair in Seattle, then continued on to Canada. As long as Joe was going to be in the Pacific Northwest, James Lee figured, he should, as he put it, "check out this cat" named Bruce Lee. So after a long day at the fair, Joe dropped his family at their hotel, then walked half a block to Ruby Chow's. Bruce was not working, but Ruby told Joe that he would probably turn up around closing time.

At 11 p.m., Bruce emerged from a side entrance wearing a carefully pressed gray flannel suit and gleaming shined shoes, looking more like a movie star than a kung fu artist. Initially he remained aloof, thinking that Joe intended to challenge him to a fight. But as the strangers grew more comfortable with each other, they slipped into Cantonese conversation, during which Bruce invited Joe out for a late-night hamburger and root beer.

After Bruce changed into more comfortable clothes, he asked Joe to show him some of his kung fu moves, then challenged him to throw a punch. When Joe obliged, Bruce blocked and grabbed his arm with what Joe would later describe as "inhuman" speed, then pulled him off balance and dragged him about helplessly. Bruce could have gone on sparring and talking kung fu all night, but Joe had to return to his family at the hotel for an early-morning departure. As soon as Joe returned to Oakland, he called James Lee. "James," he said, "the kid is amazing."[30]

James Lee in turn telephoned Bruce and invited him to visit Oakland, thus beginning a relationship that would drive Bruce to transform his body into the ultimate fighting machine.[31] Bruce visited the Bay Area periodically throughout 1963 and through James grew close to a coterie of martial artists who were seeking fresh approaches to the sport. In addition to James Lee, the group included Wally Jay, Allen Joe, Leo Fong, George Lee (no relation to Bruce or James), Ralph Castro, and Ed Parker during his Bay Area forays.

Most of these men were twenty years older than Bruce and possessed decades of experience, but none was hidebound by tradition. On the contrary, these innovators shared a commitment to finding effective methods of fighting regardless of the source, an attitude that comported well with the philosophy Bruce had begun to develop in Seattle.

≈

James Lee's split-level house at 3039 Monticello Avenue in Oakland sat atop a garage that served as a makeshift gym housing dozens of strength-building contraptions and martial arts training devices that Lee had built out of scrap metal using his welding and metalworking skills. It also contained cans of sand and ball bearings into which Lee repeatedly plunged his hands to toughen them. Despite Lee's small stature, avid weightlifting made him burly, and hand strengthening gave him mitts like blocks of steel.

Wally Jay had first met James in 1959 at a martial arts exhibition in Oakland, and the two had grown close over the years as they performed alongside each other.[32] These exhibitions made Lee famous for his ability to break bricks using the Iron Palm technique he practiced. He could break a stack of five bricks with a single blow, but even more impressively, it was said that he could stack a dozen bricks, ask an audience member to choose one, and then with a mighty strike of his palm, break the selected brick while leaving the others intact.

James Lee smashed traditions as easily as he broke bricks. His belief that knowledge of kung fu should not be hoarded but shared drove him to become perhaps the first person to write English-language books about the Chinese art in the United States. In the late 1950s, he self-published his first book, *Fighting Arts of the Orient: Elemental Karate and Kung Fu*, under his Chinese name, Kein Heir Lee.[33] He sold the fifty-four-page volume in bookstores in Chinatown and via mail order through advertisements placed in the magazines he loved to read: *Popular Science*, *Popular Mechanics*, *Ring*, and the bodybuilding magazine *Iron Man*.[34]

Jesse Glover's discovery of *Fighting Arts of the Orient* inspired his pilgrimage to Oakland. Similarly, Ralph Castro and Ed Parker met James Lee after seeing the book in a San Francisco book shop and tracking down its author.[35] Lee had deliberately used the term "kung fu" in the book's title because he thought it sounded less foreign than the Cantonese pronunciation of "gung fu" and perhaps also because of its alliteration with the better-known Japanese term "karate."

The success of James Lee's first book inspired him to write another, this one coauthored with his *sifu*, T. Y. Wong. *Modern Kung Fu Karate: Iron Palm and Poison Hand Training* appeared in 1960. In its introduction, Lee emphasized the fundamental unity of Asian fighting styles, arguing that the martial arts of Japan, China, Okinawa, and Korea, despite superficial differences, all bore resemblances not only due to their "common past influence" but also because they are performed by the human body, which does not vary greatly across nations.

Lee also promoted martial arts as a way to unify people. "Perhaps by arousing the American interest in this face of Oriental Art," he wrote, "this may in some small way become the wedge to keep open the door to understanding and good will between the different cultures of the East and the West. There is an old Chinese saying, 'Tin ha, yat gat,' which means, 'Under Heaven, there is but one family.' I, for one, certainly agree." Sadly, *Modern Kung Fu* forced a wedge between Lee and Wong, as what might have been a minor disagreement about how to split production costs and profits ended their relationship as both student-teacher and coauthors.[36]

THE GARAGE ON MONTICELLO AVENUE

After James Lee's break from Wong, he began teaching kung fu on his own out of his garage on Monticello Avenue to a mongrel pack of martial artists and weightlifters united by both a drive to find the best fighting techniques, regardless of their origins, and a devotion to strength training as a tool to hone their bodies into the most effective tools of destruction. Shouts and the sound of breaking bricks and boards inside the garage broke the evening quiet on the street, and on weekends, neighbors saw small groups of men sparring in the driveway.

Lee had begun informally teaching Sil Lum kung fu in 1958 to his weight-lifting buddy Al Novak, a hulking 280-pound white man whom Lee had convinced T. Y. Wong to accept as a student.[37] George Lee, who with Bruce, James, and Allen Joe was one of the so-called Four Musketeers, also hung out in the garage. An accomplished machinist by day, he and Allen Joe had become friends after realizing that they were the only Chinese Americans working out at a gym in El Cerrito.

Another regular was Leo Fong, a Methodist preacher who drove to Oakland from his church in Sacramento. Fong, who was born in Guangzhou and raised in Arkansas, started out as boxer and compiled a 25–4 record (with 18 knockouts) as an amateur and collegiate fighter. When he was assigned to a church in Northern California, he took the opportunity to study Choy Lay

Fut with Lau Bun and Sil Lum with T. Y. Wong, as well as a Korean martial art from a student at Sacramento State University.[38]

Fong began weightlifting in 1955 and became a devotee of the training once he discovered how much it increased the power of his punches.[39] He had met Bruce in 1962 at Wally Jay's luau and was blown away when he witnessed the power of Bruce's one-inch punch at James Lee's home.[40] (Fong would go on to publish books on Sil Lum and Choy Lay Fut; found his own style, called *wei kuen do*; and appear in more than twenty action films in the 1970s. In 2006, *Black Belt* magazine named Fong Kung Fu Artist of the Year.)[41]

The maelstrom of Oakland invigorated Bruce. Unlike Seattle, where he was the most advanced kung fu artist in his circle of students and young toughs, in Oakland he found himself among men in their forties with families, businesses, and professions, some of whom were professional martial arts teachers and even published authors. Despite Bruce's youth and braggadocio, they appreciated his doggedness, creativity, and ability to absorb and synthesize new ideas. He was a brilliant kinesthetic mimic who could faithfully reproduce movements after seeing them just once.

Perhaps most of all, they were astounded by his speed. The phrase "lightning quick" failed to capture how suddenly he moved, how he could set up outside striking distance, then seemingly teleport into close range, his fist gently brushing his opponent's forehead. On every visit to the Bay Area, Bruce talked martial arts techniques, shared ideas, verbally jousted, and physically sparred with experienced artists whose collective training spanned all manner of styles from across China, Japan, Okinawa, Korea, and the Philippines.

Bruce Lee's martial arts sophistication stood in stark contrast to his ignorance about strength training. James Lee informed him that the purpose of lifting weights is to create small tears in muscle fibers, which then heal bigger and stronger. The idea of intentionally tearing muscles dismayed Bruce, but just looking at James convinced him that his elder knew the subject well.

James put Bruce on a schedule of training his upper and lower torso on alternate days with recovery days between, and Bruce began pumping iron in earnest for the first time in his life.[42] Within months, he was telling people that his favorite meal of beef with oyster sauce was the perfect bodybuilding diet: rice providing carbohydrates for energy and beef the protein necessary to build muscles.[43]

≈

Back in Seattle, inspired by James's publication of martial arts books, Bruce set out to write one of his own. When he shuttled back to Seattle for school, he split time between classes and sessions at the *kwoon*, drafting sections, drawing illustrations, and consulting on the phone with James on layout, photography, and marketing. One weekend he enlisted a friend from Hong Kong to shoot action photos of his students Taky Kimura, Jesse Glover, Charlie Woo, and James Demile in Ruby Chow's parking lot. Bruce told James that he wanted to title his book *Chinese Gung-fu: The Philosophical Art of Self Defense*, because he thought "gung-fu" sounded closer to the Cantonese pronunciation of the name of the martial art and was therefore more faithful to tradition than James's use of "kung fu." He meant to hew to tradition in order to shake up the masters in Hong Kong, he declared.[44]

Bruce filled his visits to the Bay Area with intense training and deep conversations. In the Monticello Avenue garage, he taught Wing Chun to James, who in turn instructed him in brick breaking and weightlifting. Conversations about *kenpo* with Ralph Castro and Ed Parker, boxing with Leo Fong, and judo with Wally Jay filled James's living room and overflowed into innumerable Chinese restaurants. Perhaps most importantly for Bruce's future, he and James began planning to open a chain of martial arts schools that would be grounded in their increasingly entwined philosophy of speed, power, and efficiency.

Bruce's proudest achievement, though, was the publication in 1963 of *Chinese Gung-fu* through James's Oriental Book Sales company. Its photographs feature Bruce in black, loose-fitting pants and tunic *jing-mo* kung fu outfit but without the thick black-rimmed glasses he usually wore. The book marked a turning point on Bruce's journey, as the action shots show Lee demonstrating positions and movements with his Seattle students, but the prefatory "About the Author" notes introducing the young *sifu* were written by members of his new and more experienced Oakland crew: J. Y. Lee, Ed Parker, and Wally Jay.

≈

The following summer, having abandoned college, Bruce moved from Seattle into the Monticello Avenue home to live with James Lee; his wife, Katherine; and their children, Karena and Greglon. For months, Bruce and James had spent hours discussing opening a second branch of the Jun Fan Gung Fu Institute, and Bruce had come to Oakland to make it a reality. They found a location on Broadway Avenue on the first floor of a two-story brick building and created a studio out of the narrow space that was ten or fifteen feet wide and thirty feet deep. At the rear of the studio, a raised section of floor leading to a back room created a potential tripping hazard—and source of great future controversy.[45]

Moving to Oakland enabled Bruce to concentrate exclusively on martial arts. It must have been liberating to teach at his new school and train for hours on end with James and the gang instead of busing tables at Ruby Chow's and studying for college classes. But the monomania that had fueled the twenty-three-year-old martial artist's development of new ideas and techniques blinded him to how controversial those ideas might be among those who valued seniority, experience, and tradition. Before long, Bruce was ruffling feathers across the Bay Area.

James Lee, Leo Fong, Ralph Castro, and Ed Parker gathered in Wally Jay's backyard in Alameda at his luau in the summer of 1964, eager to watch a demonstration from their young friend, whom James had invited to perform in front of this large gathering of seasoned experts. Bruce began by showing off a dramatic northern kung fu form that featured big, round high kicks, which he immediately criticized as impractical for street fighting. No one could win a real fight by practicing such a rigid routine, he insisted, for "Classical methods like these are a form of paralysis." And, he added, "Too many practitioners are rehearsing these systematic routines and stunts."[46] Instead, he explained, the method he was developing stripped movements down to their bare essences and stressed speed and power.

Some of the martial artists in the crowd frowned at the upstart's effrontery, but James and his friends looked on with amusement. Bruce then chose a linebacker-sized volunteer from the audience and explained what would happen next: Bruce would start from a distance, and the volunteer would try to block his punch. They set up several feet apart, then Bruce flew forward and tapped the volunteer on the forehead before he could block. They returned to their positions, and Bruce asked, "Ready?" Again, he closed the distance in an instant, but this time the volunteer threw the block early in anticipation of the attack. Bruce allowed the block to pass, then touched the volunteer's forehead again. The crowd murmured in astonishment at Bruce's astounding closing speed and perhaps even more at his arrogance.[47]

This occasion marked Bruce's debut as a force to be reckoned with in the Bay Area. But unbeknownst to him, two more pivotal performances lay ahead of him in the coming months. One was a national demonstration; the other was a fight.

THE LONG BEACH INTERNATIONALS

Ed Parker threw a big party in early August 1964, the First International Karate Tournament in Long Beach, California. Envisioned as an opportunity to gather the most prominent and accomplished practitioners of a wide variety of styles from across the nation, the light-contact tournament formed only one part of the festivities, as experts in karate, tae kwon do, kung fu, and *kali* exhibited their styles to the thousands of spectators in attendance. Knowing how Bruce could electrify a crowd, Parker invited him to the tournament, not to compete but to give a demonstration.

Although Bruce arrived in Long Beach as a bit player among the luminaries, his performance remains the best-remembered part of the event. In the stifling afternoon heat, Bruce took center stage in the arena, wearing a black *jing-mo*, accompanied by Taky Kimura as his assistant. Bruce demonstrated

Wing Chun's *chi sao* exercise with Kimura, all the while explaining the principles at play: sensitivity, the reciprocal give-and-take of energy, probing for openings, and attack and defense of the center line.

Given Wing Chun's obscurity, these notions would have seemed novel to most members of the audience, although perhaps somewhat familiar to those with knowledge of kung fu. But when Bruce began to showcase physical feats, he entered entirely uncharted territory. He began by showing off his one-inch punch, which began with his arm extended, fist hovering just an inch from the chest of a volunteer. His fist shimmered almost imperceptibly, launching the unlucky guinea pig backward into a waiting chair.

Far from being a stunt, the one-inch punch proved how much power Bruce could generate instantaneously inside a tiny space, without resorting to a long windup with his arm or big movement of his lower body. Instead, he amassed kinetic energy by coordinating the explosive unleashing of each of the connected parts of his body, beginning with his feet and legs; continuing through his hips, chest, right shoulder, and arm; and finally focusing that energy to blast forward through his wrist and knuckles.

Next, Bruce dropped to the floor to demonstrate his two-finger push-ups. He braced himself on the thumb, forefinger, and middle finger of his right hand, his torso rigid in plank position, legs slightly splayed, and his left hand tucked against his thigh. He lowered himself nearly to the floor using just two fingers and a thumb. A controlled, one-handed descent would have been impressive enough, but Bruce pressed his body upward, completing the push-up, then repeated the process twice more before switching hands to repeat the feat. Like the one-inch punch, the two-finger push-up demonstrated how much strength he had built within his 135-pound frame, but it also showed off his incredible balance and control.

Bruce Lee's performance impressed a national martial arts audience, but the connections he made behind the scenes in Long Beach proved even more pivotal to his future. Ed Parker asked one of his students, Dan Inosanto, to look after the brash young kung fu artist and show him around. In response, Bruce gave Inosanto a firsthand demonstration of the one-inch punch, which left Inosanto gasping and nauseous. It was an inauspicious beginning to a life-long friendship in which the two men bonded over their joint commitment to learning from the nearly infinite diversity of fighting styles.

Inosanto, who went on to become a martial arts legend in his own right, had traveled a path parallel to Bruce's, one structured by colonialism and militarism. His grandfather Sebastian Inosanto had been born in the Philippines when Spain ruled the islands. The United States assumed control over the Philippines in 1898 after the Spanish-American War, with President William McKinley declaring a policy of "benevolent assimilation" for the colony.[48]

The Filipino revolutionaries who had been battling for independence from Spain fought with equal fervor against their new master. The assimilation of the colony hardly felt benevolent to the hundreds of thousands of Filipinos killed in the brutal Philippine-American War of 1898–1902, a conflict rife with atrocities that has been called the United States' "first Vietnam."[49] After the "pacification" of the Philippines, the US-backed government began sending promising students to college in the United States. Dan's grandfather Sebastian Inosanto was one such student, but rather than returning to the Philippines, he remained in the US, became a farm worker, and was a member of the Filipino labor union that preceded the legendary United Farm Workers led by Cesar Chavez.

≈

Dan Inosanto was born in Stockton in 1936. Despite his small stature, he was a determined athlete who dabbled in jujitsu and boxing but loved football. At just 125 pounds, he played running back in high school and college and ran track at Whitworth College in Spokane, Washington. He also began to study judo while in college and went on to earn both bachelor's and master's degrees in physical education.[50] Inosanto enlisted in the US Army after graduating and earned a spot as a paratrooper in the elite 101st Airborne Division.

While stationed at Fort Campbell in Kentucky, Inosanto witnessed the confluence of many martial arts styles, including boxing, wrestling, and karate.

He trained with Hank Slomanski, an American karate instructor who had learned his craft as part of the occupation forces in Japan and later went on to train Elvis Presley. The school on the base featured instruction in Korean, Japanese, and Okinawan styles by teachers in their various specialties. The wide variety of martial arts to be seen at Fort Campbell can be traced to the stationing of US armed forces personnel across Asia during the Cold War and their training in local fighting styles while abroad.

Devotees of each style boasted about their superiority, but one incident opened Inosanto's eyes to the idea that context matters most of all. One soldier declared that he would defeat all comers as long as he could specify the venue, then surprised everyone by choosing the deep end of the swimming pool. He proceeded to "drown" a boxer, a wrestler, a judoka (practitioner of judo), and everyone else who dared challenge him. His background as a former water polo player made him invincible under those particular circumstances. Inosanto learned from his experiences in the army to respect the parts of each discipline that were effective in particular settings. This perspective, influenced by the extensive US military presence across Asia, prepared Inosanto for his introduction to Bruce Lee.

Shortly after the 1964 Internationals, Inosanto introduced Lee to a Filipino weapon called the *tabak-toyok*, better known as the "nunchaku," two short wooden rods joined together with a rope or chain. Inosanto recalls that at the time, Lee did not think much of *escrima*, the Filipino art of stick fighting. However, when Inosanto visited Lee in Hong Kong a few years later, Lee pulled out a nunchaku and, despite having no prior training, improvised a form called "Largo Mano" that he could not have known existed. Inosanto believes that Lee's dexterity with the sticks derived from his experience with the epee, a Western fencing sword, whose powers he had learned from his older brother, Peter, a champion fencer.

≈

Bruce made another crucial connection in Long Beach when he met the tae kwon do master Jhoon Rhee. Like so many of the martial artists in Lee's circles, Rhee's presence in the United States could be traced directly to war and militarism. Rhee was born in 1932 in Asan, Korea (today part of South Korea). A small child who had been bullied in school, he began studying tae kwon do at the age of fifteen and discovered that beating up one of his tormentors gained him respect in the eyes of his classmates. Sneaking into American movies after the end of World War II convinced Rhee that he had to move to the United States. How else could he marry a gorgeous blonde like the ones he fell in love with onscreen, the fifteen-year-old wondered?

Rhee vowed to teach tae kwon do to earn a living in the United States and began studying English as avidly as he trained in martial arts. The outbreak of the Korean War diverted his plans but set him on the path that would ultimately lead him to the US. Initially he put his language skills to use by serving as an interpreter for the US Air Force, before being drafted into the South Korean Army and enrolling in the officer cadet corps. In 1956, he was selected for a spot in a course in aircraft maintenance at Gary Air Force Base in San Marcos, Texas.

A couple whom Rhee met at the Methodist church he attended in San Marcos agreed to sponsor him as a student, ensuring that he could return to the United States after completing his military service in Korea. The following year, he began college in San Marcos, before transferring to the University of Texas at Austin with plans to earn an engineering degree. Instead, in 1962, he accepted a job teaching karate in Washington, DC, then opened a tae kwon do school of his own.[51]

When Rhee met Bruce, he thought that the twenty-three-year-old "looked about sixteen years old" but discovered that the youthful appearance masked a serious artist. He was dumbfounded when Bruce performed *chi sao* blindfolded but also recognized weaknesses in Bruce's practice. "To be honest with you, though," Rhee recalls, "his kicks didn't impress me then." By contrast, Rhee's kicking demonstration wowed Bruce: Rhee broke three-inch-thick boards held seven feet in the air with a jumping front kick and performed "a triple side-jump kick in the air before landing back on the floor." Bruce called Rhee's kick a "thing of beauty," and Rhee in turn diplomatically complimented

Bruce on his punching. That evening, the two talked martial arts for an hour, recognizing in each other kindred obsessive spirits.[52]

≈

Ten days after Bruce's performance at the Long Beach Internationals, he flew to Seattle to marry Linda, who had been waiting patiently. After the modest ceremony, the newlyweds moved to Oakland to live with James Lee and his family while the Jun Fan Gung Fu Institute got off the ground. Tragically, James's wife, Katherine Lee, was diagnosed with advanced breast cancer almost immediately after they arrived and died within weeks. The loss bonded James; his children, Karena and Greglon; Bruce; and Linda into "one family," as Greglon remembered.[53]

In "Uncle Bruce," the kids gained a confidant and an exuberant presence who lifted their father's spirits and threw surprise parties for his birthday.[54] Linda did her best to provide a semblance of ordinary family life and cared for the children as if they were her own. A sixth member joined the family on February 1, 1965, when Linda gave birth to Brandon Bruce Lee. Though the baby entered the world with a head of black hair, he soon turned blond, a transition that bespoke his biracial heritage.[55] Little Brandon was as mixed as his father's martial arts.

MAKING A NAME IN THE BAY AREA

When Bruce Lee moved to Oakland, he was a relative unknown. He had just published a book, the *Chinese Gung Fu*, but his television and movie roles, write-ups in martial arts magazines, and status as instructor to the stars still lay in the future. As a result, the brash twenty-four-year-old faced an uphill battle in trying to make a name for himself. The few hundred dollars a month that the Jun Fan Gung Fu Institute cleared were sufficient to cover the couple's expenses, Linda recalled, but not enough for the couple to afford a house or even an apartment of their own.[56] To be a success, the school would have to attract more students. That required publicity.

One of the most storied events of Bruce's storied life occurred in Oakland in early January 1965. The incident has long since taken on the characteristics of a myth. All retellings agree that Bruce Lee faced off with a kung fu artist named Wong Jack Man at Bruce and James's *kwoon* on Broadway Avenue in Oakland, but they disagree about the cause of the confrontation, its nature, what happened that day, and the aftermath. The best-known version, based on the recollections of Bruce and his followers, represents the encounter as a fight that Lee won decisively, despite the fact that his opponent literally ran away from him.

The account of Bruce's wife, Linda, underscores the point that due to the history of British imperialism in China and anti-Chinese racism in the United States, Chinese and Chinese Americans viewed kung fu as a clandestine weapon to use against white aggressors. Chinese, particularly in the US, were reluctant to disclose the secrets of their marital arts to Caucasians. "It became an unwritten law that the art should be taught only to Chinese," Linda explains. She describes an unnamed kung fu practitioner who appeared with several Chinese friends at Bruce's *kwoon* in Oakland and presented Bruce with an "ornate scroll" containing an ultimatum written in Chinese, which challenged him to a match and demanded that if he lost, Bruce would cease teaching kung fu to white students. Bruce agreed to the contest but insisted instead on a full-on fight. The challenger proposed ground rules forbidding blows to the face and groin, but Bruce angrily retorted, "You've come here with an ultimatum and a challenge, hoping to scare me off. You've made the challenge—so I'm making the rules. So as far as I'm concerned, it's no-holds-barred."[57]

According to this retelling, the match began with Bruce and the challenger bowing formally, then taking their stances. Bruce established control within a minute using Wing Chun punches. As he continued his forward attack, the challenger began to backpedal, then turned and ran away. Bruce knocked him to the ground and demanded that he capitulate. "That's enough!" the vanquished foe pleaded.

But despite Bruce's decisive victory, earned in just three minutes, he felt unsatisfied. He believed that he should have been able to end the fight more quickly and was frustrated that he had become winded from chasing his opponent. Dissecting the fight convinced him that his Wing Chun was limited by its emphasis on punching, to the detriment of kicking. He began serious aerobic training, running two to six miles per day, and renewed his efforts to learn from other martial arts styles.

Bruce Lee's biographer Bruce Thomas follows Linda's narrative but adds a recollection from Dan Inosanto about what Bruce said later regarding the end of the fight: Bruce punched the challenger repeatedly in the head and back until his fists swelled. As Inosanto reports, he said, "I kept whacking him as he lay on the floor—until he gave up. I was so tired I could hardly punch him."[58]

Leo Fong did not witness the match but remembers James Lee phoning him immediately afterward. James reported that "the guy ran" and that Bruce had chased him "like a cat chasing a mouse." Bruce came on the line and confirmed that the "sumbitch ran" and went on to say that once the guy was cornered, he had yelled, "I give up, I give up!" Bruce added that his Wing Chun forward blast had been rendered ineffective against an opponent who refused to engage. Fong drove down to Oakland the next day and saw Bruce working out in James's garage, punching at a glove hung from the ceiling on a chain, shuffling "like [Muhammad] Ali" forward and backward in a style dramatically different from Wing Chun orthodoxy. As Fong concluded, "That was the day that Jun Fan Wing Chun gung fu of Bruce Lee made a transition to Jeet Kune Do"—the martial art Bruce would spend the rest of his life developing.[59]

This well-enshrined narrative contains five main points: first, that the purpose of the challenge was to prevent Bruce from teaching kung fu to non-Chinese students; second, that the encounter was a fight, not a sparring match; third, that Bruce's opponent turned and fled (indeed, Bruce and James referred to the challenger as "the runner" for years afterward); fourth, that Bruce won definitively; and finally, that Bruce's dissatisfaction with his own performance forced him to reevaluate his martial arts practice.[60]

But the other side of the story also merits consideration. Rick Wing, who decades later became a student of the challenger, presents compelling evidence that refutes the first point and context that complicates the others.

Wing's telling begins in late October or November 1964, when Bruce traveled from Oakland to the Sun Sing Theater in San Francisco's Chinatown.[61] His journey to the Sun Sing Theater marked a homecoming of sorts, for his father, Lee Hoi Chuen, had performed Cantonese opera on the stage of the building at 1021 Grant Avenue when it had housed the Mandarin Theatre.[62] Bruce went to the Sun Sing Theater to give a kung fu demonstration but played second fiddle to the main attraction, the glamorous Chinese movie star Zhang Zhongwen (Diana Chang), who was visiting San Francisco on a publicity tour. After her film played, the young actress entertained the crowd by singing and dancing the cha-cha onstage with Bruce.

As the dancing ended, Bruce hurried to the dressing room and changed into his kung fu clothes. Back onstage, he performed a number of kung fu sets and sparred with a partner. For the finale, he invited a volunteer from the audience, handed him a pad to hold against his chest, and explained that he would knock the man down with a one-inch punch. The blow normally would send a grown man flying, but on this occasion, the volunteer remained standing. Bruce flushed as he heard a chuckle from the audience and quickly threw a second punch that floored the volunteer. "Hey, that's not fair!" the man sputtered. "You said you were only going to hit me once." A few members of the audience flicked cigarette butts onto the stage to show their disapproval.

This sign of disrespect enraged Bruce, who blustered that any audience member who thought they could do better should step up onstage. Bruce's temper pushed him to the brink of decorum, and his arrogance sent him over the edge. He declared that he was the best martial artist in San Francisco and that if anyone wanted to prove him wrong, they were welcome to try.

With these words, a relative unknown had thrown down a challenge to every martial arts master in San Francisco. Members of the Gee Yau Seah martial arts school heard Bruce's tempestuous words and retired to their club to discuss them. Concluding that Bruce had issued a challenge that had to be met, they wrote a letter inviting him to come to the Gee Yau Seah school to explain himself. When Lee ignored the first invitation, a member delivered a handwritten letter to his Oakland studio. It was signed by Wong Jack Man, a twenty-three-year-old member of the Gee Yau Seah school and aspiring *sifu* of the Northern Shaolin kung fu style who had arrived recently in San Francisco from Hong Kong. Unable to disregard the personal challenge, Bruce invited Wong to settle the matter at his Oakland *kwoon*.

On the appointed day, Wong finished his shift as a waiter at a Chinese restaurant in San Francisco, piled into a car with five other men, and headed east across the Bay Bridge toward Oakland. They arrived at the *kwoon* around 6 p.m. and were joined by three more men from San Francisco. Inside the studio, the Lee contingent consisted of Bruce and Linda, James Lee, and George Lee.

Everyone agrees that Bruce Lee and Wong Jack Man faced off against each other, but even what to call the event remains subject to interpretation. Pro-Bruce stories describe a fight between Lee and Wong, but Rick Wing contends that the contest was better understood as a sparring match. The distinction is crucial. A no-holds-barred street fight would have no rules and would end only when one combatant was victorious and the loser conceded. A sparring match, by contrast, would be governed by rules, and the combatants would refrain from seriously harming each other. Wing acknowledges that Bruce insisted that there should be no rules since the group from San Francisco had challenged him.

The pro–Wong Jack Man contingent agrees that Bruce scored first, a fist to Wong's head above the eye, but believe that the punch was landed dishonorably. According to Wing, Bruce struck Wong with his right before Wong believed that the match had started. An alternate explanation is that Bruce's tremendous closing speed and lightning-quick hands enabled him to strike immediately.

The cramped *kwoon* made it impossible for anyone to see every detail of the fight. As Lee and Wong stalked each other around the room, onlookers had to scoot out of the way and peer around obstructions to watch the action. Bruce attacked in short, direct Wing Chun fashion, using chain punches and low kicks toward the shin or groin. In contrast, Wong moved evasively, left and right in his Northern Shaolin style, and only occasionally throwing punches of his own. Bruce employed a philosophy of always attacking and projecting forward energy, but Wong frustrated him by dodging, slipping away, and mostly playing defense.

The end of the encounter has become legendary in Lee lore yet remains controversial to Wong Jack Man proponents. Rick Wing alleges that Wong tripped and fell on the raised portion of the floor at the back of the room, Bruce rushed up to take advantage of the situation, and Wong dodged most of the punches that Bruce threw at him while he was down.

Wong contends that the fight ended not with a concession but in a draw, with onlookers pulling the fighters apart. By contrast, Bruce and his coterie contend that he pinned Wong on the floor and punched him repeatedly in the back of the head. Most important, they stipulate that Wong conceded, thus ending the fight or match.

≈

Many questions emerge from divergent accounts of the confrontation, one of which revolves around exactly how much damage Bruce inflicted on Wong. Bruce later claimed that he left Wong's face black and blue and that Wong took off work for three days after the fight. The San Franciscans remember differently, saying that they returned to Chinatown, bought an egg, hard-boiled it, and applied it to Wong's face (an admission of damage), but they recall his only injury as a visible cut above the eye.

Finally, questions arise about the aftermath. Bruce claimed that when he walked into a restaurant while Wong was waiting on customers, Wong panicked and spilled tea all over the floor. If the San Franciscan's account of the fight is accurate, Wong would have had no reason to fear Lee.

Finally, and perhaps most crucially, rather than disputing who would be allowed to learn kung fu, it seems more likely that Bruce Lee and Wong Jack Man fought to determine who could teach it best. But no evidence backs the claim made in many articles, movies, and books, including Linda's, that the fight was an attempt by Chinatown's elders to stop Lee from teaching kung fu to non-Chinese students, and the evidence that does exist tends to refute this allegation.

Rick Wing is fairly convincing on the point that this was a challenge to see whose kung fu was superior. But perhaps more important, posters and programs advertising kung fu demonstrations published in newspapers during this period provide contemporaneous proof that some kung fu schools in San Francisco's Chinatown were already admitting a few white students.

And indeed, what setting could have been more ideal for Bruce Lee and his philosophy of intermixing and innovation than Oakland, full of Asian American martial artists who were combining national traditions; crossing racial, ethnic, and cultural divides; and partaking in the all-American pastimes of weightlifting and bodybuilding? Yet, even before Bruce could put down roots in the Bay Area, he set off on his next quest, leaving behind his dream of a career as a martial arts teacher to pursue an even more glamorous one in show business.

"EITHER HOLLYWOOD OR HONG KONG"

THE MARTIAL ART OF SHOW BIZ

Jay Sebring had been part of the crowd at the 1964 First International Karate Tournament, transfixed by the charismatic young *sifu* with catlike reflexes, utter self-assurance, and seemingly superhuman strength. A dabbler in martial arts who had studied *kenpo* with Ed Parker, Sebring was better known as the hairstylist to the stars, a man whose client list included Henry Fonda, Red Skelton, Jackie Cooper, Steve Allen, Cliff Robertson, Mickey Rooney, Frank Sinatra, and the entire Rat Pack except for Dean Martin (a major omission since Martin boasted the best hair of the bunch). Far more than an ordinary barber, Sebring offered the ultimate in chic men's styling, charging exorbitant fees for the time: $25 for a visit to his salon and $50 for a house call.[1]

Five years later, the hard-partying playboy met a tragic end as a victim in the notorious massacre of the Manson Family, in which four other people were killed, including his former girlfriend Sharon Tate, the actress who was by then married to the director Roman Polanski.[2] But in 1964, Sebring was part of the Hollywood scene, and one of his A-list clients, the television producer William Dozier, confided that he was planning a series based on the fictional detective Charlie Chan and was searching for an actor to play Chan's eldest son. Sebring mentioned the suave performance he had seen in Long Beach and put Dozier in touch with First International Karate Tournament organizer Ed Parker, who delivered film of Bruce's demonstration. Intrigued, Dozier called the Lee home in Oakland and reached Linda, who promised to pass his message to Bruce when he got home.[3]

This phone call inaugurated a new phase in Bruce's life, one in which he would revisit old paths and chart new ones. He returned to acting for the first time since filming his final movie in Hong Kong in 1959, but this time in Hollywood, the capital of the world's biggest and most influential film industry. In Hollywood, he met, hung out with, and trained luminaries such as Steve McQueen, was introduced to and took up cannabis consumption, and indulged his playboy inclinations.

The producer Dozier and Lee agreed that Bruce would fly to Los Angeles for a screen test, but shortly before the scheduled date, Linda went into labor. Brandon Bruce Lee was born at the East Oakland Hospital on February 1, 1965, weighing eight pounds, eleven ounces, and with a head of black hair that would turn blond within three months.[4] In the birth announcement mailed to Bruce's student Taky Kimura, he boasted that his son was "a big healthy boy of course!"[5] Four days after becoming a father, Bruce took a major step toward a show-business career in the United States.

≈

Bruce's screen test at the Twentieth Century Fox studio in Hollywood, which can be seen today on YouTube, captured a natural performer in his element, a figure with a charismatic presence who exuded confidence in front of the camera.[6] The debonair twenty-four-year-old wore a close-fitting dark suit, white shirt, and skinny tie, and he spoke with a melodious Hong Kong accent mellowed by five years in the United States as he described losing sleep on the three nights since his son's birth, described shooting films between midnight and 5 a.m. in Hong Kong to avoid the city noise, and recalled studying philosophy in college. Even after having waited for seven hours to shoot the test, his eyes lit up brightly when he began expounding on the martial arts.[7]

Asked to name the best form of "Oriental fighting," he initially demurred. "Well, it's bad to say the *best*," he replied with a chuckle, "but in my opinion, I think gung fu is pretty good." He quickly dropped the modest façade, however, declaring, "Gung fu originated in China. It is the ancestor of karate and jujitsu. It's more of a complete system, and it's more fluid. By that I mean that it is more flowing; there is continuity of movement, instead of one movement, two movement, and then stop."

Asked to explain further, Bruce invoked what would become over the course of his career his most famous metaphor. "Well," he began, "gung fu, the best example would be a glass of water. Why? Because water is the softest substance in the world, but yet it can penetrate the hardest rock or anything, granite, you name it. Water also is insubstantial. By that I mean you cannot grasp hold of it. You cannot punch it and hurt it. So every gung fu man is trying to do that, to be soft like water and flexible and adapt itself to the opponent." The tiny slipups that betrayed him as a nonnative US English speaker—pronouncing "granite" as "GRA-night" and saying "adapt itself" rather than "adapt himself"—only made him seem all the more charming.

Asked to demonstrate some kung fu movements, he requested a partner, bantering, "Although accidents do happen . . ." An older, white assistant director shuffled hesitantly into the frame, eyes wide behind his thick glasses. Bruce shot rapid-fire eye-pokes, punches, and kicks so fast that they appear as mere blurs in the archival footage. With fists and feet flying perilously close to his head and body, the unwitting target flinched every time but always far too late to have avoided damage from a real attack.

When the director ordered the assistant director to back up, the room erupted in laughter. "Don't worry," Bruce reassured his nervous opponent with a smirk, patting his arm. A screaming high kick that flew in front of the man's face drew another flinch, along with laughter from the audience. "He's kind of worried," Bruce observed drily.

≈

For someone who had pursued the limelight as a child by acting in Hong Kong movies and as an adult through years of demonstrating martial arts before crowds in the United States, combining the two types of performance must have felt exhilarating. Beyond showcasing Bruce's kung fu skills, the screen test put into clear focus his rapport with the camera, his magnetic personality, and his unflappable confidence.

But Bruce had little time to bask in his success. Just a week after Brandon's birth and days after his screen test, he received news that his father had passed away in Hong Kong, and he rushed home to pay obeisance to the man whom he had both revered and feared. At the entrance of the funeral parlor, as ceremony dictated, he dropped to his hands and knees and crawled to his father's coffin, crying loud lamentations all the way.[8]

True to the pattern of cultural crossings that had produced Bruce and his world, Lee Hoi Chuen's funeral combined "Chinese custom and Catholic regulation." Bruce followed a mourning custom by not cutting his hair or shaving, which, as he confessed in a letter to Linda, left him looking "like a pirate with long hair and whiskers."[9]

Even as Bruce grieved for his father, the health of his wife and new son remained uppermost in his mind. He urged Linda to visit the doctor and ensure that Brandon received all the necessary blood tests and vaccinations, even though money was tight because their only income came from the fledgling kung fu school. After the mourning period ended, he took up visiting friends, most often Mrs. Eva Tso, the woman who was nearly his second mother, and old movie acquaintances; going to bath houses for massages; and screening kung fu movies.

Because of the high cost of transpacific telephone calls, Bruce and Linda communicated chiefly by mail. His letters to Linda, posted nearly daily, are filled with inquiries about Brandon; complaints about money amid complications with his father's will; endearments for his wife; promises to buy her clothes, jewelry, and a wig; and attempts to schedule their too-seldom phone conversations. As his stay stretched on, he proposed that Linda and Brandon should visit Hong Kong to meet their Chinese family. Despite pleas of penury,

Bruce reported that he had bought Linda a diamond ring and promised that the Hong Kong trip would include visits to Japan and Hawaii as a belated honeymoon.[10]

Bruce's rigorous exercise regimen suffered amid the chaos of family and old friends. He grumbled about losing weight and at one point declared, "To hell with the gym." Finally, after a month in Hong Kong, Bruce flew to San Francisco and on to Seattle, reuniting at last with Linda and Brandon, who had been staying with Linda's mother during his prolonged absence. The separation from his wife and newborn son took an emotional toll on Bruce but also afforded him time to contemplate his career. Three days before departing from the colony, he closed one of his final letters to Linda with a salutation signaling his budding Hollywood aspirations. "Till then, my dearest wife," he wrote, "With love from, 'China James Bond.'"[11]

≈

Planting the seeds of a Hollywood career allowed the transpacific nomad Bruce Lee to renew his Hong Kong roots. William Dozier locked up the promising young performer with a one-year retainer of $1,800, a veritable fortune to Bruce and Linda, who still lived in James Lee's Oakland home. But instead of using the money to rent their own place or solidify their finances, the couple used nearly all of the option money to buy airline tickets to Hong Kong.[12] The new family arrived in Kowloon in early May 1965 just as both Bruce's career and the local climate were beginning to heat up.

Linda had spent nearly her entire life in the temperate Pacific Northwest, and she wilted in the heat and tropical humidity of Hong Kong. But being linguistically and culturally isolated caused even greater discomfort. Bruce, Linda, and Brandon moved into the Lees' teeming Nathan Street apartment, which was already stuffed beyond capacity with an extended family still reeling from Lee Hoi Chuen's death. Despite the fact that Linda was white and spoke no Cantonese, the Lee family welcomed her without a trace of the racial animosity that the Emerys had shown Bruce. Nonetheless, the language barrier left her feeling alone and isolated. To compound matters, baby

Brandon was fussy and often ill in the heat and humidity. Linda cradled and walked him for hours every night to avoid disturbing the sleep of the other apartment dwellers.

Linda did get to enjoy some of the perks of the island, however. Eva Tso, "who was like an adopted mother to Bruce,"[13] whisked the young couple out of the crowded apartment on sightseeing excursions to the magnificent harbor and Victoria Peak (the highest point on the island, which tourists accessed by riding a funicular up a steep mountain slope to enjoy spectacular 360-degree views from the top of the peak) and shopping trips on which Linda purchased a number of bespoke outfits from Hong Kong's world-renown tailors.[14]

At this point, Bruce had one foot firmly planted in Hong Kong and the other in California. On the brink of what appeared to be a breakthrough in Hollywood, he was eager to ensure that his young wife and infant son would be welcomed into his family and network of friends in Asia.

As Bruce spent the summer of 1965 in Hong Kong awaiting word from Twentieth Century Fox about his acting future, he continued his ocean-spanning project to refine his martial art, both returning to his Wing Chun roots and trying to surpass them. He visited his *sifu*, the sixty-six-year-old Yip Man, whom Bruce and other students always called "Old Man." Bruce was planning to write and illustrate a book on Wing Chun and took more than 130 photographs of the master performing *siu lim tau* and other forms of martial arts.[15] The planned book indicates that Bruce still thought of Wing Chun as the basis of his developing fighting system, even as he challenged himself to push beyond its limitations.

His old pal Hawkins Cheung recalls a telling incident in which Bruce gave a martial arts exhibition on a popular television talk show but did not mention Yip Man at all, a sign of a developing rift between student and teacher. Cheung later learned that while Bruce had been eagerly publicizing kung fu in the media, the elderly *sifu* had declined to be filmed, as he did not wish to expose the form widely. Cheung concluded that the Old Man's "traditional thinking had come up against Bruce's Western thinking."[16]

Letters from Bruce to his Seattle student Taky Kimura capture this moment in Bruce's martial arts development, a moment when he was considering how to develop the most efficient fighting style. Amid mundane matters, such as Bruce asking Kimura to send him the dues from the school, discussing recently published martial arts books, and gossiping about mutual acquaintances, he developed his theory of fighting. For example, Bruce reflected on the surprising results of the second fight between boxing heavyweights Sonny Liston, once considered to be invincible, and the brash upstart Cassius Clay (soon to be Muhammad Ali). In this bout, which took place in Miami on February 25, 1964, Clay knocked out Liston in the first round with a mysterious punch that left many observers wondering whether Liston had taken an intentional dive. Bruce rejected the idea of foul play and attributed Clay's victory over the more powerful Liston to the advantage of speed and an evasiveness to which Liston could not adapt. "You know," Bruce concluded, "it is the style of Clay that screwed up Liston the most." Bruce could hardly view the fight any other way because he had spent his Hong Kong vacation thinking about the importance of style and doggedly refining his own. As he reported to Taky, "TIMING and DISTANCE are the basic stuffs" of his new method, "but Wing Chun principle is the nucleus (the most important foundation)."[17] At this point, he still acknowledged Wing Chun as the basis of his style but did not consider it to be a perfect system.

Bruce elaborated on his quest to perfect Wing Chun in letters to James Lee, which were filled with discussions of techniques and detailed hand-drawn illustrations. He confided, "I hope to . . . formulate my style, which I've been working on nearly every day as I've nothing else to do." Just as he had told Taky that Wing Chun remained the nucleus of his martial art, he described his efforts as the "formation of a more complete Wing Chun." Rather than abandoning his first martial art, he meant to augment, refine, and evolve it. For example, he envisioned a method called "Indirect Progressive Attack," which involved first feinting to draw a misplaced block or parry; second, closing the distance to the opponent; and third, breaking the opponent's rhythm—all accomplished with a single smoothly connected set of continuous move-ments. Bruce described his emerging system as "a combination of chiefly Wing Chun, fencing and boxing."[18]

Aside from the technical treatises, Bruce gossiped, bantered, and boasted in these letters to his close friend James Lee. One letter ended with an en-dearing closing that read, "Brandon is getting bigger—that guy's got the basic requirement and the killing instinct—he is screaming now! So long. Ah boy, got to look after the 'little sifu.'"[19]

Throughout 1965, Bruce was perched tenuously between Hollywood and Hong Kong in a liminal status that would not resolve itself until the begin-ning of the next year. His correspondence with William Dozier reveals his re-lentless effort to find work in US television and, most important, his struggle to create authentic and respectful representations of Chinese and Chinese American people. Unfortunately, those efforts would not bear fruit for Bruce or other Asian and Asian American actors for years to come. In response, Dozier reassured Bruce, "The film you shot looks very good, and when you return to San Francisco, please let me know."[20]

CHARLIE CHAN'S NUMBER ONE SON

Dozier and Lee continued to discuss the Charlie Chan project via letters, but the producer cautioned at the beginning of April that gaining final approval would take another two or three months.[21] As Dozier considered how to pitch the television series, he must have pondered Lee's dazzling screen test, for he proposed a slight change in direction. In an April 22 letter to Bruce, Dozier referred to the television series by a new title, *Number One Son*, a clear sign that the charismatic young actor would have a more important role. Furthermore, he urged Bruce to find suitable representation and introduced him to "a reputable and honest agent," William Belasco of the Progressive Management Association.[22] Dozier also forward a thirteen-page treatment of the pilot episode by Lorenzo Semple Jr., a screenwriter for the *Batman* series who went on to a long Hollywood career writing films including the 1976 movie *Three Days of the Condor.*[23]

Semple's preposterous sketch begins in San Francisco's Chinatown and sends Charlie Chan and Number One Son to Hong Kong to unravel a plot involving murder and brainwashing masterminded by a Chinese Communist villain. The episode features a martial art described as "a form of super-judo" with a decidedly Japanese-sounding but totally made-up throw called an "a'zu-taki."[24] In a further indication of Hollywood's cavalier attitude toward authenticity, Semple thanked Dozier for sending him a number of Charlie Chan books, promising that for actual scripts, he would "dip into them, browsing color & witty chinese [*sic*] sayings &c."[25] In other words, Semple intended to sprinkle his script with ersatz quips and wisecracks drawn from the condescending series of books written by the white author Earl Derr Biggers, a collection that inspired the movie series that always starred white actors in yellowface in the title role.[26] Only decades later would the yellowface in films like the Charlie Chan series and the egregiously offensive performance by Mickey Rooney as Mr. Yunioshi in *Breakfast at Tiffany's* (1961) come to be recognized as prime examples of Hollywood racism.

Bruce reacted positively, despite the thorough mediocrity of the script and the borderline-offensive treatment of Asian Americans. "I'm very enthused on the whole project," he wrote, but he also offered several of his own ideas "to add more 'coolness' and 'subtleness' to the character of Charlie Chan," as he put it. Bruce's suggested revisions sought to portray the detective as a member of modern society rather than as an inscrutable Oriental object of amusement. In rethinking Chan, Bruce returned to the theme of synthesis and combination, which undergirded everything from his philosophy papers at the University of Washington to his martial arts practice. He argued that the "uniqueness" of the TV series could be found "in the *interfusion* of the best of both the Oriental and American qualities," alongside the introduction of "never before seen Gung Fu fighting techniques." And he encouraged Dozier, echoing the sentiment he had shared with Linda, "I have a feeling that this Charlie Chan can be another James Bond success if handled properly."[27]

Bill Dozier brushed off Lee's entreaties, referring to him with mild condescension in a memo to a studio executive as "the young Chinese boy whom we wish to sign for possible use in a series" and encouraging Lee to watch television to improve his English.[28] Bruce obediently complied, informing Dozier that he was watching as many English TV programs as possible to improve his "clarity in speaking."[29]

Dozier's suggestion was telling. Bruce had grown up in Hong Kong and spoke English with the colony's mellifluous accent that so beautifully combines Cantonese and British inflections. By deeming his accent as unsuitable for US television, Dozier rejected Bruce's hybridity as undesirable and excessively foreign. Even as Dozier sought to shoehorn Bruce into monocultural norms, other players around the *Number One Son* production attempted to change its cast. One suggested introducing a second, adopted white son, as if what the Charlie Chan series needed most was more white characters.[30]

≈

In September, with Bruce's future in US television still in limbo, the Lees departed from Hong Kong after a stay of three months. They headed first to Seattle, living with Linda's mother for four months, before returning to James Lee's home in Oakland.[31] While Bruce was in Hong Kong, William Dozier had been developing a television series based on the radio show and comic book series *The Green Hornet* and was considering Bruce for a major role. The biographer Bruce Thomas writes that Lee had inquired regularly about the status of *The Green Hornet* throughout the summer but made no attempt to rekindle his Hong Kong movie career, indicating that he definitively saw his path forward leading through Hollywood.[32]

However, personal letters reveal that Bruce's vision of the future remained hazy as late as mid-December 1965, when he informed his friend George Lee, "Linda and I will be coming down to Oakland to stay for around a month before either going to Hollywood or Hong Kong." Although he estimated that the deal with Twentieth Century Fox had an 85 percent probability of coming to fruition, he hedged, "I have two contracts waiting in Hong Kong."[33] William Dozier's announcement that *The Green Hornet* would go forward finally settled the question of which Pacific shore Bruce Lee would alight on.

In March 1966, the Lees moved into a small apartment on Wilshire Boulevard in Los Angeles, near the UCLA campus and just minutes away from the Twentieth Century Fox lot. For the first time in his life, Bruce enrolled in acting classes, instructed by Jeff Corey, whom he boasted was "the best drama coach in Hollywood."[34] Lee marveled at the tuition of $70 per session, which was paid by the studio, telling a friend that he would never pay such an exorbitant fee out of his own pocket.[35]

Because Bruce did not yet draw a salary from the studio, he resumed teaching kung fu to make ends meet. For $25 an hour, he taught a roster of students drawn from the Hollywood set that would eventually include the actors Steve McQueen and James Coburn as well as the writer Stirling Silliphant. Martial arts also paved the way for the Lees to move into a much posher apartment shortly before filming began. In a letter, Bruce marveled to Taky Kimura, "By the way, I'll be moving to another really 'cool' apartment, the Barrington Plaza—a 27 stories high luxury tower with doormen and attendant parking, laundry & dry cleaning valet service, Olympic-size pool, all-wool carpeting, all electric kitchen (dishwasher, built-in range and oven, etc.), electronic huge elevators—I'll be living on the 23rd storey (the higher the more expensive) and I'm telling you it's something else."[36] The best part, he added, was that he had scored a highly discounted rent of $140 (just $20 more than he paid for the tiny apartment on Wilshire) in exchange for giving the landlord two kung fu lessons per month.

The new quarters were indeed "something else" for Bruce, Linda, and Brandon, who had been living with friends and family for the past year and a half. Beyond a chicer apartment, the Lee family's situation improved once filming of *The Green Hornet* started in June. Bruce began drawing a salary of $400 per week, which netted $313 after deductions (roughly $3,200 gross and $2,500 net in 2021 dollars). The increased income could not have come at a better time, for Linda recalls that when the first paycheck arrived, they "didn't have enough to pay the rent and other outstanding bills."[37] However, the car-loving Bruce could not resist using the windfall to buy a new Chevy Nova.[38]

THE GREEN HORNET

Bruce's debut in US television came not as Charlie Chan's Number One Son but as Kato, the sidekick in *The Green Hornet*, a series derived from the popular radio show of the 1930s and 1940s and the comic books it inspired. ABC aired twenty-six episodes constituting the show's sole season from September 1966 to July 1967. The hero operates behind a double disguise, appearing by day as Britt Reid, wealthy owner and publisher of *The Sentinel* newspaper, while masquerading at night as the notorious archcriminal, the Green Hornet. However, the Green Hornet's villainous reputation is a façade used to gain credibility with criminals and cover his crime fighting, with only District Attorney Frank Scanlon aware that Reid is the Green Hornet and that the Green Hornet is actually not a lawbreaker.

The producer William Dozier cast five main characters with performers ranging from veteran actors to newcomers. Van Williams starred as Britt Reid / the Green Hornet. The brown-haired, blue-eyed Williams boasted an athletic build developed by working on his family's ranch and performing in rodeos, and he was square-jawed and good looking but in such a generic way that publicists for the series could describe him only in the most clichéd way as "a tall, dark, and handsome Texan." Williams had already enjoyed moderate success in television, starring in early-1960s series including *Bourbon Street Beat*, *Surfside 6*, and *The Tycoon*.[39]

The prolific character actors Lloyd Gough and Walter Brooke assumed the roles of the grizzled reporter Mike Axford and District Attorney Frank Scanlon, respectively. Lenore Case, Reid's assistant at *The Sentinel*, was played by the fresh-faced and relatively inexperienced actress Wende Wagner. Dozier praised Bruce Lee as "handsome," "a natural athlete," and "one of the finest natural acting talents" that he had seen in his years in the industry.[40] Although it was true that Lee had never appeared in US films or television, his natural talent had been honed by a dozen years of acting in Hong Kong in twenty films.

Dozier worked overtime to differentiate *The Green Hornet* from his then-current hit show, *Batman*. In contrast to *Batman*'s campiness, which featured captions like "Blam!" and "Pow!" splashed across the screen in bright colors, *The Green Hornet* played it straight. Newspaper and magazine articles with headlines proclaiming, "Batman Producer Dozier Takes Hornet out of Camp," "Hornet Will Not 'Camp,'" and "Hornet Sans Camp" hammered home the point that the Hornet would forgo *Batman*'s arch tone in favor of taking itself ever so seriously.[41]

The dramatic difference stemmed from George Trendle's vigorous defense of the straightforward show that he had created for radio. *Batman* writer Lorenzo Semple and Trendle nearly came to blows over the pilot script for *The Green Hornet*, which Semple wrote as a farce and Trendle found deeply objectionable. Dozier mediated the dispute but ultimately ruled in favor of Trendle, who still owned the rights to the characters.[42] Trendle's licensing agreement, which included a clause stipulating that the television show "shall not depict *The Green Hornet* in a manner substantially different from which he or the other major characters were depicted in the radio series," guaranteed that the Hornet would indeed "not camp."[43]

For example, whereas *Batman* featured an overly dramatic narrator who concluded each episode with the catchphrase, "Tune in next week. Same bat time, same bat channel!" *The Green Hornet* eschewed an announcer. In place of *Batman*'s garish, cartoony palette, *The Green Hornet* made the Hornet's signature color a deep emerald and generally tended toward darkness, with action scenes often set in shadowy warehouses and gloomy alleys. And in contrast to Batman's knowingly arch delivery of dialogue, Britt Reid and Kato always spoke as realistically as their awkward dialogue would allow.

≈

Trying to play *The Green Hornet* as a realistic crime/adventure show, however, had disastrous artistic results, as it forced audiences to try to accept its abundant absurdity with a straight face. To begin with, the script added a layer to the superhero-in-disguise trope, invoking a superhero disguised as a millionaire disguised as a criminal. Like Batman, the Green Hornet wielded an abundance of gadgets, including a hornet gun, a hornet stinger that blasts open doors and disarms bad guys with a sonic-wave blast, and a chemical weapon that emits a green knockout gas. Unlike Batman, who takes the wheel of the Batmobile and relegates Robin to the passenger seat, the Green Hornet rides in the backseat of Black Beauty, the sleek, angular black sedan chauffeured by Kato.

Even the most ardent fans of *Superman* must give a knowing wink and engage in willful suspension of disbelief to overlook the fact that none of Clark Kent's friends and coworkers recognize that he looks exactly like the Man of Steel wearing thick-framed glasses. Batman's arsenal of outlandish gadgetry can be forgiven by the show's refusal to present itself as anything but a preposterous romp. But *The Green Hornet* demanded that its viewers not just wink and nod but watch the show as if they were seven years old.

The Green Hornet's plots range from the unimaginative to the ridiculous, with episodes in which the Hornet and Kato break up local crime rings to those in which they fight a leopard (which the Hornet subdues with his gas emitter), take on a Chinatown kung fu master (whom Kato defeats, of course), and battle Green Hornet impersonators. The most ludicrous story line aired in the two-part episode that closed the season, "Invasion from Outer Space," which features extraterrestrials who shoot electric beams from their fingers. Shockingly, the English-speaking aliens wearing shiny foil suits ultimately prove to be human criminals intent on stealing a hydrogen bomb.

≈

The Green Hornet's artistic failure prevented it from finding a broad audience. The series opened promisingly, with viewership driven by a vigorous promotion campaign that included a full-page advertisement in the immensely popular *TV Guide* and numerous publicity interviews with William Dozier. Its first three episodes were powered to the top of the ratings by exploratory ganders from viewers curious about a new show from the *Batman* producer, but audiences for subsequent episodes declined steadily. Unlike audiences, critics gave the show no quarter from the beginning, with the *New York Times* calling it "sluggishly old hat rather than divertingly awful" and *Variety* bemoaning its "unrelieved straight melodrama" and "fulsome noise and violence."[44]

As both reviews suggest, the tonal shift rendered *The Green Hornet* unwatchable to sentient adults. Whereas *Batman* became a hit by allowing wide-eyed kids to watch alongside smirking parents, *The Green Hornet* appealed mainly to children, who made up its most ardent fan base. Although the TV show never received the audience response its creator had hoped for, the fan mail that did arrive was from children to their hero, Kato.[45] Bruce's friend and publisher Mito Uyehara claims that at the peak of the show's popularity, Kato received six hundred fan letters a week. Bruce read all of the letters, but Linda sent the replies.[46]

On a show filled with gimmicky gadgetry, Kato's hand-to-hand fighting stood out as the only genuine element, and Bruce Lee received the few accolades that came the show's way. Bruce introduced an entirely different style of combat movement that stood in stark contrast to the usual form displayed in US television and movies of the time. Think of any number of John Wayne fight scenes, in which the hero starts with hands balled at his sides at chest height, cocks his fist downward and backward, then lumbers forward, swinging his arm in a wide, lethargic arc that at long last brings his fist into contact with his adversary's jaw. He might block an opponent's slowly arcing punch by throwing up a forearm that completely stops the blow, then follow up with glacial counterpunches. And John Wayne never sullies his cowboy boots by kicking. This slow-developing, ham-fisted, heavy-footed style of fighting characterized most onscreen fistfights before Bruce Lee broke onto the scene.

In *The Green Hornet*, Bruce does not adhere strictly to classic Wing Chun, but his fights resemble kung fu more than the roundhouse, haymaker style most familiar to audiences. His movements proceed directly along the center line of the body that Wing Chun prioritizes. He eschews the "block then counterpunch" routine but instead moves forward inside opponents' round-houses and strikes before they can land. He also uses his feet adroitly, landing high kicks to the face and medium-level kicks to the midsection and torso. The Green Hornet must not have studied kung fu with Kato, though, because he brawls like a drunkard in an Old Western saloon.

≈

During *The Green Hornet*'s time on the air in the 1967–68 television season, it caused a stir among martial arts aficionados by broadcasting Lee's fighting style to the widest US audience kung fu had ever enjoyed. After the first episode aired, two readers wrote separately to the editors of *Black Belt* magazine to inquire about who Bruce Lee was, what discipline he trained in, and what rank he held. William Granberry of Chicago thought he noticed aikido throws and ventured, "This was the first time I have ever seen real karate on TV." Robert Williams, who wrote from Flushing, New York, observed more accurately, "He demonstrates to me that he has a knowledge of the art" of kung fu. The magazine's editors replied that they had known about Lee for five years from his demonstrations at martial arts tournaments and that although he was highly skilled, he did not hold a rank since kung fu does not issue rankings. Granberry's statement about never having seen karate on TV before and an editors' note to inform readers of a martial arts magazine about kung fu's rankless system reinforced the groundbreaking nature of Lee's performance. The editors' understated declaration that "the Chinese art of Kung Fu is not well known in the U.S." underscored the point that kung fu remained surpassingly obscure in the 1960s. Interestingly, their assertion that most of the few kung fu schools in the US "will not teach anyone outside of their own race" suggests that they may have been unaware of the schools training non-Chinese pupils.[47]

By October 1967, Bruce Lee had graduated from the "Letters to the Editor" section of *Black Belt* magazine to its cover, where a headline asked, "Green Hornet's 'Kato': Does He Really Practice Kung-Fu?" The wording of the headline, which named "Kato" while omitting "Bruce Lee," portrayed an actor subservient to his role. But the cover imagery reversed that relationship by combining two pictures of Bruce: in the foreground, he wielded a nunchaku while wearing kung fu garb, while in the predictably green background, he holds a throwing dart from the television arsenal while wearing the chauffeur uniform, gloves, hat, and mask from the show.

Placing Bruce in the foreground while relegating Kato to the background suggests that the true character of interest is the martial arts practitioner, not the television character. This ambiguity, a muddling of the dichotomy between the person Bruce Lee and the image of "Bruce Lee," exemplifies an enduring characteristic of the complex way in which audiences have understood the man, his life, and his performances as tightly braided together in ways seldom seen with other celebrities.

"JUST WHAT HE LOOKS LIKE—AN ORIENTAL"

Despite Bruce's desire to create a fully realized, faithfully rendered Chinese American character in Hollywood, starring in *The Green Hornet* would not provide that opportunity. His appearance on the popular ABC television program *The Milton Berle Show* demonstrated the prevalence of Orientalism on mainstream television in 1966 and the impossibility of escaping it. The comedy skit that was clearly meant to introduce the new ABC network show was rife with outlandish stereotypes, supposedly Asian characters speaking broken English, and the conflation of Japan and China.[48]

≈

The writers and producers of *The Green Hornet* paid no more attention to ethnic authenticity than did the writers of *The Milton Berle Show*. Instead, they relegated Kato to a vague existence as a generic "Oriental." Kato had begun in the radio series as a Japanese houseboy played by the Japanese American actor Tokataro Hayashi, who was credited as "Raymond Toyo," the name a radio director gave him. As tensions in the Pacific built over Japan's invasion of China in 1935, the radio writers transformed Kato into a more sympathetic

Filipino character. In 1942, with Japan and the United States at war, a white actor took over the role after Toyo was imprisoned in an internment camp along with over 110,000 Japanese Americans from the West Coast, two-thirds of whom were US citizens.[49] Just as the Charlie Chan movies of this period starred white actors in yellowface, during and after World War II, the *Green Hornet* radio series featured white actors performing stereotypical accents, which might be termed "yellow voice."

The 1960s television show treated Kato's ethnicity with an indifference equal to the radio show of the 1940s. Writing to the character's creator, George Trendle, Dozier commented, "I have a superb Oriental in the bullpen for Kato and will be able to show you a piece of test film on him when you come out. He is actually an American-born Chinese, but can play any sort of Oriental or Filipino. I don't think we should ever say what sort of nationality Kato is: just let him be what he looks like—an Oriental."[50]

Descriptions for casting Kato imagine him as between five feet and five feet four inches tall, weighing about a hundred pounds, and holding himself in a way described as "Erect, easy. Lean but tough." His face appears "quiet, pleasant, *definitely oriental* [*sic*, emphasis mine]. Eyes sometimes passive, sometimes keen. Firm and intelligent looking. Clean shaven."[51] At five foot seven and 130 pounds, Lee towered over the diminutive Kato the writers had imagined, but he certainly looked the part, as doing so primarily meant looking "Oriental."

≈

If playing an undifferentiated "Oriental" challenged Bruce's attempt to portray a fully rounded character, embodying the character of Kato as sidekick to a white hero proved even more daunting. The dynamic between the Green Hornet and Kato recalls nothing more than the one-dimensional relationship between the Lone Ranger and Tonto, with the resemblance being far more intentional than accidental. In fact, George Trendle had created *The Green Hornet* radio series in 1936 as a successor to his earlier hit, *The Lone Ranger*.

Parallels between the two dramas abound. Both feature masked white heroes using memorable transportation: the Lone Ranger traversing the Old West on his faithful steed Silver and the Green Hornet prowling the night in his highly modified car, Black Beauty. Both use classical music for their themes: Rossini's "William Tell Overture" for *The Lone Ranger* and a jazzy, trumpet-based version of Rimsky-Korsakov's "Flight of the Bumblebee" for *The Green Hornet*. Even more intriguingly, a hereditary lineage links the two series, for in 1947, Britt Reid revealed that the Lone Ranger had been his father's uncle.[52]

William Dozier scrupulously avoided outright references to *The Lone Ranger* within the scripts of the 1967 television series because he did not own its TV rights. However, publicity articles framed the relationship between Britt Reid and Kato in terms that explicitly recalled the Lone Ranger and Tonto. One article noted that Reid's granduncle had "championed justice in the West with the aid of an Indian named Tonto."[53] The entertainment-industry newspaper *Variety* reported, "Where the Ranger had his Tonto, the Hornet's partner will be played by Bruce Lee."[54] The lead actor, Van Williams, explained in a newspaper interview that the series was a contemporary version of *The Lone Ranger*, including what he termed "the faithful Oriental servant, Kato," as a modern-day Tonto.[55]

≈

Bruce applied his kung fu philosophy of meeting resistance with flexibility and deflected racism with his typical brand of cornball humor. He playfully confronted the stereotype that native Chinese speakers have difficulty pronouncing the *r* sound when he discussed the name of the hero, Britt Reid. He informed a reporter that he could pronounce his *r*'s when he put his "mind to it" and teased producer Dozier, saying, "How lucky can you get—you've got a Chinaman from Hong Kong who can say 'Britt Reid.'"[56] But try as he might, Lee could not dodge headlines like the *Washington Post*'s groan-worthy "Kato Likes Puns, Preys on Words."[57]

Behind the scenes, Bruce tried valiantly to infuse Kato with humanity, but he met with little success. Reflecting back on when he was first offered the part, he recalled, "A producer wanted me to play a Chinese. I immediately could see the part—pigtails, chopsticks and 'ah-so's,' shuffling obediently behind the master who has saved my life. But it turned out to be better."[58] It may indeed have turned out better than bowing and shuffling, but it certainly did not fulfill all of Bruce's wishes.

On February 10, 1966, before shooting began, Bruce wrote to Dozier asking to be flown from Oakland to Hollywood: "I would like to talk to you (and maybe the script writer too) regarding the characterization of Kato. I believe that through this brief meeting, more 'sizzles' can be added to the Green Hornet; also, a more appropriate character will derive from better understanding of me and my ideas."[59] His stated desire to create a "more appropriate character" by enabling the producer and writer to get to know him better suggests that Bruce saw Kato as a flat character that required further development.

Dozier brushed him off, stating that the scriptwriter was working from his home in Connecticut and it would be better for Bruce to comment on the final script before shooting.[60] Bruce's being denied a meeting and learning that he was to have no input on the script must have been disappointing, as Bruce responded immediately to Dozier, insisting that he had "come up with several ideas" that he hoped would "be useful for the Green Hornet."[61]

Four months later, now living in Los Angeles and shooting the completed scripts while taking acting lessons from Jeff Corey, Bruce took another swing at the issue. Despite acknowledging that Kato serves as Britt's houseboy, he insisted, "As the crime fighter, Kato *is* an 'active partner' of the Green Hornet and not a 'mute follower.' Jeff Corey agrees and I myself feel that at least an occasional dialogue would certainly make me 'feel' more at home with the fellow players." He went on to explain that because he had so few speaking lines, he and Corey were working on nonverbal acting exercises. "I'm not complaining," he concluded, "but I feel that an 'active partnership' with the Green Hornet will definitely bring out a more effective and efficient Kato. My aim is for the betterment of the show and I bother you with this because you have been most understanding."[62]

Dozier sidestepped Lee's politic effort to obtain more dialogue for Kato in order to give his character more depth (and, not coincidentally, increase his exposure) as easily as Kato slipped a thug's punch. Like a good Jeet Kune Do practitioner, Dozier accomplished two things simultaneously with his reply. First, he blocked Bruce's thrust, stating, "We think there is great value in presenting Kato as a somewhat taciturn and enigmatic 'man of action' rather than a talker." But while justifying Kato's relative muteness, he reassured Bruce, "We have no intention of never having him say *anything*. He will have some dialogue now and then, but when he does, it will count for something," concluding diplomatically, "I think you are coming off very well on the screen. Carry on."[63]

≈

Although Dozier initially brushed off Bruce's attempts to flesh out Kato's character, he later acknowledged that doing so might improve the show. In the face of floundering ratings, he wrote a memo analyzing what *The Green Hornet* could do in order to be renewed and possibly expanded into an hour-long show. "If we could know more about [Kato] as a human being we would be more interested in his exploits as a crime fighter," he mused. He also raised a number of pertinent questions about the story line: "Where did Britt Reid first encounter Kato? Could he have met him in Korea when Britt Reid was involved in the police action there, for example? Where and how did their relationship come into being? What does Kato do in his off hours."[64] Answering these questions, he believed, would allow audiences to be more invested in Kato and thereby strengthen the show. Although Dozier had initially restricted Kato to being a generic "Oriental," he acknowledged in this memo that nailing down Kato's ethnicity as Korean and giving him a backstory would provide a badly needed level of specificity, even if he ignored the fact that Kato's martial art was not Korean.

This proposed reimagining of the Kato character shows the ties between militarism abroad and domestic racism. In Dozier's reimagination of the story, Reid and Kato initially meet in Asia because of the US presence during the Korean War (or "police action," as the memo calls it), but in the United States, their relationship falls into the decades-old racial structure of white supremacy and Asian exploitation, with Reid as millionaire-hero and Kato as servant-sidekick.

"ORIENTAL CULTURE AND OCCIDENTAL CULTURE ARE NOT MUTUALLY EXCLUSIVE"

Although Bruce's efforts to demolish stereotypes onscreen met with only limited success, he did in his personal life shatter one significant social barrier: the taboo against interracial marriage. With a white wife and a clearly biracial son, Bruce defied US laws forbidding and widespread social disapproval of interracial mixing that dated back to the Colonial era. The first antimiscegenation law, passed in Maryland in 1691, forbade marriages between whites and Blacks. As Asians began migrating to the United States in significant numbers in the nineteenth century, opposition to sex and marriage between Asians and whites became a primary component of anti-Asian racism and attempts to ban Asian immigration.

The early anti-Chinese movement pointed to the horror of perverse Chinese men luring innocent white girls into the opium dens of Chinatown to molest them in unspeakable ways. Similarly, virulent anti-Filipino hatred during the exclusion period portrayed Filipino men as suave, brown-skinned devils who would work their wiles on unwitting white women. These messages portrayed Asian men as sexual predators and deviants whom no respectable white woman would willingly marry. If Asian-white marriages were unthinkable, the fruits of those unions—biracial babies—were abominable.

In the early twentieth century, when white Californians were lobbying to prevent Japanese migrants from coming to the US, one agitator fumed before the state legislature, "Near my home is an eighty-acre tract of as fine land as there is in California. On that tract lives a Japanese. With that Japanese lives a white woman. In that woman's arms is a baby. What is that baby? It isn't a Japanese. It isn't white. It is the germ of the mightiest problem that ever faced this state; a problem that will make the black problem of the South look white."[65] Racism and anti-immigrant sentiment rendered romantic and certainly sexual intermixture between Asians and whites monstrous.

≈

Bruce and Linda were able to be married in Seattle because Washington did not have an antimiscegenation law on the books. The rest of Washington's western neighbors—Oregon, California, Idaho, Montana, North and South Dakota, Wyoming, Nevada, Utah, Colorado, and Arizona—barred interracial unions well into the mid-twentieth century, only beginning to repeal antimiscegenation laws in 1948. By the time Bruce and Linda had married in 1964, Wyoming was the only remaining western state that would have prevented their union, but antimiscegenation laws remained on the books throughout the South. Their marriage would not become possible uniformly across the nation until 1967, when the United States Supreme Court declared all antimiscegenation laws unconstitutional in its landmark ruling in the aptly named case *Loving v. Virginia*, a case in which the white Richard Loving and Mildred Loving, a woman of color, were wed in Washington, DC, then returned to their home state of Virginia.

Bruce conducted an advance publicity tour for *The Green Hornet* during the summer of 1966, a moment when antimiscegenation laws remained on the books in seventeen states. But although the publicity tour took place at a time when interracial marriage remained illegal in a third of the nation, his marriage and family garnered remarkably supportive coverage. He spoke with journalists from film and television magazines and newspapers across the country, always arriving with a stylish haircut and wearing impeccably tailored suits and flashy cufflinks. The interviews and articles portrayed Bruce as an intriguing intermixture of Chinese and Western culture, his marriage to the pretty and conspicuously blond Linda as loving rather than loathsome, and Brandon as the lucky recipient of dual cultural heritages rather than tragically caught between them.

Bruce, Linda, and Brandon Lee, 1968. (Photo by AF Archive via Alamy Stock Photo)

These newspaper and magazine articles typically set up a dichotomy between East and West, then marveled that the two could be combined, albeit only to a limited extent. One introduction to Bruce noted his "slang-tinged vernacular" that was "as jazzy and Western as a Sousa March" and his "snappy up-to-the-minute, Hollywood approved style," yet it insisted that under this hip "veneer," he was at heart "an exquisite import from Hong Kong" and "thoroughly, totally, completely Chinese."[66] This description implies that Chinese and Western cultures exist like oil and vinegar in a salad dressing; although they can be forced to emulsify, they will never dissolve together; Bruce's essential Chinese character could be concealed on the surface but never altered.

Another article opens with the rhetorical question, "How does it happen that two people from opposite ends of the earth meet, fall in love, establish a true and contented union, and bring up their children as a triumph of human grace?" The emphasis on "opposite ends of the earth" may have been geographically correct, but the author of the article had culture more than geography on her mind, for she characterized Bruce as "a fascinating blend of East and West," adding, "He had the innate personal dignity characteristic of the Orient; he had a Western sense of humor."[67]

The same author in another article uses a description of the biracial Brandon to portray the opposition between East and West, proclaiming, "He is Oriental and Occidental. . . . His personality is a fascinating blend of the thoughtfulness of the East and vigor of the West." Despite depicting "Oriental" and "Occidental" difference, the author rejects the idea that they are ultimately incompatible, concluding that the "diverse blood lines" of the Chinese Bruce and Scandinavian-English Linda "have met in Brandon Lee, and the result is superb."[68]

Even as press coverage portrayed Bruce in a positive fashion as an Asian American man who was an appropriate sexual partner for a white woman and a loving father of a beautifully biracial son, he insisted on going further by pushing back on the notion that East and West exist in opposition. Instead, he averred that they should be conceived as parts of a harmonious whole. Asked by a reporter from the publication *TV and Movie Screen* how he and

Linda raised Brandon in what was described as a "world in which prejudice is everywhere," Bruce responded, "Brandon is being brought up in the midst of two cultures. . . . Brandon will learn that Oriental culture and Occidental culture are not mutually exclusive, but mutually dependent. Neither would be remarkable if not for the existence of the other."[69] Similarly, when asked about how he would educate his son, Bruce answered, "You see, nothing is superior in every respect; the Occidental education is excellent in some ways, the Oriental in others. You will say, 'This finger is better for one purpose; this finger is better for another.' But the entire hand is better for all purposes."[70]

Throughout these interviews, Bruce sprinkled in references to yin and yang, invoking the Taoist notion of duality and mutual dependency. Rather than seeing Chinese and Western cultures as inimical to each other, he emphasized that differences could be subsumed into wholes greater than the sum of their parts. As he concluded in an interview with a television and radio publication, "I want my son to be a mixed-up kid!"[71]

It was one thing for Bruce Lee to announce his intention to freely intermix Chinese and American cultures to create a synthesis superior to both, but it was quite another for mainstream magazines not only to publish his provocative comments but more important to deem them delightful. Given that Bruce at the time was an unknown actor on a yet-to-be-aired television show, his declaration probably got scant attention. In contrast, Sidney Poitier attracted national attention the following year by starring as a Black doctor engaged to a white woman in the 1967 film *Guess Who's Coming to Dinner?*, a provocative work starring Katharine Hepburn, Spencer Tracy, and a dashing-looking Sidney Poitier that pushed the conversation about racial equality beyond civil rights into the intimate arena of intermarriage.

"CONFUCIUS SAY, 'GREEN HORNET BUZZ NO MORE'"

By early 1967, the writing was on the wall for *The Green Hornet*. ABC decided not to renew the series for a second season due to mediocre ratings and disappointing merchandise sales.[72] In breaking the news to Bruce in March, Dozier once again demonstrated that he could not see Kato except through a racial lens. His note opened with an embarrassingly clichéd passage: "Confucius say," he wrote, "'Green Hornet buzz no more.'"[73] His letter to Van Williams read quite differently: "Well, it looks like our friend The Green Hornet is just going to buzz off into oblivion."[74]

But rather than buzzing no more or into oblivion, *The Green Hornet* buzzed across oceans and borders, starting to air in Japan and several countries in Central America as early as January 1967, a development that set the stage for Bruce's next act. Although Bruce had no inkling of what lay in the future, he graciously thanked Dozier for the opportunity Dozier had given him and outlined his next steps. "Definitely I'm looking forward to work on another new series," he wrote, emphasizing that he would seek "good parts" portraying "proud Chinaman [*sic*]." His response showed that he still held hopes that he could find nondegrading Chinese roles in Hollywood, but in the meantime, he concluded, "I'm concentrating on my Gung Fu and sharpening the tools require[d] in acting."[75]

≈

Bruce viewed kung fu and acting as deeply interrelated activities. Indeed, his approach to acting mirrored his philosophy of kung fu. Just as he sought to pare down his martial art to its bare essence, he sought to simplify his performance as an actor. Mastery of both martial arts and acting demanded sanding and polishing away superfluous movements or techniques to leave only a smooth, unadorned core. During the filming of the television series, he had expressed this relationship in a letter to Dozier. "Simplicity—to express the utmost in the minimum of lines and energy—is the goal of Gung Fu, and acting is not too much different," he wrote the show's producer. "Since the first episode, I've gained actual experience. I've learned to be 'simply human' without unnecessary striving. I *believe* in Kato and am truthfully justifying the physical action economically."[76] Both kung fu and acting, he argued, entailed expressing the truth of being human as simply as possible by paring away all excess. After the show's cancellation, he reflected on his journey as an actor: "I've gained tremendous experience from the Green Hornet and believe I've improved steadily since the first show—that of minimizing and hacking away the unessential."[77]

≈

Even before the official cancellation of *The Green Hornet*, Bruce turned again to teaching, opening his third kung fu school in February 1967, with Dan Inosanto as the assistant instructor. The Los Angeles school, located at 628 College Street, was in Chinatown, just as Bruce's *kwoon* in Seattle had been.[78] At the entrance sat a tombstone inscribed with the words, "In Memory of a Once Fluid Man, Crammed and Distorted by the Classical Mess."[79] The inscription encapsulated Lee's conviction that doggedly reproducing the classical forms of kung fu and karate would produce stiff, wooden fighters unable to adapt and change their styles to meet new challenges. Instead, he created what he called Jeet Kune Do (Way of the Intercepting Fist), a discipline that stipulated "no style" so that it could adapt to any other style.[80]

Bruce's first group of students in Los Angeles "jumped ship" from training with Ed Parker, for whom Inosanto had been teaching, after hearing Bruce's philosophy and seeing what he could do. The school operated in a semiclandestine fashion with no signs or advertising, and each new student had to be vouched for by a current member. Those who were accepted were experienced and serious martial artists who endured punishing training that concentrated on flexibility, endurance, and technique. Every session ended with hard sparring.[81]

In addition to attending regular classes at the studio in Chinatown, students gathered informally at Bruce and Linda's home in Culver City, where Bruce had set up training equipment in the backyard. After warming up on heavy bags and speed bags, they would proceed to the backyard and don gloves, head protectors, chest shields, and shin guards so that they could safely practice landing full blows in all-out sparring. This training technique, the Lee biographer Matthew Polly points out, diverged from the "touch sparring" customarily used in karate, an approach in which fighters stop their strikes when it is clear that they would land.[82] In contrast, Bruce's adoption of full-speed, no-punches-pulled sparring, which resembled nothing more than the way boxers prepare for fights, showed how he was adopting not just fighting movements but also training techniques from every source he encountered.

≈

More evidence of Bruce's combining of worlds could be found in the serious competitive martial artists who turned to him in hopes of leveraging his Hollywood connections. Both Mike Stone and Joe Lewis had already won national karate championships before they met Bruce but began training with him in 1967–68. Stone, who remained too proud to call Bruce his teacher, worked out and discussed aspects of various martial arts with Bruce, though he was careful never to spar. In contrast, Lewis acknowledged that his sessions with Lee were actual lessons and credited them with raising his fighting skill to another level. During his time with Lee, Lewis won eleven consecutive tournaments (adding to the two national championships he already possessed), acknowledging, "What Bruce showed me enabled me to do that."[83]

These high-profile relationships produced mutual benefits. On the one hand, Lee's reputation soared thanks to the willingness of champion fighters to consult or study with him, while on the other, both Stone and Lewis believed that Bruce's Hollywood connections could help them break into show business. Stone and Lewis were two members of a triumvirate of champions who dominated karate tournaments in the mid-1960s, and both achieved limited success as actors. But the third member of this trio went on to make a bigger name for himself as a television and movie star than as a martial artist.

Carlos Ray Norris was born in 1940, the same year as Bruce, to an eighteen-year-old mother and an alcoholic and mostly absent father, and he shuttled between California and Oklahoma throughout an impoverished childhood. Two months after graduating from high school, he enlisted in the Air Force, which eventually stationed him at Osan Air Base in Korea. Norris by now had acquired the nickname "Chuck" and would go on to become a leading star in the martial arts firmament. At Osan, he observed, soldiers could drink, take academic classes, or study martial arts. "I'd never been a drinker, and academic studies weren't my vote," he recalled, "so delving into the martial arts seemed the best way to pass the time."[84]

Norris joined the judo club on base but broke his collarbone in the second week and was unable to train. One day, while wandering through the village of Osan, he saw a sight that changed his life: "As I walked through the village, I suddenly heard fierce yelling and saw people's heads popping up over the top of a knoll, like puppets on a string. Curious, I walked up to see what was going on. Several Koreans, dressed in what appeared to be white pajamas, were jumping up in the air and executing spectacular kicks. I had never before seen such incredible athletic maneuvers, and I could not believe that the human body was capable of such amazing feats. I stood there watching them for more than an hour, fascinated by the sight."[85]

The on-base judo instructor informed Norris that the Koreans were practicing a martial art called *tang soo do* and introduced him to the teacher, who reluctantly agreed to train him in kicking while his shoulder healed. Norris trained hard in *tang soo do* and, once fully recovered, continued studying judo, earning a black belt in the former and a brown belt (second in rank only to a black belt) in the latter by the time his Korean tour of duty ended.[86] Back in the States, some GIs spied him practicing martial arts and asked him to teach them. To obtain approval to start his sports club on the base, Norris had to use the Japanese name "karate" because nobody in the military chain of command would recognize the name of the Korean art. Thus, he began teaching "karate," despite the fact that all of his training had been in *tang soo do* and judo.[87]

After Norris's discharge, he started a karate school but soon realized that he needed good publicity to recruit students. Knowing that winning titles and trophies would earn him the credibility he needed, Norris began entering karate tournaments, eventually winning a number of national championships.[88] He recognized early on that his Korean techniques were effective because they usually took American fighters who were trained in the Japanese style by surprise. As opponents became more familiar with his moves, Norris sought out instruction in additional forms, including different variants of karate, hap-kido, jujitsu, and judo.[89]

Norris's experience shows the crucial role that military deployments in Asia played in the development of martial arts in the United States, especially through their encouragement of intermixing various national and cultural forms. Norris's nemesis in martial arts competitions, Joe Lewis, provides another example of militarism as the motivating force for the development of martial arts in the United States and the intermixing of various forms, for he had learned karate as a US Marine in Okinawa.[90] It was only in the US that Norris, Lewis, Inosanto, and innumerable other veterans wove together diverse strands of martial arts practices from far-flung regions.

≈

In 1967, Norris earned laurels as the Grand Champion of the All-American Karate Championship held in Madison Square Garden in New York City. Although Norris and Lee had met only briefly prior to this event, Lee congratulated Norris. Their conversation about martial arts and philosophies lasted hours, only ending in a sparring match at 4 a.m. in the hallway of their hotel. Back home in Southern California, Lee invited Norris to work out in his backyard, where they trained twice a week for three or four hours at a time. They exchanged techniques, with Lee showing Norris kung fu moves and Norris teaching Lee tae kwon do kicks. "Bruce had never believed in kicking above the waist," Norris recalled four decades later, "but when I demonstrated some high spinning heel kicks, he was intrigued. Within six months he could perform the high kicks as well as I could and added them to his repertoire with tremendous proficiency."[91]

SIFU TO THE STARS

While Bruce engaged in serious martial arts innovation with a cadre of dedicated and talented students, including national champion fighters, he was also developing a second circle of less experienced students: the Hollywood set. After the cancellation of *The Green Hornet* in 1967, financial concerns again loomed large as Bruce was no longer drawing a salary and the lucrative personal appearances for which he had been able to command fees of up to $4,000 dried up.[92] However, the TV role had elevated him from an unknown martial artist to a minor celebrity and, most important, strengthened his Hollywood connections.

With newfound fame, Bruce's fees rocketed from the $22 per month he had once charged for group lessons at the Chinatown studio to $50 or more per hour for private lessons, at a time when the median family income in the United States was approximately $190 per week. He was "shocked," he said, to find people willing to pay his exorbitant asking price, but the Hollywood set did not blink an eye.[93] Others may have been willing to pay even more: rumors alleged that a Greek millionaire had offered him $1,000 per hour but that Bruce had declined.[94]

Hairstylist to the stars Jay Sebring introduced Bruce to celebrities like the actors Steve McQueen and James Coburn, the crooner Vic Damone, and the director Roman Polanski. McQueen was a bona fide matinee idol who had made his name in tough-guy roles in films such as *The Magnificent Seven* (1960), *The Great Escape* (1963), and *Bullitt* (1968). He brought a survivor's mentality to his lessons with Lee, having learned to fight during an upbringing that included confrontations with physically abusive stepfathers, a period of juvenile delinquency, and time in a home for wayward boys. He would punch and kick for hours, to the point of utter exhaustion, and refused to stop even when bruised and bloody.

Because of this dogged determination and toughness, Bruce honored McQueen by calling him a "fighter."[95] McQueen became Bruce's student, mentor, and friend. What McQueen absorbed in martial arts knowledge he returned in advice about building an acting career, and the two men bonded as proud, aggressive outsiders and iconoclasts. Bruce regarded McQueen with both admiration and competitiveness, even spending $6,990 to buy a red Porsche 911S sports car like McQueen's to race down Mulholland Drive.[96] The two may also have shared a lover, Sharon Ferrell, who claims that she had an affair with Bruce during the filming of *Marlowe*. Bruce believed that she abandoned him for McQueen because of the latter's stardom.[97]

McQueen's harsh refusal to lend his celebrity to a film in which Bruce was planning to star infuriated the struggling actor. "Who the hell is he to tell me he won't do this film with me?" he raged. "I'll be a bigger star than Steve McQueen!"[98] In the aftermath of the rejection, Bruce tried unsuccessfully to recruit Paul Newman, McQueen's biggest professional rival, as a student and potential big name for his film project.[99]

≈

James Coburn was another famous pupil of Lee's. Unlike McQueen, who had developed fighting skills to survive, Coburn had learned karate while training for the fight scenes in the 1966 film *Our Man Flint*. An unusually dedicated student, he worked out with Bruce three days a week for five months straight and remained a student until Lee's death. "We'd do a thing Bruce called 'bridging the gap,'" Coburn recalls, a maneuver he understood as knowing how to close the distance to your opponent in order to strike and how to move away without being hit.[100] Developing this perceptiveness demands that practitioners conceive of themselves and their opponents not as separate but as interlinked, in effect making up two parts of a whole.

Although Bruce was teaching Coburn his newly defined art of Jeet Kune Do, bridging the gap is a concept drawn from his kung fu origins, as the name of the second form of Wing Chun, *chom kiu* (taught after the first form, *siu lim tao*), can be translated as "searching for the bridge" or "bridging the gap." It teaches a fighter how to establish contact with and break away from an opponent or how to move into and out of striking range. This was exactly the lesson Coburn learned, despite being taught an art not called kung fu. And although Bruce was happy to teach both actors, he envied Coburn's stardom as much as he had McQueen's, vowing, "One day I will be a bigger star than McQueen and Coburn."[101]

Unlike McQueen and Coburn, Roman Polanski and Dean Martin showed no affinity for the combat arts. Bruce met Polanski through Sebring, who had remained close to his former girlfriend, Sharon Tate, even after she married the director. Tate invited Lee over for a dinner at which he impressed the auteur, who began studying with him regularly.[102] Although Polanski even flew Bruce to Switzerland for private lessons, no amount of training could make a fighter out of him.

Dean Martin proved to be unteachable for different reasons. When Bruce tried to train Martin for the 1968 film *The Wrecking Crew*, he found that Martin was too drunk, "too lazy and too clumsy" to film a convincing fight scene. Bruce took the opportunity to hire his friend and sparring partner, the karate champion Mike Stone, as Martin's stunt double, and he also found small roles for his martial arts colleagues Chuck Norris and Ed Parker.[103]

A story about Vic Damone has become legendary, repeated so often that it appears as a blurb on the back cover of Bruce Thomas's *Bruce Lee: Fighting Spirit*. According to the tale, Bruce met Damone in Las Vegas in the singer's hotel suite, where they got to talking about fighting. When Damone expressed doubt about the power of martial arts, Bruce offered a demonstration: he would go outside the suite, and the singer's two massive bodyguards could try to stop him from entering. He exited, then a loud crash rang out as Bruce kicked the door off its hinges, knocking the first bodyguard to the ground. Before anyone could move, his foot flew upward, knocking a cigarette out of the second bodyguard's mouth.

In some retellings, the singer is Frank Sinatra instead of Damone, but in fact, as the masterful debunking by the journalist and Bruce Lee biographer Matthew Polly shows, the entire story seems to be an exaggeration that grew with each telling and retelling.[104] The apocryphal story of their meeting notwithstanding, Damone in fact did study with Bruce in Los Angeles and Las Vegas.

A "CHINAMAN'S CHANCE" IN HOLLYWOOD

Although Bruce could have earned a lucrative living as a martial arts teacher, he continued to pursue his dream of stardom in a Hollywood that could not conceive of an Asian American leading man. He became one more struggling actor, although he was more fortunate than most in that he had friends and students who could advocate for him. Racial and gender strictures limited him to playing minor characters on television and in film, yet even these small roles hinted at the changing place of Asian Americans within the United States.

As the cultural historian Christina Klein argues in *Cold War Orientalism: Asia in the Middlebrow Imagination, 1945–1961*, depictions of Asian Americans in American popular culture reflected the evolving world order of the Cold War. Striving for global dominance during the 1950s and 1960s, the United States vied with China and the Soviet Union for the allegiance of Third World nations in Africa, Latin America, and Asia. Communist nations pointed out to a world-wide audience of Black, brown, and yellow people that continuing racism in the United States proved that the US was unworthy of their admiration.

In response, the US argued that historical discrimination was slowly giving way to greater equality. Popular cultural forms like musicals, films, and television reconfigured Asian Americans from perpetual foreigners who could not be assimilated to an ethnic minority on the road toward acceptance and, in doing so, proclaimed that the US was on its way to building a pluralistic society. Yet despite the progress made in erasing the stain of the Yellow Peril, Asian Americans could not completely break free of Orientalist depictions that continually marked Asians as racial others. Bruce Lee's struggles in Hollywood reflected the in-between status of Asian Americans as both potentially able to assimilate on the one hand and unalterably Oriental on the other.

IRONSIDE

Bruce's 1967 guest appearance in an episode of the first season of the long-running and critically acclaimed television series *Ironside* portrays him as both belonging in the United States and remaining foreign to it. In an episode titled "Tagged for Murder," he plays Leon Soo, the US-born son of a Chinese immigrant from Canton to Seattle. Bruce's character manages to be both incongruous and internally consistent. Soo is called "a karate instructor in Chinatown," and the San Francisco phone book lists "Karate Instruction by Leon Soo. Aikido–Judo." The incongruity lies in a Chinese American offering instruction in the Japanese martial arts of karate, aikido, and judo in Chinatown, which shows the inability of the show's writers to differentiate between the ethnic origins of various forms of martial arts. However, Bruce gives a performance that hews faithfully to the script, showing off movements based in karate rather than kung fu.

The address of Soo's studio at 237 Grand Avenue gestures toward the changing place of Asian Americans in the racial order of the United States. Although no "Grand Avenue" exists in San Francisco's Chinatown, Grant Avenue is the ethnic enclave's most renowned boulevard, celebrated in Rodgers and Hammerstein's hit musical *Flower Drum Song*, which opened on Broadway in 1958, running for a year and a half, and was adapted in 1961 as a film starring Nancy Kwan and James Shigeta. Themes of generational conflict and cultural belonging suffuse the story, with characters torn between the old-world ways of their parents and their own desires for independence. As Klein argues, the musical depicts Asian Americans as having a "dual identity" of perpetual foreigners and ethnic American immigrants, occupying a middle ground within which they oscillate between continuing to be marked as others and being accepted as members of the American nation.[105]

The number "Chop Suey," which celebrates one character's progress toward attaining US citizenship, illustrates this duality. The spoken introduction to the song identifies chop suey as "the Chinese dish the Americans invented," which has "everything" in it, "all mixed up." This description is full of hybridity—a Chinese dish invented by Americans that combines diverse ingredients. The choreography reflects this hodgepodge notion, careening wildly through the cha-cha (coincidentally the dance form in which Bruce won a championship in Hong Kong), square dancing, ballroom dancing, the Charleston, and modern jazz dancing. An all–Asian American troupe performing these Western forms suggests that East and West are not antithetical but compatible. However, the number ends with what can best be called a "ching chong" musical motif that concludes with a gong hit and the dancers bowing to each other with palms pressed together—a culmination that returns the Asian Americans to their essential status as Orientals.

Similarly, the signature song "Grant Avenue" depicts a parade down Chinatown's most famous street to position Asian Americans as both accepted in the US and racial others. Like "Chop Suey," it begins with a gong hit, Chinese costumes, and lyrics describing Grant Avenue in bifurcating terms as a "western street with eastern manners." However, it goes on to argue instead that Chinatown can actually exist not apart from but as a part of the United States. The street where you can eat shark-fin soup and feel like "you're in Hong Kong" is "Grant Avenue, San Francisco, California, USA." The rousing chorus concludes, "You know you can't have a new way of living / Till you're living all the way / On Grant Avenue. Where's that? / San Francisco, That's where's that! / California USA."

The "new way of living" being created on Grant Avenue entails Chinese ethnicity that is squarely a part of the American way of life. The choreography includes running slides, high kicks, and jazzy movements, interrupted only briefly by interludes featuring the "ching chong" musical phrase during which the dancers widen their eyes using two fingers. The act of manually widening their eyes is a fascinating move that reverses a racist gesture known to every Asian American child who has ever been mocked by kids using their fingers to make "Chinese" eye slits. Widening the eyes alludes to erasing Asian racial difference in accordance with the US narrative of an increasingly plural society; yet it simultaneously highlights the facial feature that has been most widely used to discriminate against Asians in the US.

The music and choreography of "Grant Avenue" thus vacillate between portraying Asian Americans as thoroughly American and permanent Orientals. Similarly, the script of the television episode of *Ironside* wavers between portraying Bruce's character, Soo, as on the one hand an American and on the other a foreigner. On the one hand, his identity as an American is buttressed by the fact that he is the son of a US Army veteran, while on the other, he appears only as a martial arts teacher dressed in Asian clothing.

AN UNSAVORY FOOT-SWINGER

Sterling Silliphant facilitated Bruce Lee's US debut on the big screen in *Marlowe* (1969), an adaptation of a Raymond Chandler novel starring James Garner as the detective Philip Marlowe. Bruce appeared as the small-time hood and tough guy Winston Wong in a part written expressly for him by his student. The studio, Metro-Goldwyn-Mayer, and the martial arts press symbiotically promoted Bruce as a fusion of actor and martial artist. MGM courted martial arts audiences with a full-page advertisement in *Black Belt* magazine, which blared, "Two people have just been killed. . . . A karateman (Bruce Lee) has just wrecked your office. Welcome to Marlowe Country!"[106]

Conversely, *Black Belt* paid attention to showbiz because it understood the important role that films and television played in popularizing the martial arts. As one karate promoter observed, crowds at tournaments grew when Bruce appeared on *The Green Hornet* and diminished once it stopped airing.[107] *Black Belt* faithfully traced Bruce's progress in the movies from casting to filming through debut: a short item in December 1968 announced that he would appear in a film based on a Chandler novel; an article in 1969 displayed pictures of Bruce performing a high kick on the set as well as shots of him training Dean Martin, Sharon Tate, and Nancy Kwan on *The Wrecking Crew*; and after *Marlowe* was released, the magazine crowed, "Bruce Lee of Green Hornet fame as Kato portrays a 'foot-swinging, unsavory character.'"[108]

Bruce plays Winslow Wong as stylish '60s hipster in dark glasses, turtleneck sweater, and boxy, wide-lapel suit. Wong and Marlowe exchange witty banter, with Wong dropping lines like "The word is out that you're a cool cat" in his debonair Hong Kong accent. In Bruce's first scene, Wong tries to intimidate Marlowe into dropping an investigation by destroying his office. The rampage culminates with a spectacular high kick that shatters a ceiling lamp hanging eight feet above the floor. Bruce told friends how proud he was to pull off the high kick and that the lamp was constructed of stunt glass made of sugar to prevent injury from shards.[109]

The second scene finds Wong chasing Marlowe with a series of kicks onto a ledge on a balcony of a high-rise building. "You're light on your feet, Winslow," Marlowe taunts. "Are you just a little gay?" When the enraged Wong leaps at Marlowe, he sidesteps and Wong flies by screaming into the abyss.

≈

Lee's small role in *Marlowe* plays into long-standing racialized and gendered imagery of Asian men yet also opens space for new imaginations. Marlowe's dig plays into a long tradition of Asian and Asian American men being portrayed as emasculated in Western culture. As the literary scholar David Eng argues, Asian American men undergo a process called "racial castration," which undermines their status as men by rendering them as feminine or gay.[110] Wong's anger can thus be seen as a reaction against Marlowe's racist and homophobic slur, which impugns the possibility of proper Asian manhood by simultaneously devaluing gay masculinity.

Apart from the absurdity of Bruce's character being baited into jumping off a high building, the part of Wong must have pleased Bruce immensely as it enabled the undeniable clothes horse to wear slick suits and deliver lines in the hippest of slang. These may have been just the kind of character improvements he had in mind when he had proposed that Dozier "add more 'coolness' and 'subtleness' to the character of Charlie Chan" and "sizzles" to Kato. Winslow Wong managed to be both cool and sizzling.

BLONDIE

Unlike Bruce's performance in *Marlowe*, his guest role on the short-lived television series *Blondie* (1968–69) has been lost to posterity, with no known footage remaining in existence.[111] Episode 13, "Pick on Someone Your Own Size," features Bruce as Yoto, a karate instructor engaged by Dagwood to help him deal with a bully. Although the episode itself may be forgotten, Bruce left a memorable impression on the actor Will Hutchins, who starred as

Dagwood. Hutchins recalls that the obscure Asian actor entertained an audience of cast and crew members during breaks by showing off various martial arts moves and tricks.

In one instance, Bruce placed a penny on Hutchins's outstretched palm held waist high, raised his own right hand above his head, and told Hutchins that he would grab the penny before Hutchins could react. Bruce's hand whooshed down, but Hutchins could still feel the coin in his clenched fist and felt sorry for having embarrassed Bruce in front of a crowd. To his amazement, when he opened his hand, he discovered that Bruce had left a dime in place of the penny.

Lee's presence and energy left such a deep impression that Hutchins later compared him to another superstar who died prematurely. "Of all the people I've worked with in 'the showbiz,' Elvis Presley is number one and Bruce Lee is a close second. . . . Those guys worked on a different consciousness and elevation than the rest of us." The veteran character actor whose career spanned decades concluded, "Of all the actors I ever met, he was the most well-balanced in body, mind and soul."[112]

HERE COME THE BRIDES

Bruce gave his only non-martial-arts television performance in an episode of the short-lived 1969 series *Here Come the Brides*, in a story that simultaneously relies on and undermines the Orientalist trope of Chinese and American incompatibility. He plays Lin Soong, a Chinese migrant to frontier-era Seattle who has spent most of his life in the United States and has grown to admire US culture. The episode begins with Lin refusing to marry Toy, a woman to whom he has been unwillingly betrothed for an arranged marriage. Chi Pei, the leader of the local tong (known as "the Society"), threatens Lin with violence for breaking the agreement. "I just want to be left alone to live like an American," Lin pleads, to which Chi replies, "But you are Chinese; therefore, you must respect your people's traditions."

The tong boss's scripted response reinforces the notion that an immigrant from China would remain immutably Chinese regardless of his desire to fit into US society. Similarly, Lin's rejoinder—"You and this entire Society are useless in this country, Chi Pei. You are archaic."—furthers the notion that the backward East is incompatible with the modern West. These are clear expressions of the standard Orientalist East versus West framework, even if mouthed onscreen by Asian American actors.

In contrast to Lin and Chi's classically Orientalist formulations, it is the white characters who offer a more liberal perspective. After having observed Toy from afar, Lin decides that he had made a mistake by rejecting her. The white Bolt brothers, one of whom had rescued Toy and hence (according to the show's logic) owns her, hatch a scheme for Lin to save Toy's life and thereby claim her as his own. Lin's objection that "in China, this would be considered deceitful" meets with the Bolt's reassurance, "Well, you're in America now." This exchange argues that Lin can and should embrace modern US cultural norms and practices. To underscore the point, after Lin rescues Toy from drowning and takes her as his bride, he praises her by saying, "You look very American."[113]

Bruce's only straightforward acting role revealed Hollywood's racial and gender constraints. The episode begins with an Orientalist framing of a despotic East that casts women as property versus an enlightened West in which individuals are free to make their own romantic choices. But it questions the rigidity of the barrier between the two by suggesting that Lin and Toy could eventually shed the strictures of Chinese "tradition" to become American. This was a progressive message, especially in comparison with contemporaneous representations of Chinese on television, such as Hop Sing on *Bonanza*, whose fish-out-of-water routine played chiefly as comic relief. However, white men remain the active agents and magnanimous heroes who direct the Chinese man's action; perhaps most strikingly, the Chinese woman continues to be a passive subject whose ownership simply passes from one man to the next.

INTERLUDE

By 1968, Bruce was earning money from both martial arts—including private lessons to celebrities and serious fighters and revenues from the Los Angeles Chinatown branch of his Jun Fan Gung Fu Institute—and show business from wages as an actor and stunt coordinator, and residuals from *The Green Hornet*. Enjoying more income than ever before, Bruce and Linda purchased a three-bedroom ranch-style house in the exclusive enclave of Bel Air in the hills overlooking Los Angeles for $47,000, far more than they initially thought they could afford. The new home provided a perfect setting for Bruce, Linda, and Brandon to welcome the fourth member of their family. Shannon Lee was born on April 19, 1969, weighing six pounds, six ounces, and measuring nineteen inches long. The adoring father doted endlessly on his new daughter.[114] In four years in Los Angeles, Bruce had achieved a level of personal and professional success that would have satisfied many people, but he still hungered for much more.

When Bruce visited Hong Kong in early 1970, he was stunned by crowds of fans, television cameras, and newspaper reporters besieging him at every turn. He had returned briefly with five-year-old Brandon to help his mother obtain a visa to live in the US, as four of her five children now resided on the West Coast. Unbeknownst to Bruce, his mother had alerted the press that her son was coming home, a fact that would have been of little interest to the public except for one development: *The Green Hornet* had become a hit on Hong Kong television, but with a significant twist. The erstwhile sidekick had become the undeniable star of what locals called "The Kato Show."

Bruce's star shone so brightly in Hong Kong in part because he had made it in Hollywood. He reflected, "To most people [in Hong Kong], including the actors and actresses, Hollywood is like a magic kingdom. It's beyond everyone's reach and when I made it, they thought I'd accomplished an incredible feat."[115] That feat earned Bruce a guest appearance on the popular TV talk show *Enjoy Yourself Tonight*, which he filled with easy banter with the "Johnny

Carson" of Hong Kong, performing two-finger push-ups, breaking wooden boards and having little Brandon break some too, and kicking a man so hard he flew off the stage.

Beyond amazement at the kung fu demonstration, audiences took away an impression of a new kind of celebrity, which the movie director Ang Lee recalled years later as exhibiting "a very straight-forward, very Westernized, very gung-ho, can-do spirit."[116] Bruce's newfound stardom in Hong Kong was highly mediated by his ocean-spanning journeys, having been built on his relative success in Hollywood and the Western inflections he had picked up there, providing yet more evidence of the powerful transpacific forces influencing his journey.

≈

Despite all the affirming attention Bruce received in Hong Kong, he returned to his home in Los Angeles to suffer a devastating setback. In late summer of 1970, he was performing "good mornings," one of his usual exercises and one that entailed holding 125 pounds on his shoulders while bending forward, when he felt a twinge in his back. Within days, he could barely move. His physician diagnosed the problem as damage to his fourth sacral nerve, an injury so severe that doctors doubted he would ever practice martial arts again.

Being bedridden for three months, riddled with pain and unable to earn any money, threw Bruce into emotional despair and "a black cloud of depression settled over him," as Linda recalled.[117] Three more months passed with Bruce only able to move gingerly about the house. Over his objections, Linda went out and found an office job to cover expenses, a fact that the ever-proud Bruce hid from friends and acquaintances. During his convalescence, he studied diligently, reading numerous books on martial arts and recording notes and his own thoughts in eight notebooks that Linda later edited and published as *The Tao of Jeet Kune Do* after his death. A note to himself on a business card—"Walk On!"—served as inspiration and a constant reminder to persevere. And persevere he did. After six agonizing months, he began to start working out and returned to teaching. His defiant willpower and ironclad resolve enabled him to eventually regain the ability to do everything he had done before and more.[118] However, the unstoppable force of his determination to break through in show business would collide with a formidable obstacle: the immovable object of Hollywood racism.

PROJECTING FORWARD

Bruce could not defy the stereotypes that relegated him to small onscreen roles and work as a fight and stunt coordinator, so he counterattacked by attempting to create his own star vehicle. In January 1969, he and Sterling Silliphant invited James Coburn to direct, coproduce, and star in a movie that would be coproduced by Silliphant and choreographed by Lee. Bruce hoped that playing multiple costarring roles in the film would elevate his profile. Finding a writer for the project was difficult, as the team dismissed two unsuccessful scriptwriters before Silliphant himself took over. For months, the three men met from four to six every Monday, Wednesday, and Friday evening to write a narrative in which the protagonist Cord (Coburn) embarks on a globe-spanning quest for the true meaning of martial arts.[119]

The result was a trippy, gruesomely violent, and sexually explicit script entitled *The Silent Flute* that was too extreme and bizarre to be released by any mainstream US studio. Nevertheless, Warner Bros. agreed to back the film but with one major proviso: the movie had to be shot in India with rupees embargoed within that country. For three weeks in early 1971, the trio crisscrossed the Subcontinent, scouting locations from the metropolis of New Delhi to the northern desert near Pakistan to Chennai in the south and the beaches of Goa in the west. None of the locations proved suitable, nor could the filmmakers find local martial artists to fill the roles of extras. Coburn abandoned the project, and without his star power, the film withered away, leaving Bruce feeling angry and betrayed.[120]

But even the dashed dream of *The Silent Flute* illustrates the complex, interconnected world in which Bruce Lee emerged. Warner Bros. earned the rupees with which it intended to fund Bruce's project by releasing its films in India but could not transfer the money to the United States. This barrier limited the scope of the film, the making of which Bruce and his cohorts had envisioned as a worldwide jaunt to be shot in Thailand, Japan, and Morocco, a journey involving six different languages. Although barriers to travel, trade, and monetary exchange had been falling for centuries, some remained standing in 1971.

≈

Bruce also developed the idea for a television show called *The Warrior*, which would follow the itinerant adventures of a Shaolin monk wandering across the US West. Warner Bros. rejected Lee's bid to play the protagonist in what became the *Kung Fu* series (1972–75), on the grounds that he was "too Chinese" to carry the show.[121] Warner Bros. executive Fred Weintraub tells an alternative version of the story, however. According to Weintraub, two writers having nothing to do with Bruce pitched a treatment for a film about a Shaolin monk righting wrongs across the Old West with violent hands and feet but a pacifist spirit. Bruce tried out for the part, but the casting agents who met with him concluded that "the time wasn't right for an international star." Weintraub acknowledges that Bruce was short and had an accent but concludes bluntly, "In the history of Hollywood there had never been an Asian hero."[122]

Regardless of whether Bruce or two other writers developed the idea for the show, the fact remains that racial discrimination blocked him from starring in it. Instead, David Carradine, a white actor who had never studied martial arts, scored the starring role of the nomadic biracial martial artist Kwai Chang Caine over Bruce Lee, a martial arts expert with both Chinese and European ancestry who had spent his life wandering the Pacific.

Bruce understood his struggles in the larger context of white supremacy in Hollywood (and of course everywhere else), not just over Asians Americans but also over Native Americans and African Americans. He longed for roles that would let him express himself not as an Asian stereotype but as a complete person, vowing, "I have to be a real human being." And, he added, "It's about time we had an Oriental hero."[123]

Ironically, to become an "Oriental hero" in the US movie firmament, Bruce Lee had to leave Hollywood and return to Hong Kong.

6

HONG KONG TRILOGY

Raymond Chow, the man who would soon transform Bruce Lee into an international superstar, was in 1970 seeking new ways to help his new production company, Golden Harvest, make a name for itself. He was trying to lift the company out of the shadow of Shaw Brothers studio, an entertainment giant that for decades had dominated the cinema industry of not only Hong Kong but most of Asia.

In 1925, the Shaw family had begun building what would become an Asian empire when they founded the Unique Film Productions company in Shanghai. As the University of Illinois film historian Poshek Fu argues, the transnational growth of the Shaw companies throughout the twentieth century took advantage of flows of capital, technology, skilled labor, and know-how across the Chinese diaspora in Asia, Europe, and the United States.[1]

By the 1950s, audiences throughout Southeast Asia were devouring films shot and produced in Shaw studios in more than 130 Shaw-owned theaters, along with visiting Shaw theme parks and dance halls. Run Run Shaw, the youngest brother in the family, moved from Shanghai to Hong Kong in 1957 and revolutionized filmmaking in the colony by embracing new technologies such as widescreen images and color photography and instituting a vertically integrated production and distribution model.

Run Run personally made budget decisions and dictated creative directions, always with an eye toward economy and efficiency. Movietown, the expansive Shaw Brothers complex in Hong Kong's Clear Water Bay, grew to become the largest and best-equipped studio in the Sinophone cinema industry, with fifteen stages and cutting-edge technology imported from Europe and the United States.

In addition to modernizing the studio's equipment, Run Run Shaw instituted a brutally efficient production system that resembled nothing more than a factory assembly line staffed by rigidly controlled laborers. Company training programs cranked out actors and technicians to create the movies. Employees, including all but the biggest stars and directors, signed exclusive contracts for measly wages, lived in cloistered dormitories on the Movietown campus, and submitted to an exacting code of conduct that governed even romantic activities. In contrast, by the 1960s, Hollywood actors and directors were no longer bound to studios by long contracts but instead signed on to individual films as free agents.

Shaw Brothers churned out movies at an astonishing rate driven by a mass-production process that prioritized speed, efficiency, and cost controls. At its peak, the studio was working on a dozen films at a time, starting a new one every nine days and completing a film in an average of forty days. Along with its mass-produced works, the studio also produced a limited number of prestige films for international distribution, works for which it authorized more generous budgets and relaxed timelines. As a point of comparison, in 1967 Warner Bros. released eighteen films, including *Cool Hand Luke* and *Bonnie and Clyde*.

Japanese imports played a vital role in the rise of the Shaw Brothers empire. To elevate the quality of its films, the studio recruited Japanese creative and technical talent, including artists such as directors, cinematographers, and musicians, along with technical workers such as sound recording and special effects specialists. The Japanese cinematographer Tadashi Nishimoto, for example, introduced color filming to Shaw Brothers in 1957 and shot more than three dozen films in Hong Kong (though he was credited under a Chinese pseudonym). The studio also borrowed thematic content from Japanese cinema. Samurai films inspired and influenced the new genre of swordplay period pieces like King Hu's *Come Drink with Me* (1966) and Chang Cheh's *One-Armed Swordsman* (1967).[2]

≈

Raymond Chow, the executive who enabled Bruce's ascent to become a worldwide icon, had been born in Hong Kong in 1927, earned a degree in journalism in Shanghai, and after the Communist revolution returned to Hong Kong, where he worked as a journalist for various news organizations, including Voice of America. He began his film career at Shaw Brothers as a publicist and rose through the ranks to become head of production.

In 1970, however, chafing at the venerable studio's rigid, factory-like creative process, Chow and a fellow Shaw Brothers executive, Leonard Ho, broke away to form a new company, which they named Golden Harvest. Using a more flexible corporate structure, they contracted with independent producers and actors to whom they offered considerable artistic license.[3] Nonetheless, they needed new stars to challenge the Shaw Brothers behemoth.

Chow took notice when Bruce Lee blew into Hong Kong in the spring of 1970 with the force of a hurricane. Although Bruce was there just to visit his family, the massive media attention he received and the adoring crowds that gathered whenever he went out in public portended a megastar in the making. But Bruce concluded his Hong Kong visit and was back home in Los Angeles before Chow could make contact.

When the two finally spoke by telephone, Chow tried to recruit Bruce to make a film with Golden Harvest, but Bruce stuck by his plan to conquer Hollywood. Over the next year, however, as his dream faded with the collapse of *The Silent Flute* and the snub of *Kung Fu*, he picked up the phone again.

Chow remained interested in working with Bruce and offered him a contract. But Bruce wanted to keep his options open before signing with the upstart studio and reached out to Shaw Brothers kingpin Run Run Shaw through his childhood acting buddy Unicorn Chan, demanding $10,000 per movie (far above Shaw Brothers' normal rates) along with control over scripts and fight choreography. Shaw countered with an offer variously reported as $2,000 or $5,000 per film or perhaps $1,500 a month for six years or $200 per week—the standard rate for actors contracted to Shaw Brothers.

According to Bruce's friend Mito Uyehara, publisher of *Black Belt* magazine, Bruce read a newspaper article claiming that Run Run Shaw was offering him $2,000 per film, more than any Hong Kong star had ever earned. Bruce was so amused by the indirect approach that he boldly called the paper and said that he "refused to work for such a small sum." Regardless of the size of the offer, Shaw made no concessions when it came to control of scripts or choreography. Meanwhile, Chow sent a representative to close the deal. Gladys Hwa, the wife of Golden Harvest director Lo Wei, offered Bruce a two-film deal worth a total of $15,000, according to Linda Lee, though other sources quote widely divergent figures.[4] Whatever the size of the offer, Bruce signed the contract on June 28, 1971. Raymond Chow had his coveted star.

LONGSTREET

After signing with Golden Harvest but before leaving California, Bruce completed his work in the 1971 television series *Longstreet*. His onetime student Sterling Silliphant had created the show with Bruce in mind and incorporated so many of his teachings that the scripts can be taken as a virtual transcription of the Bruce Lee philosophy of fighting. His part as the thinly veiled persona, the Chinese antiques dealer and martial artist Li Tsung, was his most extensive and satisfying television role.

The pilot episode, titled "Way of the Intercepting Fist," a translation of Jeet Kune Do, introduces the eponymous Mike Longstreet (James Franciscus), a blind insurance investigator digging into corruption among longshoremen on the New Orleans waterfront. Li encounters Longstreet as he comes across three thugs savagely beating the blind man in a dark alley. After Li chases off the assailants, Longstreet begs Li to teach him how to defend himself, a request that sets off the inevitable narrative of training, tension between student and teacher, enlightenment, and finally triumph over the villain. Li starts off by denying that he can educate Longstreet, using a line reminiscent of Bruce's college essays on self-actualization: "I cannot teach you, only help you to explore yourself, nothing more." Rather than serving as an instructor, Li promises simply to be a guide on Longstreet's journey of self-discovery.

In the beginning Longstreet moves clumsily, unsure of himself and overthinking every move. When he finally delivers a powerful kick, Li asks how it felt. Longstreet's reply—"Like I didn't kick, *it* kicked"—pleases Li and echoes Bruce's emphasis in his writings that a martial artist should not try to act consciously in combat but rather flow within it. When Longstreet's assistant asks how the training is going, Li replies, "His warehouse having burned down, nothing obscures his view of the bright moon," making this the first (but certainly not the last) time Lee evoked the moon metaphor onscreen. The enigmatic statement suggests that since Longstreet's preconceptions about how to fight have been eliminated (like a warehouse destroyed by fire), he can now gaze unimpeded toward the truth, symbolized by the moon.

At one point, Li refuses to teach Longstreet anymore because the insurance investigator only wants to learn to fight. After some consideration, Longstreet visits Li at his antiques shop to beg for another shot. "It's more than just learning to defend myself," Longstreet says. "There were a couple of times when you were teaching me that I felt that my body and my head really were together. It's funny that out of a martial art, out of combat, that I feel something peaceful, something without hostility, almost as though if I knew Jeet Kune Do, it would be enough simply to know it and, by knowing it, never having to use it." The soliloquy expresses the idea that martial arts should be a practice that unites mind and body rather than a means toward fighting and that achieving that unity is an end in itself. And it is this idea that convinces Li to resume training Longstreet. When Li does so, he escorts Longstreet on a condensed version of Lee's prolonged martial arts journey, beginning with the basic Wing Chun exercise of *chi sao* and progressing to the Jeet Kune

Do–inspired notion of doing anything and everything possible to survive, including biting and even gouging out an opponent's eyes when necessary.

Finally, Li delivers his own concluding soliloquy, which in various forms would become Bruce Lee's most famous statement describing his approach to fighting and life itself: "Empty your mind. Be formless, shapeless, like water. Now you put water into a cup, it becomes the cup. Put it into a teapot, it becomes the teapot. Now water can flow or creep or drip or crash. Be water, my friend." The emphasis on the adaptability of water, which deferentially accepts the shape of its surroundings yet can "crash" so powerfully that it carves valleys out of rocks and grinds stone cliffs into sand, underlay Bruce's entire martial arts philosophy from Wing Chun to Jeet Kune Do. The power of water to both comply and resist, cede and conquer, also symbolized Lee's approach to the limitations and stereotypes of Asians and Asian Americans that he encountered in Hollywood, which in brilliant fashion he alternately flowed around and demolished.

The climactic fight scene—it is not necessary to understand the plot to know that the episode must end with a fight—starts with Longstreet taking a beating from the sneering foreman of the longshoremen. Just as things look bleakest for the blind, bruised, and battered hero, Longstreet cocks his ear to hear Li intone in an Obi-Wan Kenobi–like voice-over, "You must free your ambitious mind," a directive that prompts Longstreet's training to overtake his thinking. Longstreet finishes off the villain with a vicious elbow drop to the back as Li's voice echoes in his head: "Empty your mind. Be formless, shapeless, like water." To an onlooker who asks how he learned to fight, the victorious Longstreet replies cryptically, "Drinking tea from an empty cup."

≈

For Bruce Lee, the episode "Way of the Intercepting Fist" pointed both backward and forward. Despite acknowledging that he performed "impressively enough to justify a series of his own," the *New York Times* once again relegated Bruce Lee to the role of sidekick, calling him "a Robin for Longstreet's Batman." The paper of record went on to further describe Bruce in purely racial terms using Orientalist language to declare that "the Chinaman . . . lends a deft touch of exotica."[5]

The theme of relying on touch rather than sight also represented a link to Bruce's past, for as a Wing Chun student, he had practiced *chi sao* with his eyes covered, and as a brash young immigrant, he had once challenged rivals to fight him blindfolded. It also derived from his longtime fascination with samurai movies, for he admired Zatoichi, the blind swordsman hero of several Japanese films from the 1960s, and had mentioned to Silliphant that he dreamed of starring in a movie as a blind fighter.[6] *Longstreet*'s premise thus derived from the dreams of a Chinese martial artist inspired by Japanese films and interpreted by a white American writer. This was a quintessential example of how transpacific currents were ever more powerfully shaping cultural products of the mid-twentieth century.

While the origin of the episode derived from Bruce's past, it also foreshadowed an emblem that would become almost as closely associated with him as the phrase "Be water." In the training sessions with Longstreet, Bruce wore a red tracksuit with white racing stripes that two years later would morph into the yellow tracksuit with black racing stripes featured in *Game of Death*. The yellow tracksuit became so iconic that Quentin Tarantino adapted it to outfit Uma Thurman in his 2003 martial arts homage *Kill Bill: Volume 1*.

A GLOBAL HONG KONG TRILOGY

Bruce Lee's next act was to star in three Hong Kong films produced or coproduced by Raymond Chow and Golden Harvest. In doing so, he would alter the course of Hong Kong filmmaking by introducing a violent and visually compelling style of cinematic hand-to-hand combat and, over time, melding the aesthetics of Hong Kong and Hollywood.

Although Bruce's films are commonly understood to be lightweight movies whose appeal lies in the spectacular physicality of their fight scenes, collectively they meditate on the transpacific themes that suffused the actor's life: migration, identity, and nationality. Unpacking these films—including the characters they introduced and the styles of fighting they employed—reveals that they tackled weighty topics via the all-too-easily-dismissed medium of martial arts films. Thematically, they address how people who migrate far from home develop new senses of self and identity, argue against fixed notions of nationality, and show the power of intermixing cultures.

Two key ideas underpin Bruce's Hong Kong trilogy: diaspora and hybridity. Diaspora—derived from the same Greek root as "disperse"—refers to the scattering of a people away from their traditional homelands. Despite living in far-flung locations, the members of a diaspora retain some sense of commonality and identity. At the same time, however, people are inevitably influenced by the cultures they encounter and adapt to their new circumstances by melding their old practices with the ones surrounding them. Hybridity—or the state of being hybrid—is a powerful source of innovation that leads to the creation of novel cultural practices. Bruce's three Hong Kong films showcase diaspora and hybridity, in part by visually depicting how martial arts fighters move their bodies.

≈

Bruce's first two movies, *The Big Boss* and *Fist of Fury*, were written and directed by Lo Wei, a prolific actor, director, and producer who had been making films in Hong Kong since 1948 for the two big studios, Motion Picture and General Investment (MP&GI) and Shaw Brothers. Lo defected from Shaw Brothers in 1970 and began working with Bruce—uneasily, as it would turn out—in what was just his second Golden Harvest film.[7]

How fair is it to call these films "Bruce Lee movies" if someone else wrote and directed them? Bruce exuded such a strong star quality, composed of generous portions of charisma and unique style, that he branded everything he appeared in as his own. The film scholar Eric Pellerin labels him a "starteur," combining the word "star" with "auteur," the term used to describe directors who exert total creative control to enact their personal cinematic vision. Even before the release of Bruce's initial martial arts film, he was a major celebrity in Hong Kong because of the popularity of *The Green Hornet* (a.k.a. "The

Kato Show") along with articles in newspapers and appearances on Hong Kong television. As a "starteur," Bruce bent the films he starred in to express his individuality and unique point of view through his prodigious celebrity, tenacity, and sheer force of will.[8]

Bruce flew to Hong Kong after completing the *Longstreet* episode and, because Raymond Chow feared that someone might steal his newfound prize and had ordered him not to set foot outside the airport, proceeded directly to Thailand. From Bangkok, Bruce traveled to the small town of Pak Chong, where he arrived on July 13, 1971, and greeted his new boss in inimitable Bruce Lee form. "You just wait," he assured Chow. "I'm going to be the biggest Chinese star in the world." Despite his visions of personal glory, Bruce hated Pak Chong. In letters home to Linda, he complained about mosquitoes and cockroaches, the scarcity of meat, two directors he viewed as incompetent, slicing his right hand on a broken glass, and spraining his ankle while performing a stunt.[9] He lost ten pounds due to the stifling humidity and the limited diet of rice and vegetables. But the environment was not his biggest worry. Although a farce like *The Green Hornet* may have been less than a masterpiece, Bruce's years in Hollywood had accustomed him to an aesthetic that differed from that typical of Chinese filmmaking. He judged the script for *The Big Boss* to be "overplayed" rather than nuanced and in response helped to rewrite portions of it.[10]

One of the primary ways that Bruce remade Hong Kong martial arts films was by instilling a direct and even brutal style of cinematic hand-to-hand combat. The director initially slated to helm the film intended that Bruce would perform the style of film fighting that predominated at the time: elaborately choreographed dance-like routines staged in the style of martial Cantonese opera. Bruce, however, demanded the realism of short, decisive fights based on street combat. After all, this was supposed to be a gory film about physical mayhem; after Bruce's salary, the second-largest budget item was for fake blood.

With the star and director intractably at odds over the aesthetics of fighting, Chow intervened by firing the director and replacing him with the veteran

Lo Wei, who decided to reshoot everything. This did not solve the problem, however, as Bruce quarreled repeatedly with Lo, reflecting an animosity that he would feel for the rest of his life.[11]

≈

The Big Boss, which opened in Hong Kong in 1971 and in 1973 was released in the United States as *Fists of Fury*, dwells on themes of movement and identity, asking what binds people together across distance and migration. In the film, Bruce plays Cheng Chao-An, a country bumpkin from the Chinese countryside who travels to Thailand to find work. This journey reflects a centuries-long pattern of outmigration from southern China, a phenomenon that has created communities of ethnic Chinese dispersed throughout Southeast Asia. Cheng obtains a job in an ice-making factory that turns out to be a drug-smuggling operation run by the titular Big Boss. Although he promised his mother before leaving home that he would stay out of trouble and not get into fights, circumstances eventually force his hands (and feet), and he ends up kicking all kinds of ass. The film explores such sweeping themes as loyalty, ambition, romance, and revenge, but most important, it depicts the creation and endurance of a diasporic community.

The film opens by showing Cheng arriving on a ferryboat and quickly being apprised of the dangers of this new land. "Life here is very different from back home," warns the uncle who greets him at the dock, "so be careful." The warning proves prophetic, for when the pair stop at a roadside stand for shaved ice treats, four local thugs accost both the pretty female proprietor (played by Nora Miao, who would go on to portray Bruce's love interest in his next two films) and a little boy selling rice cakes. Reminding Cheng that he has promised not to fight, the uncle pulls out a jade pendant from under Cheng's shirt. Throughout the film, this locket symbolizes the promise of pacifism that Cheng made to his mother.

Fortunately, another man arrives and single-handedly dispatches all four hoodlums. The newcomer turns out to be Cheng's cousin Hsu Chien (James Tien), who throughout the film functions as Cheng's alter ego, mirroring

Cheng in the following senses: he is an awesome fighter, he resembles Cheng facially, he wears dark Chinese garb identical to Cheng's uniform, and he ardently seeks justice for his community.

Hsu Chien leads Cheng and Uncle to a household that stands in stark contrast to the alienation suggested in the opening scene and introduces Cheng to six more male "cousins" and Hsu Chien's sister, Chiao Mei, who eventually becomes Cheng's romantic interest and throughout the film represents both family and community. The male cousins, who are loosely related or may even be friends from the same village in China, live, work, eat, and sleep communally, a reflection of their close bonds.

Cheng joins his cousins in working at the ice-making factory run by the Big Boss. Two of the cousins discover that the factory is a front for a drug-smuggling operation and then disappear suddenly. Hsu Chien searches high and low for them, confronts the Big Boss, and eventually falls victim himself to the Boss's henchmen. When Cheng and the remaining cousins go on strike to protest the disappearances, the factory manager orders a band of thugs to attack them.

Cheng is mindful of his promise to his mother and simply watches the mayhem, even while the workers take the brunt of the beatings and his cousins plead for help. But when a hoodlum rips the locket off Cheng's chest, the trademark Bruce Lee snarl emerges. He emits a fierce howl and jumps into the fray. The fight ends with the thugs fleeing from Cheng, but he finds both his jade pendant and his promise shattered.

Rather than punishing Cheng, the manager promotes him to foreman and takes him to a dinner where he is plied with food, liquor, and prostitutes. Cheng wakes up in the morning to find a naked woman snuggled up against him, but he dresses quickly, only to bump into a disapproving Chiao Mei as he scurries out of the brothel. Cheng returns to the factory and orders the laborers to resume working, but they accuse him of selling out and refuse. These juxtapositions show that Cheng has betrayed the trust of his surrogate family and strained his ability to belong to the diasporic community that they have built.

≈

When Cheng returns to grill the prostitute about the whereabouts of his missing cousins, she informs him that the factory is in fact a drug-shipping operation. After he leaves, the Boss's son kills the prostitute and kidnaps Chiao Mei to add to his father's harem of drug-addled sex slaves. Cheng goes to the factory, where he discovers the drugs and Hsu Chien's body encased in blocks of ice. Just as he is processing this devastating revelation, the Boss's son and a gang of knife-wielding henchmen attack. In a pitched battle, Cheng defeats them and kills the Boss's son. He then rushes home, only to discover that all of his male cousins have been massacred and Chiao Mei is missing.

The morning finds Cheng sitting beside the river, contemplating the slaughter. "I promised my mother I'd keep out of trouble," a voice-over intones, externalizing his inner thoughts. "If I had any sense, I'd get out of here. If anything happened to me, who would take care of Mom? . . . She's over seventy, but I can't just walk away from this. I just can't do that. I can't." A vision of his slain cousins and Chiao Mei appears in the water as he ponders his promise to his mother.

Torn between the vow made in the homeland and allegiance to his newfound community in a new land, Cheng tosses his packet of belongings into the river, a gesture that symbolizes a fundamental break. He is casting aside the things he brought from the motherland and making a new start, declaring that his primary allegiance belongs to the community of expatriates he has joined. He stares heavenward and vows vengeance, an act that will cement his place in the new nation.

In the climactic scene, Cheng runs to the Big Boss's compound, where he faces off with half a dozen guards armed with knives, all of whom are Thai rather than Chinese and clad in gloriously garish 1970s Western-style slacks and shirts, in contrast to Cheng's simple black and white Chinese garb. The fight takes place on a lawn in front of a reflecting pool, behind which is a Thai-style Buddhist shrine, a visual reminder that the combatants are not in China but in a foreign land.

After briskly defeating the guards, Cheng takes on the Big Boss himself. Cheng and the Big Boss mirror each other's garb, both wearing collarless, wide-cuffed Chinese coats, and alternating shots of their feet show Cheng and the Boss to be wearing dark, flowing Chinese pants and canvas shoes. When they begin to fight, the two match each other unarmed, punch for punch and kick for kick, further emphasizing their similarity. When the Boss grabs two knives from the fallen guards, he begins to get the best of Cheng. The fight ends when the Boss flings a knife at Cheng, but Cheng kicks it back and buries it in the Boss's gut. Cheng then thrusts eight fingers, piercing deep into the Boss's chest, and punches him in the head repeatedly until both collapse, Cheng motionless atop the dead body of the Boss in a symbolic death of his own.

After Cheng finally manages to kill the Boss, Chiao Mei arrives with two cars full of Thai police officers, who rush out to capture Cheng. He shakes them off and appears ready to fight, but when Chiao Mei cries, "Listen, Cheng, give up!" he looks up, as if suddenly conscious of his situation, and raises his blood-stained hands to the sky to be arrested.

The film concludes with Chiao Mei and the handcuffed Cheng, flanked by the officers, walking toward the police cars. This ending is unsatisfying in that it presumes that Cheng will have to face trial for murder, but in other ways, it represents a new beginning for him. To begin with, when he fights the Big Boss, Cheng takes on his evil doppelganger. By slaying the Boss, Cheng not only exacts revenge for his cousins but also eliminates his old self.

Similarly, Cheng's good alter ego, Hsu Hsien, lies buried in ice. With both symbolic doubles dead, Cheng must build a new identity. The film ends before defining that identity but implies that the new beginning will occur in Thailand with Chiao Mei. Cheng's submission to Thai justice suggests that whatever fate awaits him, he will face it not in China but in the land that will become his new home.

Cheng and Chiao Mei walking together arm in arm toward the police car also suggests that the two of them will enter the future together and that the family they build will replace the lost community represented by the cousins.

The Big Boss thus represents how people create new senses of identity and belonging when they leave their homelands behind.

≈

Although Bruce had faith that *The Big Boss* would find an audience, he never dreamed of the success it would achieve.[12] Sitting anxiously next to Linda at the midnight premiere in Hong Kong in early September 1971, he fretted that the film would not connect with the audience. But when the closing credits rolled and "the audience rose to its feet with thunderous, cheering applause," then "absolutely mobbed" the couple as they left the theater, Bruce knew that he had entered a new stage of his life as a "glittering star."[13]

An American critic judged Bruce's performance as "one of the most outstanding examples of sheer animal magnetism on the celluloid ever produced," likening him to Clint Eastwood (an apt comparison, as we shall see), his friend and rival Steve McQueen, and the James Bond he had imagined himself as years earlier.[14] *The Big Boss* became an immediate smash hit, selling out midnight openings in five theaters throughout Hong Kong.

During the film's nineteen-day run, sixteen theaters screened the movie seven times per day to packed houses.[15] Its earnings of $3.2 million in Hong Kong dollars shattered box-office records, helping the movie replace *The Sound of Music* as the highest grossing film in Hong Kong history.[16] The film also topped box-office charts throughout Asia, becoming a smash hit in Malaysia, Singapore, and the Philippines and even sparking a martial arts demonstration and competition in Manila.[17]

After completing *The Big Boss*, Bruce returned to Hollywood to shoot three more episodes of *Longstreet* over nine days at a rate of $2,000 per episode, a sharp increase over his *Green Hornet* salary of $400 a month.[18] Despite his strong performance in the series premiere, the role of Li Tsung shriveled with each subsequent episode, his dialogue shrinking from nineteen lines to twelve and finally to five.[19] It was becoming clear that *Longstreet* would never propel Bruce to the heights he desired, and audiences across the Pacific were clamoring for more from Asia's newest star.

On October 11, 1971, after just a month back in California, Bruce, Linda, and Brandon returned to Hong Kong.[20]

THE GLOBALIZATION OF MARTIAL ARTS IN *FIST OF FURY*

Bruce Lee's second film, *Fist of Fury* (1972), came out shortly after *The Big Boss*. The two were scheduled for release in the United States close together, and a mix-up resulted in their titles being switched. *The Big Boss* was supposed to be called *The Chinese Connection*, a reference to the 1971 movie *The French Connection*, a film about narcotics trafficking, while the title of the second film was mistranslated as *Fists of Fury* (note the pluralization of "fists"). During export or import, the reels were placed in the wrong cans and the titles thus swapped, so the first film became known in the United States as *Fists of Fury* and the second as *The Chinese Connection*, despite having nothing to do with drug smuggling.[21] The titling blunder shows how travels across national borders and cultural and linguistic boundaries can deform meanings, but *Fist of Fury* also demonstrates how the transnational migrations can result in wondrous new hybrid forms.

Fist of Fury departed from *The Big Boss*'s meditation on diaspora to examine colonialism and Chinese pride. In contrast to the US-centric literature that emphasizes Lee's resistance to racism, Asian studies scholarship sees Lee as a symbol of Chinese nationalism. The widely influential Singapore-based film critic Stephen Teo argues that the "nationalistic theme in his films [had] nothing to do with his adoptive country" of the United States, describing his appeal as "an abstract kind of cultural nationalism" binding together Chinese people across the diaspora.[22] *Fist of Fury* does indeed project Chinese strength, but it does so in ways that refer to Lee's globe-spanning travels.

In this film, Lee plays Chen Zhen, a student at the Jing Woo school of martial arts in an early twentieth-century Shanghai riven by colonialism. The historical Jingwu school arose out of the nexus between Chinese nationalism and martial arts. In the mid- to late 1800s, Western powers and Japan forced China to sign a series of unequal treaties, under which China ceded territory and trading rights to foreigners. In the International Settlement district of Shanghai, foreigners were exempt from Chinese laws and subject to the laws of their own nations.

The Boxer Rebellion (1900–1901), which aimed to expel outsiders from China and eradicate foreign influences, was named after its adherents, who practiced martial arts in the mistaken belief that such skills could provide protection against Western bullets. A multinational force crushed the rebellion, but the Jingwu school was created to ensure that kung fu would continue to be taught.[23] In *Fist of Fury*, Ho Yuan-chia, Chen's beloved teacher and founder of the kung fu school, has been murdered by members of a rival Japanese karate school. The quest for vengeance fuels the plot, which moves forward through a series of gorgeously ballet-like fight scenes.

Chinese national humiliation and subsequent redemption form a major theme of the film. At Ho's funeral, an acolyte equates the teacher and his Jing Woo school with the future of China, declaring, "He died for us," adding, "He aimed to strengthen minds and the bodies of you, the young people, for the sake of China, our land." Wu, a Chinese interpreter for the Japanese played by Wei Ping-ao as a weasely and effeminate traitor to his people, interrupts the solemn ceremony along with two karatekas to present the gathered mourners with a framed scroll reading, "Sick Man of Asia," a profoundly insulting moniker used historically to refer to China's geopolitical weakness during the late nineteenth and early twentieth centuries, an era of unequal treaties. (The phrase would continue to rankle well into the twenty-first century. In the midst of the coronavirus pandemic of 2020, the Chinese government condemned as "racially discriminatory" a *Wall Street Journal* op-ed article bearing the headline, "China Is the Real Sick Man of Asia," and in response expelled three of the paper's reporters.)[24]

Wu further baits the funeral-goers. "Chinese are a race of weaklings, no comparison to us Japanese," he sneers. "Just look at yourselves. You're pathetic, you know that?" Chen balls his fist, his mouth twitching with rage, as Wu slaps his cheek and demands tauntingly, "What's holding you back? Are you yellow or something? Sick man of Asia?" Although Chen maintains his composure during the funeral, afterward he goes alone to the karate dojo to confront two dozen Japanese fighters in a beautifully choreographed scene in which the Japanese students, clad in *gi* (the traditional robe donned for martial arts practice), swirl around Chen, converging and dispersing like synchronized swimmers in a violent Esther Williams water ballet.

Chen lays waste to the lot of them with his hands, feet, and nunchaku, which he whirls about in deadly arcs. To his opponents lying helpless on the mats, he proclaims, "We are not sick men," and to underscore the point, he shatters the glass frame of the scroll and forces the two karatekas who had disrupted Ho's funeral with Wu to eat the scroll.

The film's most famous scene occurs when Chen tries to visit a park at an entrance with a sign that reads, "No Dogs and Chinese Allowed." The turban-wearing Gurkha guard stops Chen but allows a white woman walking a dog to enter. A group of kimono-clad Japanese people notice his predicament, and one man says with a smirk, "You were wanting to get in there? There's only one thing you need do. Pretend you're a dog, and I'll take you in."

Chen erupts into violence, beating the taunter, kicking the offensive sign into the air, and destroying it with a flying high kick. A crowd of Chinese onlookers surround Chen and usher him away as the Gurkha blows his whistle to summon help. The messages of the scene are clear: Chinese are treated as lower than dogs in their own country, Chen is a hero for defying the racial order, and the Chinese people support his resistance.

Beyond the Japanese-Chinese dynamic, however, lurks the specter of British imperialism. The guard at the park in is a Gurkha soldier, one of the many Nepalese serving in the British Army deployed throughout Asia to police British colonial holdings. Thus, although it is the Japanese who mock Chen by telling him to act like a dog, they do so within the International Settlement carved out in part by the unequal treaties Great Britain forced China to sign.

Hong Kong audiences thrilled to the movie's message of Chinese strength. One viewer at an early screening noted that when Chen declared, "We are not the sick man of Asia!" the packed crowd let out a "mighty roar," and "deafening applause and stamping of feet shook the theater." In response, a Westerner in the audience "scrunched lower in his seat, suddenly feeling very much the foreigner in an alien land."[25]

In retaliation for the mayhem Chen unleashed, a contingent of Japanese fighters lay waste to the Jing Woo school and its students. The interpreter Wu threatens to close down the school and have the fighters arrested if they do not hand over Chen, invoking the power that the Japanese hold over the Chinese. Chen's friends urge him to flee Shanghai; but before he leaves, he confides in Yuan that he intended to ask her to marry him, and she promises to wait for him until he returns. On his way out, he hears two cooks boasting about having poisoned teacher Ho. Chen kills both of them with his bare hands and hangs them from a lamppost. Now wanted as a murderer, he goes into hiding at a cemetery, where Yuan finds him at night roasting a dog over an open fire. They declare their love for each other and fantasize about the future they had planned together, the children they would have had, and running the Jing Woo school. Chen and Yuan gaze deeply into each other's eyes and share a bittersweet kiss in the last moment of intimacy for the doomed lovers. Despite being a heartthrob, this was Bruce Lee's one and only onscreen kiss.

Although the film sets up a conflict between the righteous Chinese of the Jing Woo school and the invidious Susuki and his Japanese minions, this rigid distinction fails to cohere. The two cooks at the Jing Woo school who poison teacher Ho are revealed to be Japanese in disguise, a substantial slippage between the two identities that are meant to be posed in opposition to each other. The status of Wu is even more tenuous, for as the scholar Paul Bowman notes, the interpreter describes himself in ambiguous ways. In the English-dubbed version of the film, Wu says, "The Chinese are a race of weaklings, no comparison to us Japanese," with the use of the first-person pronoun "us" including Wu within the category of Japanese. By contrast, in the subtitled version of the film, he states, "Even though we are of the same kind, our paths in life are vastly different," which indicates that he is Chinese. To ask which version is more faithful to the original is futile, since films like *Fist of Fury* were shot without sound and subsequently dubbed into Cantonese, Mandarin, English, and numerous other languages. Even more confounding, the actor Wei Ping-ao, who plays Wu, dubbed his own lines in both the Cantonese and English versions, thus serving as an interpreter of the interpreter.[26]

Wu's eventual demise further clouds the picture. He meets his fate after a party at the Japanese dojo, replete with a stripper whose kimono ends up crumpled on the floor. Wu joins in the feasting and heavy drinking, but when he stands to leave, Susuki orders, "If you really want to go out the door, go out like a Chinese, on your hands and knees!" Wu crawls obediently across the tatami mat floor, playing the part of a dog, just as the Japanese man at the park had urged Chen to do.

The clear symbolism of kimonos and tatami mats marks a Japanese space that Wu tries desperately to leave. He functions as both insider and outsider, accomplice and object of ridicule. Chen lies in wait for Wu outside the party and kills him in an alley. This confrontation is unsurprising, but even after, as Chen tries to cement Wu's identity as an enemy to the Chinese people (and therefore like the Japanese), he introduces more ambiguity by hanging Wu's body on the same lamppost where he had hung the two cooks. Chen thus stages the death of Wu, a Chinese acting like and in the interests of the Japanese, to mirror the cooks, who were Japanese acting like Chinese.

The film concludes with Chen making the ultimate sacrifice for the Jing Woo school and, by extension, for China. While Chen is off fighting and killing Susuki, Japanese villains return to the school and massacre the students. A Japanese representative demands that the Jing Woo school turn Chen over to face charges for killing Wu, ignoring the murdered Chinese students on the floor around him. The inspector, a Chinese police officer played by director Lo Wei himself, argues in vain that the true crime is the slaughter of the students, but the Japanese representative insists on arresting all of the survivors.

Chen sneaks in through a second-story window, views the carnage, alternating between fury and anguish, and overhears the Japanese representative telling the inspector, "I'm the law in Shanghai. You should know that." Understanding that he must surrender himself to save the school, he descends the stairs, exchanging a lingering glance with his sweetheart, Yuan, as he passes—a sorrowful acknowledgment that none of their dreams will come to pass. He extracts a promise from the inspector that if he turns himself in, the inspector will spare the Jing Woo school. "I shall accept punishment for the lives I took," he declares. "You just leave this school alone!"

Flanked by the inspector and the Japanese representative, with Yuan and the other Jing Woo students on the portico behind him, Chen walks out to the front door, bare-chested and empty-handed but resolute, to face the armed police arrayed at the entry gate. A close-up shows the mournful expression on his face as he grieves his dead friends and unfulfilled future with Yuan twist into pure fury at the injustice of it all. He rushes forward, leaping into a fusillade of bullets, the final frame frozen on his snarling face and taut body suspended midair in a flying kick. Chen ultimately sacrifices his present and future life to preserve the Jing Woo school and the hope for China that it symbolizes.[27]

≈

Given that the most straightforward reading of the movie thus focuses on the restoration of Chinese pride in the face of Japanese imperialism, *Fist of Fury* might seem to be an ill-suited vehicle for exploring the notion of hybridity. In that vein, Stephen Teo highlights Bruce Lee's nationalism as the most important characteristic of his films, calling him "an ardent nationalist" whose work "stir[s] the hearts of Chinese audiences everywhere, while foreign critics talk of jingoism and chauvinism."[28]

However, a more intriguing story lurks beneath the surface of *Fist of Fury*, one that complicates its seemingly straightforward nationalism with hybridity and transnational crossings. In this film, Bruce Lee introduces the use of nunchaku (also known as "nunchuks"). The most captivating sequences feature Chen sending the nunchaku twirling in rapid arcs through the air and striking opponents with blink-and-you-miss-it quickness. At that time, the nunchaku was a relatively obscure Okinawan weapon, but Lee's dazzling usage made it seem like the coolest thing on Earth. Within a few years, nunchaku had become so popular that it was banned as a deadly weapon in parts of the United States and throughout all of Canada and England.

The story of how the nunchaku came to play a starring role in this movie once again demonstrates the transnational flows of martial arts and artists. The independent scholar M. T. Kato traces the evolution of Okinawan martial arts to cultural and commercial exchanges between China and the Ryukyu Islands (the archipelago of which Okinawa is the largest island) in the fifteenth century CE. The ruling Sho clan demilitarized the nobility and disarmed the populace of the Ryukyu Kingdom, a policy that continued after the Japanese Shimazu clan conquered the islands. During this period, the kingdom functioned as a dual vassal state of both China and Japan. Because of the disarmament policy, peasants adapted rice flails into the nunchaku to defend themselves against samurai wielding *katana* swords.[29] The climactic battle between Chen's nunchaku and Suzuki's *katana* entangles the histories of Okinawan and Chinese anticolonialism, resuscitating a make-do weapon of the weak against overwhelming military power. Given the alternate genealogy of the nunchaku as the Filipino weapon *tabak-toyok*, to which Bruce had been introduced by his pupil Dan Inosanto, the fight can also be read as a reference to Filipino resistance to the Japanese invasion in World War II. Rather than simply helping Chinese people affirm their relationship with the "mother culture," as Teo suggests, an alternate reading of the film shows how it build transnational identifications through references to cultural interflows and multiple instances of anticolonial struggle.[30]

Other influences of Lee's time in the United States peek out at various points in *Fist of Fury*. To begin with, Bruce's American student Robert Baker plays the Russian villain Petrov, whom Chen of course kills.[31] More intriguingly, at the park entrance with the "No Dogs and Chinese Allowed" sign, a white man with a long shaggy haircut, wearing a gaudy tie and 1970s-style suit, strolls arm in arm with an African American woman who has an outsized Afro. This glaring anachronism seeps through the film's artifice of early twentieth-century Shanghai to subtly remind viewers of Lee's sojourn in the United States.

Finally, *Variety* magazine's review of the movie places it within the context of global American filmmaking, calling it "an Oriental paraphrase" of the spaghetti westerns starring Clint Eastwood and directed by Sergio Leone.[32] This was an apt comparison, as Bruce admired Eastwood's crooked path to Hollywood stardom, which like his own, began with an American television show (*Rawhide*, in Eastwood's case) followed by exile abroad, Eastwood to Italy and Bruce to Hong Kong.

Bruce could only hope that, like Eastwood, he could ride favorable currents back to the US. *Fist of Fury* followed the box-office success of *The Big Boss*, setting a new record for box-office receipts in just thirteen days and eventually garnering $4.5 million Hong Kong dollars.[33] Perhaps even more importantly for Golden Harvest, the success of *Fist of Fury* came at the expense of the biggest competing Shaw Brothers film, which dropped from twenty theaters to eleven, with revenues plummeting by over 80 percent in just a week. As a headline in the *Hong Kong Post Herald* announced with a smirk, "Shaw Brothers' epic takes a beating from Bruce Li film."[34]

HYBRIDITY IN *THE WAY OF THE DRAGON*

Bruce Lee's third Hong Kong martial arts film, the 1972 *The Way of the Dragon*, marked a dramatic departure from his prior works. Having broken box-office records with both of the movies in his two-film contract with Golden Harvest, he was a free agent and the biggest movie star in Asia, which he leveraged to demand total artistic freedom. He and Raymond Chow formed a jointly owned company, Concord Productions, to create his next project. Lee wrote, coproduced, choreographed, and starred in a film that expressed his martial arts philosophy of entangling Chinese and Western techniques and bodies. Unlike before, he had no disagreements with the director, as he directed the film himself.

In this most ambitious of Lee's Hong Kong films, themes of migration and hybridity take center stage. (Because it was released in the United States in 1974, after the Hollywood-produced *Enter the Dragon*, US audiences know this film as *Return of the Dragon*.) Like its predecessors, the film invokes imperialism and race, but more prominently, it undermines the rigid distinction between East and West.

With extensive scenes filmed on location in Rome, *The Way of the Dragon* was the first Hong Kong production to be shot in Europe.[35] In 1972, even by air, the trip from Hong Kong to Italy was a nineteen-hour journey that required refueling stops in Bangkok, Burma, and Israel.[36] Bruce arrived in Rome on May 5, 1972, with the producer Raymond Chow, the coproducer Chaplin Chang, and Tadashi Nishimoto, the Japanese cinematographer who had shot the classic 1963 film *Love Eterne* and many other movies under the Chinese pseudonym of Ho Lan Shan. While awaiting the arrival of the rest of the cast and crew, a group that included the leading lady Nora Miao, the early arrivals toured Tuscany, visited Florence, and took pictures in front the Leaning Tower of Pisa.[37] Shooting began on May 7, 1972.

Lee plays Tang Lung, a country boy who travels from Hong Kong to Rome to aid the owners of a Chinese restaurant—Chen Ching-hua, the lovely damsel in distress played by Nora Miao, revisiting her role as Bruce's love interest in *Fist of Fury*, and her Uncle Wong—who are under attack by an Italian mob boss. The mob boss is trying to force them to sell their business by having his thugs harass and drive off potential customers. Despite the best efforts of the Chinese cook and waiters to defend the restaurant, it teeters close to failure. Tang takes on the hoodlums and ultimately faces off with imported mercenaries played by martial arts champions, including the karate expert Chuck Norris.

Diaspora constitutes one major theme of the film. The film's opening credits announce its interest in migration. Wavy lines scroll across the screen from left to right, suggesting flowing water, and a stop-motion animated cutout of a dragon boat and its rowing crew traverse the waters in the opposite direction until it crashes onto a rocky shore and the boat transforms into a dragon.

The opening scene underscores the sense of alienation, beginning with a close-up of Tang Lung's face and then panning out to reveal him standing in the Rome airport surrounded by Europeans. Tang is wearing charcoal-colored

Chinese clothing of loose pants and a collarless, wide-cuffed shirt, while the Europeans are clad in turtlenecks, jeans, polyester shirts, suede jackets, and 1970s suits with wide lapels. An older white woman invades Tang's personal space, gaping unblinkingly at him as if she has never seen a more curious sight. Other passengers cast more discreet glances at Tang, but they, too, clearly see him as an oddity. The scene showcases Lee's acting talent, for he silently conveys his discomfort with uncomfortable gulps, a downcast gaze, cocking of the eyebrow, awkward smiles, and a nervous hand to the face. It is a performance worthy of silent-film giants such as Buster Keaton and Charlie Chaplin.

Chen arrives to drive Tang to the restaurant, passing celebrated Roman tourist sites like the Trevi Fountain and the Colosseum along the way. Many of the locations they see evoke the imperial past of the Eternal City, including the Piazza del Popolo, which features the towering Flaminio Obelisk, which was plundered from Egypt after the Roman conquest, and the Arch of Constantine, spanning the Via Triumphalis, through which Roman emperors led their armies when returning victorious from battle.

This jaunt through the city emphasizes Tang's distance from home by firmly placing the narrative among the famous sights of imperial Rome and also conjures tourism, which involves travel and temporary stays in unfamiliar locales. (Incidentally, these outdoor scenes and others, like the one in which Tang meets an Italian prostitute at the fountain at Piazza Navona and another that shows him strolling with Chen through the gardens at Villa d'Este, were shot without acquiring the necessary permits, to avoid bureaucracy and costs.)[38]

≈

In the film's depiction of a diasporic community, *The Way of the Dragon* resembles *The Big Boss*. As in the earlier film, Lee plays an unsophisticated country boy who in this case hails from the New Territories, a rural area of Hong Kong far from the big city. It is obvious that he does not belong in Italy: he is suspicious of depositing his meager earnings in a bank, unwittingly cavorts with a prostitute, and squats over the toilet Chinese-style instead of sitting on it like a Westerner.

Tang's naïveté signals that he is a fish out of water, but all the Chinese characters (save for the complicated figure of the translator, Mr. Ho) form a diasporic community around the restaurant—they are in an alien land far from home, bound together by their common homeland. Uncle Wong expresses this idea when Tang arrives at the restaurant. After inquiring about Tang's flight from Hong Kong, he says wistfully, "It's ages since I was there." For him and the other Chinese characters, Hong Kong is the home to which they intend to return one day.

The film draws distinctions between members of the diasporic community and the people surrounding them by highlighting differences of race, nationality, and martial arts disciplines. Racially, the Chinese restaurant workers stand in contrast to the Italian boss and his thugs, who are both white and Black. In addition, the thugs tower over the diminutive Chinese. The national distinction becomes clear when Uncle Wong cautions, "Thugs are safest at home. This is their home. Where we are now, we're all foreigners. All around us is their territory." Finally, the restaurant workers practice the Asian martial arts of karate and kung fu, in contrast to the thugs, who fight like Western boxers.

The first big fight scene begins with an Italian tough guy assuming a three-quarter boxing stance, with left foot forward and left fist high. When a waiter comes at him with a karate approach, the thug knocks him out with a single overhand right. The thugs sneer, "Chinese boxing!" a clear indication that they do not understand the distinction between karate and kung fu, but more important, their derision establishes a firm hierarchy of West over East. Because Tang cannot let this stand, he uses kung fu–style high kicks to knock out the boxer and then defeats another thug who bobs and weaves in classic boxing style.

≈

In *Fist of Fury*, the triumph of kung fu over karate symbolized the recuperation of Chinese national pride, but *The Way of the Dragon* proceeds in a much more complex way, setting up dichotomies only to subvert them. Rather than making simplistic statements of Chinese superiority over Japanese, or Asian superiority over the West, the film argues for the power of hybridity and cultural intermixture and ultimately demonstrates the untenable nature of rigid dichotomies.

The first potential dichotomy differentiates between Chinese kung fu and Japanese karate. When Tang arrives at the restaurant, he observes the waiters practicing karate, which they plan to use to defend themselves against the thugs who are scaring away customers. They scorn "Chinese boxing" (as the movie labels kung fu) as lacking power. Conversely, the cook, who is the only kung fu aficionado, dismisses karate as foreign and therefore uninteresting. After the fight in which Tang uses kung fu to demolish the Italian boxers, the waiters abandon karate and beg him to teach them the Chinese art.

This might be seen as the triumph of kung fu over karate, but Tang insists otherwise. In response to the cook's labeling of karate as "foreign," Tang counters, "Foreign or not, if it helps you to look after yourself when you're in a fight, then you should learn to use it. It doesn't matter at all where it comes from." This is not the nationalist dichotomy of kung fu versus karate posited in *Fist of Fury* but rather the hybridity that incorporated nunchaku into Lee's choreography in that same film, as well as the do-anything-necessary philosophy of Jeet Kune Do as expressed in *Longstreet*.

The second possible dichotomy could be drawn between the Asians as good guys versus Westerners as villains. The film initially appears to follow this formula, as the Chinese restaurant workers appear to be innocent victims of the Italian mob boss and his white and Black hoods. However, the neat categorization of Asian as good and European as evil falls apart quickly, as shown by two characters: Mr. Ho and Uncle Wong.

A Chinese man named Mr. Ho serves as the Italian boss's right-hand man and interpreter. Ho is portrayed as an effeminate individual who dresses flamboyantly, prances, minces, giggles flirtatiously, and coyly admires Tang's muscular physique. The most problematic aspect of this representation is that it equates his implied homosexuality with his duplicity and disloyalty toward his fellow Chinese.[39] Similarly to Mr. Ho, Uncle Wong is a Chinese character who betrays his community. At the climax of the film, Uncle Wong literally stabs two waiters in the back and reveals that he has been conspiring to sell the restaurant all along so that he can return home to his wife and children in Hong Kong. Ho and Uncle Wong's treachery undermines the dichotomy of Chinese as good and Westerners as evil.

The third and final dichotomy that fails to hold up equates Asians with kung fu and karate and Europeans and Americans with boxing. Although as we have seen, the film begins by making this distinction clear, its conclusion muddies things considerably. After Tang defeats all of the local thugs in Rome, the boss imports three highly skilled martial artists to take care of him. The first is played by the hapkido expert Whang Ing Sik, who is portrayed inexplicably as a karateka. The second, also a karate master, is played by Robert Wall, a white American billed as "World Professional Karate Champion 1970" in the credits. Whang and Wall are each determined to be the one to take on Tang Lung and are sparring against each other for the honor of fighting the man referred to as "that Chinaman" when the boss returns with the third, and most fearsome, martial artist.

Colt, played by the conspicuously white Chuck Norris, has flown in from the United States expressly to fight Tang. In reality, when Norris landed at the airport in Rome, Bruce had a film crew shooting as he deplaned and included the footage in the movie as Colt's arrival. Norris looks appropriately dashing and intimidating, especially for a man who had not expected to be filmed. Having never visited Europe before, Norris had asked his friend and karate school coowner Bob Wall to accompany him, and Bruce took advantage of Wall's presence by putting him into the film as well.[40]

When the boss grants Whang the honor of fighting Norris, he slaps himself on the chest and demands, "Who can do karate better than Japanese?" The unstated humor here is that the Korean Whang is neither a karateka nor Japanese. Norris and Whang fight each other, with the American besting the supposed Japanese at karate. In the final analysis, the best karate master is not Asian at all but a white American. The film thus subverts crude equations of race with martial artistry and destabilizes dichotomies of Japanese karate versus Chinese kung fu and Asian heroism versus Western villainy.

≈

The climactic fight between Tang Lung and Colt in the Colosseum is arguably the most iconic scene in the history of martial arts films. It would be easy to see the clash of the Chinese Tang versus the American Colt—set in the two-thousand-year-old masterpiece of Roman architecture in the cradle of Western civilization—as emblematizing East versus West in a battle of modern-day gladiators. This interpretation is bolstered by the fact that "Tang" can be a synonym for the word "Chinese." Indeed, the huge success of *The Way of the Dragon* among Chinese audiences in Hong Kong and throughout Asia is owed in no small part to an interpretation of the film as a restoration of ethnic pride, a statement that China could stand up against any nation on Earth.

However, just as with *Fist of Fury*, an alternative reading reveals complexity rather than simplicity and hybridity rather than purity. Bruce revealed to Norris his vision of the fight as "two gladiators in a fight to the death," a comment that demonstrates his framing of the conflict in terms of individuals, not civilizations. When Bruce offered Norris the role of Colt and outlined the climactic fight, he claimed the victory for himself because, as he said, "I'm the star!" Norris, who at the time held the title as world karate champion, protested the plot, objecting that Bruce was proposing that in the film he would beat up "the current world karate champion." Bruce replied cockily, "No, I'm going to *kill* the current world karate champ." Norris could only laugh and accept the part.[41]

Once the cast and crew were setting up in the Colosseum, Norris was overcome by the realization that "not so long ago gladiators had gone out there to fight to the death before a cheering crowd." But even this recognition was mediated through a cinematic lens, as he recalls, "I was reminded of movies like *Spartacus*, in which Kirk Douglas fought in the arena."[42] Although parts of the fight were filmed in the Colosseum, a lack of time and permits dictated that it be completed elsewhere, so the crew took photographs of the Colosseum that were used to construct a replica set at the Golden Harvest studios in Hong Kong.[43]

Bruce Lee and Chuck Norris on the set of *The Way of the Dragon* (1972) (Photo by Concord Productions Inc. / Golden Harvest Company / Sunset Boulevard / Corbis via Getty Images)

The film establishes a stark visual distinction between Tang and Colt, who prepare for combat by stripping to their waists and limbering up. Colt unveils his muscular upper body, thick rounded shoulders and biceps, and hair, so much hair, covering his shoulders, chest, stomach, arms, and back. In contrast, Tang reveals a smooth torso, not a hair in sight, and the famed Bruce Lee physique—lean and extraordinarily defined. Colt appears powerful, whereas Tang makes Michelangelo's statue of David look fat and out of shape.

The contrast was intentional, as Norris had remade his body at Bruce's behest. He discovered a favorite restaurant in the Trastevere neighborhood, where he ate mounds of pasta and gelato night after night to pack on the twenty pounds Bruce had requested.[44] Once Tang and Colt begin sparring, the American's physical advantage becomes clear as his superior size enables him to strike Tang before Tang can get within reach.

After being knocked down twice, Tang realizes the futility of his approach and makes a quick adaptation that signals his rejection of purity in favor of intermixing. When Tang rises, instead of assuming a kung fu stance, he begins to dance like a boxer. Colt throws a series of kicks and punches, but Tang bobs and weaves away. Bruce Lee was known to admire the boxer Muhammad Ali and avidly studied his movements on film. Perhaps not surprisingly, his movements in this scene resemble the "float like a butterfly" strategy of The Greatest.[45]

As a further example of how cultures flow in unpredictable and intriguing ways, Amy Ongiri, a film scholar at Lawrence University, notes the immense popularity of kung fu movies in African American communities in the 1970s, due in no small part to their portrayal of "the body as a raw tool for the articulation of violent retribution against societal inequities and personal wrongs."[46] This phenomenon illustrates an extended circuit: Bruce Lee incorporated the movements of a Black boxer to fight against the white Norris (who has absorbed the Japanese style of karate), and in turn, Black audiences in the US embraced kung fu cinema. The influence of Asian martial performances lasted far beyond the 1970s, extending, for example, to the hip-hop group Wu-Tang Clan, which emerged in the 1990s.

When Tang Lung changes his fighting style to boxing, it marks the turning point of the battle in the Colosseum. From then on, Tang bobs and weaves, using speed to elude Colt's strikes and get inside the bigger man's reach. Tang destroys Colt's knees, leaving him immobile, and urges him to stop fighting, but the valiant American refuses to give up and insists on fighting to the death like the gladiators of old. Reluctantly, Tang breaks Colt's neck, gently lays down the body of the champion, and sorrowfully covers him with his *gi*. This gesture signals Tang's respect for his opponent, whom he recognizes as a master of his own discipline. The combination of Tang's adaptation of boxing methods, last seen in the film being used by the hapless thugs, and show of esteem for the karateka reveals Lee's ideology of synthesis and cultural intermixture.

≈

The Italian setting of *The Way of the Dragon* conjures the spaghetti westerns to which *Variety* had compared *Fist of Fury* and also evokes sword-and-sandals epics such as *Ben-Hur* and *Spartacus* (as Chuck Norris remembered), which featured bare-chested male bodies onscreen. Lee puts Kirk Douglas to shame when he poses and flexes, naked to the waist, impossibly ripped and lean. Lee's films introduced this brawny aesthetic to Hong Kong *wuxia* (martial arts) films, which had never before focused the gaze so centrally on an overtly sexualized male body.[47]

Prior to Bruce Lee's return to Hong Kong, the long-running and wildly popular Wong Fei Hung (Huang Feihong) series dominated not just *wuxia* films but all of Hong Kong cinema, with ninety-nine films made between 1949 and 1994, the vast majority in the 1950s.[48] The twenty-five Wong Fei Hung films made in 1956 alone constituted 12 percent of that year's entire cinematic output. The series portrayed the heroic Master Wong as a gentlemanly Confucian scholar and herbal doctor who always remained properly clad.[49] Wong embodied Chinese *wen* masculinity, which emphasizes scholarly achievement and literary refinement and stands in contrast to *wu* masculinity, which values physical or martial prowess.[50]

In contrast to Wong's staid and proper masculinity, a "new style" of martial arts films rose to dominate the Hong Kong market in the 1970s, ushering in a new form of masculinity.[51] Chris Berry and Mary Farquhar, professors of film studies in the United Kingdom and Australia, respectively, argue that Lee's unveiling of his body represented a new form of what they call "neo-*wu* masculinity," a combination of the traditional Chinese *wu* with US codes of muscularity.[52] In each of Lee's movies, he plays an unimposing character whose ferocity remains concealed until he rips off his shirt. The emphasis on his corporeal form is highlighted when he suffers a cut, touches his bleeding wound, and tastes his own blood—then goes off to wreak havoc.

In *The Way of the Dragon*, salacious stares by both an Italian prostitute and Mr. Ho make it obvious that Tang's body is an object of sexual desire for women and men. The film showcases the male body, combining aesthetics drawn from Italian and Hollywood sword-and-sandal epics with Hong Kong *wuxia* productions.

≈

The ending of *The Way of the Dragon* departs from its predecessors, both of which set up a Confucian moral universe in which Lee's character atones for his violence in order to restore the social order. *The Big Boss* concludes with Cheng surrendering to the Thai police after killing the Boss, and *Fist of Fury* ends with Chen essentially committing suicide by running headlong into a hail of police bullets. In contrast, at the end of *The Way of the Dragon*, the cook muses, "In this world of guns and knives, wherever Tang Lung goes, he will always travel on his own."

Indeed, as the credits roll, Tang strolls off into the distance like a cowboy riding off into the sunset, evidence of how the sensibility of the genre of western films seeps into this Hong Kong *wuxia* production. Rather than idealizing the return to the homeland by diasporic sojourners—after all, Uncle Wong's treachery is motivated by a desire to return home—*The Way of the Dragon* highlights transnational migrations that may or may not return home at all.

The Way of the Dragon became the first Hong Kong film to gross more than $5 million Hong Kong dollars, besting *Fist of Fury* by more than $600,000. As a partner in Concord Productions, as well as writer, director, and star, Lee netted an estimated $3 million Hong Kong dollars. Despite the film's wild popularity, the *China Mail* deemed *The Way of the Dragon* to be less "tight in structure" than Lee's two previous Lo Wei–directed efforts, chalking up its success to Lee's status as a superstar and its "masterful" publicity campaign.[53] This opinion may have reflected the newspaper's refusal to accept the film's Western-inflected aesthetics and morality, but the box-office record shows that adoring Hong Kong audiences eagerly embraced these transpacific cross-pollinations.

≈

After wrapping up the filming on *The Way of the Dragon*, Bruce began sketching out a new film that he called *Game of Death*, which he intended to be a parable of his martial arts philosophy. Although he had not yet developed a script, he envisioned the climactic scene as a series of fights ascending the floors of a five-story pagoda. At each level, he would encounter a martial artist using one particular style and adapt his fighting style accordingly. This pattern of modifying his approach to changing circumstances showcased his admonition to "be water," as he took the forms that were required rather than stubbornly adhering to a single fixed style.

Bruce more or less improvised as he went along, swapping out ideas for whom he would face on each floor depending on the availability of friends and martial artists. The third-floor scene starred Dan Inosanto, his friend and student from Los Angeles, who deployed the Filipino stick-fighting discipline of *escrima*. On the fourth floor, he faced off against Ji Han Jae, an expert in the Korean martial art of hapkido who happened to be under contract with Golden Harvest at the time. Bruce's dramatic fifth-floor opponent was the seven-foot-two professional basketball center Kareem Abdul Jabbar, who had trained with Bruce when he was starring in college at UCLA.

The physical incongruity of the five-foot-seven Bruce trying to combat the length and reach of the seven-footer made an unforgettable spectacle. Bruce even pulled a groin muscle trying to kick Kareem in the face. In the end, Bruce defeats his gargantuan opponent by grappling him on the ground and choking him, thus enacting his philosophy of doing what is necessary given the conditions. The scenes for the bottom two floors were never shot, though Bruce considered for the roles his Seattle friend and student Taky Kimura, his Wing Chun *sihing* Wong Shun Leung, and his Hollywood pupil James Coburn.[54]

Filming for *Game of Death* was interrupted after Warner Bros. green-lighted the movie that would become *Enter the Dragon*. Five years after Bruce's death, Golden Harvest released an execrable movie built on the thirty minutes of edited footage of the fight scenes, onto which it layered a ludicrous plot. The film creates Bruce's character, Billy Lo, through a variety of methods ranging from the dubious to the absurd. Much of the footage uses a Bruce Lee look-alike actor who resembles him not at all. More egregiously, the movie intersperses repurposed footage from his previous films (some with redubbed dialogue to

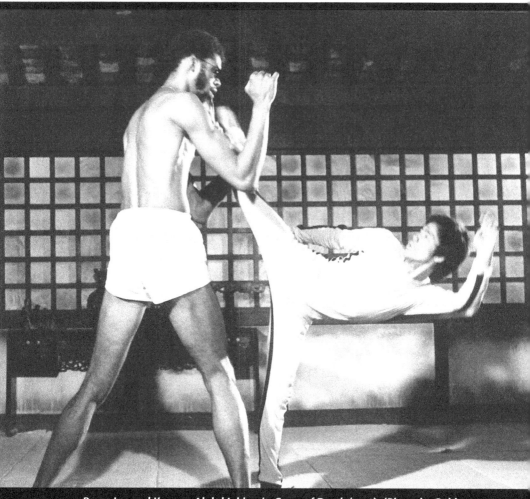

Bruce Lee and Kareem Abdul Jabbar in *Game of Death* (1978). (Photo by Golden Harvest Group via Alamy Stock Photo)

fit the new plot). Even more embarrassing is the scene in which a cardboard cutout of Bruce's face is filmed in front of the actor playing him. The ludicrous plot includes Billy being shot in the face, forcing him to cover his entire face in bandages and undergo plastic surgery. The image of Billy whipsaws wildly among footage of Bruce Lee recycled from *The Way of the Dragon*, a double who resembles him only vaguely and cannot fight convincingly, a bandaged or disguised figure, and the actual Bruce Lee in scenes he filmed for the project.

The effect is so ghastly that in *Bruce Lee: The Biography* (1988), Robert Clouse, who wrote and directed the debacle, describes it entirely in the third person as "tasteless and fraudulent," never once noting the central role he played in creating it.[55] But in 1972, the travesty of *Game of Death* remained in the future, as Bruce put the project on hiatus to pursue the opportunity that had eluded him for so long.

7

ENTER AND EXIT THE DRAGON

By 1972, Bruce's star in Asia blazed so brightly that it could be spied over the horizon on the other side of the Pacific. And fittingly, the same ocean-spanning entertainment industry that led to Bruce appearing in a Chinese movie while an infant in San Francisco propelled his transnational rise to fame in the final chapter of his life. That chapter would prove to have a devastatingly premature ending that revealed his drug use and marital infidelity. But until that moment, his vulnerabilities remained shrouded, and the trajectory of his career and the extent of his fame seemed to know no bounds.

That rise to fame was fueled by Raymond Chow, the Golden Harvest executive who was trying to expand the international distribution of his company's films to match that of the Hong Kong cinema giant Shaw Brothers studios, which had already succeeded in distributing a kung fu film, *King Boxer* (also known as *Five Fingers of Death*), to Europe and the United States.

Six months after Bruce had departed for Hong Kong, Chow sent a print of *The Big Boss* to Warner Bros. executive Fred Weintraub, a move that generated some interest at the studio, although not enough to spark action. However, after a print of *Fist of Fury* arrived, Weintraub recalls, "I knew we had something going."[1] He was finally convinced that Bruce was a bankable star. Chow offered to sell Weintraub the right to distribute the two films throughout the United States (except for the Chinatown theaters that Chow owned in San Francisco, Chicago, and New York) for $25,000. Weintraub declined, citing the cost, although he came to regret the decision, as he later estimated that the movies eventually grossed up to $20 million.

However, with Warner Bros. producing the television series *Kung Fu* and distributing *Five Fingers of Death*, Weintraub saw an opening. Along with his coproducer, Paul Heller, he created a rough four- to five-page treatment of a kung fu vehicle that would star Bruce and perhaps be a moneymaker for his studio. For financing, Weintraub turned to Dick Ma, the studio's head of Far East distribution, who said he could guarantee $250,000 in foreign sales.

That was enough money for the chief executive officer of Warner Bros. to greenlight the project, although not enough to actually make a movie. Estimating that the budget would be double what Ma could provide, Weintraub settled on Hong Kong, with its lower costs of production, as an ideal filming location and promptly went looking for a local partner to put up the other half of the money.

During Weintraub's time in Hong Kong, he spent two weeks unsuccessfully negotiating with Raymond Chow, who insisted that making a movie with a US studio would be bad for Bruce's career, because he did not relish losing control of his biggest star (at least according to Weintraub's reasoning). The breakthrough came at a dinner party where the guests were Bruce and Linda, Weintraub and his wife, and Chow. Weintraub told Bruce that he could not reach a deal with Chow, implicitly suggesting that Bruce leave Chow and sign instead with him. In response, Bruce stared at Chow and said simply, "Sign the contract, Raymond." To which Chow assented, "I think it's a wonderful idea." The deal Chow agreed to was to jointly produce the film that Weintraub had been developing, at the time titled *Blood & Steel*.[2]

Bruce pushed hard for a different title. His preference was for *Enter the Dragon*, a reference to his nickname, Siu Lung (Little Dragon).[3] He even threatened to break off his relationship with Warner Bros. if the studio did not accept the title change.[4] His insistence reveals an important aspect about how Bruce was growing his personal brand, for his moniker as "the dragon" was already in circulation throughout Asia with his earlier film *The Way of the Dragon*. He hoped that this Hollywood-backed film would help him build on his fame in Asia as "the dragon" to crack into the cultural consciousness not just of Asia but of the entire planet.

ENTER THE THIRD-WORLD DRAGON

Americans shooting a movie in Hong Kong offered a window into how differently filmmakers on opposite sides of the Pacific approached their craft. The expectations of the producer, Fred Weintraub, and the director, Robert Clouse, often ran headlong into Hong Kong filmmaking practices that gave priority to speed, efficiency, and improvisation, an approach that sometimes led to less-than-perfect results. For example, in one of the first scenes, Lee is sitting on a green couch while being recruited by a British agent of a secretive spy organization. Shooting wound up for the day, and when Weintraub returned to the set the next morning, a red couch had replaced the original green one.

As Weintraub ultimately discovered, the green couch had been rented for only a day because the Chinese prop master had assumed that filming the brief scene would take no longer than that, a reasonable assumption based on the normal pace of shooting in Hong Kong. So in the dark of night, Weintraub, Clouse, and the prop master piled into a van and headed to a remote warehouse in the Kowloon hills to retrieve the green couch, relieved that it had not been sold in the meantime.[5] Clouse relates the same story except that in his account, it was blue-upholstered furniture in another room that disappeared.[6]

Other surprises included the fact that the extras cast as prostitutes cost more than almost any other personnel. Because Hong Kong actresses refused to play women of ill repute, the filmmakers had to hire real-life prostitutes at their usual rates, which outstripped the wages of crew members.[7] And just as Weintraub and Clouse clashed with Chinese filmmakers, Bruce quarreled with the scriptwriter, Michael Allin, who was on the set during filming and objected to dialogue changes that the star suggested. Allin later claimed that he rewrote lines to force Bruce to say as many *r*'s as possible in an attempt to embarrass the native Cantonese speaker.[8] However, the joke was on Allin, for as Bruce had jested years earlier when he played Britt Reid's sidekick on *The Green Hornet*, he was a "Chinaman" who could pronounce his *r*'s.

≈

Despite differences with the Hong Kongers, Weintraub and Clouse came to appreciate the spirit of Chinese filmmaking. In one case, the producer and director were blocking the scene in which Lee's sister kicks one of the hood-lums chasing her off a ledge into a dirty canal four feet below. A group of stuntmen accompanied Weintraub and Clouse to a rooftop opposite the canal from which the scene was to be shot, but all adamantly rejected doing the stunt. After some cajoling, one man finally said, "O.K., I do it. But it's going to be hard to reach from here." Weintraub was blown away by the Chinese can-do spirit when he realized that the stuntman was agreeing to be kicked into the canal from the rooftop instead of from a ledge near ground level.[9]

Similarly, building the prison cells below Han's fortress showcased how Chinese workers made do with less. In Hollywood, the bars would have been made of dowels spray-painted black, but on the set of *Enter the Dragon*, a crafts-man laboriously hand-planed two-inch-wide pieces of scrap wood to make round bars because using leftover materials was cheaper than buying dowels.[10] And because Clouse, the director, had to make other adjustments to filming Bruce Lee in action because of the speed of his movements, one scene had to be shot at an accelerated rate of thirty-two frames per second rather than the standard twenty-four to adequately capture Bruce's rapid-fire punches.[11]

Ironically, despite being coproduced by Warner Bros., written and directed by white Americans, and featuring white and African American actors in key roles, *Enter the Dragon* reflects Hong Kong more directly than any of Lee's films completed during his lifetime. For one thing, *Enter the Dragon* was the first to be shot exclusively in Hong Kong. (*The Big Boss* had been filmed in

Thailand; *Fist of Fury* included scenes shot in Macau, such as one in the park with the "No Dogs or Chinese Allowed" sign; and much of *The Way of the Dragon* had been shot in Italy.) In addition, the villain Han was played by Shek Kin (also known as Shih Kien or Shi Jian), beloved by Hong Kong audiences for having portrayed the antagonist in the immensely popular Wong Fei Hung series of movies. Despite playing bad guys, the sixty-year-old actor was a fan favorite because he always accepted defeat graciously and promptly abandoned his wicked ways.[12]

≈

Enter the Dragon opens with a scene that both expresses the Bruce Lee philosophy and summarizes his years of martial arts and geographical exploration. And because Bruce both wrote and directed the scene, it differs markedly in tone and substance from the rest of the film.[13] Surrounded by monks at a Shaolin temple, Bruce squares off with a much burlier and surprisingly agile opponent. Although they begin by exchanging punches and kicks, Lee wins the match by grappling and pinning his opponent to the ground, forcing him to tap out in submission and thus end the match. This scene, the only instance of grappling in the film, shows Bruce's commitment to highlighting the idea that all techniques must be embraced when they are effective. Instead of going toe-to-toe with a stronger opponent, he renders his opponent's size disadvantage meaningless by going to the ground.

After the victory, Bruce's master praises his progress as having advanced beyond the physical realm into a spiritual level and poses a series of questions that Bruce answers by enunciating the Bruce Lee philosophy. To the master's query, "What is the highest technique you hope to achieve?" he replies by essentially defining Jeet Kune Do: "To have no technique." Bruce proceeds to elaborate on combat as an activity that allows an individual to transcend the self by becoming one with the opponent and eliminating the barrier between conscious thought and unconscious action. As he puts it, "There is no opponent . . . because the word 'I' does not exist. . . . A good fight should be like a small play but played seriously. A good martial artist does not become tense but ready, not thinking but not dreaming, ready for whatever might come. When the opponent expands, I contract. When he contracts, I expand. And when there is an opportunity, I do not hit; it hits all by itself." The final line is a near-verbatim recapitulation of Longstreet's line, "I didn't kick; it kicked," words that Sterling Silliphant undoubtedly cribbed from his lessons with Bruce.

Imagining himself as a Shaolin fighter allowed Bruce to incorporate more of his philosophy of combat. While instructing a young acolyte, he demands that the pupil infuse his kicks with "emotional content, not anger." After the student delivers an acceptable kick, Bruce asks, "How did it feel to you?" The boy responds, "Let me think," a comment that earns him a smack on the head and the admonition, "Don't think. Feel." Pushing a student to describe how a good kick felt echoes the scene in *Longstreet* in which Li asks the same question of the blind insurance investigator, just as Lee's statement, "I do not hit; it hits all by itself," echoes Longstreet's comment, "I didn't kick; it kicked."

Finally, Lee describes the purpose of martials arts instruction to the student: "It is like a finger pointing a way to the moon. . . . Don't concentrate on the finger, or you will miss all that heavenly glory." The finger that the youngster stares at is analogous to Longstreet's burned-down warehouse, which Bruce had explained was obscuring a view of the "bright moon." In both *Longstreet* and *Enter the Dragon*, Bruce cautions against getting bogged down with the mechanics of training because doing so reduces one's ability to gaze unimpeded at the beautiful moon, which symbolizes the state in which mind and body are unified. The similarities in the two scenes, the first written by his student, the second that he wrote himself, reveals the consistency of Bruce's vision throughout his journey as a martial artist, a journey that had taken him from his college essays to what would prove to be the final turbulent months of his life. During that concluding period, his vulnerabilities and imperfections were put on full display—a body that was outwardly perfect but breaking down under stress, use of illegal drugs to cope with tremendous psychological stress, and philandering. But in late 1972 and early 1973, only the flawless veneer was visible.

≈

Enter the Dragon wove Third World solidarity into the fabric of the martial arts genre, a move that the widely published author Vijay Prashad attributes to the "anti-imperialism of kung fu."[14] Understanding that anti-imperialism requires understanding how Bruce's transpacific life in Hong Kong and the United States enabled him to interweave a critique of colonialism with the ideology of Black Power.

Produced in partnership between Concord Productions and Warner Bros. Studios, *Enter the Dragon* bears witness to its transpacific origins. Bruce plays a martial artist named Lee who has been recruited by a shadowy British intelligence agency to infiltrate a deadly tournament being held on an island near Hong Kong and sponsored by a mysterious man named Han. (This was the closest Bruce would ever get to playing the James Bond–like figure he had dreamed of since *Number One Son*.) To carry out his mission, he forges alliances with two American contestants in the tournament: Williams, an African American fighter who is intimately familiar with police harassment, and Roper, a white playboy who is on the run from gambling debts.

Williams, a self-assured martial artist who sports an enormous Afro matched by an outsized libido, is played by Jim Kelly, a Kentuckian born in 1946 who had been a gifted athlete in high school. Kelly had won a scholarship to play football at the University of Louisville but left the team abruptly in protest of the coach's racist treatment of another player. He began studying the Okinawan style of *shorin ryu* karate in 1964 in Lexington, Kentucky, continued to train in Chicago, and earned a black belt studying with a Marine Corps sergeant in San Diego—yet another example of the role of the military personnel in spreading martial arts around the globe.

In 1970, Kelly attended the Long Beach International Karate Championships, the tournament where six years earlier Bruce had made his debut on the national martial arts scene. Watching the matches inspired Kelly, and he resolved to become a champion within a year. As he told an interviewer many years later, "My ultimate goals were to get into the movie business, to become famous, to make a lot of money and motivate and inspire young people, people of all nationalities and colors." But, he added, "I didn't know anything about acting. And there weren't a lot of black heroes in the movies at that time. I felt that with the martial arts, I could offer Hollywood something different. So my goal was to become a world-champion martial artist and try to get noticed."[15]

Kelly achieved his first goal in 1971 when he was crowned middleweight champion at the Long Beach Internationals, just as he had predicted. He moved to Los Angeles, where he opened a karate studio in the largely African American Crenshaw district and broke into the movies when he was hired to train an actor in the film *Melinda*. He must have been noticed on the set because he also had a small role as a martial arts teacher.

Kelly was a late addition to *Enter the Dragon*, replacing an actor who dropped out just days before shooting was scheduled to begin. Upon landing the part, he was asked, "How soon can you leave for Hong Kong?" Two days later, he was on a plane crossing the Pacific.[16]

The character of Williams ties martial arts practice to the Black Power movement in the United States. He is introduced in a flashback that shows a karate dojo filled with Black students. He enters and exchanges a Black Power closed-fist salute with the instructor. The dojo's logo, painted on the wall and embroidered on the students' uniforms, consists of a flared king cobra within an outline of a fist laced with red, green, yellow, and black stripes. After Williams leaves the dojo, two racist police officers try to arrest him, but Williams beats them and flees in their cruiser.

The martial arts and culture scholar Maryam Aziz notes that the instructor in the scene is played by Steve Sanders, who took the name Steve Muhammad upon converting to Islam and was the cofounder of the Black Karate Federation, known as the BKF.[17] Muhammad, like Norris and Inosanto a military veteran, had learned karate in Okinawa before being deployed to Southeast Asia. Despite the danger he faced in Vietnam, Muhammad developed sympathy for the Viet Cong, stating, "As far as I am concerned, those people just want to be left alone to do their thing."[18] Along with his fellow

BKF cofounders and a host of other Black teachers, Muhammad viewed martial arts as a way to provide opportunities for Black youth, instill pride and discipline, and prepare communities to struggle for justice.[19] The film's logo is an early version of the BKF emblem, which conjures Pan-Africanism with its colors and deadliness with the snake.[20] The presence of the logo on the dojo wall was no accident, as the scene was filmed in Kelly's Crenshaw studio.[21]

In the film, Bruce confronts a cobra, but rather than killing the snake, he captures it and later releases it to frighten two guards who impede his progress. And rather than treating the snake as an enemy, he enlists it as a confederate. While filming the scene with the cobra, Bruce would whack it on the head to make it angry enough to flare its hood. After a few of these episodes, the snake had enough and bit Bruce on the knuckle; fortunately its venom gland had been removed.[22]

Williams proves to be a trusted collaborator who gives his life to avoid imperiling Lee. *Enter the Dragon*'s evocation of Black antiracism can further be seen in the casting of Kelly, a talented athlete who lost opportunities due to protesting racism and embraced martial arts as form of self-determination in the realm of the body.

Kelly's charismatic turn in the role of Williams impressed Warner Bros. enough for the studio to offer him a three-movie contract, making him the first martial artist to land such a deal. Through the rest of the 1970s, Kelly became a staple of Blaxploitation films, starring in *Black Belt Jones, Three the Hard Way, Hot Potato*, and *Black Samurai*. His trajectory from *Enter the Dragon* into Blaxploitation films was hardly accidental, for as the film scholar Amy Abugo Ongiri argues, kung fu theater brought together Asian Americans and African Americans in unexpected ways. The attraction of martial arts films for Black audiences lay in antiracist readings of the films, which portray underdogs struggling for survival against oppression, using the body as an instrument of self-defense. Because of these resonant themes, Ongiri observes, "Images of Bruce Lee were at least as popular in many Black homes as were images of Martin Luther King, possibly even more so."[23]

The affinity of Black viewers for the body politics of martial arts films spilled over to the genre of Blaxploitation, which featured larger-than-life African American heroes (rather than sidekicks) who were propelled by the Black Power ideal of self-determination and were more than willing to put their bodies on the line while engaging in necessary violence. Perhaps unsurprisingly, in 1973, the film critic Gene Siskel observed that in downtown Chicago movie theaters, "approximately three-fourths of the audience" for kung fu films was Black.[24]

≈

In contrast to Kelly, John Saxon was an experienced white actor. He was born in 1936 as Carmen Orrico to Italian American parents and grew up in a working-class neighborhood of Brooklyn that was home to Irish, Italian, Jewish, and Greek Americans. Carmen began studying acting at the age of sixteen and started to get small jobs, one of which was posing for dime-store confessions magazines like *True Romance, Modern Romance,* and *True Story.*

Carmen Orrico became John Saxon, transforming himself from an ethnic kid from Brooklyn to a potential all-American movie star. As a white actor, he enjoyed a privilege that Bruce Lee would never enjoy, one that reflected the history of race and ethnicity in the United States. European immigrants like the Irish, Jews, and Italians were able to assimilate into whiteness, while Asian immigrants like the Chinese, Japanese, and Filipinos remained perpetually marked as racial others. Chinese immigration began in earnest in 1850 and continued until the 1882 Chinese Exclusion Act, whereas Italian immigration ramped up in 1880 and accelerated rapidly in 1900. As a group, Chinese had thus been in the United States decades longer than Italians, yet in 1972, an ethnic Chinese born in the US was still deemed to be less American than an Italian son of immigrants.

Saxon's brooding looks and street-smart edginess were meant to launch him on a path following figures like Marlon Brando and James Dean. He found his first significant work, though, in pretty-boy heartthrob roles in beach-party pictures, and he made three movies with Sandra Dee. In 1962, Saxon left Universal to try his luck in the burgeoning Italian film industry. Although he landed a number of roles, he discovered that his Italian looks worked against him because filmmakers desired more stereotypically American-looking actors. So he returned to Hollywood, where he found regular work in films and television. In 1973, he was thirty-eight years old, an experienced actor who had been studying martial arts for only about four years. He nearly backed out of *Enter the Dragon* after initially agreeing to take the part but before signing a contract. The original script was only about forty pages long, and he felt that the role of Roper was more suited to a stuntman than an actor.[25]

≈

Although in the film both Roper and Williams ally with Lee, their relationship to the local people and milieu could not be more different. Roper arrives at the Hong Kong airport with dozens of pieces of luggage and leaves in a rickshaw trailed by four more rickshaws laden with his baggage, the drivers serving as beasts of burden. Riding a gondola wending its way through the Aberdeen Harbor, he stares impassively at his surroundings.

By contrast, Williams arrives empty-handed and explores the city streets on foot. On the gondola ride to the island, he glances around inquisitively and prompts excited laughter by making eye contact with and waving at nearby children. "Ghettos are the same all over the world," says Williams, recognizing the poverty that surrounds him. "They stink." Decades later, speaking of Bruce Lee and his frustrations with Hollywood, Kelly recalled, "He knew my struggle, and I knew his."[26]

The characterization of Williams as a Black radical relating to Asian people on the basis of shared exploitation and oppression invokes Afro-Asian solidarity. Lee and Williams's interracial solidarity cinematically enacts the connection between the Asian American and Black Power movements in the late 1960s and early 1970s—a relationship forged within the United States through consciousness of Third World struggles in Asia and Africa.[27]

Williams's cultural nationalism and its congruence with Asian martial arts was eminently legible to Black audiences in the United States, for as Ongiri notes, kung fu theater provided "visual narratives of the body as an instrument of social justice," a tool honed through discipline and deployed by those who possessed few other means for resistance.[28]

Just as *Enter the Dragon* appealed to African American audiences with a narrative of antiracism, it offered Hong Kong viewers an anticolonial message. The premise of the film is based on the eroding power of colonial authorities: Han's island lies partially outside the jurisdiction of British authorities, and the agency that recruits Lee acknowledges that it cannot enforce laws but only gather intelligence. Lee is the one who uncovers Han's drug dealing and sex trafficking, bringing to light what agency officials only suspected.

Furthermore, only after Lee kills Han does the help promised by the agency arrive. As the helicopters fly into view, Lee surveys the carnage left on the island and shakes his head ruefully, knowing that he could never have counted on them. Lee proves himself more powerful than the British by accomplishing what they could not and doing so with his bare fists and feet. The portrayal of an ill-equipped Asian man triumphing where modern Western military technology had failed also raised the specter of the Vietnam War, for the United States signed the Paris Peace Accords and nearly completed the withdrawal of its troops from Southeast Asia the same year that *Enter the Dragon* was released.[29]

≈

Audiences in the United States flocked to *Enter the Dragon*, which became the highest grossing movie in the United States in its first week in wide distribution; it spent three weeks atop the rankings and nine weeks in the top ten.[30] It went on to gross $90 million worldwide, a figure that by 1987 swelled to $150 million.[31] *Variety* raved, "Lee socks over a performance seldom equaled in action."[32] The *New York Times* concurred, saying, "The picture is expertly made and well-meshed; it moves like lightning and brims with color." The paper also described Lee as "a fine actor" who delivers a "downright fascinating" performance.[33] However, Bruce's most American-influenced film fared less well in Hong Kong, grossing only $3.3 million Hong Kong dollars despite intense publicity centering on the star.[34]

As it would turn out, however, Bruce Lee was unable to enjoy the accolades he had sought for so long. He died suddenly six weeks before the release of *Enter the Dragon*. The circumstances surrounding his death remain controversial even half a century later. But the fact that they are still debated speaks to the enduring legacy of a singular man who lived and worked during a transformative period in history.

EXIT THE DRAGON

In the spring of 1973, Bruce Lee stood on the precipice of international stardom. He had become the biggest movie star in Hong Kong, broken box-office records throughout Asia, and signed a contract with Warner Bros. that promised to help him achieve the Hollywood success that had eluded him for so long. Despite outward appearances, however, all was not well with either his mind or his body. Early warning signs pointed to deterioration that was invisible to his adoring public and perhaps even to himself.

Even before Bruce returned to Hong Kong to shoot the Golden Harvest films, his friend the judo champion Hayward Nishioka noticed that something amiss. Nishioka recalled a couple of phone calls during which Bruce uncharacteristically sounded as if he were "real high" on drugs. From Hong Kong, Bruce sent "sloppily written" letters to his friend the martial arts publisher Mito Uyehara, a departure from his normally "beautiful penmanship," which had deteriorated to the point of being nearly indecipherable.[35]

During the filming of *Enter the Dragon*, Bruce drove himself to the brink of exhaustion. Unable to sleep at night, he compulsively choreographed fight scenes at the home on Cumberland Road where he, Linda, Brandon, and Shannon lived. By day, he obsessed over every detail to ensure that everything went perfectly, and he demanded that action scenes be shot up to fourteen times in a row before he was satisfied. He also lost weight rapidly and suffered from dehydration. His skin became pale, and people whispered that he did not look well.[36] Over Linda's objections, he avoided solid food for four months during the filming, subsisting on apple and carrot juice to lose weight. He believed that doing so would enable him to jump higher and longer in the fighting scenes.[37]

≈

After shooting was completed for *Enter the Dragon* and the film moved into postproduction, Bruce suffered a frightening collapse that foreshadowed the event that would end his life two months later. The episode occurred on May 10 while he was recording dialogue for the film's audio track. The noisy air conditioner in the dubbing room at Golden Harvest had been turned off, even though the day was especially sweltering. Half an hour into the session, Bruce complained of feeling ill and headed to the bathroom, where he ate some hashish—a concentrate made from the resin of the cannabis plant— and then collapsed. As would become clear later, he continued the habit that he had acquired in Hollywood of orally ingesting hashish, despite the much greater legal and social stigma against the substance in Hong Kong. When a studio employee entered the bathroom, Bruce struggled to his hands and knees, pretending to be searching the floor for his eyeglasses. The worker helped him to his feet and guided him back to the recording room, where he promptly fainted, vomited, and began convulsing.

Raymond Chow telephoned his physician, Dr. Donald Langford, who urged him to rush Bruce to nearby Baptist Hospital. Bruce arrived in the backseat of Chow's car, unconscious, sweating profusely with a high fever, barely breathing, and having seizures so violent that several doctors and nurses had to hold his body down. Langford feared that his patient might stop breathing and used an ambu bag (a manually operated breathing apparatus), evacuated the contents of Bruce's stomach, and intubated him to help him breathe. Doctors administered the drug Mannitol to combat what they suspected was a swelling of the brain, but since Baptist had no available beds, they decided to transfer their patient to St. Teresa's Hospital.[38] There the neurosurgeon Dr. Peter Wu diagnosed Bruce as suffering from cerebral edema (swelling of the brain).

By the next day, Bruce had regained consciousness and recovered his ability to move and speak. He admitted that he had ingested hashish, and indeed cannabis was found in his stomach contents. Dr. Wu cited drug overdose or sensitivity as the cause of the seizure and warned Bruce that he would have died without immediate and drastic medical intervention.[39] Bruce, however, rejected the diagnosis outright and promptly flew to Los Angeles to consult American doctors who were less judgmental about marijuana usage. After conducting a full neurological examination at UCLA Medical Center, Dr. David Reisbord uncovered no abnormalities and declared that Bruce not just was physically fit but had the body of an eighteen-year-old.

The American doctor's diagnosis of a seizure arising from an unknown cause left unsolved the mystery of just what had occurred in the Golden Harvest recording room on that disturbing afternoon.[40] To old friends, Bruce appeared less healthy than the neurologist's comment suggested. Mito Uyehara observed that when they met at the Beverly Hills Hotel in Los Angeles, Bruce had dropped ten pounds from his usual weight of about 130 pounds. But Bruce was pleased with the way he looked on camera, boasting that he had retained all of his muscles and that his waist was just twenty-six inches in circumference.[41]

≈

An incident about two months later at the Golden Harvest studio demonstrated how Bruce's mental state was deteriorating along with his physical health. His nonstop sprint toward achieving his goal of becoming the biggest star in the world took its toll as he drove himself relentlessly past exhaustion and self-medicated on cannabis.

His biographers disagree about the severity of the confrontation between Bruce and Lo Wei, the director of *The Big Boss* and *Fist of Fury*, that took place in early July, but there is no disagreement about the issue under dispute.[42] Bruce harbored a deep resentment toward Lo, whom he believed was claiming too much credit for the success of his films. One afternoon while Bruce was "slightly stoned" on hashish in his office at the studio, he discovered that Lo and his wife, Gladys, were screening a new film on the premises. He burst into the screening room, screaming insults at Lo in Cantonese, calling him a "beast in human clothing," then stood over him menacingly until onlookers dragged him from the room.

About ten minutes later, Bruce returned, this time brandishing a knife with a four-inch blade nearly touching Lo's chest while announcing, "Do you believe that I can kill you with one stab?" Raymond Chow and the producer Andre Morgan pulled Bruce away. Lo called the police, telling them that he feared for his life and demanding that Bruce be arrested. Exactly what happened next is unclear, but when the police arrived, no weapon could be found. They offered to let the incident go in exchange for Bruce writing a letter confessing that he had made a mistake and promising not to harm the director in the future. Bruce signed the letter to avoid adverse publicity but later publicly denied pulling a knife. "If I wanted to kill Lo Wei, I would not use a knife," he said. "Two fingers would be enough."

As evidence of Bruce's growing paranoia, Tom Bleecker, author of an antagonistic biography of Bruce, *Unsettled Matters: The Life and Death of Bruce Lee*, claims that he had begun carrying a .22-caliber Derringer pistol loaded with hollow-point bullets and keeping a .44-caliber Magnum revolver handy, despite the fact that possessing firearms was a serious crime in Hong Kong. Although Bleecker's animosity toward Bruce is evident in his writing, Jim Kelly corroborates that Bruce did carry a gun for self-defense while filming *Enter the Dragon*.[43]

≈

Bruce spent the morning of his last day on Earth planning his next career moves.[44] The action scenes of *Game of Death* had already been shot, but the film lacked both a solid story line to connect these scenes and a bankable star to play opposite him. He and the producer Andre Morgan met with George Lazenby, the Australian actor who had starred as James Bond in the 1969 movie *On Her Majesty's Secret Service*, to discuss a possible role. Bruce must have identified with Lazenby, an outsider from the colonies who had risen to play the iconic character in a blockbuster series, because he told Raymond Chow that he wanted to offer Lazenby a part.[45] The three made plans to have dinner that evening.

In the meantime, Bruce headed to the apartment of Betty Ting Pei, a small-time twenty-six-year-old actress with a pixie haircut known primarily for playing sexpots, with whom he had been conducting an illicit affair for several months. The fact that Bruce was a devoted husband and father did not mean that he maintained marital fidelity. Indeed, rumors—veracious or not—of his philandering dated back to his years in Hollywood and continued to dog him in Hong Kong. He was a beautiful man, strikingly handsome with an exceptionally chiseled physique, a star whose charisma drew in everyone around him. Whether by gossip or because women claimed to have carried on with him, over time Bruce was linked to actresses and women associated with the entertainment industry on both sides of the Pacific. Linda, for her part, dismissed these rumors publicly at the time and has continued to do so.

Bruce and Betty spent the afternoon having sex and enjoying hashish. Bruce also offered the role of his love interest in his new film to the woman who considered herself to be his "girlfriend." Raymond Chow interrupted them at Betty's apartment at about six in the evening, perhaps to get Bruce back on track of finalizing an offer to Lazenby. Bruce was so hyped about the movie that he acted out the entire story in an animated fashion that left him hot and exhausted. He asked for a drink of water, complaining that his head hurt and he felt dizzy.

Chow, Bruce, and Betty (who could be seen in public with Bruce because she was slated to appear in his next film) were scheduled to pick up Lazenby for dinner at 7:30, but Bruce insisted that he needed to rest. Betty gave him a pill of the common nonprescription painkiller Equagesic and put him to bed in her bedroom. Chow left and took Lazenby to a Japanese restaurant, where they waited at the bar for Bruce and Betty to arrive. After half an hour, Chow called Betty, who said that Bruce was still asleep and suggested that they proceed to dinner without them.

≈

After dinner, the seriousness of whatever ailed Bruce became much clearer. Chow called at 9:30 p.m. to check in on Bruce, and Betty reported that he had not roused but promised to awaken him. Her soft whispers gave way to gentle nudges, increasingly urgent shaking, and finally to desperate screams of "Bruce! Bruce!" Chow rushed back to the apartment, where he was greeted with the sight of his star lying undressed and unresponsive on the mattress of a starlet who was not his wife. He dressed Bruce in his shirt, pants, and boots and ordered Betty to call her personal physician, Dr. Eugene Chu.

The doctor arrived to find Bruce not breathing and with no discernible heartbeat. Ten minutes of effort failed to revive him. Dr. Chu called an ambulance and ordered the paramedics to transport Bruce not to nearby Baptist Hospital but to Queen Elizabeth Hospital, more than twice as far away. "I spent at least ten minutes trying to revive him," he later said in explaining his decision. "When he did not show any signs of improvement, it did not occur to me that time was of great importance."[46] The paramedics continued resuscitation efforts on the drive to the hospital, but it was apparent that no life remained.

Linda was waiting when the ambulance arrived at Queen Elizabeth, having been told by Chow only that Bruce had collapsed. She watched as doctors administered CPR and tried to shock his heart into restarting, but his EKG remained ominously flat.[47] Bruce Lee was declared dead at 11:30 p.m. on July 20, 1973. He was thirty-two.

≈

The sudden demise of a major star at the apartment of his paramour presented both a public-relations challenge for Golden Harvest and a potential source of embarrassment to his family. Raymond Chow and Linda Lee agreed on an acceptable narrative, which Andre Morgan wrote into an official press release. It stated that Bruce Lee had collapsed while walking in the garden of his home with his wife, Linda, had been rushed to the hospital, and died there. The *China Mail* ran the bogus story on page one, and the front-page account in the *South China Morning Post* also said that Bruce had fallen ill at home.[48]

The fiction cracked within three days. An enterprising reporter located ambulance logs and spoke to the ambulance driver, who revealed that Bruce had not been picked up at his home at 41 Cumberland Road but from Flat A3 in the Pik Wah Court at 67 Beacon Hill Road. The reporter went on to uncover the identity of the apartment resident as Betty Ting Pei. Not surprisingly, the Hong Kong press quickly pounced, printing salacious innuendos connecting Bruce to Betty, who maintained that she only knew Bruce professionally and had last seen him "several months ago."[49] This fiction too cracked under the intense scrutiny of the rapacious press, as neighbors attested that Bruce had visited Betty at the apartment regularly for several months, and in fact their relationship was only a loosely held secret, as they were spotted on dates in public.[50]

These revelations forced Chow and Linda to revise their initial story. In the new version, Chow and Bruce had worked at the Lee residence before going together to Betty's apartment to offer her a role in the new film, before Bruce lay down complaining of a headache. With Chow supposedly present, the meeting of Bruce and Betty would have been entirely professional with no opportunity for questionable activities. Years later, Linda continued to stick by the revised story, which denied the notion of Bruce as a playboy despite the clear evidence.[51]

Hong Kong turned out in full force to bid farewell to its prodigal son. At Bruce's funeral, an "army of fans" estimated as between ten thousand and twenty thousand strong mobbed the small Kowloon Funeral Parlor, generating an atmosphere more like "a carnival," as the *South China Morning Post* noted, than a funeral.[52] A police force of three hundred officers held the crowd—lined up a dozen deep—at bay behind barricades. Many had waited overnight to get prime spots on the street, while others flocked to rooftops of nearby buildings. The crowd cheered wildly as celebrities entered the chapel.

Inside, a banner reading, "A Star Sinks in the Sea of Art," hung above an altar bearing a photograph of Bruce. Some five hundred floral arrangements sent from around the world spoke to his global influence.

Linda, wearing a traditional Chinese white mourning gown and headpiece, stood with eight-year-old Brandon, and three-year-old Shannon greeted visitors including George Lazenby (who left the cryptic message, "Have a [nice] one Bruce," in the visitor book), actor Nancy Kwan, costar Nora Miao, director Lo Wei, and Bruce's childhood friend and actor Unicorn Chan. A band played "Auld Lang Syne," and as the *South China Morning Post* noted, Bruce's funeral "was identical to the scene" depicting the funeral of his teacher in *Fist of Fury*. Bruce lay in a white silk suit, his face visibly swollen and puffy.[53]

≈

Death could no more confine Bruce Lee than could life. His final Pacific crossing began on a dreary day at Kai Tak Airport in Hong Kong as his coffin was loaded in the rain onto a Northwest Orient Airlines jet bound for Seattle via Japan.[54] (Fittingly, Northwest played a leading role in transpacific commercial flight after World War II, pioneering the use of the Great Circle route, which shortened the distance between North America and Asia by flying over Alaska.)[55] When the Boeing 747 landed in Seattle, Bruce's mother, sister, brother, mother-in-law, and sister-in-law met Linda and the children.[56]

During transit, the outside of the coffin had been damaged and the white silk liner stained blue by Bruce's burial suit—the navy-blue tunic and pants that he had worn in *Fist of Fury* and considered to be a lucky charm. As a result of these mishaps, the coffin had to be replaced, leading conspiracy theorists to speculate that the body had been swapped with another corpse or that perhaps Bruce Lee was not dead after all.[57] A Hong Kong newspaper described the mishap as "a traditional Chinese omen that the soul of the man to be buried will not rest in peace."[58]

Bruce Lee's global travels ended at Lakeview Cemetery in Seattle in a peaceful, private ceremony attended by a hundred friends and relatives that stood in stark contrast to the pandemonium of the Hong Kong memorial service. Pallbearers Steve McQueen, James Coburn, Dan Inosanto, Taky Kimura, Peter Chin, and Bruce's brother Peter bore his casket, which was adorned by a yin-yang emblem made up of red, white, and yellow flowers.[59] The floral image signified the doctrine of mutuality that Bruce had embraced in his philosophy, martial arts, and personal life: that artificial boundaries should be bridged and that opposites do not exist in isolation but rather in relationship to each other.

As one of his students explained, "Night and day, woman and man . . . they are not opposites but instead are complementary. We say that there is a little hardness in the softness and a little softness in the hardness."[60] Along the same lines, Coburn eulogized, "Farewell brother. As a friend and teacher you brought my physical, spiritual and psychological being together. Thank you and peace be with you." Similarly, Linda recalled, "He believed the individual represents the whole of mankind, whether he lives in the Orient or elsewhere."[61] Their sorrowful statements paid fitting tribute to a man who had conceptualized, practiced, and symbolized the impossibility of dividing mind from body and East from West. Even the location of Bruce's grave reflected his all-encompassing philosophy. Like Seattle of the late nineteenth and early to mid-twentieth century, the cemetery's gravesites of that period are segregated, with Chinese bodies isolated in a ghetto of the dead adjacent to a Japanese section. Today, under a marble headstone identifying Bruce as the "Father of Jeet Kune Do," his body rests on a hillside overlooking the Chinese subdivision, not among his coethnics but nearby, as if drawing comfort from their proximity. (Tragically, his grave adjoins that of his son, Brandon, who was killed at the age of twenty-eight in a stunt accident on the set of *The Crow* in 1993. Brandon was trying to follow in his father's footsteps by starring in martial arts movies.) Like Ruby Chow's, the first restaurant to loosen the borders of Chinatown and introduce white Seattleites to Chinese cuisine back in the late 1940s, Bruce Lee broke boundaries even in death.

AFTERMATH

Back in Hong Kong, it was hardly surprising that intense scrutiny over Bruce's death generated massive publicity. A coroner's inquest convened to investigate the cause of death for the colony's biggest celebrity. Wild speculation about what could have killed the man who appeared to be the epitome of physical fitness and the intense interest of the public boosted newspaper sales by an average of 20 percent, with the circulation of some newspapers doubling and even tripling.[62] The inquest began on September 3, 1973, with Coroner Egbert C. K. Tung presiding at Tsunwan Coroner's Court over a three-member jury that would hear expert testimony, witness accounts, and cross-examinations before rendering a verdict.[63]

On the first day of the proceedings, reporters and eager observers jammed the courtroom, while outside, police struggled to contain a crowd that included more than a hundred people from the media and several thousand raucous fans. That Bruce had died of cerebral edema, or swelling of the brain, was never in doubt. The key question was what had caused that cerebral edema.

Shortly after Bruce's death, the clinical pathologist at Queen Elizabeth Hospital, Dr. R. R. Lycette, had performed an autopsy that found no signs of external injuries or abnormalities except for an enlarged brain. Examination of Bruce's stomach contents revealed two important substances: the Equagesic pill that Betty Ting Pei had given Bruce and the cannabis that he had eaten. Lycette concluded that "the most likely cause of death is cannabis intoxication." At the time of the autopsy, Dr. Langford and Dr. Wu, who had treated Bruce when he collapsed on May 10, agreed with Lycette that marijuana had killed Lee. The press ran wild with the story about Bruce's use of marijuana, an illegal drug widely viewed in Hong Kong as dangerous, and intimated that he been a drug fiend addicted to hallucinogens and opioids.[64] Although the allegations of drug use other than hashish were false, the matter of when Bruce had begun to ingest cannabis became a major point of contention.

Bruce held two life-insurance policies, one for $200,000 taken out on February 1, 1973, the other for $1.35 million taken out on April 30, 1973. The policies would be voided if it were determined that he had lied on the applications, since in both cases he had declared that he had never used illegal drugs. Linda had to acknowledge the fact that Bruce used cannabis prior to his death because cannabis appeared in his stomach contents on both May 10 and July 20 and he had admitted using it to doctors. However, she maintained on the witness stand that she had no idea that he ever used it upon returning to Hong Kong in 1972 and learned about his usage only in March or April 1973, thus preserving the validity of the life-insurance policies.[65]

Medical experts zeroed in on an implausible theory as to what had caused the cerebral edema that felled Bruce. In the time between the autopsy and the inquest, Dr. Lycette backed away from his earlier conclusion that cannabis intoxication was the cause of death, a turnabout that occurred after he reached out to toxicology experts in the United States and New Zealand who rejected the notion that cannabis could cause a fatal overdose. Now Dr. Lycette speculated instead that Bruce had suffered from what he described as a "hypersensitivity" to the ingredients in the Equagesic pill that Betty Ting Pei had given him.[66]

Under questioning, Dr. Langford and Dr. Wu also retreated from their earlier opinions on cannabis overdose, with Langford saying, "It may or may not have been drug intoxication," and Wu admitting, "I am not in the position as an expert to talk about cannabis."[67] An expert witness flown to Hong Kong to offer testimony, Dr. Ronald Teare, a professor of forensic medicine at the University of London, dismissed outright the assertion that Bruce had died of an overdose of cannabis. Citing a report by Dr. Ira Frank, a researcher in the Department of Psychiatry at UCLA's School of Medicine, Teare characterized cannabis as a nonlethal drug. As for the finding of cannabis in Bruce's stomach contents, he sniffed, "I regard that about as significant as if I had been told that Li had taken a cup of tea or a cup of coffee." Like Lycette, he pointed to "hypersensitivity" to the two ingredients in Equagesic, aspirin and meprobamate, either alone or in combination.[68]

≈

The coroner's inquest concluded on September 24 that Bruce Lee had died of "death by misadventure," a variation of accidental death. The verdict thus ruled out homicide, suicide, or natural causes in favor of mishap, relying on the theory of hypersensitivity to Equagesic offered by the expert medical witnesses. Adopting this hypothesis meant accepting the fact that Bruce died from a single dose of an innocuous painkiller composed of aspirin combined with meprobamate (a mild sedative used to lower anxiety) prescribed by the millions in Asia. But Bruce had been prescribed meprobamate, under the trade name Miltown, after a surgery in November 1972 and showed no signs of hypersensitivity then.[69]

Furthermore, there is no evidence that he took Equagesic during the May 10 episode that presaged his death, and on July 20, he took Equagesic after complaining of a headache, thus eliminating that drug as a cause. In both cases, he experienced a headache and dizziness or nausea, ate hashish, and suffered severe brain swelling. The strikingly similar symptoms strongly suggest that whatever caused Bruce to be hospitalized in May killed him three months later. Although his use of hashish in both cases indicates how regularly he partook of the drug, it does not provide a causal explanation, since millions of people around the world ingest cannabis with no reports of it causing cerebral edema.

With only a far-fetched medical explanation for Bruce Lee's death, rumors understandably abounded suggesting more fantastic causes. He had died of an overdose of LSD or heroin or too much sex. His move to Kowloon Tong had angered spirits: when Lee Siu Lung moved to the neighborhood "Nine Dragon Pond" (in English), he became the tenth, and the others slew him because he was, after all, only a Little Dragon. The home he purchased was an unlucky house, rumored to have financially ruined previous owners and damaged their health. Bruce installed a mirror on the roof to deflect bad feng shui, but it was blown away by a typhoon on July 18; and he died two days later.

More theories tumbled out, each more fantastic than the last. The name of Bruce's film project, *Game of Death*, tempted fate and he lost the confrontation. He was assassinated by a jealous martial artist using the *dim mak*, or vibrating palm technique, which enables killers to concentrate and transmit chi (energy) through their palms into victims who drop dead days, months, or years later.[70] As to the latter theory, Bruce did indeed feud with members of the kung fu community of Hong Kong, just as he had in California. He once appeared on television with several prominent masters, one of whom took a stance and challenged the others to shove him off balance. This master was rooted so firmly that no one could dislodge him, but Bruce stood up, walked over, and punched him in the face. The master toppled over. "Anybody can defend themselves if they dictate how they are going to be attacked," Bruce announced.[71]

Bruce's arrogance did not go unnoticed, for his declaration of Jeet Kune Do as superior to the traditional martial arts affronted practitioners of these older forms.[72] Even members of his Wing Chun brotherhood excommunicated him. When grandmaster Yip Man died on December 2, 1972, his students, including the top disciples, kept the news from Bruce, who as a result did not attend Yip Man's funeral. This serious breach of etiquette was widely seen and even publicized in the press as a gesture of contempt for the *sifu* and the kung fu style he personified. Those same students then had the gall to criticize Bruce as too arrogant to pay proper respects. Naturally, he was both furious and deeply disappointed when he learned of their duplicity.[73]

Public grief took more bizarre forms than rumor mongering. At least three fake bombs purporting to avenge Bruce's death were planted around the city. In one case, a supposed bomb was found by police on the hood of taxicab in Mongkok, wrapped in a brown paper packing bearing Chinese characters reading, "Revenge for Bruce Li's death." However, the package turned out to contain garbage.[74] The label on another fake bomb proclaimed, "Betty Ting knows the cause of Bruce Lee's death."[75]

≈

If Betty knew what killed Bruce, she was privy to a secret shared by no one else. Toxicology reports refuted the notion that Bruce had died of an overdose of hallucinogens or opioids, though death from too much sex was impossible to prove or disprove. Accepting the tenth dragon or feng shui or vibrating palm theories requires faith in forces that remain unverified by science. The autopsy ruled out death by violence. Even the theory that he had been killed for his money fails to hold water. After Bruce died, the press discovered that many of his assets, including the Cumberland Road house and his stock in Concord Productions, were held in the name of his butler and childhood friend, Wu Ngan. But why would Wu Ngan murder Bruce in July 1973, with brighter stardom and bigger paychecks on the horizon?

Tom Bleecker, who was married briefly to Linda in the 1980s, contends that Bruce died of withdrawal from anabolic steroids.[76] Indeed, he had taken prescribed steroids as an anti-inflammatory treatment for his severe back injury in 1970, and his physique was extraordinarily muscular. However, he boasted sinewy, lean muscle mass that was neither bulky nor swollen. He did not grow from a skinny kid into a thick, bloated specimen like the baseball slugger Barry Bonds. And though symptoms of steroid withdrawal can include dizziness and nausea, the medical literature does not cite cerebral edema as one of the symptoms.

≈

If all these theories are untenable, the question remains: What killed Bruce Lee? Matthew Polly, the author of the definitive biography *Bruce Lee: A Life*, argues persuasively, "Bruce Lee died from heatstroke. It is the most plausible scientific theory for his death." His symptoms—dizziness, nausea, vomiting, and high body temperature—typify those of hyperthermia. The dubbing room at Golden Harvest was sweltering, and the air conditioner had been turned off because it was too noisy; and at Betty Ting Pei's apartment, he had worn himself out excitedly acting out scenes.[77]

In addition, Bruce had had the perspiration glands in his underarms surgically removed in November 1972 so that he would not look so sweaty onscreen, which would have diminished his ability to shed body heat.[78] Even this theory has holes. Why would Bruce have become overheated from dubbing lines in a hot room or performing scenes in an apartment but not under the scorching lights of the movie set while filming endless takes of high-exertion fights? Yet heat stroke remains the most reasonable explanation for why this archetype of physical fitness died so suddenly.

THE SUMMER OF KUNG FU (1973)

Bruce Lee was poised to surf a wave of martial arts films crashing onto US shores in early 1973, but naysayers thought he was already too late. Bruce's own *Fists of Fury* (i.e., *The Big Boss*) debuted at number one on *Variety*'s box-office chart on May 16, 1973.[79] And it was not alone in achieving this lofty position. In fact, three Hong Kong martial arts films topped the box-office charts at the time: *Fists of Fury* stood as the highest earner, grossing $3.8 million in its opening week, followed by Golden Harvest's *Deep Thrust—The Hand of Death* and Shaw Brothers' *Five Fingers of Death*. Their success sent "American distributors scrambling for Hongkong-made 'kung fu' films," as the press on the island colony boasted.[80] In all, five Hong Kong films rose to number one on US charts in 1973, with one or another occupying the top spot during the kung fu craze of late spring through early fall. In addition, fifteen kung fu films ranked in the top fifty.[81]

Gene Siskel commented on the success of three "karate films" (as he mistakenly called them) in downtown Chicago theaters in early May. Although he disdained the lot as "terribly short on story material, badly dubbed, and unintentionally hilarious," he acknowledged that they could be "decidedly entertaining, providing you enjoy feats of violence." He judged *Five Fingers of Death* as "the best, or at least the funniest" of the genre, a further indication of his dismissive attitude, although he found *Fists of Fury* to be morally "the most sophisticated of the lot." In Siskel's eyes, the spate of martial arts films constituted a mere fad. Like beach-party or motorcycle-gang or gladiator or Blaxploitation pictures, they would be a short-lived "epidemic" or a "bandwagon," he predicted, to be jumped on and then just as quickly abandoned.[82] Even some Warner Bros. executives thought that the martial arts fad had played out, and in fact, one of them warned *Enter the Dragon* director

Robert Clouse that his movie would arrive a year too late.[83] Naturally, Clouse disagreed, as did his coproducer Paul Heller, who predicted, "The genre will take its place alongside the Western and the chase film, demanding improved stories and better production values."[84]

Enter the Dragon defied prophecies that the martial arts film wave had crested. Before its premiere in Los Angeles on August 24, 1973, a large crowd gathered on Hollywood Boulevard in front of Grauman's Chinese Theater, cheering as teams of dragon dancers from Los Angeles and San Francisco paraded past the iconic theater amid the crackling explosions and acrid-smelling smoke of fireworks.[85] Costar John Saxon recalls that when he arrived at the premiere in his limousine, he "saw lines and lines of people, and the lines didn't end." Indeed, the ticket line snaked around the block, with some people having queued up the night before.[86] The lines continued after opening night, and the movie set a new record for first-week sales at the theater on a nonholiday week.[87]

Enter the Dragon divided critics, who could not make heads or tails of the martial arts genre, yet most recognized Bruce Lee's charisma. Writing in the *New York Times*, the critic Howard Thompson called the film "expertly made and well-meshed; it moves like lightning and brims with color." He also praised Bruce as "a fine actor" who was "downright fascinating."[88] Thompson offered the most complimentary opinion among New York critics, as a roundup of reviews found three mixed and three negative evaluations aside from Thompson's.[89]

However, even hostile critics recognized Bruce's charisma, physical magnetism, and acting chops. A London critic pooh-poohed the film as a "mutant" mash-up of a James Bond–like thriller and kung fu fight film with "shoddy production values and a director and scriptwriter who fundamentally misunderstand the appeal and rules of the genre." However, he acknowledged Bruce's screen power, noting, "Bruce Lee's fight scenes come as near as anything could to saving the day."[90] Similarly, a redundantly redundant review in *Boxoffice* exclaimed, "Lee's athletic skill and an intriguing quality as an actor comes through intriguingly."[91]

≈

Enter the Dragon landed in the United States like a typhoon, and not just in coastal cities. It topped the box-office charts on September 5, 1973, and held its place the next week, grossing even more money.[92] It broke opening-week box-office records in places as diverse as the Grand Theatre in Cincinnati, Ohio, the State Lake theater in Chicago, and the Pinehaven Cinema/Theatre in Charleston, South Carolina.[93]

A karate demonstration accompanied the opening of *Enter the Dragon* in Kansas City, Missouri, where the film played in eleven theaters simultaneously. A small airplane flew over shopping centers in Omaha, Nebraska, dropping Ping-Pong balls that could be exchanged for free passes to the movie at two drive-in theaters. A Chinese restaurant in Washington, DC, lured diners by giving away records of Lalo Schifrin's soundtrack. In Denver, an "Enter the Dragon Day" promoting the film featured tae kwon do and karate demonstrations, along with radio disk jockeys participating in a dragon race.[94] The inventiveness of the film's publicity machine seemed to know no bounds.

Beyond the United States, *Enter the Dragon* inspired audiences around the globe, grossing $90 million worldwide in 1973, an astounding take for a movie that cost only $850,000 to make. Fans in Israel formed lines to buy tickets amid the chaos of the 1973 Arab-Israeli War.[95] *Enter the Dragon* fared more poorly in Hong Kong than in the rest of the world. It grossed only $3.3 million in Bruce's home territory, good for fourth place on the 1973 box-office chart, trailing *The Way of the Dragon* by $2 million. The *China Mail* labeled this disappointing performance the year's "biggest shock as far as box-office takings are concerned."[96]

Worldwide audiences, however, demanded more Bruce Lee even after *Enter the Dragon* closed. *The Way of the Dragon* was released in the United States as *Return of the Dragon*, a retitling that reflected the fact that it would be the second Lee film most viewers outside Asia would encounter. In Tokyo, *The Way of the Dragon* attracted 90,901 viewers at three theaters in its first week, making such a strong showing that Warner Bros. resolved to reissue

Enter the Dragon over a year after its initial closing, and a distributor snapped up rights to *Game of Death* before its completion.[97]

Fans progressed from devouring films to clamoring for Bruce Lee paraphernalia. In Great Britain, his picture adorned pillowcases, sheets, T-shirts, blouses, knickers, key rings, stickers, alarm clocks, and life-size posters. Teenage girls constituted Bruce's biggest fan base in the UK, forming a fan club with over thirteen thousand members and snapping up souvenirs so quickly that one merchant declared, "We're having to restock continually because the interest is phenomenal." Raymond Chow promised that Bruce Lee handkerchiefs and neckties would be available soon in Hong Kong.[98]

A year and a half after the so-called kung fu summer of 1973, the fever remained hot enough for Carl Douglas to top the Billboard Hot 100 chart with "Kung Fu Fighting."[99] Those "funky China men from funky Chinatown" may have been "fast as lightning," as Douglas sang, but they took their time exiting the scene.

≈

Although Bruce Lee's life ended in drama and confusion, his impact was clear. The product of transpacific currents that washed people, goods, and ideas both eastward and westward, he further contributed to connecting diverse cultures and nations. His incessant shuttling across the great ocean enabled him to synthesize martial arts in ways never seen before, to combine Asian and Western philosophies, to remake Hong Kong and Hollywood action films, and to break racial boundaries in both his personal life and professional career. His impact on the world was as brilliant as a flash of lightning, but it lasted much longer.

CONCLUSION

On July 31, 1973, at Bruce Lee's modest, private graveside service in Lakeview Cemetery in Seattle, Linda Lee eulogized her husband by quoting his perspective on death: "The day of death is the day of awakening. The spirit lives on."[1] History has validated Bruce's pronouncement, for nearly five decades later, he remains as relevant as ever. His dedication to bringing people together across cultures and national boundaries and to fighting for justice and equality endures today and continues to inspire people around the globe.

Within weeks of Bruce's passing, speculation ran rampant about who in the world of martial arts would succeed him in spirit, if not in body. Headlines in the *China Mail* blared, "Following in Li's Footsteps" and "Director to Groom New Bruce Li" over articles pondering who would "take up the throne that has been left empty by Bruce Li's death."[2] Innumerable pretenders approached his vacant seat, but none could ascend to take it. The University of Virginia film scholar Sylvia Chong argues that the urge to reanimate the figure of "Bruce Lee" persisted but failed because he embodied "a contradictory and multiple set of identifications with both movement and stillness, activity and passivity, life and death." Would-be heirs of the '70s and '80s—from Sammo

Hung in *Enter the Fat Dragon* and Jackie Chan in *New Fist of Fury* to Bruce K. L. Lea, Bruce Li, Bruce Le, Bruce Lea, Bruce Leong, and Bruce Rhee— reminded audiences that Bruce Lee was dead yet continually resurrected him in ghastly form with their pale imitations.[3]

Remakes and homages also kept the Bruce Lee flame alive. Jet Li's *Fist of Legend* (1994) reproduces *Fist of Fury*, with Li starring in Bruce's role as Chen Zhen. Although the movie reprises the main plot of revenge for the killing of a beloved *sifu*, it offers a more nuanced view of the rivalry between China and Japan by portraying both sympathetic and nefarious Japanese characters. Li's Chen learns of his teacher's death while studying in Japan, he loves a Japanese woman, and he meets a different fate in the end. Whereas Bruce's Chen sacrifices his life for Chinese honor, Li's Chen escapes with the help of the anti-militarist Japanese ambassador.[4]

More recently, the 2008 film *Ip Man*, the first installment in what became an immensely popular franchise of four movies starring Donnie Yen, lionizes Yip Man, the grandmaster of Wing Chun, by highlighting his victorious fights against the despicable Japanese conquerors of China. Yip's true importance comes into clear focus only at the end of the film, when the camera pans across a picture of the master with his most famous disciple, a young Bruce Lee. This coda establishes Yip's significance by establishing him as the forebear of the anticolonial Lee. *Ip Man 4: The Finale* (2019) centers on the grandmaster taking a fictional trip to San Francisco. It depicts a version Bruce's performance at the 1964 Karate Internationals (relocated from Long Beach), features the martial arts elders of Chinatown expressing their displeasure to Ip that his student is teaching kung fu to non-Chinese, and closes on a Bruce bowing to his master's picture at his funeral in 1972.

Bruce's dream of starring in the *Kung Fu* television series was thwarted in the 1970s but revived in spirit five decades later. The action-packed Cinemax show *Warrior* (2019) is "based on the writings of Bruce Lee," according to the credits and co-executive-produced by his daughter, Shannon Lee. The excellent Andrew Koji stars as Ah Sahm, a nineteenth-century Chinese immigrant to San Francisco. Ardent Bruce Lee fans can spot Ah Sahm recapitulating his mannerisms, including the signature swipe of the thumb across his nose and an anguished grimace when he stomps a man to death. Callbacks to Bruce's movies including the jade pendant from *The Big Boss*, the iconic image of the hero posing with nunchaku strung taut in his right hand and his left arm extended with an outstretched palm shielding forward, and episodes titled "The Chinese Connection" and "Enter the Dragon." Bruce's life also echoes throughout the show, with Ah Sahm revealing that he has a white grandfather and pursuing a romantic relationship with a white woman. He even laments that it took three minutes to defeat an opponent, which drives him to train harder and fight more frequently to improve his technique. In addition to *Warrior*, the 2021 remake of *Kung Fu* airing on The CW network updates the old show by centering as the hero Nicky Shen (Olivia Liang), a Chinese American young woman who uses her Shaolin training to fight for justice in her San Francisco community.

Bruce Lee's spirit lives on beyond revivifications of his body and invocations of his ghost. It also survives, more profoundly and enduringly, in his influence on filmmaking and fighting around the world. Paul Heller's prediction that martial arts films would become a durable genre did not come to fruition in the United States, but the *wuxia* aesthetic went on to suffuse global cinema. Lumbering John Wayne–style rumbles have given way to action scenes that feature speed, agility, and stylish moves. Hollywood badasses such as Tom Cruise in the *Mission Impossible* series, Matt Damon in the *Bourne* movies, Uma Thurman in the *Kill Bill* films, Keanu Reeves in the *John Wick* franchise, and even the light-saber wielders of *Star Wars* use styles drawn from across the globe, including Brazilian jiu-jitsu, Thai boxing (muay thai), Filipino kali, Israeli krav maga, Korean tae kwon do, Chinese kung fu, Okinawan karate, Japanese judo and kendo, and Bruce's own Jeet Kune Do.

In addition to remaining a staple of Hong Kong cinema, martial arts films have created stars in other countries, including Thailand's Tony Jaa of the Thai *Ong-Bak* series and Indonesia's most famous *silat* practitioner, Iko Uwais of *The Raid* and *The Raid 2*. Jaa and Uwais have gone on to star in films shot outside their native countries, including US series such as the *Fast and Furious* and *Star War* franchises as well as Chinese productions. Local martial arts styles have gone global along with their stars. The popularity of mixed martial arts, which Bruce Lee pioneered, has skyrocketed in the decades since his demise, with the Ultimate Fighting Championship rivaling and at times surpassing boxing in attendance and pay-per-view purchases.

Nearly half a century after Bruce Lee's physical death, he remains an immensely impactful and admired icon whose image appears in video games, commercials, documentaries, and museum exhibitions; on paraphernalia; and as a tourist attraction on two continents. However, his influence transcends popular culture and motivates people around the world to strive for justice and democracy.

ECHOES OF BRUCE LEE IN MOSTAR, COVID-19, HONG KONG, AND BLACK LIVES MATTER

On the eve of what would have been Bruce's sixty-fifth birthday, November 26, 2005, a life-sized bronze statue was unveiled in Mostar, a small city in southern Bosnia and Herzegovina. He appeared shirtless (of course), one rod of a nunchaku clenched in his right fist and the other tucked under his armpit, left hand extended and open palmed in a pose that is both poised for offense and ready for defense.

Although Mostar would seem an unlikely place for a Bruce Lee statue, the fighter symbolized something important to the people of this war-torn eastern European city: unity. The Bosnian war that followed the dissolution of Yugoslavia in 1992 tore apart this cosmopolitan, multicultural metropolis where Serbs, Croats, and Muslims once coexisted peacefully.

In 1995, a decade after the war's end, Mostar still sought to heal its wounds by creating cultural institutions and artifacts that all its residents could embrace. A group of artists called the Urban Movement conceived the Bruce Lee statue as part of a project titled "De/construction of Monument," which critiqued the use of monuments to create and foment ethnic and religious divisions. Instead, the Lee statue was intended as an antimonument, in the sense that its goal was not to memorialize any particular ethnic, national, or religious hero but to bridge differences among groups.

The writer Veselin Gatalo and the artist Nino Raspudić selected Bruce Lee as a symbol from outside the region's culture and history of strife yet one that would be popular among all camps. Even the placement of the statue was significant. As Raspudić explained, "If he faces East, they will say, 'It is a Croat Bruce Lee, threatening eastern Mostar where Muslims live.' If he faces West, they'd say. 'It's Muslim Bruce Lee against Croat people.' So we decided he will face the North!"[5]

The figure of Bruce Lee bridged time as well as ethnicity and religion, connecting the present to the 1970s, a moment when his popularity in the former Yugoslavia represented a new form of global popular culture and a period during which ethnic and religious groups coexisted peacefully. And whereas monuments, especially bronze statues, customarily venerate major figures of officially sanctioned national history, the Bruce Lee statue disrupted the concept of memorialization itself by celebrating a figure made famous in lowbrow popular culture. As Gatalo concluded, "We will always be Muslims, Serbs, or Croats, but the one thing we all have in common is Bruce Lee." Sadly, vandals did not honor the artists' lofty vision, and the night after the statue's unveiling, they broke Bruce's nunchaku and stole one of the rods. Vandals continued to attack the statue for several months, until the Urban Movement removed it for repairs and safekeeping.[6] Yet just as the spirit of Bruce Lee persisted after his death, his statue was repaired and reinstalled. Today it is a popular tourist destination.

≈

Over five thousand miles and two continents away from Mostar, Bruce Lee inspired pro-democracy protesters in his childhood home of Hong Kong. The island of Hong Kong, along with the New Territories on the Asian mainland, had remained a colony of Great Britain while Lee was growing up. But on July 1, 1997, Great Britain returned sovereignty over the area to the People's Republic of China, which incorporated Hong Kong within the larger nation as a "special administrative region." The Chinese government imposed a doctrine of "one country, two systems," which granted Hong Kong a modicum of self-governance while reserving ultimate authority for China. Unsurprisingly, this contradiction fueled tensions between pro-democracy forces and the government of the mainland.

In 2014, hundreds of thousands of Hong Kong residents took to the streets to protest a proposed law that would require that candidates for the post of chief executive be preapproved by Chinese officials in Beijing. Demonstrators occupied several blocks and barricaded streets in the Central District, and their protests came to be known as the "Umbrella Movement" for the brightly colored umbrellas they used to ward off assaults of tear gas and pepper spray by the police.[7]

Mass protests flared again five years later, this time motivated by opposition to a proposed law that would allow Hong Kongers to be extradited and tried for crimes on the mainland. Although the extradition law provided the spark, the reinvigorated Umbrella Movement was in fact driven by a broad ideology embracing democratic governance and opposing police violence and the authoritarian state.[8]

Bruce Lee's influence could be seen and heard as the Umbrella Movement refined its protest tactics between the summer of 2019 and early 2020. The slogan "Be water," drawn from Bruce's dictum, "Be formless, shapeless like water," impelled protesters to create a fluid, adaptable, and ever-changing resistance that eschewed rigid confrontations in well-defined spaces in favor of coalescing at rally points, then disappearing into the city. The leaderless uprising used the secure communication app Telegram to alert participants to collect in one location, then melt away when the police presence became too great.

Like water, which Bruce said could crash or flow, protesters clashed with armed authorities, then flowed away to the next confrontation. The insurgents expanded to fill the empty spaces unfilled by police, then contracted once they arrived. One piece of protest art by an anonymous artist and circulated on Telegram tied the movement specifically to Bruce. The words "Be Water Hong Kong" float above imagery of umbrella-wielding, gas-mask-clad

Graphic from Hong Kong protest adopting Bruce Lee's motto, "Be Water," circa 2019 (Artist unknown, distributed on Telegram)

demonstrators, and the image is rendered in yellow and black, reminiscent of the iconic colors of the track suit Bruce wore in *Game of Death*.

To drive home the connection between Bruce's adage and the second Umbrella Movement, a rally placard rendered in yellow and black read, "Be Water! We are formless. / We are shapeless. / We can flow. / We can crash. / We are like water. / We are HONGKONGERS!"[9] Umbrella Movement tactics traveled the globe, attracting the attention of protest movements in places as diverse as Catalonia in Spain, Belarus in eastern Europe, and Indonesia.[10] It was fitting that these movements adopted tactics provoked by the antiauthoritarian Bruce Lee, who rejected rigid orthodoxy and taught students to always adapt to both their opponents and changing circumstances.

≈

Bruce Lee remains relevant even amid a worldwide pandemic of disease and racism. COVID-19 began sweeping the globe in early 2020 during an era of heightened international tensions in the Pacific and around the world. Notably, Donald Trump won the US presidency in 2016 by promising to erect barriers to both trade and immigration. His famous call to build a wall spanning the entire seventeen-hundred-mile Mexico-US border (and make Mexico pay for it) never came to fruition, but the symbolism of raising a highly visible barricade emblematized his disdain of the other, the Mexican and Central American migrants whom he called drug smugglers, criminals, and rapists. This dehumanization led the Customs and Border Protection agency to separate children from their parents and detain undocumented minors in cages.

Trump's response to the COVID-19 pandemic began with denial, then turned xenophobic when the deadly spread of the virus could no longer be ignored. The man who rose to power through fomenting racism blamed China for the global dispersion of the novel coronavirus, calling it the "Chinese virus," the "Wuhan virus," and the "kung flu"—to the acclaim of his supporters.[11]

This campaign of fearmongering and disinformation that singled out Asian people as vectors of disease transmission harked back to the anti-Chinese movement that culminated in the passage of the 1882 Chinese Exclusion Act. The racism of that nineteenth-century movement, which scathingly conceived of Chinese people as bearers of disease, sexual depravity, and opium and as labor competition, reverberated in the twenty-first century.

The number of incidents of anti-Asian harassment, discrimination, vandalism, and physical assault skyrocketed during the pandemic. Nearly thirty-eight hundred incidents of anti-Asian bias were reported to the group Stop AAPI (Asian American / Pacific Islander) Hate between March 19, 2020, and February 28, 2021.[12] (Because the reporting system was not in place earlier, it is not possible to know with certainty how this figure compares with that of the previous year. As one measure of contrast, however, in 2019 the Federal Bureau of Investigation reported 158 anti-Asian hate crimes.)[13]

These offenses, which occurred from coast to coast, ranged from verbal harassment to deadly assault. An elderly man who died after being beaten in the Chinatown neighborhood of Oakland, California, was one of the victims of eighteen crimes targeting Asian Americans in the area during a two-week period in February 2021.[14] In New York City, Asian Americans suffered from a nearly tenfold increase in racially motivated crimes. Tellingly, the New York Police Department attributed the great majority of the incidents in 2020 to what it described as "coronavirus motivation."[15]

In the nation's deadliest attack, eight women, six of whom were Asian American, were murdered in Atlanta-area massage parlors. Cherokee County Sheriff Captain Jay Baker, who had previously hawked T-shirts calling coronavirus "COVID 19 Imported Virus from Chy-Na," declined to characterize the killings as a hate crime.[16] Because the murderer claimed that he killed to quell his sexual addiction, it is hardly surprisingly that it was widely noted that most of his victims were Asian women who for centuries have been stereotyped and exploited as exotic and sexually alluring.

The racism and xenophobia that spurred this resurgence of anti-Asian violence is exactly what Bruce Lee fought against throughout his life as a martial artist and actor. His constant admonition to learn from our neighbors around the globe could hardly be more apropos and needed today.

≈

There is liberating power in overturning the schema that divides the world into "us" versus "them," into "insiders" who live within our borders versus "outsiders" who live on the other side. Justice seekers have historically sought to demolish this mind-set, which has long been a centerpiece of systems of political, social, and economic domination. The Reverend Dr. Martin Luther King Jr. argued in his supremely eloquent "Letter from a Birmingham Jail," written on April 16, 1963, when he was in jail for opposing segregation, that when it comes to matters of justice and equality, all people are intertwined. "Injustice anywhere is a threat to justice everywhere," he wrote. He went on to say, "We are caught in an inescapable network of mutuality, tied to a single garment of destiny. Whatever affects one directly, affects all indirectly." King rejected the concept of insiders and outsiders based on geographical location. "Never again can we afford to live with the narrow, provincial 'outside agitator' idea," he wrote. "Anyone who lives inside the United States can never be considered an outsider anywhere within its bounds."[17] Later in his career, he would extend his notion of justice and the "single garment of destiny" beyond the borders of the United States to encompass the entire globe.

In what became known as his "Beyond Vietnam" sermon, delivered at Riverside Church in New York City on April 4, 1967, one year to the day before his assassination, King spoke both as a "citizen of the world" and "one who loves America" to outline a new dream for a peaceful revolution to create a planet free of poverty, racism, and national chauvinism, a planet governed by democracy and justice. King advocated for "an all-embracing and unconditional love of mankind" that would produce "a worldwide fellowship that lifts neighborly concern beyond one's tribe, race, class, and nation."[18]

≈

In April 2020, with the novel coronavirus sweeping the globe, the Bruce Lee statue stood guard once again in the central park of Mostar, a surgical mask covering his face and a purple latex glove on his outstretched hand as if warding off an unseen threat.[19] The peril he defended himself against may have been the virus, as the personal protection equipment indicated, but in truth, it was much more. In a multitude of ways, the life of Bruce Lee illustrated the dangers of racism, ethnocentrism, xenophobia, and national oppression.

The Jeet Kune Do principle of simultaneous defense and offense remains apropos: Bruce defended himself and the underdogs he personified by going on the offensive to break barriers and incorporate the best practices he could find, regardless of their origin. His character Tang Lung

Bruce Lee statue wearing COVID-19 personal protective equipment in Mostar, Bosnia and Herzegovina, 2020. The statue was made by the Croatian sculptor Ivan Fijolic and was erected in Mostar's central park in 2005. (Photo by STR/AFP via Getty Images)

expressed this idea in *The Way of the Dragon* when he remonstrated one of the Chinese waiters for refusing to learn the "foreign" Japanese martial art of karate. "Foreign or not," he declared, "if it helps you to look after yourself when you're in a fight, then you should use it," adding, "It doesn't matter at all where it comes from."

Just as borders cannot contain effective fighting styles, crossing them can spark new ideas and powerful solidarities. The remarkable resurgence in 2020 of the Black Lives Matter movement in the wake of the killing of George Floyd by the Minneapolis police officer Derek Chauvin and of Breonna Taylor by Louisville police officers galvanized many Americans of all races to enmesh themselves in Dr. King's "inescapable network of mutuality," in which Black people's lives, dignity, and well-being are valued and nurtured.

That year, half a million people took part in more than five hundred protests that erupted on June 6 across the United States, and between fifteen million and twenty-six million Americans reportedly participated in what the *New York Times* estimated to be "the largest movement in the country's history."[20] Black activists demanding an end to police violence encountered angry opposition, to be sure, yet perhaps more importantly also mustered support from a broadly multiracial coalition.[21] Asian Americans activists challenged their communities to confront their anti-Black racism and participated in solidarity actions across the nation.[22] Sikh volunteers practicing *langar*—the custom of providing meals as an act of service—fed Black Lives Matter (BLM) protesters in Queens, New York; Fremont and Los Angeles, California; and Norwich, Connecticut.[23]

Carlos Montes, cofounder of the Chicano Movement–era organization the Brown Berets, attended Black Lives Matter solidarity events in the venerable Chicano neighborhood of Boyle Heights in East Los Angeles. Some five thousand people, including former members of the Puerto Rican Movement–era Young Lords Party, marched in New York City in solidarity with BLM.[24] The National Native American Bar Association declared, "Hasapa Wiconi Hecha (Black Lives Matter)," noting that Native people also suffer from disproportionate rates of police violence. At a BLM protest at the state capital in Lansing, Michigan, Native American speakers linked the mistreatment of Black people to what they described as the "systemic brutality" and "genocide" suffered by Indigenous people.[25]

A number of polls conducted in June 2020 revealed that roughly two-thirds of Americans, including six in ten whites, approved of the BLM protests.[26] This widespread support represented a significant uptick from the first wave of BLM protests sparked by the killing in 2014 of Michael Brown in Ferguson, Missouri. A poll conducted by the Pew Research Center in 2016 revealed that only 43 percent of Americans, including four in ten whites, supported BLM at the time.[27]

Beyond the United States, demonstrators rallied by the thousands in London, Hamburg, Berlin, Paris, Brisbane, Sydney, Tokyo, Seoul, Bangkok, Bogotá, Trinidad, Rio de Janeiro, Johannesburg, Nairobi, and many other locations. These global protests decried racism in the United States, as well as local racism against Black and Indigenous people and ethnic minorities, police brutality, and colonialism.[28]

≈

Bruce Lee fought against racism during his lifetime. As a young teacher, he assembled a motley crew of students that included Black, Latino, Asian American, and white students. As a celebrity teacher in Hollywood, he developed a friendship with Kareem Abdul Jabbar, whom he not only trained as a fighter but also cast in the film *Game of Death*. As an actor, he vocally objected to depictions of Asians as weak and subservient and instead sought roles as a star rather than sidekick. Critically, he recognized that Asian Americans shared a common plight with Black and Native American people, who also suffered from demeaning stereotypes.

As a martial arts philosopher, Bruce rejected the idea that "there is such thing as a Chinese way of fighting, or a Japanese way of fighting or whatever way of fighting," which led him to conclude, "I do not believe in styles anymore." This declaration was based on the notion that people share a common humanity because we all occupy the same bodily form. He argued that only if some "human beings have three arms and four legs" would we have "different form[s] of fighting. But basically, we have only two hands and two feet."[29] This position, that human beings are all the same, is challenged by the campaign for disability rights, in which advocates have fought to achieve full human and civil rights for people with vision or hearing impediments or who suffer paralysis or diminished use of limbs. Indeed, not all people have "two hands and two feet."

Disability rights was not a well-known term in the 1970s. But if Bruce Lee were alive today, it is hard not to believe that he would forcefully embrace disability rights and modify his statement to say, "Basically, [as human beings] we all have bodies." On *Longstreet*, in a role written by his student that ventriloquized Lee's philosophies and teachings, he guided a blind man toward using his body as an effective fighting tool. In a 1971 interview, Bruce was asked, "Do you still think of yourself as Chinese, or do you ever think of yourself as North American?" He replied, "I want to think of myself as a human being. Because I don't want to sound like 'As Confucius say,' but under the sky, under the heaven, there is but one family. It just so happens that people are different."[30] Throughout his life and his career, Bruce Lee embraced a common humanity that recognizes and respects human differences.

On National Public Radio's always-fascinating podcast *Hidden Brain*, the network's social science correspondent Shankar Vedantam examines how working in intercultural settings and building relationships that cross lines of difference spurs creativity. Studies have shown that musicians, scientists, business students, and entrepreneurs who live abroad, date or marry people from outside their own cultures, or collaborate in diverse work groups generate more innovative ideas than those who do not. Social scientists believe that immersion in cultures other than our own enables us to envision new possibilities by forcing us to question our base assumptions and to see how others conceive of the world in different ways. Diverse groups come up with more creative solutions to problems, they have found, because their differences help them avoid groupthink by combining ideas drawn from diverse traditions.[31]

≈

Bruce Lee's life and career, tragically brief as they were, show how a singular remarkable individual became a global icon by crossing borders and embracing and synthesizing the cultural diversity offered by our wonderfully varied world. The enduring truth of Bruce's assertion that "the spirit lives on" after death can be seen by the fact that nearly half a century after his death, he lives on as a supremely popular cultural icon across the planet.

Zooming outward from a close-up focus on Bruce Lee as an individual to a wider view of the world he inhabited reveals that the forces of migration, militarism, racism, xenophobia, and transpacific trade that surrounded his rise to global fame still pertain in the twenty-first century. More important, the resiliency of people who migrate despite barriers, oppose militarism, fight racism, and join hands across difference also endures, perhaps more powerfully than ever before.

After the coroner's inquest into the cause of Bruce's death concluded in Hong Kong, his wife, Linda Lee, boarded an airplane to return to Seattle. High above the Pacific, the ocean that Bruce had crossed so many times, she gazed out the window and recalled a Chinese poem he had once translated for her:

> Do you not see
> That you and I
> Are as the branches
> Of one tree.
> With your rejoicing
> Comes my laughter;
> With your sadness
> Start my tears.
> Love,
> Could life be otherwise
> With you and me?[32]

She remembered the moving passage as a love poem expressing the intertwining of two souls. Yet the work holds greater significance as a statement about the interconnectedness of all humanity. Despite cultural, linguistic, racial, political, and national differences, not to mention the vast geographic distances separating people like branches of a tree, all living people share the one common root of basic humanity. May that spirit of Bruce Lee live on forever.

ACKNOWLEDGMENTS

Just as martial arts cannot be practiced alone, writing requires partners. Larry Hashima gave an enthusiastic thumbs-up when I asked him over a decade ago whether he thought a cultural history of Bruce Lee would make for a scholarly yet accessible book. Since then, I have benefited enormously from the guidance, suggestions, and encouragement of many people, including Arturo Aldama, Maryam Aziz, Yu-Fang Cho, Shilpa Davé, Rudy Guevarra, Tom Guglielmo, Masumi Izumi, Gina Marchetti, Leilani Nishime, Tasha Oren, Tom Romero, Seema Sohi, Andy Chih-ming Wang, and my students, colleagues, and friends in the Department of Ethnic Studies and College of Arts and Sciences at the University of Colorado Boulder. Sifu Stephen Joffe of Martialworks in Boulder, Colorado, introduced me to the physical aspects of Wing Chun. Audiences and commentators at conferences and talks at the American Studies Network–China, Japanese Association of American Studies, Organization of American Historians, Pacific Coast Branch of the American Historical Association, University of the Ryukyus, Doshisha University, University of California, Berkeley, University of Denver, University of Colorado Boulder, University of Colorado Denver, and Arizona

State University pushed the book forward in important ways. I am especially indebted to the scholars who compose the American Studies Association's partnership with the Japanese Association of American Studies, which is a shining example of how academic work can bridge national boundaries. I appreciate the aid of librarians and archivists at the University of Hong Kong, Hong Kong Film Institute, University of Wyoming, Wing Luke Asian Museum, Ingi House of the National Archives at San Francisco, and the interlibrary loan staff at CU Boulder. The University of Colorado supported the research and writing of the book through the College Scholar Award, Arts and Sciences Fund for Excellence, and the LEAP Associate Professor Growth Grant. Students in my undergraduate class on Bruce Lee and the transpacific proved to be an endless source of creative questions, confirmation that Bruce Lee continues to inspire young people, and joy in pursuing the project. Sincere appreciation to Eric Zinner and Furqan Sayeed at NYU Press, who have been staunch and patient advocates of this project, and Constance Rosenblum, whose incisive editorial suggestions improved the book in innumerable ways.

Thank you to the many nonacademic folks who eagerly engaged with me about Bruce Lee and his meaning; your enthusiasm convinced me to strive toward writing an accessible account explaining his life and significance. Finally, this book would never have come to fruition without the encouragement and unwavering support of my immediate and extended family. The people who especially helped me to protect and project from my center line (to reference a Wing Chun concept) are Alex and Tohru Dutro-Maeda and, most of all, Elizabeth Dutro.

NOTES

INTRODUCTION

1   Clouse, *Making of "Enter the Dragon,"* 187–93. Clouse relates an identical description of the mirror set, in *Bruce Lee,* 159–61. Internet discussions of this scene demonstrate the proliferation of inaccurate and unverified lore, as numerous sites claim that "over 8,000" mirrors were used in constructing the set. This is probably a misinterpretation of Clouse's figure of $8,000 spent on mirrors.

2   A note on terminology: although "Wing Chun" and "Jeet Kune Do" are not recognized by *Webster's Collegiate Dictionary,* 11th edition, as English words, both terms are so integral to the Bruce Lee story that they are not italicized as foreign terms in this book.

3   Matsuda, "Afterword," 326.

4   Matsuda, *Pacific Worlds*; Igler, *Great Ocean*; Sinn, *Pacific Crossing.*

5   Nguyen and Hoskins, introduction to *Transpacific Studies,* 24.

6   Deleuze and Guattari, *Thousand Plateaus,* 382.

7   In *Beyond Bruce Lee: Chasing the Dragon through Film, Philosophy, and Popular Culture,* Paul Bowman argues convincingly that Bruce Lee must be studied as a supremely intertextual figure.

8   For hagiography, see L. Lee, *Bruce Lee Story*; for character assassination, see Bleecker, *Unsettled Matters.* While acknowledging the deep commodifications of, and contestations over, the figure of Lee (which has appeared in films, merchandise, advertisements, and video games and continues to inspire imitation and remakes of his films), I seek to unpack how this multifarious figure establishes rhizomatic connections across national and regional boundaries, racial categories, and scholarly literatures.

9   For a discussion of parallax distortions, see Byrd, *Transit of Empire*, 29–31, 79.

10 Chan, *Chinese American Masculinities*, 76–77, 89.

11 Shimizu, *Straitjacket Sexualities* 33–81.

12 Chong, *Oriental Obscene*, 211–12.

13 Desser, "Diaspora and National Identity."

14 Teo, *Hong Kong Cinema*, 110–13.

15 Prashad, "Bruce Lee and the Anti-imperialism of Kung Fu."

16 Frazier, *East Is Black*.

17 Maeda, "Black Panthers, Red Guards, and Chinamen," 1089.

18 Fujino, *Samurai among Panthers*; Fujino, *Heartbeat of Struggle*.

19 Wu, *Radicals on the Road*.

20 Mullen, *Afro-Orientalism*.

21 Onishi, *Transpacific Antiracism*; Horne, *Facing the Rising Sun*.

22 Stein, "Bruce Lee," 118.

23 Polly, *Bruce Lee*, 490.

24 Yap, "Bruce Lee's Protégé Recalls His Humility"; Yap, "Bruce Lee's Daughter Says Quentin Tarantino 'Could Shut Up.'"

25 L. Lee, *Bruce Lee Story*, 74.

26 Clouse, *Making of "Enter the Dragon,"* 148.

27 Chaw, "Why Are You Laughing at Bruce Lee?"

CHAPTER 1. NEITHER EAST NOR WEST

1   Many sources cite Glover as a nurse, while others credit her as a physician. This question seems to be settled by the fact that a Dr. Mary Glover was listed as a member of an organization of women physicians in California in 1922. See Lyons and Wilson, *Who's Who among the Women of California*, 170.

2   Ruskola, "Canton Is Not Boston," 867–68.

3   Y. Chen, *Chinese San Francisco*, 16–18.

4   E. Lee, *Making of Asian America*, 59.

5   Daniels, *Asian America*, 69–71.

6   Stephenson, "Quantitative History of Chinatown, San Francisco," 82.

7   Lei, *Operatic China*, 8.

8   Lei, 10–11.

9   Ng, *Rise of Cantonese Opera*, 144–45.

10 Information on early performances of Cantonese opera in California is drawn from Lei, "Production and Consumption of Chinese Theatre"; Lei, *Operatic China*, 30–50; Riddle, *Flying Dragons*; Riddle, "Cantonese Opera"; Y. Chen, *Chinese San Francisco*, 90–94; Ng, *Rise of Cantonese Opera*; Rao, *Chinatown Theater in North America*. The name of the original opera company varies widely across and even within original sources: Lei argues that "Tong Hook Tong" is the correct transliteration, while Ronald Riddle refers to it as "Hong Took Tong," and Nancy Rao refers to the "Fook Hook Tong" company.

11 Ng, *Rise of Cantonese Opera*, loc. 2297.

12 R. Riddle, *Flying Dragons*, 18.

13 R. Riddle, 20.

14 Y. Chen, *Chinese San Francisco*, 90–94.

15 R. Riddle, *Flying Dragons*, 55.

16 R. Riddle, 48.

17 R. Riddle, 48.

18 Martin, *Verdi at the Golden Gate*.

19 *San Francisco Post*, 9 October 1877, quoted in Riddle, *Flying Dragons*, 39.

20 E. Lee, *Making of Asian America*, 91.

21 On the Workingmen's Party of California, see Saxton, *Indispensable Enemy*. Quotes from the rally appear on page 118.

22 E. Lee, *Making of Asian America*, 93–4.

23 Wunder, "Anti-Chinese Violence in the American West."

24 E. Lee, *Making of Asian America*, 91.

25 Daniels, *Asian America*, 33–35; E. Lee, *Making of Asian America*, 91.

26 Information on Chuen and Ho's bond posting, journey through San Pedro, and departure from the US drawn from their exclusion files: Lee Hoi Chuen (39707/8-26; Box 3820; C-26-1-8-6) and Ho Oi Yee (39707/8-26; Box 3820; C-26-1-8-6), housed at the San Bruno branch of the National Archives and Records Administration. Many thanks to the archivist Ingi House for tracking down their exclusion files. Description of the Mandarin in Rao, *Chinatown Theater in North America*, 215–16. Information on performers' ability to enter the US in Ng, *Rise of Cantonese Opera*, 145.

27 Information on Chuen and Ho's journey and arrival drawn from "Passenger Lists of Vessels Arriving at San Francisco, California," ARC 4498993, Records of the Immigration and Naturalization Service, 1787–2004, Record Group 85, National Archives, Washington, DC, accessed via Ancestry.com, "California, Passenger and Crew Lists, 1882–1959" (database online). Their entries appear on lines 25–26 of list 8, SS *President Coolidge*, arriving on 8 December 1939. For their bond entries, see lines 25–26 of "Lists of Chinese Applying for Admission to the United States through the Port of San Francisco, California, compiled 07/07/1903–01/07/1947," National Archives Microfilm Publication M1476, 27 rolls, ARC 4482916, Records of the Immigration and Naturalization Service, Record Group 85, National Archives, Washington, DC, accessed via Ancestry.com, "San Francisco, California, Chinese Passenger Arrivals and Disposition, 1903–1947" (database online).

28 US Bureau of the Census, *Sixteenth Census of the United States, 1940*, Census Place: San Francisco, California, roll T627_299, p. 7A, Enumeration District 38-15, accessed via Ancestry.com, "1940 United States Federal Census" (database online). Salary calculations and inflation adjustment are my own. In the Ancestry.com index entry for Lee, his personal name has been mistranscribed as "Hoi Chuel," but the document clearly shows it written as "Hoi Chuen."

29 Teng, *Eurasians*, 8.

30 L. Lee, *Bruce Lee Story*, 20.

31 Eric Ho, *Tracing My Children's Lineage*, 26–38; Teng, "Hong Kong's Eurasian 'Web.'"

32 Guterl, *American Mediterranean*, 98.

33 On Shi Tai, in addition to the sources cited later in this chapter, see Teng, *Eurasians*, 98.

34 Eric Ho, *Tracing My Children's Lineage*, 42–44.

35 Eric Ho, 9, 17n5.

36 Eric Ho, 12–16, 44–45.

37 Eric Ho, 7–12. For a fascinating and detailed account of growing up in the extended Ho family, see Cheng, *Clara Ho Tung*.

38 Tsang, *Modern History of Hong Kong*, 64–65.

39 Cheng, *Clara Ho Tung*, xvi.

40 Eric Ho, *Tracing My Children's Lineage*, 96–106.

41 Tsang, *Modern History of Hong Kong*, 48–49.

42 Teng, *Eurasians*, 188–90.

43 *New York Times*, 14 April 1901, quoted in Eric Ho, *Tracing My Children's Lineage*, 123.

44 Eric Ho, *Tracing My Children's Lineage*, 108; "Chinese gentleman" description in Teng, *Eurasians*, 188.

45 On Walter Bosman, see Eric Ho, *Tracing My Children's Lineage*, 150–57.

46 Eric Ho, 45–48, 136–37.

47 Eric Ho, 34–38. Ancestry.com documents confirm his marriage, children, naturalization, and death.

48 Liu, *Ho Kom-Tong*, 53 (on 1914 and Mid-Levels), 97–145.

49 Liu, 53 (on jewelry and at least twelve concubines). Liu mentions the thirteenth concubine on page 89.

50 Liu, 151–57.

51 Liu, 184–89.

52 Liu, 190.

53 Liu, 89.

54 Liu, 231.

55 Liu, 89; Eric Ho, *Tracing My Children's Lineage*, 140.

56 Liu, *Ho Kom-Tong*, 217–25.

57 Law and Bren, *Hong Kong Cinema*, 5–20; see also appendix 1, 297–304.

58 Teo, *Hong Kong Cinema*, 40.

59 Information on Brodsky (whose name was sometimes rendered as Brasky or Polaski) is drawn from Law, "American Connection," 45–46; Law and Bren, *Hong Kong Cinema*, 29–42; Curry, "Benjamin Brodsky: Part One"; Curry, "Benjamin Brodsky: Part Two"; and Bren, "Fabulous Adventures." Scholars often disagree on details of the life and career of Brodsky, who over time listed various places and dates of birth and made a number of unverifiable, self-aggrandizing claims. His film company's name is translated variously as "Huamei," "Asia Film Company," and "Variety Film Exchange." However, Brodsky remains an important and intriguing figure in Chinese, Japanese, and US film history.

60 Curry, "Benjamin Brodsky: Part One."

61 Law and Bren assert that Brodsky produced these films, while Curry casts doubt on this assertion. Furthermore, Law and Bren argue that *Roast Duck* was not made until 1914 and was the fourth, not first, Hong Kong film. See Bren, "Fabulous Adventures"; and Bren and Law, "Ben Brodsky and the Real Dawn."

62 On the Lai brothers and China Sun, see Law and Bren, *Hong Kong Cinema*, 47–56; and Law, "American Connection," 47–49; Kam, "From *South Pacific* to *Shanghai Blues*," 14.

63 Information on Moon Kwan found in Law and Bren, *Hong Kong Cinema*, 77–79; Law, "American Connection," 48–50; and Teo, *Hong Kong Cinema*, 267–8.

64 Information on Grandview drawn from Law, "American Connection," 50–59; and Law and Bren, *Hong Kong Cinema*, 80–87.

65 Fu, "Between Nationalism and Colonialism," 217.

66 Law, "American Connection," 52.

67 Mitter, *Forgotten Ally*, 87.

68 The best account of Eng's life and career can be found in Law, "In Search of Esther Eng."

69 Eng is credited as director in the English-language version, while the Cantonese version credits Kwan. See Law and Bren, *Hong Kong Cinema*, 98; and Law, "In Search of Esther Eng," 321.

70 American Film Institute, *American Film Institute Catalog*, 399.

71 On the Chinese hospital, see S. Chen, *Being Chinese*, 165–67.

72 For an excellent discussion of *In re Ah Yup, United States v. Wong Kim Ark*, and the prerequisite cases, see López, *White by Law*.

CHAPTER 2. A HONG KONG CHILDHOOD

1 Fleming, *Thrilling Cities*, 19–20.

2 Tsang, *Modern History of Hong Kong*, 16; Welsh, *History of Hong Kong*, 105.

3 Thomas, *Bruce Lee*, 7.

4 L. Lee, *Bruce Lee Story*, 20–21; Thomas, *Bruce Lee*, 6–7.

5 L. Lee, *Bruce Lee Story*, 27; Thomas, *Bruce Lee*, 8; Campbell and Lee, *Dragon and the Tiger*, vol. 2, 11.

6 Campbell and Lee, *Dragon and the Tiger*, vol. 2, 4–6.

7 L. Lee, *Bruce Lee Story*, 26.

8 Robert Lee's recollection in *Curse of the Dragon*.

9 Uyehara, *Bruce Lee*, 143.

10 L. Lee, *Bruce Lee Story*, 21–22.

11 Hong Kong Movie Database, "Lee Hoi-Chuen."

12 Campbell and Lee, *Dragon and the Tiger*, vol. 2, 2, 13; Thomas, *Bruce Lee*, 299. The titles and dates of many of Bruce Lee's early films vary across sources. The most definitive list of Hong Kong films is Hong Kong Film Archive, "Hong Kong Filmography (1914–2010)." The filmography lists no film called *The Birth of Mankind* or *The Beginning of a Boy* (as Linda Lee calls the film) in 1946. Linda Lee (*Bruce Lee Story*) and Thomas (*Bruce Lee*) date *The Kid* to 1948, but the filmography lists it as a 1950 release.

13 Campbell and Lee, *Dragon and the Tiger*, vol. 2, 21.

14 L. Lee, *Bruce Lee Story*, 22; Thomas, *Bruce Lee*, 11.

15 L. Lee, *Bruce Lee Story*, 22, 26, 31; Thomas, *Bruce Lee*, 11–12; Polly, *Bruce Lee*, 40–45.

16 Tsang, *Modern History of Hong Kong*, 167.

17 Carroll, *Concise History of Hong Kong*, 144–46.

18 L. Lee, *Bruce Lee Story*, 26; Pollard, "Is 'The Green Hornet's' Version of Gung Fu Genuine?," 18.

19 Judkins and Nielson, *Creation of Wing Chun*, 8–9.

20 Judkins and Nielson, 180–83.

21 Judkins and Nielson, 113.

22 Judkins and Nielson, 164–65.

23 Wong, "Bruce Lee and His Friendship."

24 L. Lee, *Bruce Lee Story*, 26–31; Campbell and Lee, *Dragon and the Tiger*, vol. 2, 6.

25 Hawkins Cheung, in Chu, "Bruce Lee's Hong Kong Years."

26 Wong, "Bruce Lee and His Friendship."

27 Cliff Ah-Yeung, interview with Daryl Maeda, Hong Kong, 13 November 2013.

28 Interview in *Death by Misadventure*.

29 Wong, "Bruce Lee and His Friendship"; Cheung, "Bruce Lee's Hong Kong Years," part 1; L. Lee, *Bruce Lee Story*, 31.

30 Interview in *Death by Misadventure*.

31 L. Lee, *Bruce Lee Story*, 30; Campbell and Lee, *Dragon and the Tiger*, vol. 2, 6–7. Some sources, including this Campbell and Lee, translate Pearl's surname as "Cho," but in his own writings, Bruce use the form "Tso."

32 Cheung, "Bruce Lee's Hong Kong Years," part 1.

33 Campbell and Lee, *Remembering the Master*, 172.

34 Rubinstein, "In the Shadow of a Legend."

35 L. Lee, *Bruce Lee Story*, 31.

36 Thomas, *Bruce Lee*, 25, 29.

37 Interview in *Death by Misadventure*; Wong, "Bruce Lee and His Friendship."

38 Cheung, "Bruce Lee's Hong Kong Years," part 1.

39 Wong, "Bruce Lee and His Friendship."

40 Cheung, "Bruce Lee's Hong Kong Years," part 1; Thomas, *Bruce Lee*, 29.

41 Bruce's destination address of 654 Jackson is listed in the "Passenger and Crew List" of the SS *President Wilson* in "Passenger and Crew Lists of Vessels and Airplanes Arriving at Honolulu, Hawaii, compiled 01/1954–12/1981, National Archives Microfilm Publication A3571, roll 60, Records of the Immigration and Naturalization Service, 1787–2004, Record Group 85, National Archives, Washington, DC, accessed via Ancestry.com, "Honolulu, Hawaii, Passenger and Crew Lists, 1900–1959." Charles Russo notes that address as Quan Ging Ho's apartment, in *Striking Distance*, 30.

42 Bruce Lee to unknown adviser, November 1958, in *Letters of the Dragon*, 20.

43 Cheung, "Bruce Lee's Hong Kong Years," part 3.

CHAPTER 3. AN IMMIGRANT IN SEATTLE

1 On Chin Chun Hock (who is alternately known as Chun Ching Hock) and the Wa Chong Company, see S. Lee, *Claiming the Oriental Gateway*, 26; Taylor, *Forging of a Black Community*, 110–11; Chew, *Reflections of Seattle's Chinese Americans*, 126–27, 130; M. Riddle, "Chun Ching Hock Opens the Wa Chong Company."

2 Lew-Williams, *Chinese Must Go*, 6.

3 Pfaelzer, *Driven Out*, xxiv; Lew-Williams, *Chinese Must Go*, 1, 40.

4 Daniels, *Asian America*, 61–62.

5 Lew-Williams, *Chinese Must Go*, 120–25; Wilcox, "Anti-Chinese Riots in Washington."

6 Daniels, *Asian America*, 63–64; Wilcox, "Anti-Chinese Riots in Washington," 208–11; Karlin, "Anti-Chinese Outbreaks in Seattle"; Taylor, *Forging of a Black Community*, 111–12.

7 On immigration policy and the shifting demographics of Asian migration, see Hing, *Making and Remaking Asian America*.

8 S. Lee, *Claiming the Oriental Gateway*, 39–45; Taylor, *Forging of a Black Community*, 115–25.

9 On "Uncle Fook," see Campbell and Lee, *Dragon and Tiger*, vol. 2, 66–68. See also Skip Ellsworth in Bax, *Number One*, loc. 502. Bax renders his surname as Yeung, while the 1940 census form, Glover (*Bruce Lee*), and Campbell and Lee (*Dragon and Tiger*, vols. 1 and 2) transliterate it as Young.

10 Ruby Chow's Restaurant menu, ca. 1955, ID #2016.20.7, Museum of History and Industry, http://digitalcollections.lib.washington.edu.

11 Information on Ruby Chow drawn from Ron Chew, "Interview with Ruby Chow," 28 February 1994, Seattle, Folder "Chow, Ruby" (March 31, 1994 draft), Wing Luke Museum of the Asian Pacific American Experience; Chin, "Three Kingdoms"; K. Chen, "Legend in Her Own Time," 8, 14; Estes, "Ruby Chow," 4, 5; *Pacific*, "Ruby Chow," 4–7, 11–13; Chew, *Reflections of Seattle's Chinese Americans*, 105–6. In case of conflicting information, I prioritize the Ron Chew interview, as it is drawn directly from Chow herself and contains her corrections and annotations. My thanks to the Wing Luke Museum for assistance in accessing these sources.

12 *Pacific*, "Ruby Chow," 1.

13 Ruby Chow states in *Northwest Asian Weekly* that her father died (K. Chen, "Legend in Her Own Time") but told Chew that her father returned to China ("Interview with Ruby Chow").

14 The description of Bruce's living space comes from Skip Ellsworth's recollections in Bax, *Disciples of the Dragon*, loc. 465–78. Ellsworth describes him living on the second floor, but Cheryl Chow, Ruby and Ping's daughter, states that he lived on the third floor, along with two Chow brothers, in Kimura, *Regards from the Dragon*, 222.

15 Shelton Chow in *Curse of the Dragon*; Cheryl Chow in Kimura, *Regards from the Dragon*, 223.

16 Glover, *Bruce Lee*, 2–7.

17 Glover, 2–7.

18 Glover, 8–12.

19 Glover, 13–18.

20 Skip Ellsworth in Bax, *Disciples of the Dragon*, loc. 413–39.

21 Glover, *Bruce Lee*, 9.

22 Glover, 20.

23 Skip Ellsworth in Bax, *Disciples of the Dragon*, loc. 439.

24 Glover, *Bruce Lee*, 38–39.

25 Halpin, "Little Dragon," 424. Halpin purports that Demile was twenty years old in 1960, which would make his year of birth 1940. Other sources cite his year of birth as 1935 or cite his age as thirty-five in 1973, which would make 1938 the year of his birth. Eugene Ho, "Hypnotism in Self-Defense," 28.

26 wcdvid, "Bruce Lee—Seattle Years."

27 Demile in *Curse of the Dragon*.

28 Glover in *Curse of the Dragon*.

29 Glover, *Bruce Lee*, 76.

30 Skip Ellsworth in Bax, *Disciples of the Dragon*, loc. 457.

31 Glover, *Bruce Lee*, 31.

32 Bax, *Disciples of the Dragon*, loc. 320.

33 Ed Hart in Bax, loc. 329–30; James Demile in Bax, loc. 1541.

34 Glover, *Bruce Lee*, 55.

35 Kimura, *Regards from the Dragon*, 224.

36 Kimura, 218, 240–41.

37 Glover, *Bruce Lee*, 38.

38 Skip Ellsworth in Bax, *Disciples of the Dragon*, loc. 493.

39 Glover, *Bruce Lee*, 39–40.

40 Thomas, *Bruce Lee*, xix.

41 Glover, *Bruce Lee*, 48–49.

42 Glover, 47–48.

43 Glover, 48.

44 Glover, 48.

45 Glover, 49.

46 Glover, 76.

47 Kimura, *Regards from the Dragon*, 184.

48 Glover, *Bruce Lee*, 77.

49 Skip Ellsworth in Bax, *Disciples of the Dragon*, loc. 589.

50 Kimura, *Regards from the Dragon*, xviii–xxi.

51 Kimura, xxiii.

52 Glover, *Bruce Lee*, 12, 16.

53 Glover, 14.

54 Glover, 14–15.

55 Glover, 40.

56 Glover, 40.

57 Ed Hart in Bax, *Disciples of the Dragon*, loc. 330.

58 Weldon Johnson, "Mike Lee Hope for Rotsa Ruck: U Introduced to Gung Fu," *Seattle Times*, n.d., reprinted in Little, *Bruce Lee*, 24–27.

59 Skip Ellsworth in Bax, *Disciples of the Dragon*, loc. 460–68.

60 Glover, *Bruce Lee*, 41.

61 Glover, 41–43.

62 Glover provides the most detailed description (40–45); see also L. Lee, *Bruce Lee Story*, 45; and Jesse Glover in Bax, *Disciples of the Dragon*, loc. 287–95.

63 Kimura, *Regards from the Dragon*, 280, 284–85; Doug Palmer in Bax, *Disciples of the Dragon*, loc. 1066.

64 Skip Ellsworth in Bax, *Disciples of the Dragon*, loc. 497–505.

65 Skip Ellsworth in Bax, loc. 529–30.

66 Doug Palmer in Bax, loc. 1082–85.

67 Skip Ellsworth in Bax, loc. 535–45.

68 University of Washington report card, dated 16 March 1962. On display at the *Do You Know Bruce?* exhibit at the Wing Luke Museum, visited 1 August 2015.

69 Bruce Lee, "The Tao of Gung Fu: A Study of the Way of the Chinese Martial Art," 16 May 1962, Bruce Lee Papers (in possession of the Bruce Lee Foundation), reprinted in B. Lee, *Artist of Life*, 3–12. Unless otherwise noted, quotations in this section are drawn from this essay.

70 Bruce Lee, "How to Choose a Martial Arts Instructor," handwritten manuscript of the book *The Tao of Gung Fu*, Bruce Lee Personal Papers, reprinted in B. Lee, *Artist of Life*, 25–26.

71 Doug Palmer in Bax, *Disciples of the Dragon*, loc. 1089–91.

72 Pat Strong in Bax, loc. 1190–93.

73 Bruce Lee, "Any Color I Want," philosophy essay, University of Washington, ca. 1964, reprinted in B. Lee, *Artist of Life*, 66–88.

74 Bruce Lee, "Descartes," University of Washington, 24 January 1964, reprinted in B. Lee, *Artist of Life*, 65; and Bruce Lee, "Cogito Ergo Sum," philosophy notebook, 7 January 1964, reprinted in B. Lee, *Artist of Life*, 65.

75 Kimura, *Regards from the Dragon*, 190.

76 B. Lee, "Tao of Gung Fu," 9; Bruce Lee, "A Moment of Understanding," undated handwritten essay for a class at the University of Washington, reprinted in B. Lee, *Artist of Life*, 15–17; Bruce Lee, "All Streams Flowing East or West," handwritten poetry, reprinted in B. Lee, *Artist of Life*, 98.

77 Unless otherwise noted, information on Linda and her early relationship with Bruce drawn from L. Lee, *Bruce Lee Story*, 7–19.

78 Information on Palmer's experiences with Lee in Hong Kong drawn from Doug Palmer in Bax, *Disciples of the Dragon*; an interview with Palmer in Kimura, *Regards from the Dragon*, 287–291; and Wesselhoeft, "What It Was Like."

79 Wesselhoeft, "What It Was Like."

80 Erskine, "Polls."

81 L. Lee, *Bruce Lee Story*, 49.

82 L. Lee, 47–48.

83 L. Lee, *Bruce Lee*, 18.

84 Uyehara, *Bruce Lee*, 143.

85 Additional information on the engagement and marriage drawn from Thomas, *Bruce Lee*, 59–60.

CHAPTER 4. OAKLAND TRANSITIONS

1 Russo's portrait of Lau Bun appears in *Striking Distance*, 21–27.

2 Information on Wong drawn from Russo, 37–39 (*le tai* quote, 38); Campbell and Lee, *Dragon and the Tiger*, vol. 1, 94–96.

3 Russo, *Striking Distance*, 37.

4 Information on James Yimm Lee's life drawn from Campbell and Lee, *Dragon and the Tiger*, vol. 1, 6–12. I regard this book as unreliable in its rendition of Bruce Lee's life, as it describes episodes that are either unconfirmed by other sources or directly contradicted. For example, it contends that Bruce made an extended visit to New York City in 1959 between arriving in San Francisco and departing for Seattle, during which he met his father, who was performing opera. However, I can find no immigration or transportation records for Lee Hoi Chuen returning to the United States. It also contains an extended narration of Ruby Chow meeting Bruce at the airport, whereas other accounts specify that a friend of the family drove from Seattle to San Francisco to fetch Bruce. Despite these discrepancies, I consider the book to be definitive on its discussions of James's life and experiences because it is cowritten by his son, Greglon.

5 Dan Inosanto, quoted in Russo, *Striking Distance*, 88.

6 J. C. Beaglehole's definitive biography of Cook is *The Life of Captain James Cook*.

7 Haley, *Captive Paradise*, 11–27.

8 Wharton, "Dynamics of Participatory Conservation." The actual clothing represented in the statue would also contain vermilion elements made of feathers from the ʻIʻiwi bird. Splendid examples of the royal clothing and feather work can be seen at the Bishop Museum in Honolulu.

9 On the Great Mahele, see Kent, *Hawaii*, 29–35; and Haley, *Captive Paradise*, 159–66.

10 Kent, *Hawaii*, 39.

11 E. Lee, *Making of Asian America*, 74.

12 E. Lee, 74.

13 E. Lee, 111.

14 Sharma, "The Philippines," table 10.1, 339.

15 Bonacich, "Some Basic Facts," table 2.5, 65.

16 Dan Inosanto, quoted in Russo, *Striking Distance*, 88.

17 Corcoran and Farkas, *Martial Arts*, 355–36.

18 Corcoran and Farkas, 64, 230, 314–15; Russo, *Striking Distance*, 95.

19 Corcoran and Farkas, *Martial Arts*, 230, 367; Russo, *Striking Distance*, 95–96.

20 Russo, *Striking Distance*, 93–94.

21 Russo, 89.

22 Russo, 88–90.

23 Wally Jay recollection in Campbell and Lee, *Remembering the Master*, 75; Russo, *Striking Distance*, 85, 91–92.

24 Gentilcore, *Pomodoro!*, 3–4.

25 Campbell and Lee, *Remembering the Master*, 76–77; Campbell and Lee, *Dragon and Tiger*, vol. 1, 224–36.

26 Joe, with Kim and Bobkov, *Last of the Four Musketeers*, loc. 175.

27 Joe, loc. 139, 175.

28 Joe, loc. 292.

29 Joe, loc. 577.

30 Joe, loc. 834–82; Campbell and Lee, *Dragon and Tiger*, vol. 1, 236–42.

31 Campbell and Lee, *Dragon and Tiger*, vol. 1, 249–51.

32 Jay recollection in Campbell and Lee, *Remembering the Master*, 74.

33 Publication under the Chinese name cited in Campbell and Lee, *Dragon and Tiger*, vol. 1, 97.

34 Dan Inosanto recollection in Campbell and Lee, *Remembering the Master*, 91; Campbell and Lee, *Dragon and Tiger*, vol. 1, 91.

35 Ralph Castro recollection in Campbell and Lee, *Remembering the Master*, 84; Campbell and Lee, *Dragon and Tiger*, vol. 1, 109–10.

36 Campbell and Lee, *Dragon and Tiger*, vol. 1, 92–111. Excerpt from the introduction to *Modern Kung Fu* on page 104.

37 Campbell and Lee, 78–79, 88.

38 Leo Fong in Bax, *Disciples of the Dragon*, loc. 1555–56.

39 Leo Fong in Rafiq, *Bruce Lee Conversations*, 63.

40 Hobart, "Integrated Ideas of a Life Warrior," 75.

41 *Black Belt*, "Leo Fong."

42 Campbell and Lee, *Dragon and the Tiger*, vol. 2, 23–25.

43 Campbell and Lee, 93.

44 Campbell and Lee, 8.

45 Russo, *Striking Distance*, 138.

46 Russo, 7–8.

47 Russo, 1–9.

48 S. Miller, *Benevolent Assimilation*.

49 The historian Gabriel Kolko cites estimates ranging from two hundred thousand to six hundred thousand killed, in *Main Currents in Modern American History*, 278. Luzviminda Francisco speculates that up to one million may have been killed by combat, rampant disease, and horrific conditions within concentration camps, in "First Vietnam."

50 Information on Dan Inosanto drawn from Kelly, *Dan Inosanto*.

51 Rhee, *Bruce Lee and I*, 23–28, 36–38.

52 Rhee, 9–10.

53 L. Lee, *Bruce Lee Story*, 51.

54 Campbell and Lee, *Remembering the Master*, 98–100, 108.

55 L. Lee, *Bruce Lee Story*, 55.

56 L. Lee, 51.

57 Linda's account appears in L. Lee, 51–54.

58 Thomas, *Bruce Lee*, 62–63.

59 Leo Fong in *My Friend Bruce Lee*.

60 For one example among countless others of this canonical retelling, see Gong, *Bruce Lee*, 56–58.

61 Wing, *Showdown in Oakland*. Chapter 2 describes events at the Sun Sing Theatre, chapter 3 discusses the fight in Oakland, and chapter 4 recounts the battle in the press.

62 The Mandarin Theatre closed and reopened as the Sun Sing Theatre in 1948.

CHAPTER 5. "EITHER HOLLYWOOD OR HONG KONG"

1 Thomas, *Bruce Lee*, 67; Oppenheimer, "Would You Pay $50 for a Haircut?," 3.

2 On the Manson Family's murders and trials, see Buglioso with Gentry, *Helter Skelter*.

3 L. Lee, *Bruce Lee Story*, 70–71. One example of how memories fade and retellings become hazy can be seen in Linda's account in the video documentary *I Am Bruce Lee*, dir. Pete McCormack. She recalls fielding the call in Oakland from William Dozier's office before Bruce even arrived home from Long Beach. But Linda still lived in Seattle at the time of the tournament (August 2) and did not move to Oakland until after their wedding on August 12.

4 L. Lee, *Bruce Lee Story*, 71.

5 Bruce Lee to Taky Kimura, February 1965, in *Letters of the Dragon*, 43.

6 Synai Rockz, "Bruce Lee."

7 Bruce Lee to William Dozier, 21 February 1965, Box 6, Folder "Correspondence—1965," William Dozier Papers, Collection #06851, American Heritage Center, University of Wyoming, Laramie (hereafter Dozier Papers).

8 Thomas, *Bruce Lee*, 71.

9 Bruce Lee to Linda Lee, 15 February 1965, in *Letters of the Dragon*, 45.

10 Bruce Lee to Linda Lee, 15, 17, 21, 22, 25, 26, 26, and 29 (*sic*) February and 3 March 1965, in *Letters of the Dragon*, 45–54.

11 Bruce Lee to Linda Lee, 21 February and 3 March 1965, in *Letters of the Dragon*, 48, 54.

12 L. Lee, *Bruce Lee Story*, 71.

13 L. Lee, 72.

14 Bruce reported these trips in a letter to Taky Kimura, reprinted in Kimura, *Regards from the Dragon*, 70; and in an interview years later (1967), in Little, *Bruce Lee*. But Linda subsequently denied buying lots of clothes: in Little, *Bruce Lee*.

15 Bruce Lee to James Yimm Lee, 29 July 1965, in *Letters of the Dragon*, 58.

16 Thomas, *Bruce Lee*, 72–73.

17 Bruce Lee to Taky Kimura, 7 June 1965, in *Letters of the Dragon*, 56–57.

18 Bruce Lee to James Lee, 29 and 31 July 1965, in *Letters of the Dragon*, 57–58, 59–61.

19 Bruce Lee to James Lee, 16 August 1965, in *Letters of the Dragon*, 65.

20 William Dozier to Bruce Lee, 17 February 1965, Box 6, Folder "Correspondence—1965," Dozier Papers.

21 William Dozier to Bruce Lee, 1 April 1965, Box 6, Folder "Correspondence—1965," Dozier Papers.

22 William Dozier to Bruce Lee, 22 April 1965, Box 6, Folder "Correspondence—1965," Dozier Papers.

23 Weber, "Lorenzo Semple Jr."

24 Lorenzo Semple, "Number One Son: Story Outline, 'The Dragon-Thread Thing,'" 2, Box 6, Folder "Correspondence—1965," Dozier Papers.

25 Lorenzo Semple to William Dozier, 26 April 1965, Box 6, Folder "Correspondence—1965," Dozier Papers.

26 On the cultural phenomenon of Charlie Chan, including the books by Biggers and the movies starring white actors in yellowface, see Huang, *Charlie Chan.*

27 Bruce Lee to William Dozier, 28 April 1965, Box 6, Folder "Correspondence—1965," Dozier Papers.

28 William Dozier to Maurice Morton, 8 May 1965, Box 6, Folder "Correspondence—1965," Dozier Papers.

29 Bruce Lee to William Dozier, 10 August 1965, Box 6, Folder "Correspondence—1965," Dozier Papers.

30 Sheldon Abend to William Dozier, 4 January 1966, Box 6, Folder "Correspondence—January and February 1966," Dozier Papers.

31 L. Lee, *Bruce Lee Story*, 72–73.

32 Thomas, *Bruce Lee*, 72.

33 Bruce Lee to George Lee, 18 December 1965, in *Letters of the Dragon*, 66.

34 Bruce Lee to George Lee, 31 March 1966, in *Letters of the Dragon*, 68.

35 Bruce Lee to Fred Sato, 9 April 1966, in *Letters of the Dragon*, 69.

36 Bruce Lee to Taky Kimura, 18 April 1966, in *Letters of the Dragon*, 71–72.

37 L. Lee, *Bruce Lee Story*, 81.

38 Thomas, *Bruce Lee*, 76.

39 "Van Williams," Box 1, Folder: "Biographical Sketches—Actors," Dozier Papers.

40 "Bruce Lee," Box 1, Folder: "Biographical Sketches—Actors," Dozier Papers.

41 Kay Gardella, "Batman Producer Takes Hornet Out of Camp," *Daily News*, 17 August 1966; Dave Kaufman, "'Hornet' Will Not 'Camp': New CBS Development Deals," *Variety Daily*, 6 July 1966, 11; "'Hornet' Sans Camp," *New York Herald Tribune*, 4 March 1966; all in Box 5, Folder: "Clippings—Green Hornet," Dozier Papers.

42 Grams and Salomonson, *Green Hornet*, 315–17.

43 Grams and Salomonson, 308–9.

44 Grams and Salomonson, 331–33.

45 Grams and Salomonson, 349.

46 Uyehara, *Bruce Lee*, 69–70.

47 *Black Belt*, "Letters to the Editor," 61.

48 *The Milton Berle Show*, created by Milton Berle, season 1, episode 2, aired 16 September 1966.

49 Grams and Salomonson, *Green Hornet*, 74–81.

50 Grams and Salomonson, 318.

51 "Green Hornet Characterizations," Box 49, Folder: "Miscellaneous," Dozier Papers.

52 Erickson, *From Radio to the Big Screen*, 134–43.

53 Glenn Hawkins, "'Batman' Boss Will Unleash 'Green Hornet,'" *Los Angeles Herald Examiner, TV Weekly*, 26 June–2 July 1966, 7, Box 5, Folder: "Clippings—Green Hornet," Dozier Papers.

54 Kaufman, "'Hornet' Will Not 'Camp,'" 11.

55 Richard K. Shull, "Holy Hero, Batman! Don't Let the Gung-Fu Get You," unknown newspaper, 1966, reprinted in Little, *Bruce Lee*, 57.

56 Bernie Harrison, "A Swinging 'Kato' Pays a Visit," *Washington Star*, 1966, reprinted in Little, *Bruce Lee*, 62; P. M. Clepper, "Deadly Simple Fighter," *St. Paul Dispatch*, 18 July 1968, reprinted in Little, *Bruce Lee*, 66.

57 Willard Clopton, Jr., "Kato Likes Puns, Preys on Words," *Washington Post*, May 1967, reprinted in Little, *Bruce Lee*, 80.

58 Ian Glass, "Chop Talk with an Actor: Mayhem Up His Sleeve," *Miami News*, Florida Report, 24 October 1969, reprinted in Little, *Bruce Lee*, 93.

59 Bruce Lee to William Dozier, 10 February 1966, Box 6, Folder "Correspondence—January and February 1966," Dozier Papers.

60 William Dozier to Bruce Lee, 14 February 1966, Box 6, Folder "Correspondence—January and February 1966," Dozier Papers.

61 Bruce Lee to William Dozier, 16 February 1966, Box 6, Folder "Correspondence—January and February 1966," Dozier Papers.

62 Bruce Lee to William Dozier, 21 June 1966, Box 7, Dozier Papers.

63 William Dozier to Bruce Lee, 23 June 1966, Box 7, Dozier Papers.

64 Author unlisted, no title, n.d., Box 12, Folder "Manuscripts by William Dozier," Dozier Papers. Dozier is the presumed author given its placement in this folder.

65 Quoted in Daniels, *Politics of Prejudice*, 59.

66 Flora Rand, "I Want My Son to Be a Mixed-Up Kid!," *TV/Radio Mirror*, November 1966, reprinted in Little, *Bruce Lee*, 48.

67 Fredda Dudley Balling, "Bruce Lee: Love Knows No Geography," *TV Picture Life*, 1966, reprinted in Little, *Bruce Lee*, 35, 38.

68 Fredda Dudley Balling, "Bruce Lee: 'Our Mixed Marriage Brought Us a Miracle of Love,'" *TV and Movie Screen*, 1966, reprinted in Little, *Bruce Lee*, 42–43.

69 Balling, 43.

70 Balling, 45.

71 Rand, "I Want to My Son," 48.

72 Grams and Salomonson, *Green Hornet*, 348–52.

73 William Dozier to Bruce Lee, 7 March 1967, Box 8, Dozier Papers.

74 William Dozier to Van Williams, in Grams and Salomonson, *Green Hornet*, 348–52.

75 Bruce Lee to William Dozier, 13 May 1967, Box 8, Dozier Papers.

76 Bruce Lee to William Dozier, 21 June 1966, Box 7, Dozier Papers

77 Bruce Lee to William Dozier, 13 May 1967, Box 8, Dozier Papers.

78 Thomas, *Bruce Lee*, 89; L. Lee, *Bruce Lee Story*, 62.

79 Pollard, "In Kato's Gung Fu Impact Is Instant," 16.

80 B. Lee, *Tao of Jeet Kune Do*, 12.

81 Polly, *Bruce Lee*, 197–98.

82 Polly, 199–200.

83 Polly, 212.

84 Norris, *Against All Odds*, 32.

85 Norris, 33.

86 Norris, 42.

87 Norris, 45.

88 Norris, 47–49.

89 Norris, 50–56.

90 Norris, 56.

91 Norris, 64–65.

92 Polly, *Bruce Lee*, 217.

93 Linda Lee quotes the figure of $50 per hour, in *Bruce Lee Story*, 81; Matthew Polly cites $150 per hour, or $500 for ten lessons, in *Bruce Lee*, 219; Felix Dennis and Don Atyeo quote Bruce as saying he charged $500 for ten lessons, then doubling the price when he met no resistance to that price point, in *Bruce Lee*, 35. Weekly wages calculated from median family annual income of $9,870 in US Bureau of the Census, "Median Family Income Up in 1970."

94 Stom, "Budo Breeze," 43.

95 L. Lee, *Bruce Lee Story*, 82.

96 Polly, *Bruce Lee*, 228, 233, 237.

97 Polly, 251–55.

98 Polly, 261.

99 Polly, 262.

100 L. Lee, *Bruce Lee Story*, 83–84.

101 Polly, *Bruce Lee*, 275.

102 Polly, 245.

103 Polly, 244–46; on Polanski, see Thomas, *Bruce Lee*, 101; *Wrecking Crew*, dir. Phil Karlson.

104 Polly, *Bruce Lee*, 220–22.

105 Klein, *Cold War Orientalism*, 226–41.

106 *Black Belt*, January 1970, 15.

107 Stom, "Budo Breeze," 25.

108 *Black Belt*, December 1968, 21; *Black Belt*, "Budo Goes Hollywood," 45–46; *Black Belt*, "Black Belt Times" (January 1970), 11.

109 Uyehara, *Bruce Lee*, 69–70.

110 Eng, *Racial Castration*.

111 Scherling, *Blondie Goes to Hollywood*, cites the episode title and number as season 1, episode 14, "Pick on a Bully Your Own Size" (loc. 2624). I have chosen, however, to rely on the Internet Movie Database (imdb.com) listing.

112 Scherling, loc. 2756; Hutchins, "Touch of Hutch."

113 *Here Come the Brides*, created by N. Richard Nash, "Marriage Chinese Style," aired 9 April 1969.

114 Polly, *Bruce Lee*, 235–38.

115 Polly, 292.

116 Polly, 294; Uyehara, *Bruce Lee*, 75–77.

117 L. Lee, *Bruce Lee Story*, 88.

118 Polly, *Bruce Lee*, 269–71.

119 Linda Lee reports the 4–6 p.m., Monday, Wednesday, and Friday sessions in *Bruce Lee Story*, 90.

120 Polly, *Bruce Lee*, 262–63, 268–69, 271–75.

121 Thomas, *Bruce Lee*, 144.

122 *Black Belt*, "Enter the Dragon"; Weintraub, *Bruce Lee, Woodstock and Me*, 6.

123 J. D. Bethea, "Don't Call It Karate—It's Martial Art," *Washington Star*, 16 August 1970, reprinted in Little, *Bruce Lee*, 98.

CHAPTER 6. HONG KONG TRILOGY

1 Fu, "Shaw Brothers Diasporic Cinema," 2–6.

2 Fu, 10; Davis, "Questioning Diaspora," 53–54; Desser, "Globalizing Hong Kong Cinema through Japan"; Chung, "Moguls of the Chinese Cinema"; Kong, "Shaw Cinema Enterprise," 32–33.

3 V. Chow, "Golden Harvest's Raymond Chow."

4 L. Lee, *Bruce Lee Story*, 100; Polly, *Bruce Lee*, 301–5. Polly reports the counteroffer of $5,000 per film. The figure of $2,000 per film is reported in Thomas, *Bruce Lee*, 120; and L. Lee, *Bruce Lee Story*, 97. The figure of $200 per week appears in Desser, "Kung Fu Craze," 33. Dennis and Atyeo report the offer of $1,500 per month, citing Golden Harvest executive Andre Morgan, in *Bruce Lee*, 45. The newspaper story reporting an offer of $2,000 per film appears in Uyehara, *Bruce Lee*, 85; Uyehara reports Chow's offer as three films for $10,000 apiece (85). Clouse purports that Bruce signed for $10,000 for the first picture and $15,000 for the second, in *Making of "Enter the Dragon,"* 25. Linda's account is the most credible on the amount, since she was party to payments, as well as on the length of the deal, given that after completing two movies, Chow made major concessions to keep Bruce in the fold. These would have been unnecessary if Bruce had been locked up for a third film.

5 O'Connor, "In the Name of the Law," D19.

6 Uyehara, *Bruce Lee*, 42, 116.

7 Stokes and Braaten, *Historical Dictionary of Hong Kong Cinema*, 312–13.

8 Pellerin, "Bruce Lee as Director."

9 L. Lee, *Bruce Lee Story*, 100–103.

10 Dennis and Atyeo, *Bruce Lee*, 48–49.

11 Polly, *Bruce Lee*, 308–12.

12 Dennis and Atyeo, *Bruce Lee*, 49; L. Lee, *Bruce Lee Story*, 112.

13 L. Lee, *Bruce Lee Story*, 107.

14 Jack Moore, "Superstar Bruce Lee? Who's He? Well, He's to 'Easterns' What Ol' John Wayne Was to Westerns," *Off Duty/Pacific*, November 1972, reprinted in Little, *Bruce Lee*, 152–53.

15 Teo, *Chinese Martial Arts Cinema*, 78.

16 "Bruce Lee's $1 Million Punch," *The Star* (Hong Kong), 4 November 1971, reprinted in Little, *Bruce Lee*, 108; "The Big Boss Takes a Record Profit," *China Mail* (Hong Kong), 19 November 1971, reprinted in Little, *Bruce Lee*, 115.

17 Richard, "'Big Boss' Big Hit in Malaysia," 11; Mendoza, "Bruce Lee and *Big Boss* Hit in Manila," 14.

18 Polly, *Bruce Lee*, 316.

19 Polly, 319.

20 Polly, 329.

21 Thomas, *Bruce Lee*, 304. I use the films' original titles, simply because they make more sense.

22 Teo, *Hong Kong Cinema*, 110.

23 Kennedy and Guo, *Jingwu*.

24 Xiao, "China Expels 3 Wall Street Journal Reporters."

25 Moore, "Superstar Bruce Lee?," 153–54.

26 Bowman, "Sick Man of Transl-Asia."

27 I have always found it incongruous that the police unleash a volley not only toward Chen but also toward the crowd behind him, which includes the Japanese representative, the inspector, and the students. The framing of the shot is masterful, the logic less so.

28 Teo, *Hong Kong Cinema*, 110–11.

29 Kato, "Burning Asia."

30 Teo, *Hong Kong Cinema*, 111.

31 *Black Belt*, "Black Belt Times" (September 1972), 12.

32 *Variety*, "Jingwu Men," 49.

33 H. S. Chow, "Bruce's Fists Smash $3.5M Mark"; *Black Belt*, "Bruce Lee Shatters Own Hong Kong Movie Record," 12.

34 *Hong Kong Post Herald*, "Shaw Brothers' Epic Takes a Beating," 1.

35 Donovan, *Asian Influence on Hollywood Action Films*, 90.

36 Kerridge, *Bruce Lee Chronicles*, loc. 481.

37 Kerridge, loc. 400, 419–24.

38 Kerridge, loc. 432, 546, 578, 617, 635–36.

39 Interestingly, Wei Ping-ao, the actor who plays Ho, is reprising his role as the traitorous translator in *Fist of Fury*.

40 Norris, *Against All Odds*, 78–80; shooting at the airport described in Kerridge, *Bruce Lee Chronicles*, loc. 624.

41 Norris, *Against All Odds*, 78.

42 Kerridge, *Bruce Lee Chronicles*, loc. 663.

43 Kerridge, loc. 544.

44 Norris, *Against All Odds*, 80.

45 Thomas, *Bruce Lee*, 96–97.

46 Ongiri, "Bruce Lee in the Ghetto Connection," 255–56.

47 Berry, "Stellar Transit," 227.

48 Williams, "Kwan Tak-Hing and the New Generation," 71.

49 Rodriguez, "Hong Kong Popular Culture"; Teo, *Chinese Martial Arts Cinema*, 65.

50 Louie and Edwards, "Chinese Masculinity"; Louie, *Theorising Chinese Masculinity*.

51 Desser, "Diaspora and National Identity," 145–46.

52 Berry and Farquhar, *China on Screen*, 201.

53 *China Mail*, 25 January 1973.

54 Polly, *Bruce Lee*, 382–86.

55 Clouse, *Bruce Lee*, 135–36.

CHAPTER 7. ENTER AND EXIT THE DRAGON

1 Clouse, *Making of "Enter the Dragon,"* 25.

2 Clouse, 26; Weintraub, *Bruce Lee, Woodstock and Me*, 12.

3 Weintraub, *Bruce Lee, Woodstock and Me*, 17.

4 Clouse, *Bruce Lee*, 161.

5 Weintraub, *Bruce Lee, Woodstock and Me*, 18–20.

6 Clouse, *Making of "Enter the Dragon,"* 160.

7 Clouse, 152–58.

8 Clouse, 60.

9 Weintraub, *Bruce Lee, Woodstock and Me*, 25; Clouse, *Making of "Enter the Dragon,"* 72.

10 Clouse, *Making of "Enter the Dragon,"* 84.

11 Clouse, 136.

12 Stokes, *Historical Dictionary of Hong Kong Cinema*, 379–80.

13 Weintraub, *Bruce Lee, Woodstock, and Me*, 40.

14 Prashad, "Bruce Lee and the Anti-imperialism of Kung Fu."

15 Ryfle, "DVD Set Is Devoted."

16 Information on Jim Kelly drawn from Yardley, "Jim Kelly," A22; Ryfle, "DVD Set Is Devoted"; Calhoun, "Jim Kelly"; Horn, "Jim Kelly." Weintraub's recollection of the casting appears in Weintraub, *Bruce Lee, Woodstock and Me*, 15–16.

17 Aziz, "Our Fist Is Black."

18 Prashad, "Anti-imperialism of Kung Fu," 70.

19 Prashad, 74–76.

20 Aziz, "Our Fist Is Black."

21 Weintraub, *Bruce Lee, Woodstock and Me*, 17.

22 Clouse, *Making of "Enter the Dragon,"* 138–42; Weintraub, *Bruce Lee, Woodstock and Me*, 34.

23 Ongiri, "He Wanted to Be Just Like Bruce Lee," 33.

24 Siskel, "Click, Chop, Ring, Chop, Chop," E4.

25 Verswijver, *"Movies Were Always Magical,"* 163.

26 Quoted in Prashad, "Anti-imperialism of Kung Fu," 58.

27 Maeda, *Chains of Babylon*; Ho and Mullen, *Afro Asia*; Watkins, *Black Power*; Onishi, *Transpacific Antiracism*.

28 Ongiri, "He Wanted to Be just like Bruce Lee," 38.

29 Marchetti, "Immigrant Dreams, Marginal Fantasies," 14, quoted in Chan, *Chinese American Masculinities*, 94–95.

30 Desser, "Kung Fu Craze," 34.

31 Weintraub, *Bruce Lee, Woodstock and Me*, 24; Clouse, *Making of "Enter the Dragon,"* 194.

32 *Variety Film Reviews*. Although the review is dated July 31, 1973, it appears in the entries marked August 22.

33 Thompson, "Enter Dragon."

34 H. S. Chow, "Film Profits Soar."

35 Uyehara, *Bruce Lee*, 66.

36 Clouse, *Bruce Lee*, 152; Thomas, *Bruce Lee*, 180.

37 L. Li, "Violent World of Bruce Li: He Prowled the Neon Jungles," 12.

38 Langford interview in *Death by Misadventure*, dir. Toby Russell.

39 Wu interview in *Death by Misadventure*.

40 Account of this alarming incident drawn from L. Lee, *Bruce Lee Story*, 151–54; Dennis and Atyeo, *Bruce Lee*, 70–71; Clouse, *Bruce Lee*, 163–66. Discussion of hashish use in Polly, *Bruce Lee*, 425–29.

41 Uyehara, *Bruce Lee*, 79.

42 Thomas characterizes it as a relatively minor incident, in *Bruce Lee*, 193–94. Bleecker considers it more serious, in *Unsettled Matters*, 108–12. Polly treats it as an indication that "something was wrong with Lee," in *Bruce Lee*, 434–36. See also Clouse, *Bruce Lee*, 174–77. Polly makes the assertion of hashish use, citing an interview with Andre Morgan in which Morgan describes Bruce as "slightly stoned" (*Bruce Lee*, 434).

43 *Death by Misadventure*.

44 Unless otherwise cited, the account of Lee's death is drawn from Polly, who interviewed numerous witnesses (*Bruce Lee*, 439–53).

45 According to a story published on 20 July in the *China Mail* newspaper, Lazenby had signed a contract for the film the day before, a small discrepancy with the most widely accepted chronology of Bruce Lee's final day. *China Mail*, "Dynamic Duo's Game of Death," 4.

46 Dennis and Atyeo, *Bruce Lee*, 74.

47 L. Lee, *Story of Bruce Lee*, 158.

48 *China Mail*, "Li's Death—Heart Attack May Be the Cause," 1; *South China Morning Post*, "Sudden Death of Bruce Li," 1.

49 *China Mail*, "Who's Lying about Bruce Li's Last Hours?," 1; Ting Pei's address detailed in *South China Morning Post*, "Doctor Found Bruce in Deep Coma," 7.

50 Polly, *Bruce Lee*, 373.

51 L. Lee, *Story of Bruce Lee*, 156–57.

52 *South China Morning Post*, "Final Bow for Bruce Li," 1. This article has the figure of twenty thousand.

53 *China Mail*, "10,000 Good-Byes," 1; *South China Morning Post*, "Final Bow for Bruce Li," 1; Dennis and Atyeo, *Bruce Lee*, 76–77.

54 *China Mail*, "Linda: Please Let Bruce Rest in Peace," 4.

55 Corbett, "Donald W. Nyrop," 144.

56 *China Mail*, "Bruce Will Be Near to Linda," 4.

57 L. Li, "Violent World of Bruce Lee: When a Doctor Warned Him," 12; L. Lee, *Story of Bruce Lee*, 162; Polly, *Bruce Lee*, 452; Dennis and Atyeo, *Bruce Lee*, 80.

58 H. S. Chow, "Bruce Li's Coffin Is Damaged," 4.

59 L. Lee, *Story of Bruce Lee*, 162.

60 Block, *Legend of Bruce Lee*, 124.

61 *China Mail*, "Farewell Brother . . . ," 4.

62 H. S. Chow, *China Mail*, 1 August 1973, 7.

63 H. S. Chow, "Bruce's Coffin Is Damaged," 4.

64 Polly, *Bruce Lee*, 448–50.

65 Polly, 456, 461–62; *South China Morning Post*, "Widow Says She Was Aware," 6.

66 *South China Morning Post*, "Hypersensitivity to a Drug Could Have Killed Li," 9.

67 Polly, *Bruce Lee*, 468–69.

68 *South China Morning Post*, "Li's Collapse Not Caused by Cannabis," 7. The story consistently misidentifies the second ingredient of Equagesic as "metrobanate," but the meaning is clear. Dr. Frank is named as the author of the report in Polly, *Bruce Lee*, 467. Duncan Alexander McKenzie, a registered nurse, advocates for the theory of an adverse reaction to Equagesic, in *Death of Bruce Lee*.

69 Bleecker, *Unsettled Matters*, 69–70.

70 Discussion of the outlandish theories appears in Dennis and Atyeo, *Bruce Lee*, 80, 88–90. On *dim mak*, see also Block, *Legend of Bruce Lee*, 136; and Thomas, *Bruce Lee*, 224.

71 Rhee, *Bruce Lee and I*, 60.

72 Block, *Legend of Bruce Lee*, 132.

73 Polly, *Bruce Lee*, 397, 399–400.

74 *China Mail*, "Bruce Li Bomb a Fake," 1.

75 Dennis and Atyeo, *Bruce Lee*, 81.

76 Bleecker, *Unsettled Matters*, 95–98.

77 Polly, *Bruce Lee*, 473–75.

78 Bleecker, *Unsettled Matters*, 45, 69–70.

79 Desser, "Kung Fu Craze," 22–23.

80 Desser, 19; H. S. Chow, "Chinese Movies Take Top Places in U.S." Like *The Big Boss*, the other films were retitled for US release: *Lady Whirlwind* as *Deep Thrust—The Hand of Death* and *King Boxer* as *Five Fingers of Death*.

81 Desser, "Kung Fu Craze," 34.

82 Siskel, "Click, Chop, Ring, Chop, Chop," E4.

83 Clouse, *Making of "Enter the Dragon,"* 194.

84 *China Mail*, "No Business like Dragon Business," 1.

85 Clouse, *Making of "Enter the Dragon,"* 197.

86 Polly, *Bruce Lee*, 478.

87 *Variety*, "'Enter the Dragon' Enters the Record Books!," 10–11.

88 Thompson, "Enter Dragon," 26.

89 *New York Times*, "What's Opened Lately at the Movies?," 16.

90 Rayns, "Enter the Dragon," 5–6.

91 *Boxoffice*, "Enter the Dragon," B7.

92 Desser, "Kung Fu Craze," 34.

93 *Variety*, "'Enter the Dragon' Enters the Record Books!," 10–11.

94 *Boxofffice*, "Diversified Promotions Aid 'Enter the Dragon,'" 13.

95 *Atlanta Constitution*, "Bruce Lee Cult Booming All Over," 4 T.

96 H. S. Chow, "Film Profits Soar."

97 *Variety*, "Bruce Lee Pix Still Big at Japanese B.O.," 7.

98 Westberg, "Bruce Lee Cult Sweeps Britain," 5.

99 Billboard, "Chart History: Carl Douglas."

CONCLUSION

1 L. Lee, *Story of Bruce Lee*, 162.

2 H. S. Chow, "Following in Li's Footsteps," 7; *China Mail*, "Director to Groom New Bruce Li," 7.

3 Chong, *Oriental Obscene*, 212, 221.

4 S. Li, "Kung Fu," 529.

5 Bolton and Muzurvić, "Globalizing Memory in a Divided City," 191.

6 Bolton and Muzurvić, 181.

7 Ortmann, "Umbrella Movement."

8 F. Lee et al., "Hong Kong's Summer of Uprising."

9 Hale, "Be water"; Wright, "Be Water"; Hui, "One Hong Kong protester."

10 Hui, "Hong Kong Is Exporting"; Zaeiets and Borresen, "What Is Happening in Belarus?"

11 D. King, "We Shouldn't Need to Explain"; *Guardian*, "Donald Trump Calls Covid-19 'Kung Flu.'"

12 Stop AAPI Hate, "Stop AAPI National Report."

13 Federal Bureau of Investigation, "2019 Hate Crimes Report."

14 KPIX 5 CBS, "Oakland Police Arrest Suspect."

15 Sturla et al., "Attacks against People of Asian Descent."

16 Baer, "Cop Who Said the Spa Shooter Had a 'Bad Day.'"

17 M. King, *Why We Can't Wait*, 65.

18 M. King, "Beyond Vietnam."

19 Getty Images, "Bosnia-Health-Virus."

20 Buchanan, Bui, and Patel, "Black Lives Matter May Be the Largest Movement."

21 Arora, Stout, and Kretschmer, "What Helps Non-Black People Support Black Lives Matter?"

22 Savitch-Lew, "Beyond 'Model Minority'"; Samson, "Massive Crowds of Asian Americans."

23 Krishna, "How to Feed Crowds in a Protest or Pandemic?"

24 L. Miller, "Latino Activists Push for Solidarity"; Parra, "Why 'Black Lives Matter.'"

25 National Native American Bar Association, "Declares Takomni Hasapa Wiconi Hecha"; Banta and Lyons, "This Is a Bill Come Due."

26 Sparks, "Polls Show Widespread Support"

27 Horowitz and Livingston, "How Americans View the Black Lives Matter Movement."

28 Reuters, "Protests Worldwide Embrace Black Lives Matter Movement"; Drayton, "Global Protests Reveal."

29 *Pierre Burton Show*, aired 9 December 1971.

30 *Pierre Burton Show*.

31 Vidantham, "Edge Effect."

32 L. Lee, *Story of Bruce Lee*, 163–64.

BIBLIOGRAPHY

ARCHIVAL SOURCES

Dozier, William. Papers. Collection #06851. American Heritage Center, University of Wyoming, Laramie

National Archives at San Francisco

Records of the Immigration and Naturalization Service, 1787–2004, National Archives, Washington, DC

Wing Luke Museum of the Asian Pacific American Experience, Seattle, WA

NEWSPAPERS AND MAGAZINES

Black Belt
Boxoffice
Chicago Tribune
China Mail
Independent
Los Angeles Herald Examiner
Los Angeles Times
New York Times
Northwest Asian Weekly
Pacific
Post Herald
South China Morning Post
Variety

BOOKS, ARTICLES, AND OTHER SOURCES

American Film Institute. *The American Film Institute Catalog of Motion Pictures Produced in the United States: Within Our Gates: Ethnicity in American Feature Films, 1911–1960*. Berkeley: University of California Press, 1997.

Arora, Maneesh, Christopher Stout, and Kelsy Kretschmer. "What Helps Non-Black People Support Black Lives Matter? A Signal from Someone in Their Own Ethnic Group." *Washington Post*, 18 June 2020. www.washingtonpost.com.

Atlanta Constitution. "Bruce Lee Cult Booming All Over." 17 August 1974.

Aziz, Maryam. "Our Fist Is Black: Martial Arts, Black Arts, and Black Power in the 1960s and 1970s." *Kung Fu Tea*, 21 January 2016. https://chinesemartialstudies.com.

Baer, Stephanie K. "The Cop Who Said the Spa Shooter Had a 'Bad Day' Previously Posted a Racist Shirt Blaming China for the Pandemic." *Buzzfeed*, 17 March 2021. www.buzzfeed-news.com.

Banta, Megan, and Craig Lyons. "'This Is a Bill Come Due': Speakers Demand Change at Black Lives Matter Rally Focused on Peace, Healing, Celebration." *Lansing State Journal*, 29 June 2020. www.lansingstatejournal.com.

Bax, Paul. *Disciples of the Dragon: Reflections from the Students of Bruce Lee*. Denver, CO: Outskirts, 2008. Kindle ed.

———. *Number One: Reflections from Bruce Lee's First Student, Jesse Glover*. CreateSpace, 2016. Kindle ed.

Beaglehole, J. C. *The Life of Captain James Cook*. Stanford, CA: Stanford University Press, 1974.

Belkin, Gary, and Chic Young, creators. *Blondie*. Season 1, episode 13, "Pick on Someone Your Own Size." Aired 9 January 1969, CBS.

Berle, Milton, creator. *The Milton Berle Show*. Season 1, episode 2. Aired 16 September 1966, on American Broadcasting Company.

Berry, Chris. "Stellar Transit: Bruce Lee's Body or Chinese Masculinity in a Transnational Frame." In *Embodied Modernities: Corporeality, Representation and Chinese Cultures*, edited by Fran Martin and Larissa Heinrich, 218–34. Honolulu: University of Hawaii Press, 2006.

Berry, Chris, and Mary Farquhar, *China on Screen: Cinema and Nation*. Hong Kong: Hong Kong University Press, 2006.

Billboard. "Chart History: Carl Douglas." Accessed 12 May 2020. www.billboard.com.

Black Belt. "Black Belt Times: A Report of the Martial Arts World." January 1970.

———. "Black Belt Times: A Report of the Martial Arts World." September 1972.

———. "Bruce Lee Shatters Own Hong Kong Movie Record." September 1972.

———. "Budo Goes Hollywood." February 1969.

———. "Enter the Dragon: Exclusive Interview with Fred Weintraub, Producer of the Bruce Lee Blockbuster." 26 July 2013. www.blackbeltmag.com.

———. "Leo Fong: Kung Fu Artist of the Year (2006)." 21 March 2011. www.blackbeltmag.com.

———. "Letters to the Editor." April 1967.

Bleecker, Tom. *Unsettled Matters: The Life and Death of Bruce Lee*. Lompoc, CA: Gilderoy, 1996.

Block, Alex Ben. *The Legend of Bruce Lee*. New York: Dell, 1974.

Bogart, Paul, dir. *Marlowe*. Metro-Golden-Mayer, 1969.

Bolton, Grace, and Neria Muzurvić. "Globalizing Memory in a Divided City: Bruce Lee in Mostar." In *Memory in a Global Age: Discourses, Practices and Trajectories*, edited by Aleida Assmann and Sebastian Conrad, 181–98. London: Palgrave Macmillan, 2010.

Bonacich, Edna. "Some Basic Facts: Patterns of Asian Immigration and Exclusion." In *Labor Immigration Under Capitalism: Asian Workers in the United States before World War II*, edited by Lucie Cheng and Edna Bonacich, 60–78. Berkeley: University of California Press, 1984.

Bowman, Paul. *Beyond Bruce Lee: Chasing the Dragon through Film, Philosophy, and Popular Culture*. New York: Wallflower Press, 2013.

———. "Sick Man of Transl-Asia: Bruce Lee and Rey Chow's Queer Cultural Translation." *Social Semiotics* 20, no. 4 (September 2010): 393–409.

Boxoffice. "Diversified Promotions Aid 'Enter the Dragon.'" 17 September 1973.

———. "Enter the Dragon." 27 August 1973.

Bren, Frank. "The Fabulous Adventures of Benjamin Brodsky: China's First Films—Really." *Asian Cinema* 20, no. 2 (Fall–Winter 2009): 1–17.

Bren, Frank, and Law Kar. "Ben Brodsky and the Real Dawn of Hong Kong Cinema." *China Daily* (Hong Kong ed.), 3 March 2010. www.chinadaily.com.cn.

Buchanan, Larry, Quoctrung Bui, and Jugal K. Patel. "Black Lives Matter May Be the Largest Movement in U.S. History." *New York Times*, 3 July 2020. www.nytimes.com.

Buglioso, Vincent, with Curt Gentry. *Helter Skelter: The True Story of the Manson Murders*. 1974. Reprint, New York: Norton, 2001.

Burton, Pierre, host. *The Pierre Burton Show*. Bruce Lee interview (a.k.a. "The Lost Interview"). Aired 9 December 1971, Screen Gems. Posted to YouTube by Be water, 24 October 2019. www.youtube.com/watch?v=qLXYFEa0q58.

Byrd, Jodi. *Transit of Empire: Indigenous Critiques of Colonialism*. Minneapolis: University of Minnesota Press, 2011.

Calhoun, Bob. "Jim Kelly, 'Enter the Dragon's' Baddest Mother." *Salon*, 13 April 2010. www.salon.com.

Campbell, Sid, and Greglon Yimm Lee. *The Dragon and the Tiger*. Vol. 1, *The Birth of Bruce Lee's Jeet Kune Do, the Oakland Years*. Berkeley, CA: Frog Ltd., 2003.

———. *The Dragon and the Tiger*. Vol. 2, *Bruce Lee: The Oakland Years: The Untold Story of Jun Fan Gung-fu and James Yimm Lee*. Berkeley, CA: Frog Ltd., 2005.

———. *Remembering the Master: Bruce Lee, James Yimm Lee, and the Creation of Jeet Kune Do*. Berkeley, CA: Blue Snake Books, 2006.

Carroll, John M. *A Concise History of Hong Kong*. Lanham, MD: Rowman and Littlefield, 2007.

Chan, Jachinson. *Chinese American Masculinities: From Fu Manchu to Bruce Lee*. New York: Routledge, 2001.

Chaw, Walter. "Why Are You Laughing at Bruce Lee?" *Vulture*, 2 August 2019. www.vulture.com.

Chen, Katy. "A Legend in Her Own Time: Ruby Chow." *Northwest Asian Weekly*, 15–21 March 1997.

Chen, Shehong. *Being Chinese, Becoming Chinese American.* Urbana: University of Illinois Press, 2002.

Chen, Yong. *Chinese San Francisco, 1850–1943: A Trans-Pacific Community.* Stanford, CA: Stanford University Press, 2000.

Cheng, Irene. *Clara Ho Tung: A Hong Kong Lady, Her Family and Her Times.* Hong Kong: Chinese University of Hong Kong, 1976.

Chew, Ron. *Reflections of Seattle's Chinese Americans.* Seattle: Wing Luke Asian Museum, 1994.

Chin, Frank. "The Three Kingdoms: Ruby Chow (1921–)." In *Washingtonians: A Biographical Portrait of the State*, edited by David Brewster and David M. Buerge, 360–80. Seattle: Sasquatch Books, 1989.

China Mail. "Bruce Li Bomb a Fake." 28 July 1973.

———. "Bruce Will Be Near to Linda." 27 July 1973.

———. "Director to Groom New Bruce Li." 8 August 1973.

———. "Dynamic Duo's Game of Death." 20 July 1973.

———. "Farewell Brother . . ." 31 July 1973.

———. "Linda: Please Let Bruce Rest in Peace." 26 July 1973.

———. "Li's Death—Heart Attack May Be the Cause." 21 July 1973.

———. "No Business like Dragon Business." 24 October 1973.

———. "10,000 Good-Byes." 25 July 1973.

———. "Who's Lying about Bruce Li's Last Hours?" 24 July 1973.

Chong, Sylvia. *The Oriental Obscene: Violence and Racial Fantasies in the Vietnam Era.* Durham, NC: Duke University Press, 2012.

Chow, H. S. "Bruce Li's Coffin Is Damaged." *China Mail*, 1 August 1973.

———. "Bruce's Fists Smash $3.5M Mark." *China Daily Mail*, 5 April 1972.

———. "Chinese Movies Take Top Places in U.S." *China Mail*, 19 May 1973.

———. "Film Profits Soar." *China Mail*, 28 December 1973.

———. "Following in Li's Footsteps." *China Mail*, 6 August 1973.

Chow, Vivienne. "Golden Harvest's Raymond Chow Recalls Glory Days of Hong Kong Film." *South China Morning Post*, 23 March 2013. www.scmp.com.

Chu, Robert. "Bruce Lee's Hong Kong Years." *Inside Kung-Fu*, part 1, November 1991; part 2, December 1991; part 3, January 1992; part 4, February 1992. Posted at http://hawkin-scheung.com.

Chung, Stephanie Po-Yin. "Moguls of the Chinese Cinema: The Story of the Shaw Brothers in Shanghai, Hong Kong and Singapore, 1924–2002." *Modern Asian Studies* 41, no. 4 (2007): 665–82.

Clouse, Robert. *Bruce Lee: The Biography.* Burbank, CA: Unique Publications, 1988.

———, dir. *Enter the Dragon.* Warner Bros. and Concord Productions, 1973.

———, dir. *Game of Death.* Columbia Pictures and Golden Harvest, 1978.

———. *The Making of "Enter the Dragon."* Burbank, CA: Unique Publications, 1987.

Corbett, Donna M. "Donald W. Nyrop: Airline Regulator, Airline Executive." In *Airline Executives and Federal Regulation: Case Studies in American Enterprise from the Airmail Era to the Dawn of the Jet Age*, edited by W. David Lewis, 125–68. Columbus: Ohio State University Press, 2000.

Corcoran, John, and Emil Farkas. *Martial Arts: Traditions, History, People*. New York: Gallery Books, 1988.

Curry, Ramona. "Benjamin Brodsky (1877–1960): The Trans-Pacific American Film Entrepreneur—Part One, Making *A Trip Thru China*." *Journal of American-East Asian Relations* 18, no. 1 (March 2011): 58–94.

———. "Benjamin Brodsky (1877–1960): The Trans-Pacific American Film Entrepreneur—Part Two, Taking *A Trip Thru China* to America." *Journal of American-East Asian Relations* 18 (2011): 142–80.

Daniels, Roger. *Asian America: Chinese and Japanese in the United States since 1850*. Seattle: University of Washington Press, 1988.

———. *The Politics of Prejudice: The Anti-Japanese Movement in California and the Struggle for Japanese Exclusion*. Berkeley: University of California Press, 1977.

Davis, Darrell William. "Questioning Diaspora: Mobility, Mutation, and Historiography of the Shaw Brothers Film Studio." *Chinese Journal of Communication* 4, no. 1 (2011): 40–59.

Deleuze, Gilles, and Félix Guattari. *A Thousand Plateaus: Capital and Schizophrenia*. Translated by Brian Massumi. Minneapolis: University of Minnesota Press, 1987.

Dennis, Felix, and Don Atyeo. *Bruce Lee: King of Kung-Fu*. San Francisco: Straight Arrow Books, 1974.

Desser, David. "Diaspora and National Identity: Exporting 'China' through the Hong Kong Cinema." In *Transnational Cinema: The Film Reader*, edited by Elizabeth Ezra and Terry Rowden, 143–56. New York: Routledge, 2006.

———. "Globalizing Hong Kong Cinema through Japan." In *A Companion to Hong Kong Cinema*, edited by Esther M. K. Cheung, Gina Marchetti, and Esther C. M. Yau, 168–85. Chichester, UK: Wiley Blackwell, 2015.

———. "The Kung Fu Craze: Hong Kong Cinema's First American Reception." In *The Cinema of Hong Kong: History, Arts, Identity*, edited by Poshek Fu and David Desser, 19–43. Cambridge: Cambridge University Press, 2000.

Donovan, Barna William. *The Asian Influence on Hollywood Action Films*. Jefferson, NC: McFarland, 2008.

Drayton, Tiffanie. "Global Protests Reveal That White Supremacy Is a Problem Everywhere." *Vox*, 23 June 2020. www.vox.com.

Eng, David. *Racial Castration: Managing Masculinity in Asian America*. Durham, NC: Duke University Press, 2001.

Erickson, Hal. *From Radio to the Big Screen: Hollywood Films Featuring Broadcast Personalities and Programs*. Jefferson, NC: McFarland, 2014.

Erskine, Hazel. "The Polls: Interracial Socializing." *Public Opinion Quarterly* 37, no. 2 (Summer 1973): 283–94.

Estes, Jane. "Ruby Chow: The Council's Good Fortune." *Northwest*, 21 January 1979.

Federal Bureau of Investigation. "2019 Hate Crimes Report." 2019. https://ucr.fbi.gov.

Fleming, Ian. *Thrilling Cities*. London: Jonathan Cape, 1963.

Francisco, Luzviminda. "The First Vietnam: The Philippine-American War of 1899." *Bulletin of Concerned Asian Scholars* 5, no. 4 (December 1973): 2–16.

Frazier, Robeson Taj. *The East Is Black: Cold War China in the Black Radical Imagination*. Durham, NC: Duke University Press, 2014.

Fu, Poshek. "Between Nationalism and Colonialism: Mainland Emigres, Marginal Culture, and Hong Kong Cinema, 1937–1941." In *The Cinema of Hong Kong: History, Arts, Identity*, edited by Poshek Fu and David Desser, 199–226. Cambridge: Cambridge University Press, 2000.

———. "The Shaw Brothers Diasporic Cinema." In *China Forever: The Shaw Brothers and Diasporic Cinema*, edited by Poshek Fu, 1–25. Urbana: University of Illinois Press, 2008.

Fujino, Diane C. *Heartbeat of Struggle: The Revolutionary Life of Yuri Kochiyama*. Minneapolis: University of Minnesota Press, 2005.

———. *Samurai among Panthers: Richard Aoki on Race, Resistance, ad a Paradoxical Life*. Minneapolis: University of Minnesota Press, 2012.

Fung Fung, dir. *The Kid*. Datong Film Company, 1950.

Gentilcore, David. *Pomodoro! A History of the Tomato in Italy*. New York: Columbia University Press, 2010.

Getty Images. "Bosnia-Health-Virus." Accessed 10 April 2020. www.gettyimages.co.uk.

Glover, Jesse. *Bruce Lee: Between Wing Chun and Jeet Kune Do*. Seattle, 1976.

Gong, Tommy. *Bruce Lee: The Evolution of a Martial Artist*. Los Angeles: Bruce Lee Foundation, 2013.

Grams, Martin, Jr., and Terry Salomonson. *The Green Hornet: A History of Radio, Motion Pictures, Comics, and Television*. Churchville, MD: OTR, 2010.

Guardian. "Donald Trump Calls Covid-19 'Kung Flu' at Tulsa Rally." 20 June 2020. www.theguardian.com.

Guterl, Matthew Pratt. *American Mediterranean: Southern Slaveholders in the Age of Emancipation*. Cambridge, MA: Harvard University Press, 2008.

Hale, Erin. "'Be Water': Hong Kong Protesters Adopt Bruce Lee Tactic to Evade Police Crackdown." *Independent*, 6 January 2020. www.independent.co.uk.

Haley, James L. *Captive Paradise: A History of Hawaii*. New York: St. Martin's, 2014.

Halpin, James. "The Little Dragon: Bruce Lee (1940–1973)." In *The Washingtonians: A Biographical Portrait of the State*, edited by David Brewster and David M. Buerge, 424. Seattle: Sasquatch Books, 1988.

Hing, Bill Ong. *Making and Remaking Asian America through Immigration Policy, 1850–1990*. Stanford, CA: Stanford University Press, 1993.

Ho, Eric Peter. *Tracing My Children's Lineage*. Hong Kong: University of Hong Kong Press, 2010.

Ho, Eugene H. "Hypnotism in Self-Defense." *Black Belt*, October 1973.

Ho, Fred, and Bill Mullen, eds. *Afro Asia: Revolutionary Political and Cultural Connections between African Americans and Asian Americans*. Durham, NC: Duke University Press, 2008.

Hobart, Peter. "Integrated Ideas of a Life Warrior—An Interview with Leo Fong." *Journal of Asian Martial Arts* 15, no. 4 (2006): 73–79.

Hong Kong Film Archive. "Hong Kong Filmography (1914–2010)." Accessed 15 November 2011. www.lcsd.gov.hk.

Hong Kong Movie Database. "Lee Hoi-Chuen." Accessed 15 November 2011. http://hkmdb. com.

Hong Kong Post Herald. "Shaw Brothers' Epic Takes a Beating from Bruce Li Film." 26 March 1972.

Horn, John. "Jim Kelly, 'Enter the Dragon' Star, Dies at 67." *Los Angeles Times,* 1 July 2013. http://articles.latimes.com.

Horne, Gerald. *Facing the Rising Sun: African Americans, Japan, and the Rise of Afro-Asian Solidarity.* New York: New York University Press, 2018.

Horowitz, Julianna Menasce, and Gretchen Livingston. "How Americans View the Black Lives Matter Movement." Pew Research Center, 8 July 2016. www.pewresearch.org.

Huang, Yunte. *Charlie Chan: The Untold Story of the Honorable Detective and His Rendezvous with American History.* New York: Norton, 2011.

Hui, Mary. "Hong Kong Is Exporting Its Protest Techniques around the World." *Quartz,* 16 October 2019. https://qz.com.

———. "One Hong Kong protester channelling Bruce Lee philosophy." Twitter, 25 June 2019. https://twitter.com/maryhui/status/1143717367521824768.

Hutchins, Will. "A Touch of Hutch." Western Clippings, April 2010. www.westernclippings. com.

Igler, David. *The Great Ocean: Pacific Worlds from Captain Cook to the Gold Rush.* New York: Oxford University Press, 2013.

Joe, Allen, with Svetlana Kim and Dmitri Bobkov. *Last of the Four Musketeers: Allen Joe's Friendship with Bruce Lee.* Bloomington, IN: Balboa, 2015. Kindle ed.

Judkins, Benjamin N., and Jon Nielson. *The Creation of Wing Chun: A Social History of the Southern Chinese Martial Arts.* Albany: SUNY Press, 2015.

Kam, Tan See. "From *South Pacific* to *Shanghai Blues*: No Film Is an Island." In *Hong Kong Film, Hollywood and the New Global Cinema: No Film Is an Island,* edited by Gina Marchetti and Tan See Kam, 13–34. New York: Routledge, 2007.

Karlin, Jules Alexander. "The Anti-Chinese Outbreaks in Seattle, 1885–1886." *Pacific Northwest Quarterly* 39, no. 2 (April 1948): 103–30.

Karlson, Phil, dir. *The Wrecking Crew.* Columbia Pictures, 1968.

Kato, M. T. "Burning Asia: Bruce Lee's Kinetic Narrative of Decolonization." *Modern Chinese Literature and Culture* 17, no. 1 (2005): 65–70.

Kelley, Robin D. G., and Betsy Esch. "Black like Mao: Red China and Black Revolution." *Souls* 1, no. 4 (Fall 1999): 6–41.

Kelly, Perry William. *Dan Inosanto: The Man, the Teacher, the Artist.* Boulder, CO: Paladin, 2000.

Kennedy, Brian, and Elizabeth Guo. *Jingwu: The School That Transformed Kung Fu.* Berkeley, CA: Blue Snake Books, 2010.

Kent, Noel J. *Hawaii: Islands under the Influence.* 1983. Reprint, Honolulu: University of Hawaii Press, 1993.

Kerridge, Steve. *The Bruce Lee Chronicles: An Inside Look at "The Way of the Dragon."* Vol. 1. N.p.: Tiger Rock, 2011. Kindle ed.

Kimura, Taky. *Regards from the Dragon: Seattle*. Los Angeles: Empire Books, 2009.

King, Daniel. "We Shouldn't Need to Explain Why Trump's 'Chinese Virus' Tweet Is Wrong. But Here We Are." *Mother Jones*, 16 March 2020. www.motherjones.com.

King, Martin Luther, Jr. "Beyond Vietnam." Martin Luther King Jr. Research and Education Institute, Stanford University. Accessed 31 May 2020. https://kinginstitute.stanford.edu.

———. *Why We Can't Wait*. New York: Signet Classic, 2000.

Klein, Christine. *Cold War Orientalism: Asia in the Middlebrow Imagination, 1945–1961*. Berkeley: University of California Press, 2003.

Kolko, Gabriel. *Main Currents in Modern American History*. New York: Harper and Row, 1976.

Kong, Lily. "Shaw Cinema Enterprise and Understanding Cultural Industries." In *China Forever: The Shaw Brothers and Diasporic Cinema*, edited by Poshek Fu, 27–56. Urbana: University of Illinois Press, 2008.,

KPIX 5 CBS. "Oakland Police Arrest Suspect Who Allegedly Made Online Threats to Asian Americans." 23 February 2021. https://sanfrancisco.cbslocal.com.

Krishna, Priya. "How to Feed Crowds in a Protest or Pandemic? The Sikhs Know." *New York Times*, 8 June 2020. www.nytimes.com.

Law Kar. "The American Connection in Early Hong Kong Cinema." In *The Cinema of Hong Kong: History, Arts, Identity*, edited by Poshek Fu and David Desser, 44–70. Cambridge: Cambridge University Press, 2000.

———. "In Search of Esther Eng: Border-Crossing Pioneer in Chinese-Language Filmmaking." Translated by Chris Tong. In *Chinese Women's Cinema: Transnational Contexts*, edited by Lingzhen Wang, 313–29. New York: Columbia University Press, 2011.

Law Kar, and Frank Bren. *Hong Kong Cinema: A Cross-Cultural View*. Lanham, MD: Scarecrow, 2004.

Lee, Bruce. *Artist of Life*. Edited by John Little. Hong Kong: Tuttle, 1999.

———. *Letters of the Dragon: The Original 1958–1973 Correspondence*. Edited by John Little. Hong Kong: Tuttle, 2016.

———. *The Tao of Jeet Kune Do*. Burbank, CA: Ohara, 1975.

———, dir. *The Way of the Dragon*. Golden Harvest and Concord Productions, 1972.

Lee, Erika. *The Making of Asian America: A History*. New York: Simon and Shuster, 2015.

Lee, Francis L. F., Samson Yuen, Gary Tang, and Edmund W. Cheng. "Hong Kong's Summer of Uprising: From Anti-Extradition to Anti-Authoritarian Protests." *China Review* 19, no. 4 (November 2019): 1–32.

Lee, Linda. *Bruce Lee: The Man Only I Knew*. Warner Books, 1978.

———. *The Bruce Lee Story*. Santa Clarita, CA: Ohara, 1989.

Lee, Shelley Sang-Hee. *Claiming the Oriental Gateway: Prewar Seattle and Japanese America*. Philadelphia: Temple University Press, 2011.

Lee Sun-Fang, dir. *Orphan, The*. Hua Lien, 1960.

Lei, Daphne Pi-Wei. *Operatic China: Staging Chinese Identity across the Pacific*. New York: Palgrave Macmillan, 2006.

———. "The Production and Consumption of Chinese Theatre in Nineteenth-Century California." *Theatre Research International* 28, no. 3 (2003): 289–302.

Lew-Williams, Beth. *The Chinese Must Go: Violence, Exclusion, and the Making of the Alien in America*. Cambridge, MA: Harvard University Press, 2018.

Li, Linda. "The Violent World of Bruce Li: He Prowled the Neon Jungles." *South China Morning Post*, 9 February 1975.

———. "The Violent World of Bruce Lee: When a Doctor Warned Him Not to Inflict Too Much Violence on His Body." *South China Morning Post*, 16 February 1975.

Li, Siu Leung. "Kung Fu: Negotiating Nationalism and Modernity." *Cultural Studies* 15, nos. 3–4 (2001): 515–42.

Little, John, ed. *Bruce Lee: Words of the Dragon: Interviews, 1958–1973*. Hong Kong: Tuttle, 1997.

Liu, Frances Tse. *Ho Kom-Tong: A Man for All Seasons*. Hong Kong: Compradore House Limited, 2003.

López, Ian F. Haney. *White by Law: The Legal Construction of Race*. New York: New York University Press, 1996.

Louie, Kam. *Theorising Chinese Masculinity: Society and Gender in China*. Cambridge: Cambridge University Press, 2002.

Louie, Kam, and Louise Edwards. "Chinese Masculinity: Theorizing *Wen* and *Wu*." *East Asian History* 8 (1994): 135–48.

Lo Wei, dir. *The Big Boss*. Golden Harvest, 1971.

———, dir. *Fist of Fury*. Golden Harvest, 1972.

Lyons, Louis S., and Josephine Wilson, eds. *Who's Who among the Women of California: An Annual Devoted to the Representative Women of California, with an Authoritative Review of Their Activities in Civic, Social, Athletic, Philanthropic, Art and Music, Literary and Dramatic Circles*. San Francisco: Security Publishing, 1922.

Maeda, Daryl J. "Black Panthers, Red Guards, and Chinamen: Constructing Asian American Identity through Performing Blackness, 1969–1972." *American Quarterly* 57, no. 4 (December 2005): 1079–1103.

———. *Chains of Babylon: The Rise of Asian America*. Minneapolis: University of Minnesota Press, 2009.

Marchetti, Gina Marchetti. "Immigrant Dreams, Marginal Fantasies: Subcultural Perspective and Bruce Lee's *Return of the Dragon*." Unpublished paper.

Martin, George Whitney. *Verdi at the Golden Gate: Opera and San Francisco in the Gold Rush Years*. Berkeley: University of California Press, 1993.

Matsuda, Matt K. "Afterword: Pacific Cross-Currents." In *Pacific Histories: Ocean, Land, People*, edited by David Armitage and Alison Bashford, 326–34. Basingstoke, UK: Palgrave Macmillan, 2014.

———. *Pacific Worlds: A History of Seas, Peoples, and Cultures*. Cambridge: Cambridge University Press, 2012.

McCormack, Pete, dir. *I Am Bruce Lee*. Network Films Two, 2012.

McKenzie, Duncan Alexander. *The Death of Bruce Lee: A Clinical Investigation*. CreateSpace, 2012. Kindle ed.

Mendoza, Antonio V. "Bruce Lee and *Big Boss* Hit in Manila." *Black Belt*, July 1972.

Miller, Leila. "Latino Activists Push for Solidarity with Black Community as They Confront Racism." *Los Angeles Times*, 14 July 2020. www.latimes.com.

Miller, Stuart Creighton. *Benevolent Assimilation: The American Conquest of the Philippines, 1899–1903*. New Haven, CT: Yale University Press, 1984.

Mitter, Rana. *Forgotten Ally: China's World War II, 1937–1945*. Boston: Houghton Mifflin Harcourt, 2013.

Mullen, Bill V. *Afro-Orientalism*. Minneapolis: University of Minnesota Press, 2004.

Nash, N. Richard, creator. *Here Come the Brides*. Season 1, episode 24, "Marriage Chinese Style." Aired 9 April 1969, American Broadcasting Company.

National Native American Bar Association. "The National Native American Bar Association Declares Takomni Hasapa Wiconi Hecha (Black Lives Matter)." 15 June 2020. www.nativeamericanbar.org.

New York Times. "What's Opened Lately at the Movies?" 2 September 1973, section 2.

Ng, Wing Chung. *The Rise of Cantonese Opera*. Urbana: University of Illinois Press, 2015. Kindle ed.

Nguyen, Bao, dir. *Be Water*. ESPN, 2020.

Nguyen, Viet Thanh, and Janet Hoskins. Introduction to *Transpacific Studies: Framing an Emerging Field*, edited by Janet Hoskins and Viet Thanh Nguyen, 1–38. Honolulu: University of Hawaii Press, 2014.

Norris, Chuck. *Against All Odds: My Story*. Nashville, TN: Broadman and Holman, 2004.

O'Connor, John J. "In the Name of the Law Is the Name of the Game." *New York Times*, 19 September 1971.

Ongiri, Amy Abugo. "Bruce Lee in the Ghetto Connection: Kung Fu Theater and African Americans Reinventing Culture at the Margins." In *East Main Street: Asian American Popular Culture*, edited by Shilpa Davé, LeiLani Nishime, Tasha G. Oren, 249–61. New York: New York University Press, 2005.

———. "'He Wanted to Be Just like Bruce Lee': African Americans, Kung Fu Theater and Cultural Exchange at the Margins." *Journal of Asian American Studies* 5, no. 1 (February 2002): 31–40.

Onishi, Yuichiro. *Transpacific Antiracism: Afro-Asian Solidarity in 20th Century Black America, Japan, and Okinawa*. New York: New York University Press, 2013.

Oppenheimer, Peer J. "Would You Pay $50 for a Haircut? Hollywood Actors and Texas Millionaires Do—Making Jay Sebring One of the Best-Paid Cutups in His Profession." *Sarasota Herald-Tribune*, 4 August 1963.

Ortmann, Stephan. "The Umbrella Movement and Hong Kong's Protracted Democratization Process." *Asian Affairs* 46, no. 1 (2015): 32–50.

Pacific. "Ruby Chow." 9 December 1984.

Parra, Daniel. "Why 'Black Lives Matter' to NYC's Latino Police-Reform Marchers." CityLimits, 2 July 2020. https://citylimits.org.

Pellerin, Eric. "Bruce Lee as Director and the Star as Author." *Global Media and China* 4, no. 3 (2019): 339–47.

Pfaelzer, Jean. *Driven Out: The Forgotten War against Chinese Americans*. Berkeley: University of California Press, 2008.

Pollard, Maxwell. "In Kato's Gung Fu Impact Is Instant." *Black Belt*, November 1967.

———. "Is 'The Green Hornet's' Version of Gung Fu Genuine?" *Black Belt*, October 1967.

Polly, Matthew. *Bruce Lee: A Life*. New York: Simon and Schuster, 2018.

Prashad, Vijay. "Bruce Lee and the Anti-imperialism of Kung Fu: A Polycultural Adventure." *positions: east asia cultures critique* 11, no. 1 (Spring 2003): 51–90.

Rafiq, Fiaz. *Bruce Lee Conversations: The Life and Legacy of a Legend*. Manchester, UK: HNL, 2009.

Rao, Nancy Yunhwa. *Chinatown Theater in North America*. Urbana: University of Illinois Press, 2017.

Rayns, Tony. "Enter the Dragon." *Monthly Film Bulletin* (London), 1 January 1974.

Reuters. "Protests Worldwide Embrace Black Lives Matter Movement." 6 June 2020. www.reuters.com.

Rhee, Jhoon. *Bruce Lee and I: An Intimate Portrait by Bruce Lee's Training Partner and the Father of Taekwondo in the United States*. CreateSpace, 2011.

Richard, A. W. "'Big Boss' Big Hit in Malaysia." *Black Belt*, September 1972.

Riddle, Margaret. "Chun Ching Hock Opens the Wa Chong Company in Seattle on December 15, 1868." Essay 10800. HistoryLink.org. Accessed 17 April 2017. www.historylink.org.

Riddle, Ronald. "The Cantonese Opera: A Chapter in Chinese American History." In *The Life, Influence and the Role of the Chinese in the United States, 1776–1960: Proceedings/Papers of the National Conference Held at the University of San Francisco, July 10, 11, 12, 1975*, edited by Chinese Historical Society of America, 40–47. San Francisco: Chinese Historical Society of America, 1976.

———. *Flying Dragons, Flowing Streams: Music in the Life of San Francisco's Chinese*. Westport, CT: Greenwood, 1983.

Rodriguez, Hector. "Hong Kong Popular Culture as an Interpretive Arena: The Huang Feihong Film Series." *Screen* 38, no. 1 (1997): 1–24.

Rubinstein, Steve. "In the Shadow of a Legend." *Black Belt*, August 1974, 17–21.

Ruskola, Teemu. "Canton Is Not Boston: The Invention of American Imperial Sovereignty." *American Quarterly* 57, no. 3 (September 2005): 859–84.

Russell, Toby, dir. *Death by Misadventure*. Unsilent Minority Productions, 1993.

Russo, Charles. *Striking Distance: Bruce Lee and the Dawn of Martial Arts in America*. Lincoln: University of Nebraska Press, 2016.

Ryfle, Steve. "DVD Set Is Devoted to '70s Martial Arts Star Jim Kelly." *Los Angeles Times*, 10 January 2010.

Said, Edward W. *Orientalism*. New York: Vintage Books, 1978.

Samson, Carl. "Massive Crowds of Asian Americans Across the Country March in Support of #BlackLivesMatter." NextShark, 9 June 2020. https://nextshark.com/hoards-of-asian-americans-across-the-country-march-in-support-of-blacklivesmatter/ (accessed 15 July 2020.

Savitch-Lew, Abigail. "Beyond 'Model Minority.'" Asian American Writers' Workshop, 15 July 2020. https://aaww.org.

Saxton, Alexander. *The Indispensable Enemy: Labor and the Anti-Chinese Movement in California*. Berkeley: University of California Press, 1971.

Scherling, Carol Lynn. *Blondie Goes to Hollywood: The "Blondie" Comic Strip in Films, Radio, and Television*. Duncan, OK: BearManor Media, 2014. Kindle ed.

Sharma, Miriam. "The Philippines: A Case of Migration to Hawaii, 1906–1946." In *Labor Immigration under Capitalism: Asian Workers in the United States before World War II*, edited by Lucie Cheng and Edna Bonacich, 337–58. Berkeley: University of California Press, 1984.

Shimizu, Celine Parreñas. *Straitjacket Sexualities: Unbinding Asian American Manhoods in the Movies*. Stanford, CA: Stanford University Press, 2012.

Silliphant, Stirling, creator. *Longstreet*. Aired 1971–72 on American Broadcasting Company.

Sinn, Elizabeth. *Pacific Crossing: California Gold, Chinese Migration, and the Making of Hong Kong*. Hong Kong: University of Hong Kong Press, 2013.

Siskel, Gene. "Click, Chop, Ring, Chop, Chop Go the Ribs and the Register." *Chicago Tribune*, 13 May 1973.

South China Morning Post. "Doctor Found Bruce in Deep Coma—Inquest." 4 September 1973.

———. "Final Bow for Bruce Li: Tears Flow in Farewell to the Little Dragon." 26 July 1973.

———. "Hypersensitivity to a Drug Could Have Killed Li." 21 September 1973.

———. "Li's Collapse Not Caused by Cannabis, Says Pathologist." 22 September 1973.

———. "Sudden Death of Bruce Li." 21 July 1973.

———. "Widow Says She Was Aware Li Sometimes Took Cannabis." 18 September 1973.

Sparks, Grace. "Polls Show Widespread Support of Black Lives Matters Protests and Varied Views on How to Reform Police,. *CNN*, 18 June 2020. www.cnn.com.

Stein, Joel. "Bruce Lee." *Time*, 14 June 1999.

Stephenson, John W. "A Quantitative History of Chinatown, San Francisco, 1870–1880." In *The Life, Influence and the Role of the Chinese in the United States, 1776–1960: Proceedings/ Papers of the National Conference Held at the University of San Francisco, July 10, 11, 12, 1975*, edited by Chinese Historical Society of America, 71–88. San Francisco: Chinese Historical Society of America, 1976.

Stokes, Lisa Odham. *Historical Dictionary of Hong Kong Cinema*. Lanham, MD: Scarecrow, 2007.

Stokes, Lisa Odham, and Rachel Braaten. *Historical Dictionary of Hong Kong Cinema*. 2nd ed. Lanham, MD: Rowman and Littlefield, 2020.

Stom, Mitch. "Budo Breeze." *Black Belt*, July 1970.

Stop AAPI Hate. "Stop AAPI National Report." Accessed 23 April 2021. https://secure-servercdn.net.

Sturla, Anna, Mirna Alsharif, Kristina Sgueglia, and Laura Ly. "Attacks against People of Asian Descent Are on the Rise in NYC: The City Is Pushing to Combat It," *CNN*, 27 February 2021. www.cnn.com.

Synai Rockz. "Bruce Lee." YouTube, 25 August 2017. www.youtube.com/watch?v=uOE3P7kDdgo.

Taylor, Quintard. *The Forging of a Black Community: Seattle's Central District from 1870 through the Civil Rights Era*. Seattle: University of Washington Press, 1994.

Teng, Emma Jinhua. *Eurasians: Mixed Identities in the United States, China, and Hong Kong, 1842–1943*. Berkeley: University of California Press, 2013.

———. "Hong Kong's Eurasian 'Web' Viewed through the Lens of Inter-Asian Studies: Comments on Engseng Ho's 'Inter-Asian Concepts for Mobile Societies.'" *Journal of Asian Studies* 76, no. 4 (November 2017): 943–51.

Teo, Stephen. *Chinese Martial Arts Cinema: The Wuxia Tradition*. Edinburgh: Edinburgh University Press, 2009.

———. *Hong Kong Cinema: The Extra Dimension*. London: British Film Institute, 1997.

Thomas, Bruce. *Bruce Lee: Fighting Spirit*. Berkeley, CA: Blue Snake Books, 1994.

Thompson, Howard. "'Enter Dragon,' Hollywood Style: The Cast." *New York Times*, 18 August 1973.

Trendle, George W., creator. *The Green Hornet*. Aired 1966–67 on American Broadcasting Company.

Tsang, Steve. *A Modern History of Hong Kong*. London: I. B. Tauris, 2004.

US Bureau of the Census. "Median Family Income Up in 1970 (Advance Data from March 1971 Sample Survey)." Series P-60, no. 78, 20 May 1971. Department of Commerce. Washington, DC: US Government Printing Office.

———. *Sixteenth Census of the United States, 1940*. Washington, DC: National Archives and Records Administration, 1940.

Uyehara, Mitoshi. *Bruce Lee: The Incomparable Fighter*. Santa Clarita, CA: Ohara, 1988.

Variety. "Bruce Lee Pix Still Big at Japanese B.O." 5 March 1975.

———. "'Enter the Dragon' Enters the Record Books!" 12 September 1973.

———. "Jingwu Men." 1 January 1972.

———. *Variety Film Reviews*. Vol. 13, *1971–1974*. New York: Garland, 1983.

Verswijver, Leo. *"Movies Were Always Magical": Interviews with 19 Actors, Directors, and Producers from the Hollywood of the 1930s through the 1950s*. Jefferson, NC: McFarland, 2003.

Vidantham, Shankar. "The Edge Effect." *Hidden Brain* (podcast), 2 July 2018.

Warrener, Don, dir. *My Friend Bruce Lee*. Starring Leo Fong. Rising Sun Productions, 2014.

Watkins, Rychetta. *Black Power, Yellow Power, and the Making of Revolutionary Identities*. Jackson: University Press of Mississippi, 2012.

wcdvid. "Bruce Lee—Seattle Years." YouTube, 29 November 2009. www.youtube.com/watch?v=7SXfk3yv2Bo.

Weber, Bruce. "Lorenzo Semple Jr., Creator of TV's 'Batman,' Dies at 91." *New York Times*, 1 April 2014. www.nytimes.com.

Weintraub, Fred. *Bruce Lee, Woodstock and Me: From the Man behind a Half-Century of Music, Movies and Martial Arts*. Los Angeles: Brooktree Canyon, 2011.

Weintraub, Fred, and Tom Kuhn, dirs. *The Curse of the Dragon*. Warner Bros., 1993.

Welsh, Frank. *A History of Hong Kong*. New York: HarperCollins, 1993.

Wesselhoeft, Conrad. "What It Was Like to Have Bruce Lee as a Houseguest." *Seattle Weekly*, 24 November 2015. http://archive.seattleweekly.com.

Westberg, Charles. "Bruce Lee Cult Sweeps Britain." *Sunday Post-Herald*, 25 August 1974.

Wharton, Glenn. "Dynamics of Participatory Conservation: The Kamehameha I Sculpture Project." *Journal of the American Institute for Conservation* 47, no. 3 (2008): 159–73.

Wilcox, B. P. "Anti-Chinese Riots in Washington." *Washington Historical Quarterly* 20, no. 3 (July 1929): 204–8.

Williams, Tony. "Kwan Tak-Hing and the New Generation." *Asian Cinema* 10, no. 1 (Fall 1998): 71–77.

Wing, Rick L. *Showdown in Oakland: The Story behind the Wong Jack Man-Bruce Lee Fight*. CreateSpace, 2013. Kindle ed.

Wong Shun Leung. "Bruce Lee and His Friendship with Wong Shun Leung." Wong Shun Leung Ving Tsun. Accessed 24 January 2018. www.wongvingtsun.co.uk/wslbl.htm.

Wright, Rebecca. "'Be Water': Hong Kong Protest Mantra Influences How Art is Designed and Distributed," *CNN*, 8 August 2019. https://edition.cnn.com.

Wu, Judy Tzu-Chun. *Radicals on the Road: Internationalism, Orientalism, and Feminism during the Vietnam Era*. Ithaca, NY: Cornell University Press, 2013.

Wunder, John R. "Anti-Chinese Violence in the American West, 1850–1910." In *Law for the Elephant, Law for the Beaver: Essays in the Legal History of the North American West*, edited by John McLaren, Hamar Foster, and Chet Orloff, 212–36. Pasadena, CA: Ninth Judicial Circuit Historical Society, 1992.

Xiao, Eva. "China Expels 3 Wall Street Journal Reporters over 'Sick Man of Asia' Op-Ed Headline." *Hong Kong Free Press*, 19 February 2020. www.hongkongfp.com.

Yap, Audrey Cleo. "Bruce Lee's Daughter Says Quentin Tarantino 'Could Shut Up' about Her Father's Portrayal (Exclusive)." *Variety*, 14 August 2019. https://variety.com.

———. "Bruce Lee's Protégé Recalls His Humility amid 'Once Upon a Time' Criticism." *Variety*, 31 July 2019. https://variety.com.

Yardley, William. "Jim Kelly, 67, Star of Martial Arts Movies." *New York Times*, 2 July 2013.

Yip, Raymond, and Manfred Wong, dirs. *Bruce Lee: My Brother*. Media Asia Films, 2010.

Young, Collier, creator. *Ironside*. Season 1, episode 7, "Tagged for Murder." Aired 1967, National Broadcasting Company.

Zaeiets, Karina, and Jennifer Borresen. "What Is Happening in Belarus? We Explain the Historic Pro-Democracy Protests." *USA Today*, 15 September 2020. www.usatoday.com.

INDEX

Page numbers in italics refer to images.

ABOUT THE AUTHOR

DARYL JOJI MAEDA is Dean and Vice Provost of Undergraduate Education and Professor of Ethnic Studies at the University of Colorado Boulder. He is the author of *Chains of Babylon: The Rise of Asian America* and *Rethinking the Asian American Movement.*

CPSIA information can be obtained
at www.ICGtesting.com
Printed in the USA
LVHW041031210822
725786LV00001B/1/J